CALENDAR
AND TIME DIARY
Methods in Life Course Research

CALENDAR AND TIME DIARY
Methods in Life Course Research

Robert F. Belli
University of Nebraska

Frank P. Stafford
University of Michigan

Duane F. Alwin
Pennsylvania State University

Los Angeles • London • New Delhi • Singapore • Washington DC

For information:

SAGE Publications, Inc.
2455 Teller Road
Thousand Oaks, California 91320
E-mail: order@sagepub.com

SAGE Publications India Pvt. Ltd.
B 1/I 1 Mohan Cooperative
  Industrial Area
Mathura Road, New Delhi 110 044
India

SAGE Publications Ltd.
1 Oliver's Yard
55 City Road
London, EC1Y 1SP
United Kingdom

SAGE Publications Asia-Pacific Pte. Ltd.
33 Pekin Street #02-01
Far East Square
Singapore 048763

Printed in the United States of America

Library of Congress Cataloging-in-Publication Data

Calendar and time diary methods in life course research / edited by
Robert F. Belli, Frank P. Stafford, Duane F. Alwin.
    p. cm.
Includes bibliographical references and index.
ISBN 978-1-4129-4063-4 (pbk.)

1. Social sciences—Biographical methods. 2. Life cycle, Human—Research—
Methodology. 3. Event history analysis. 4. Calendars. 5. Diaries. I. Belli,
Robert F. II. Stafford, Frank P. III. Alwin, Duane F. (Duane Francis), 1944-

H61.29.C35 2009
001.4'33—dc22   2008022784

This book is printed on acid-free paper.

08   09   10   11   12   10   9   8   7   6   5   4   3   2   1

Acquisitions Editor:	Vicki Knight
Associate Editor:	Sean Connelly
Editorial Assistant:	Lauren Habib
Production Editor:	Carla Freeman
Copy Editor:	Kristin Bergstad
Typesetter:	C&M Digitals (P) Ltd.
Proofreader:	Jenifer Kooiman
Indexer:	Jean Casalegno
Cover Designer:	Gail Buschman
Marketing Manager:	Stephanie Adams

Brief Contents

Detailed Contents

Acknowledgments

Two meetings have helped to identify the need to coalesce the expertise of life course researchers who use calendar and time diary methods into one volume. The 2004 Nebraska Symposium on Survey Science, "Exposures and Well-Being: Emerging Methodologies in Life Events Research," held in Omaha and sponsored by the University of Nebraska–Lincoln Gallup Research Center in conjunction with the Gallup Organization, initiated a dialogue among many of the contributors to this volume. In 2006, the Panel Study of Income Dynamics at the University of Michigan sponsored a conference in Ann Arbor titled "Using Calendar and Diary Methodologies in Life Events Research." This latter conference finalized the framework of what was to become this volume. The Nebraska symposium received generous funding through the Othmer Foundation, and the Michigan conference was generously supported by the National Science Foundation, the National Institute on Aging, and the Survey Research Center at the University of Michigan's Institute for Social Research.

The editors thank the following reviewers, who offered a number of valuable suggestions for improving the manuscript:

David Campos
University of the Incarnate Word

Cynthia S. Jacelon
University of Massachusetts, Amherst

Melinda Mills
University of Groningen, the Netherlands

John B. Nezlek
College of William & Mary

Carolyn N. Stevenson
East-West University

Arland Thornton
University of Michigan

1

Introduction

The Application of Calendar and Time Diary Methods in the Collection of Life Course Data

Robert F. Belli, Duane F. Alwin, and Frank P. Stafford

To make important discoveries about the life course via the verbal reports that are elicited from survey respondents, social, health, and behavioral scientists are keenly aware that the quality of reports—and their validity—depends on the methods used to collect them. This book focuses on two data collection methods—the use of calendars and of time diaries—that are similar in the extent to which they encourage respondents to incorporate temporal changes as cues in the reporting of events and to which they have shown the ability to provide data of remarkably high quality. With these methods, people have been asked questions on their parental status, childhood experiences, schooling, marriages, residences, relationships, wealth, work, stressors, health conditions (and their behaviors that can impact their health), levels of happiness, what they have taught others, and how they have spent their time during the past day. The researchers who have contributed chapters to this volume have asked questions along these lines, and some others as well. Although their primary aim is to document those key events that govern people's behavior, health, and social interactions, some also seek to gain a sense of what well-being is and what leads to well-being.

Theoretical and Historical Roots

During the past half century, a "life span perspective" on human development and behavior has flourished across virtually all of the disciplines of the social and behavioral sciences (see Featherman, 1983). This perspective has spawned a number of new approaches to studying human behavior through the enrichment of theory and the development of new methods of collecting data, as well as innovative methods for their analysis. In addition, and perhaps as important as new theory and methods, the life span perspective has contributed via the generation of new bodies of data, especially large-scale panel data sets, that will allow the examination of research hypotheses grounded in the emerging theories. The life course perspective is embodied in a diverse set of disciplinary studies, from the life cycle theories of consumption, training, and labor supply in economics (Modigliani & Brumberg, 1954; Ryder, Stafford, & Stephan, 1976); to life span theories of psychological development and adaptation to the environment (Baltes, 1987; Baltes, Staudinger, & Lindenberger, 1999; Bronfenbrenner, 1979); to sociological theories of age stratification and the life course (Cain, 1964; Dannefer, 1984; Elder, 1985; Elder, Johnson, & Crosnoe, 2003; Elder & Shanahan, 2006; Mills, 1959; Riley, Johnson, & Foner, 1972); evolutionary theories of aging (Kaplan, Hill, Lancaster, & Hurtado, 2000; Lee, 2003); and demographic models of cohort succession (Ryder, 1965) and population aging (Vaupel & Yashin, 1985; Weiss, 1990).

The concepts of "life cycle," "life span," "life course," and "life history" all have been applied interchangeably to the study of human lives, but each concept means something quite distinct, as articulated within the disciplines in which they originate (see Alwin, 2008; Bryman, Bytheway, Allatt, & Keil, 1987; Carey, 2003; Elder, 2000; Olshansky, Carnes, & Brody, 2002). We do not engage in discussion of their differences here, and simply note that they share a common life span perspective, which emphasizes the power of both biographical and historical forces at work in creating the unique biographies of individuals. These forces produce outcomes that can be predicted given the trajectories of experiences, the timing of events (in both a historical and a biographical sense), their sequence, and their meaning. These multidisciplinary strains of research have resulted in a number of theoretical and methodological developments that are just beginning to reap the benefits of understanding the dynamics of life course change.

One of the key insights of such life span developmental perspectives on behavior and development is that human lives are uniquely shaped by the timing and sequence of life events and experiences across rather lengthy periods of time. It is now a commonplace assumption that events occurring in the past can have powerful influences on present and future well-being. Thus, Elder, Shanahan, and Cliff (1994) could convincingly argue that the point in a young man's life cycle when he was called into active duty during World War II had lifelong consequences for employment, schooling, and other aspects of well-being. And, for example, considerable research has shown that individual differences in childhood adversity have lasting consequences for health in adulthood (Elo & Preston, 1992; Preston, Hill, & Drevenstedt, 1998). Early life events relating to unplanned fertility have been shown to be powerful predictors of labor market outcomes and poverty of British women (Ermisch & Francesconi, 2001). Such findings—which establish linkages between various strands of individual life course events, transitions, and trajectories across domains of childhood experiences, adolescence, schooling, employment, military service, marriage, family, wealth, and health—point to the inexorably interconnected nature of life events and processes.

In addition to conceptualizing the entire life span as composed of a series of life stages—childhood, adolescence, early adulthood, midlife, and old age—within which life course events and role transitions (e.g., during the transition to adulthood, or during the transition into retirement) can have important consequences at a later time, the emergent life span perspective has also turned attention to microsettings and the dynamics involved in activities, roles, relationships, settings, and their interconnections. Conceptualizing the environmental influences on behavior within "real-time" social settings that produce events and experiences that contribute to well-being, incentives for behavior, and that produce long-term socialization (or "learning generalization") effects, has strengthened the life span developmental perspective (Bronfenbrenner, 1979).

Several life course theorists (e.g., Elder, 1985; Harris, 1987) have argued that the empirical study of the life course involves primarily the study of events that occur not only across a person's life, but also occurring in historical time, as well as their intersection (Alwin, 1995). In order to understand how earlier life events may influence the present and future of individual development, or to understand the processes by which the various life pathways affect one's destiny, it is essential that social scientists studying these processes have accurate information about both the past and the present. Early discussions of the need for accurate data on life histories emphasized the need for "a lifetime chronology of events and activities that typically and variably combine data records on education, work life, family, and residence" (Elder, 1992, p. 1122).

The specific terrain of "life course" research—where the *life course* is defined as "trajectories of events and transitions within and across life stages" (Elder, 1985, p. 32)—emphasizes the importance of studying what are essentially demographic events (Harris, 1987). Indeed, some have argued that demography is almost exclusively an "event-centered" science, and it is therefore not surprising that demographers have made a unique contribution to the collection and analysis of data involving event histories. Willekens (1999) observed that "most events that occur between birth and death and that have a notable impact on a person's life are *demographic*" (p. 23; emphasis added). He went on to list the following as the unique province of demographers: "Leaving the parental home, marriage, marriage dissolution by divorce or widowhood, migration, labor force entry and exit" as the most important life events (p. 23).

It is within the demographic context of seeking to accurately measure the trajectories and event transitions that constitute the unfolding of the life course that led to the development of calendar and event-centered measurement (e.g., Freedman, Thornton, Camburn, Alwin, & Young-DeMarco, 1988). Remarkably, during the same era in which demographers were gaining insights on the characterization of life course events and on how best to measure them (Elder, 1985; Freedman et al., 1988), cognitive psychologists who measured autobiographical memory were likewise observing that the narrative reconstructions of one's past were marked by recalling extended periods of life (trajectories) and the transitional points between these extensions of stability (Barsalou, 1988; Conway, 1996). In addition, Belli (1988) observed that this structure of autobiographical memory afforded memory cues that could be optimized via calendar interviewing to assist respondents to reconstruct past events more completely and accurately. Complementing a richer understanding of the basic temporal and thematic elements that structure the life course, alongside methodologies that best assist respondents to recall autobiographical events, statistical tools, such as event history models, event-centered growth modeling strategies, and latent class models of life pathways (e.g., Alwin & Campbell, 2001; Alwin, Hofer, & McCammon, 2006; Macmillan & Eliason, 2003; Teachman, 1983) have been developed to analyze life course interactions.

Although designed to capture "snapshots" of daily events, time diaries also have had an important role to play in this life course perspective, as they have revealed important associations among different demographic characteristics and their typical use of time, and especially as they have been applied to the full age span of populations. For example, children 3–18 and their caregivers were the respondents in a 1982 pilot study (Timmer, Eccles, & O'Brien, 1985), and children 0–12 were the focus of diaries in the 1997 Child Development Supplement to the Panel Study of Income Dynamics (Hofferth & Sandberg, 2001). Diary data show distinct life course patterns—such as the concentration of educational and leisure activities in the early life course (Hill, 1985, Table 7.5), and diary patterns show the increase in nonmarket work as people transition into retirement (American Time Use Survey, 2007, www.BLS.gov). The time diaries of children show both their life circumstances and the companion activities of their caregivers, siblings, and other family members (Stafford & Yeung, 2005).

Calendar and Time Diary: Methods for Event and Timeline Measurement

Whereas calendars seek the retrospective reporting of events that happened months or years previously, time diaries typically ask participants to report on events that happened the previous day or a week prior. Yet, because they encourage respondents to report on the timing of occurrences of events as well as the duration of various conditions, states, or activities, researchers with both methods gain insights into causes and consequences that govern life course development. Further, it is precisely the encouragement of reporting on the temporal and spatial locations and the context of events in which improvements in the quality of reports have been shown. As temporal information helps to structure autobiographical memory, the temporal cues that are engendered in calendar and time diary interviews help respondents to remember their pasts more completely and accurately in comparison to more traditional standardized interviewing methods (Belli, Shay, & Stafford, 2001; Csikszentmihalyi & Larson, 1992; Engel, Keifer, & Zahm, 2001; Juster, 1985; Robinson, 1985; Yoshihama, Gillespie, Hammock, Belli, & Tolman, 2005). This better remembrance then appears to support the portrayal of dimensions of the spell of time, such as the occurrence of other elements such as who was present and companion conditions for time diaries and, for event history calendars, aspects of a spell such as the nature of relations with a partner during a spell of co-residence or training programs and wages during a spell of employment.

Calendar and time diary methods have been used by researchers who represent many disciplines. In this volume, chapters are written by experts from diverse fields including criminology, demography, economics, education, marketing, nursing, psychiatry, psychology, social epidemiology, social work, social research methodology, sociology, and survey methodology. The volume is divided into five parts. Part I of the volume provides a foundation for the remaining chapters by exploring the emergence of calendar and diary data collection methods historically, and with regard to the rationales underlying their use. Part II provides examples of substantive areas that have been explored using calendar- and diary-based methodologies. In Part III, the focus centers on assessing the data quality of calendar and diary instruments. Part IV of the volume explores fundamental methodological issues, including the collection, reliability, and validity of time-based data. Finally, in Part V, which consists of a single chapter, speculations on the future directions of calendar- and diary-based data collection methods are offered. To assist readers to navigate through the various interconnections among the chapters, each part has an introduction that presents the main themes of the chapters and how these chapters integrate with others in their respective parts and with other chapters throughout the book. In addition, at the end of each part is a section that provides comments on issues for further thought. At times these issues are practical, such as assisting readers with thinking about various facets that are involved in designing calendar and time diary instruments; at other times these comments examine critical concerns surrounding calendar and time diary methods that are not directly addressed elsewhere.

Despite the disparate topics that are covered in this volume and the different disciplines in which this work is conducted, the research is commonly framed by questionnaire-based methodologies that incorporate temporal changes as cues in the reporting of events. Readers are encouraged to examine the specific data collection approaches that are illustrated and to assess their strengths and weaknesses for the research questions that are being approached. The value of this edited volume arises from revealing—via different examples—common problems, solutions, and strategies in the methods by which researchers collect data designed to measure key events that govern the life course.

References

Alwin, D. F. (1995). Taking time seriously: Studying social change, social structure and human lives. In P. Moen, G. H. Elder, Jr., & K. Lüscher (Eds.), *Examining lives in context: Perspectives on the ecology of human development* (pp. 211–262). Washington, DC: American Psychological Association.

Alwin, D. F. (2008). *Integrating varieties of life course concepts.* Unpublished manuscript. [Available from Center on Population Health and Aging, Pennsylvania State University, University Park, PA 16801]

Alwin, D. F., & Campbell, R. T. (2001). Quantitative approaches: Longitudinal methods in the study of human development and aging. In R. H. Binstock & L. K. George (Eds.), *Handbook of aging and the social sciences* (5th ed., pp. 22–43). New York: Academic Press.

Alwin, D. F., Hofer, S. M., & McCammon, R. J. (2006). Modeling the effects of time: Integrating demographic and developmental perspectives. In R. H. Binstock & L. K. George (Eds.), *Handbook of aging and the social sciences* (6th ed., pp. 20–38). New York: Academic Press.

American Time Use Survey, U.S. Department of Labor. (2007). Retrieved June 5, 2008, from http://www.bls.gov/tus/atususersguide.pdf

Baltes, P. B. (1987). Theoretical propositions of life span developmental psychology: On the dynamics between growth and decline. *Developmental Psychology, 23,* 611–626.

Baltes, P. B., Staudinger, U. M., & Lindenberger, U. (1999). Lifespan psychology: Theory and application to intellectual functioning. *Annual Review of Psychology, 50,* 471–507.

Barsalou, L. W. (1988). The content and organization of autobiographical memories. In U. Niesser & E. Winograd (Eds.), *Remembering reconsidered: Ecological and traditional approaches to the study of memory* (pp. 193–243). New York: Cambridge University Press.

Belli, R. F. (1998). The structure of autobiographical memory and the event history calendar: Potential improvements in the quality of retrospective reports in surveys. *Memory, 6,* 383–406.

Belli, R. F., Shay, W. L., & Stafford, F. P. (2001). Event history calendars and question list surveys: A direct comparison of interviewing methods. *Public Opinion Quarterly, 65,* 45–74.

Bronfenbrenner, U. (1979). *The ecology of human development: Experiments by nature and design.* Cambridge, MA: Harvard University Press.

Bryman, A., Bytheway, B., Allatt, P., & Keil, T. (Eds.). (1987). *Rethinking the life cycle.* London: Macmillan.

Cain, L. D., Jr. (1964). Life course and social structure. In R. E. L. Faris (Ed.), *Handbook of sociology* (pp. 272–309). Chicago: Rand McNally.

Carey, J. R. (2003). The life span: A conceptual overview. *Population Development and Review, 29,* S1–S18.

Conway, M. A. (1996). Autobiographical knowledge and autobiographical memories. In D. C. Rubin (Ed.), *Remembering our past: Studies in autobiographical memory* (pp. 67–93). New York: Cambridge University Press.

Csikszentmihalyi, M., & Larson, R. (1992). Validity and reliability of the experience sampling method. In M. W. de Vries (Ed.), *The experience of psychopathology: Investigating mental disorders in their natural settings* (pp. 43–57). Cambridge, UK: Cambridge University Press.

Dannefer, D. (1984). Adult development and social theory: A paradigmatic reappraisal. *American Sociological Review, 49,* 100–116.

Elder, G. H., Jr. (1985). Perspectives on the life course. In G. H. Elder, Jr. (Ed.), *Life course dynamics: Trajectories and transitions, 1968–1980* (pp. 23–49). Ithaca, NY: Cornell University Press.

Elder, G. H., Jr. (1992). Life course. In E. F. Borgatta & M. L. Borgatta (Eds.), *Encyclopedia of sociology* (Vol. 3, pp. 1120–1130). New York: Macmillan.

Elder, G. H., Jr. (2000). The life course. In E. F. Borgatta & R. J. V. Montgomery (Eds.), *Encyclopedia of sociology* (2nd ed., Vol. 3, pp. 1614–1622). New York: Macmillan Reference USA.

Elder, G. H., Jr., Johnson, M. K., & Crosnoe, R. (2003). The emergence and development of life course theory. In J. T. Mortimer & M. J. Shanahan (Eds.), *Handbook of the life course* (pp. 3–19). New York: Kluwer Academic/Plenum.

Elder, G. H., Jr., & Shanahan, M. J. (2006). The life course and human development. In W. Damon & R. M. Lerner (Eds.), *Handbook of child psychology: Vol. 1: Theoretical models of human development* (6th ed., pp. 665–715). New York: John Wiley.

Elder, G. H., Jr., Shanahan, M. J., & Cliff, E. C. (1994). When war comes to men's lives: Life course patterns in family, work, and health. *Psychology and Aging, 9,* 5–16.

Elo, I. T., & Preston, S. H. (1992). Effects of early-life conditions on adult mortality: A review. *Population Index, 58,* 186–212.

Engel, L. S., Keifer, M. C., & Zahm, S. H. (2001). Comparison of traditional questionnaire with an icon/calendar-based questionnaire to assess occupational history. *American Journal of Industrial Medicine, 40,* 502–511.

Ermisch, J. F., & Francesconi, M. (2001). Family structure and children's achievements. *Journal of Population Economics, 14,* 249–270.

Featherman, D. L. (1983). Life span perspectives in social science research. In P. B. Baltes & O. G. Brim, Jr. (Eds.), *Life span development and behavior* (Vol. 5, pp. 1–57). New York: Academic Press.

Freedman, D., Thornton, A., Camburn, D., Alwin, D. F., & Young-DeMarco, L. (1988). The life history calendar: A technique for collecting retrospective data. In C. C. Clogg (Ed.), *Sociological methodology* (pp. 37–68). Washington, DC: American Sociological Association.

Harris, C. (1987). The individual and society: A processual approach. In A. Bryman, B. Bytheway, P. Allatt, & T. Keil (Eds.), *Rethinking the life cycle* (pp. 17–29). London: Macmillan.

Hill, M. (1985). Investments of time in houses and durables. In F. T. Juster & F. P. Stafford (Eds.), *Time, goods, and well-being* (pp. 205–243). Ann Arbor: University of Michigan, Institute for Social Research.

Hofferth, S. L., & Sandberg, J. F. (2001). How American children spend their time. *Journal of Marriage and the Family, 63,* 295–308.

Juster, F. T. (1985). The validity and quality of time use estimates obtained from recall diaries. In F. T. Juster & F. P. Stafford (Eds.), *Time, goods, and well-being* (pp. 63–91). Ann Arbor: University of Michigan, Institute for Social Research.

Kaplan, H., Hill, K., Lancaster, J., & Hurtado, A. M. (2000). A theory of human life history evolution: Diet, intelligence and longevity. *Evolutionary Anthropology, 9,* 1–30.

Lee, R. D. (2003). Rethinking the evolutionary theory of aging: Transfers, not births, shape senescence in social species. *Proceedings of the National Academic of Sciences, 100,* 9637–9642.

Macmillan, R., & Eliason, S. R. (2003). Characterizing the life course as role configurations and pathways. In J. T. Mortimer & M. J. Shanahan (Eds.), *Handbook of the life course* (pp. 529–554). New York: Kluwer Academic/Plenum.

Mills, C. W. (1959). *The sociological imagination.* New York: Oxford University Press.

Modigliani, F., & Brumberg, R. H. (1954). Utility analysis and the consumption function: An interpretation of cross-section data. In K. K. Kurihara (Ed.), *Post-Keynesian economics* (pp. 388–436). New Brunswick, NJ: Rutgers University Press.

Olshansky, S. J., Carnes, B. A., & Brody, J. (2002). A biodemographic interpretation of life span. *Population and Development Review, 28,* 501–513.

Preston, S. H., Hill, M. E., & Drevenstedt, G. L. (1998). Childhood conditions that predict survival to advanced ages among African-Americans. *Social Science & Medicine, 47,* 1231–1246.

Riley, M. W., Johnson, M. E., & Foner, A. (1972). *Aging and society: A sociology of age stratification* (Vol. 3). New York: Russell Sage.

Robinson, J. P. (1985). The validity and reliability of diaries versus alternative time use measures. In F. T. Juster & F. P. Stafford (Eds.), *Time, goods, and well-being* (pp. 33–62). Ann Arbor: University of Michigan, Institute for Social Research.

Ryder, H. E., Stafford, F. P., & Stephan, P. E. (1976). Labor, leisure and training over the life cycle. *International Economic Review, 17,* 651–674.

Ryder, N. B. (1965). The cohort as a concept in the study of social change. *American Sociological Review, 30,* 843–861.

Stafford, F. P., & Yeung, W. J. (2005). The distribution of children's developmental resources. In D. S. Hamermesh & G. A. Pfaan (Eds.), *The economics of time use* (pp. 289–318). Amsterdam: Elsevier.

Teachman, J. (1983). Analyzing social processes: Life tables and proportional hazards models. *Social Science Research, 12,* 263–301.

Timmer, S. G., Eccles, J., & O'Brien, K. (1985). How children use time. In F. T. Juster & F. P. Stafford (Eds.), *Time, goods, and well-being* (pp. 353–382). Ann Arbor: University of Michigan, Institute for Social Research.

Vaupel, J. W., & Yashin, A. I. (1985). Heterogeneity's ruses: Some surprising effects of selection on population dynamics. *American Statistician, 39,* 176–185.

Weiss, K. M. (1990). The biodemography of variation in human frailty. *Demography, 27,* 185–206.

Willekens, F. J. (1999). The life course: Models and analysis. In L. J. G. van Wissen & P. A. Dykstra (Eds.), *Population issues: An interdisciplinary focus* (pp. 23–51). New York: Kluwer Academic/Plenum.

Yoshihama, M., Gillespie, B., Hammock, A. C., Belli, R. F., & Tolman, R. (2005). Does the life history calendar method facilitate the recall of domestic violence victimization? Comparison of two methods of data collection. *Social Work Research, 29,* 151–163.

PART I

Foundations

Time diary and calendar interviewing methods have fairly long histories of implementation, having been first administered in the early and mid-20th century, respectively. Although these two methods have been developed independently, they intersect in several ways with regard to similarities in data collection and the underlying data structures that are created from their use. These observations are illustrated by the chapters by Stafford (Chapter 2) and Belli and Callegaro (Chapter 3). Stafford notes that both types of instruments illustrate one or more timelines graphically with prescribed time units that link to conventional temporal metrics (e.g., years, months, weeks, days, or hours, which are selected depending on the length of the reference period), and during data entry will visually depict reported activities or statuses as encompassing some subset of these time units. Both methods pose interesting challenges for data management and analyses as temporally continuous information results from data collection, unlike the more discrete data entries that typify standardized interviews. The interviewing in both methods is typically more nondirective, conversational, and flexible than what is observed in conventional standardized interviewing. Belli and Callegaro (Chapter 3) note that the flexible interviewing approaches of both time diaries and calendars promote better data quality as naturalistic conversational properties help to disambiguate meaning, and the temporal structures of these instruments provide effective recall cues. With both methods, the resulting data structures can store variations in variables across time in the smallest discrete time units in which the data were collected, depicting a pieced-together chronology of event trajectories and transitions. If desired, variable aggregations within larger time units can be created. Of importance to researchers is that the richness of the data collected by these methods permits detailed analyses of how the timing of specific life experiences governs life course development.

2

Timeline Data Collection and Analysis

Time Diary and Event History Calendar Methods

Frank P. Stafford

Introduction

Often we are interested in measuring time devoted to different activities over some reference period—such as weeks worked for pay in a year or hours per day spent in housework or child care. And, besides the elapsed time in a certain domain, we may also want some characterization of the activity, such as attributes of a spell of time or information on the timing of external events or transitions from one activity or state to another. The purpose of such measures is to construct variables that capture the level of designated time allocations and responses for the purpose of understanding behavior in the context of a model. In turn, the model portrays the choices of individuals with respect to a type of behavior, ranging from work, leisure, health states, and investment (Juster, 1985; Juster & Stafford, 1991) to episodes of violence or periods in various affective states. In such analyses a goal can be to understand factors shaping well-being.

To illustrate, how do certain types of time use (e.g., child care, elder care from the perspective of a provider or recipient) connect to contact with other persons over the day or how does time in compound activities (multitasking) affect mental health and stress (Bittman & Wacjman, 2000; Gershuny, 2000; Michelson, 2005)? Another purpose is to provide descriptive aggregates for assessing time trends or to create a system of social accounts, such as for satellite nonmarket gross domestic product accounts (Abraham, 2005; M. Hill, 1985). Or, as a blend between accounting and hypothesis testing, has time in personal contact with others throughout the day changed across the decades as a result of the growth of new media forms?

In this chapter an overview of some of the similarities and differences between time diaries and event history calendars (EHCs) is developed.[1] These two approaches share a common theme, which is the collection of timeline data—for diaries the timeline is a 24-hour day, and for EHCs the timeline can commonly range from months to years or even over long sections of the life course. For these different applications, how successful have they been in terms of data quality and resulting research? The questions of whether the project was a research success or whether the data were of high quality almost always have equivocal answers, and in these chapters only some of the answers are given. The strength of the volume is the provision of the methods as applied to a given study and some indication of how these methods supported research findings.

The chapters in this volume demonstrate that EHCs and time diaries and their variants are becoming applied to large, national infrastructural databases as well as to more focused, investigator-initiated research projects. In conjunction with application to more diverse samples, different variants of the instruments have emerged and are likely to continue emerging. To illustrate, the American Time Use Survey (ATUS) (see Phipps & Vernon, Chapter 7, this volume) provides a national sample and a particular model for data collection. Investigators working with diaries for special populations can compare their descriptive results with ATUS. This will provide a benchmark for situations where their sample or methods give rise to questions of how generalizable their study findings may be.

As an example of a more focused study, the Child Development Supplement of the Panel Study of Income Dynamics has collected time diary data on children age 0–12 as of 1997, 6–18 as of 2002/2003, and 11–18 in 2007/2008. Since ATUS has diaries on individuals in the age range of 15 and older, some comparisons of those in the common age range, 15–18, can be made between CDS and ATUS. In a similar fashion, market work hours as measured in the work hours via EHC in the PSID can be compared to market hours as reported in the Current Population Survey (CPS). For innovative designs such as the Consumption and Activities Mail Survey (CAMS) (see Hurd & Rohwedder, Chapter 12, this volume), measures of the time estimates can be compared with ATUS.

From these smaller investigator-initiated projects there will be feedbacks to improvements in the larger infrastructural collections. This will in turn benefit such goals as providing satellite GDP accounts. Two examples come to mind. Intangible investments in human capital have been shown to be a key to economic growth. And much of the input to human capital is time of the individual, caregivers in the family, and those who are providing out-of-home instruction. A focused study of children's time use and cognitive gains could support the construction of satellite GDP accounts.

Themes in Common

This chapter identifies similarities in the data collection methods from both diaries and calendars and in the use of the resulting data for research. Moreover, both methods have a long prior history. The well-known landmark EHC study by Freedman, Thornton, Camburn, Alwin, and Young-DeMarco (1988) was preceded by other earlier efforts (see Belli & Callegaro, Chapter 3, this volume). For diaries, the systematic use of the method appears to date back to the Soviet academician S. G. Strumilin in 1924 (Juster & Stafford, 1991). The next major period of activity was in the mid-1960s led by the Hungarian sociologist, Alexander Szlai (1972), who organized diary projects in the United States, the USSR, Hungary, the Federal Republic of Germany, East Germany, France, Peru, and several other countries. A number of methodological studies were carried out to explore the properties of diaries (Juster, 1985). A related development was the application of experiential sampling methods (Csikszentmihalyi & Csikszentmihalyi, 1988; Csikszentmihalyi & Larson, 1992; Schneider & Stevenson, 1999). This work also had the benefit of providing support for the validity of time diaries.

Since the 1960s, many countries have had regular national data collections based on time diaries. The United States has had a number of smaller-scale diary collections, and starting in January 2003 the U.S. Bureau of Labor Statistics began an ongoing, national diary project based on a sample of the participants in the CPS. For access to multinational diary data archives, see Gershuny and Fisher (2008).

The collection of such timeline data from diaries or calendars can be highlighted by reference to the experiences using both methods in the Panel Study of Income Dynamics (PSID) and the other studies in this volume. The similarities are a matter of the extent to which diary and calendar methods share their basic collection characteristics and application. For each method the types of data collection range from large infrastructural data collections such as the ATUS (see Phipps & Vernon, Chapter 7, this volume) and the PSID to investigator-initiated analysis or methods projects such as the diary-based Day Reconstruction Method (DRM) (see Schwarz, Kahneman, & Xu, Chapter 9) studies and the calendar-based Intimate Partner Violence Study (IPVS) (see Yoshihama, Chapter 8), the study of health risk behavior (see Martyn, Chapter 5) or the study of violent individuals (see Roberts & Mulvey, Chapter 11).

Most uses of diary data are based on a summation of time across the activity records to provide a measure of the share of time allocated to different activities. An example of this is the creation of population estimates of time use for the purpose of national descriptors (Juster, Ono, & Stafford, 2003) and social accounts (Abraham, 2005). Across a wide range of users, the analysis of the time diary data is based on temporal sequencing. A recent study examined time in shopping, at work, and in leisure over days of the week and time periods within days. The goal of the study was in part to examine the effect of changes in shopping-hour laws in the Netherlands (Jacobsen & Kooreman, 2005). Another example of timing analysis is the extent to which time use over the day is varied or routine across different levels of income.

Consider time diary data for children age 6–18 in the NICHD-funded Child Development Supplement (CDS) of the PSID. National time diary data were collected for children age 0–12 as of 1997 and the again when they were reinterviewed 5 to 6 years later, 2002–2003, when they were approximately age 6–18. The reinterview rate for the second set of two diaries was 88%. The CDS data were collected partly in person but largely over the phone by an interviewer who recorded the diary information on paper—with post-field coding and processing. Often researchers use data on the parents' time diaries (Hallberg & Klevmarken, 2001), but an advantage of diaries for the children themselves is the interaction with others in and out of the home, which may be contributing to the child's development. Moreover, diaries for adults need to be modified to account for "with whom" when there are multiple children in the home.

A timeline portrayal of the diary data from CDS II is presented in Figure 2.1. The diurnal pattern of personal care in getting ready for school is shown to be similar for boys and girls, with a pronounced weekday peak at about 7:30 a.m. and again around midevening. For weekends, personal care time is midmorning to noon and then again in midevening. These patterns are similar for boys and girls. In contrast to personal care, time in sports and work differs by gender. Girls spend more time working in the labor market, and this is concentrated in the late afternoon during weekdays and midday to afternoon on weekends.

From such timeline portrayals boys are shown to have somewhat more time in sports than girls at young ages. This difference is most evident at midday on weekends with almost 45% of young boys in active leisure or sports by the midday peak. This differential is much wider at older ages (12.0–17.9), where the time in such activities drops sharply for girls. For computer time outside of school and jobs, both boys and girls have similar total weekly hours and coincident diurnal patterns on weekdays and weekend days. Using the children's diaries is essential in learning about the timing of their activities as well as aggregate descriptors of their time use (Hofferth & Sandberg, 2001; Timmer, O'Brien & Eccles, 1985).

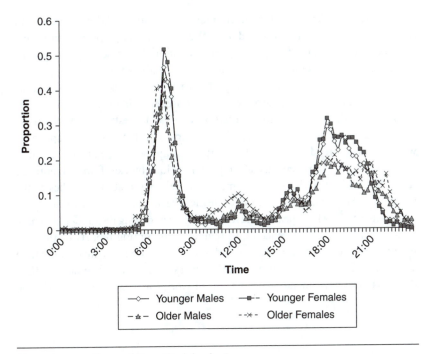

Figure 2.1   Personal Care, Weekday, by Sex

There are some obvious gaps in time diary methods at present. Most respondent-based diaries give only a superficial measure of elapsed time at school and at market work. Time on task has long been seen as a critical measure of learning input in schools. Individual diaries can be replaced with teacher diaries. The CDS attempted this in 1997. This was a national sample, so it was primarily a single teacher for each pre–high school child. A school-based sample may improve this since there should be better opportunities to train the teachers in the methods to be used. School-based studies of the sort by Rowan, Camburn, and Correnti (see Chapter 10, this volume) may be combined with an in-home component to capture a more accurate and comprehensive learning time measure. To highlight this issue, Figure 2.2 shows a tempogram of daily educational activity of African American and other children by school day versus the weekend. The superimposed figure shows a virtual coincidence of time in school and other educationally related activities during weekdays for African American and other students—for both age groups, 6–12 and 12–18. For weekends the story differs. Among the older children (12–18), from noon (.5 on the horizontal axis) on, there is a noticeably wider gap in educational activities between African American and other children. Here we can see the need for both in-school and out-of-school diaries to capture educational exposure. Moreover, the fine-grained activity within the school day can be captured only by a teacher log or other school-based diary method.

One possible approach to within-school activity in a diary is to have a topics module after the diary is completed. For those reporting segments of time at school in the diary records, there could be a series of questions that would ask about share of time in different subject matters. If such a post-diary approach were successful in educational settings, it might apply to time at market work. Here, too, diary respondents usually report quite long blocks of undifferentiated time "at work." There have been some small-scale observational studies of the workplace (Stafford, 1987, from data in the Effectiveness in Work Roles pilot study). Just as CAMS appears to have had success in getting respondents to have a temporal frame of reference as a prelude to attempting reports of time, so might a time diary with reported episodes provide a more specific framing than a generic question series on activities at work. A further advantage of time diaries is that they can capture the spells of work (or study) for those with no

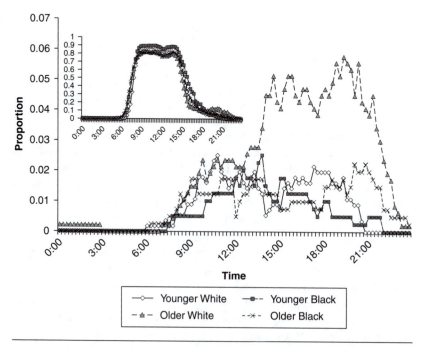

Figure 2.2   Education and Training, Weekend (large graph), and Weekday (inserted graph), by Race

fixed work (or school) location for the growing many who devote time to market work while at home or away from their normal place of work.

Besides the tempograms in Figures 2.1 and 2.2, the diary data could be used to study transitions during the day just as an EHC data file can be used to study transitions across states. In 2003, the PSID initiated national data collection of a 2-year EHC of labor market activity and residential domains. This computer-assisted telephone interviewing (CATI) EHC application was based on methodology work funded by the National Science Foundation and the National Institute on Aging. The EHC CATI software is a tabular graphical user interface for the interviewer and is a separate software component that merges into and from a more comprehensive BLAISE application, which collects information on other content areas. Based on the validity and design studies summarized by Belli and Callegaro (see Chapter 3, this volume), the EHC CATI instrument has been a part of PSID core interviewing since 2001. In 2007, the PSID implemented a health history calendar to capture early life health conditions of the adult respondents.

Both EHCs and time diaries provide vastly more information than stylized questions or what have been called question list or Q-list approaches. Here with EHCs or time diaries we have more of a chronology pieced together by the respondent with the aid of CATI or other collection tools. With high-power desktop tools (SAS, Oracle) users are free to innovate with more complex variable constructions and data alignments that are targeted to their specific research purposes such as sequence analysis (Wilson, 2006). For example, the timing of (re)employment and vehicle purchases may differ for those in poverty and more affluent consumers.

To see the nature of the microdata produced from the 2003 and 2005 EHC application in the PSID, I present data in Figure 2.3 on transitions on a one-third-of-the-month basis, starting at the beginning of January (January:1, January:2, . . . December:3). The one-third-of-a-month data is from our initial methods work (Belli, Shay, & Stafford, 2001) in which respondents were found to be able to answer "beginning," "middle" and "end" of the month, and that strongly suggests that the beginning, middle, and end of the month could be more easily recalled than weeks. Weeks have the troublesome feature of often crossing over into the next month or carrying over from the prior month. Here I consider four states: employed (including multiple job holding and not "other"), E; vacation, V; unemployed, U; and out of the labor force, O; and I am looking one calendar year back within the 2-year window transitions on a third-of-a-month basis for both data collected in 2003 and data collected in 2005. This produces 36 possible transitions over the period January:1, 2002, to December:3, 2002, and 36 more for the period January:1, 2004, to December:3, 2004. In which months do transitions among the different labor statuses occur most frequently?

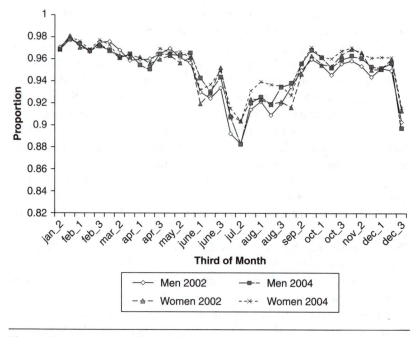

Figure 2.3   Fraction of Sample Not Transitioning

Figure 2.3 depicts the percentage *not* transitioning to a different labor market state, where the states are: at work for pay, on vacation from work, on strike, unemployed, on sick leave from an employer, and out of the labor force. For both calendar years 2002 and 2004, restricting the individuals to be age 30–60 and using the reports with complete data (about 90% of the cases), the overwhelming number of transitions are from working for pay to being on vacation (E to V) and returning (V to E). Moreover, most of the short periodicity transitions are concentrated around the last third of May (Memorial Day), the first third of July (July 4), and the last third of December. Hence one can see, not surprisingly, but comfortingly, the share of nontransitions on a third-of-a-month basis is lowest in July (after the 4th of July), November, and late December. This reflects the obvious fact these are common vacation times near major holidays, and that the EHC captures the major, known patterns in a fashion we would expect. How well an EHC so designed might be in capturing joint transitions onto and off welfare, schooling, and employment or nonmarket care giving by household members remains to be seen.

EHCs are proving to be an extremely flexible data collection tool. In a sense, the 24-hour time diary is a type of EHC. This can be seen by comparing the timeline portrayals of a *24-hour day* with respect to certain activities as in

Figure 2.1 for educational activity participation, and then considering the *12-month, 36-transition point* interview window in the EHC of the PSID as depicted in Figure 2.3. The 12-month time window is broken into fixed grids of 36 thirds-of-a-month, a practice similar to that in time use studies that have broken each hour into four fixed grids of 15 minutes each.

EHCs have the property of more fully capturing coincident activities of interest. Unlike time diaries, where there have been ongoing issues of how to treat secondary and even tertiary activities, with EHCs it is normally the case that several domains of activity or states prevail at a given time, and that within each domain there can be multiple activity forms. So a person can be a student and work at the same time (which one might judge as the primary or secondary is possible with some modification of the EHC), and one could hold two jobs simultaneously to support the ongoing school enrollment. Note that such an EHC is providing far richer information than simple questions like "Did you work last year (month)? Did you go to school last year (month)? Are you in school now? Are you working now?" Depending on the purpose, such short questions may be better, but EHCs (or time diaries) provide a great deal more information in a clearer layout even if one is interested in overall schooling activity of different population groups.

EHCs have been applied to a very wide and growing range of time windows, ranging from large segments of a person's entire life to shorter periods. For example, there have been EHC applications to obtain health conditions and events of an individual's youth. Educational histories seem particularly well suited to EHCs. Again one may be content with much less information, such as the highest grade the respondent has attained as of the date of the interview. But in an EHC design it is possible to capture the timing of specific spells of education, or within a spell any changes in the subject matter studied. Then there are distinct events such as graduation or dropping out, temporarily or otherwise. The time points of these can be marked. Health histories illustrate another area of application. For illnesses with a distinct onset and treatment period the EHC seems well suited. Some conditions such as arthritis, however, may come on gradually so there is not a distinct event that marks the onset. Health history calendars may be refined to capture the distinction between onset and diagnosis or may be better if designed to capture both for some health conditions.

Time Diary and EHC Measures: A Comparison

One phrase that has been used to describe the diary is that the responses are ideally nondirected. There is no question about work or child care or housework—ideally just an objective chronology of the events on the randomly sampled day.

The idea is that respondents can think of distinct time or activity segments in different activities over a recall period of a few days. They give a verbal description of the activity sequences and the hard work—just as in occupation coding—is the post-field transformation of what are sometimes vague answers into one of many codes by the research and processing team. When the respondent is asked to process, as with a domain-specific diary that asks for all the spells of a given type over a 24-hour day, the result is generally a strong upward bias, as illustrated in studies on media use.

The diary system is also driven by location. Changing activities often involves a change in location within the residence or travel to a different location. A parallel in EHC is the common conjunction between changes in residence and changes in employment. These location changes provide a cognitive anchor or landmark that promotes better recall for both diaries and calendars. Validity studies have often found time diaries to provide unbiased measures compared to the estimates from an identical population using experience sampling method[2] (ESM) or random paging of time samples (Robinson, 1985).

Time diary studies have shown the importance of secondary activities within each diary segment. A parallel for EHCs could be thought of as applying to people who have a lot going on in their lives in the domains under question. For example, people may hold multiple jobs at a given time or may have multiple partners or members of their family in residence. Do such coincident conditions induce stress in a manner parallel to multitasking as recorded in time diaries? Ideally, EHC measures should support event history analysis (Stafford & Sundström, 1996).

Collection and Use of Data

The use of the resulting timeline data from a time diary or an EHC ranges from creating simple individually aggregated summaries to what can be termed customized, "complex constructions." The use of EHC methods appears to allow the construction of summary measures that are similar to the aggregates from respondent-based methods—in terms of the basic allocation of the 52 weeks of the year into various statuses such as weeks of employment, out of the labor force, on vacation, and so on.

In a similar fashion the time diary records from the individual 24-hour diary (or *diaries* if more than one per person as with CDS), can be processed in a great variety of ways, starting with the most basic aggregates of an individual's time to complex timelines. The activity records are the fundamental data element collected in diaries. Each represents a nonoverlapping segment or spell of time in a given (primary) activity, and the location of an activity is both a descriptor and often the basis for delineating a new spell. Descriptors of the spell, such as secondary[3] activity or who else was present, are often key to the study of social interactions, such as child care. An interesting descriptor used in the Australian time diaries is a "for whom" indicator.[4]

The activity records are first used to create files of hours and minutes per day in specific time use codes for each respondent. These basic aggregations of the records into a file with daily time into a set of activity codes constitute a basic "processed" or flat file per person day, which is helpful to many analyses, especially for descriptive purposes and often explaining a particular time use as a dependent variable.[5] For diaries the codes are often fine grained—as many as 300 to 400 categories—and are possibly beyond the level of detail as reported by the respondent. These need to be aggregated to some higher level for any meaningful analysis. Even with aggregation to 20 code categories or so, while some respondents will have multiple episodes of an activity per day, many respondents may not have participated in a given activity on the diary day or days even in common activities such as housework—only sleep and rest (almost!) invariably show up as activities at the individual level. This issue of reliability or what Alwin (see Chapter 16, this volume) would refer to as sampling variability of time in different days, has been discussed in numerous writings (Juster et al., 2003; Kalton, 1985).

One descriptive tool is creation of similarity indices for the aggregated time use categories for population subgroups, parallel to the application of occupational dissimilarity comparisons between males and females. These dissimilarities indices can capture the extent to which time use patterns differ across the specified groups (Stewart, 2004).

Besides supporting creation of overall time use measures, the other value of the microdiary activity record data is the creation of what may be called "complex constructions"—that is, compound use of the activities *and* descriptors of the activity (where, who else was present, were you doing anything else at the same time, and—rather specific to CDS—what program were you watching [if viewing a video screen was reported], etc.) to create such special measures. There have been measures of media content exposure to learning (Wright et al., 2001) or interactive development time with parents on weekdays versus weekend days, based on the presence and involvement columns in the CDS diaries. Diaries of adults are commonly used to measure child care through the use of who-was-present indicators. In families where there are multiple children being cared for or caregivers other than the sampled adult, an incomplete picture of the child care received by the child is a likely result. Regardless of the respondent, child care measures require a set of judgments about what activity types constitute child care and which other person's direct involvement should be included in a specific definition.

Using these "with whom" and "involvement" descriptors and a set of activities regarded as developmentally valuable, it can be shown that young children living with both biological parents get more than twice as much direct interactive developmental time (Stafford & Yeung, 2005). The value of the diary is in the ability to obtain a sample of elapsed time under a particular definition of *development time.* Direct questioning about how involved the parents are might provide a possible ranking measure, but could not support a cardinal measure of how much time parents are involved with their children as is available from time diary data collections.

Both EHC and time diary data can also be designed to capture descriptors associated with a given spell or episode. For example, one can characterize a spell of employment as full-time or part-time or by the rate of compensation or extent of on-the-job learning. While complex constructions have been created and analyzed for CDS time diaries, use of the EHC data in PSID is of very recent vintage. To date they have been used to construct summary measures of annual market workweeks, unemployment, and time out of the labor force. Methodology work indicates that the EHC can provide more valid measures of a 2-year employment window than traditional question list recall of labor market activity from 2 years back (Belli et al., 2001).

Just as with diary descriptors of time, EHC data could be used to create more complex constructions such as number of weeks during the past 2 years during which the respondent worked more than one job, or had a second job at a lower wage rate. These constructions would support descriptive characterizations of multiple job holdings. A deeper use of the EHC files is to study transitions across domains (Stafford & Sundström, 1996). In conjunction with measures of financial holdings and expenditures in the PSID, such job holding constructions could also support the investigation of the use of second job activity as a way of meeting cash flow needs. As noted, a number of financial variables in the PSID have monthly activity indicators or "month strings." For example, there are month strings on the receipt of transfer payments or purchase/lease initiation of autos. These joint timeline data on residence and employment (from EHC) and vehicle acquisition and transfer payment receipt (from month strings) could be used to support analysis of the timing of exit from welfare and securing transportation for employment.

A difference between diaries and EHCs in the PSID and in other applications is the commonly far greater omnibus character of diaries compared to the selected domains common in EHC designs (see Martyn, Chapter 5; Yoshihama, Chapter 8; Roberts & Mulvey, Chapter 11, this volume). The EHC is usually designed to target specific types of activities, since, unlike time diaries, it is not, in concept, a real time measure. In an EHC, when a person reports working over some spell or spousal abuse over some time period, the activity is not occurring 24/7 and is in conjunction with other life domains. With time diaries there is, by definition, only a single primary activity at a point in time. On the other hand, diary activity records invariably incorporate additional descriptors, including with whom (CDS), affect (see Schwarz, Kahneman, & Xu, Chapter 9, this volume) and may target activities such as child care or nonmarket work (see Phipps & Vernon, Chapter 7, this volume), and as noted above, it is these descriptors that give rise to complex constructions—but constructions in a domain chosen in the research design.

With diaries, while there is often an omnibus character to the primary time uses, there is much more direction behind the choice of activity descriptors.[6] Further, in the application of teacher logs (see Rowan, Camburn, & Correnti, Chapter 10, this volume), the teachers themselves are asked to code the class time. While this may give rise to some bias in reporting their teaching time, responses to 24 items on an annual survey show far higher frequencies of teaching than do the same items recorded in the teacher logs. The teacher logs are a variant of diaries. They ask the teacher to focus on a specific teaching episode and record, from a set of items, those that occurred during the lesson. In principle, these data could be used to study the timing of teaching methods over a school day. Studying school days themselves is important. In a general purpose diary, both time at work and time at school get reported as largely an undifferentiated block of time.

Timeline analysis of diary data is also possible but is less common among economic studies. For example, time diary data have been used to study the daily patterns of time in one's residence as a way of evaluating the potential for energy saving on heating and cooling and possible peak load pricing responsiveness (D. Hill, 1985). A number of timeline portrayals of diary data are reviewed by Michelson (2005). These are presented as tempograms of percentage of percentages of workers engaged in main paid work across a 24-hour day (pp. 116–119) and can also be used to characterize the daily patterns of social contact of children during school days. Other newly emerging tools can be applied to the analysis of diary files as timeline data. One approach that has been used with success is software to portray sequencing (Wilson, 2006). Possibly tempograms and sequencing software will become applied to EHC data.

Conclusion: Calendar and Diary Data Compared to What?

Commonly, we hope to phrase a question or question sequence and rely on the respondent to construct a summary measure of elapsed time for us. The summary measure is often readily used by the research community with few concerns—but then some limitations of the summary measure come to light. Or we would like to characterize the elapsed time in some way such as, say, productive, enjoyable, or representing an investment in children. Further still, we may be interested in the sequencing of episodes that add up to the total elapsed time. To illustrate, of the weeks of unemployment during a calendar year, was this one spell or several shorter spells, and what was the timing?

In respondents' direct reports of elapsed time over a year or a "typical week" or "typical day" or recent weeks, there can be a bias in their processing to come up with an average, particularly when the time category is not well delineated as with emerging employment patterns with less structure as to time and place—as a contrast to market work on a regular schedule at a given location or a daily housework routine. For example, particularly when the work is variable with respect to effort, location, and content, respondents may exaggerate socially desirable time as a part of the construction process or rely on stereotypic or stylized answers such as 8 hours of work or of sleep, or 2 hours of housework a day. So, for example, time allocated to the care of one's own children—which has an inherent ambiguity as to what is time in child care itself or possibly including time "on call" as part of child care as a secondary time use (as a reported activity descriptor)—and a large social desirability element—is found to be reported at levels way beyond amounts as measured in a validation study with paging devices (Hofferth, 1999). Further, this time exaggeration is greater for more educated parents—evidently because care for children is seen as important and who would say, "I barely notice my children—most of *my* time is spent channel surfing!" "And, by the way, what do you *really mean* by care of my child?" On the other hand, the use of carefully designed nondiary sequences asking for recall over recent months and weeks have been implemented with notable success (see Hurd & Rohwedder, Chapter 12, this volume).

Some time constructions of interest to researchers are simply too demanding for respondents to provide from direct questions. A classic distinction in economics is between time in employment and unemployment versus time out of the labor force—for extended periods, perhaps because of illness or injury. The respondent may know only that work was missed for 6 months because of an injury. The respondent may think of this as "unemployment" but researchers would consider most of the 6 months to be time "out of the labor force"—because of injury—not unemployment: not 26 weeks of illness—since shorter periods of time away from work on accident or sick leave (but paid) is another matter. Moreover, during a calendar year a respondent may have several segments of time out of the labor force. While these may add up to 6 months, those segments may be too much to process into a report of "6 months" in an interview situation.

Many times a Q-list sequence or more detailed sequences can be used to get "good answers." An interesting illustration is years and spells of smoking behavior collected in the PSID. In 1986, respondents were asked for their current smoking behavior and smoking history—do they currently smoke and how many cigarettes do they currently smoke per day? When did they start and, if they have quit (dozens of times, it's easy), when was that? Again in 1999—13 years later and in 2001—15 years later—they were asked similar questions on current smoking behavior and their smoking history. Here we can use their prior (at-the-time reports—which we assume to be accurate) and compare with their recall over a 13-year interval. In comparing the reports from the two waves it was found that about 10% gave inconsistent answers (Grafova & Stafford, 2008). Why might this happen? Possibly a lot of attention is given—both by the smoker and also by friends—to attempts to quit and by the onset of or cessation of a distinct and visible habit. The transition creates its own landmark—"I haven't smoked a cigarette since New Year's Day of 1994" or "I quit on my birthday in 1997." Quitters often refer to the duration of their success, and those who smoke often keep a mental note of how long they have been smoking. So perhaps it is these natural mental landmarks that appear to make this smoking recall quite accurate (Patrick et al., 1994). It is a open question of whether, let us suppose, a smoking history calendar (SHC) would provide data as good or better (but see Belli, Smith, Andreski, & Agrawal, 2007, for evidence that collecting smoking via an EHC approach is better), but a calendar may be possible while a panel over prior years is not possible or is more expensive. If so, an advantage of the SHC is that long panel observations would not be necessary. A key aspect of long span EHCs is that they may be a substitute for an expensive panel project.

Another example of what seems effective for some diary-based measures is the use of an extensive set of questions about a particular time use but calibrated over a shorter horizon for regularly occurring events and over a longer period for less frequently occurring activities. The CAMS in the Health and Retirement Study (HRS) is an example of a nondiary-based time use study that appears to do quite well. At the other side of the diary-type spectrum is the Daily Inventory of Stressful Events (DISE). There respondents were asked to report the presence of a set of stressful events over the prior 24 hours on 8 contiguous days (see Wethington & Almeida, Chapter 6, this volume). The goal of the project was to record the incidence of stressful events in daily life and the extent of stress in each episode, not the elapsed time of the stressful event. Given the panel nature of the approach, the time path of stressors and well-being can be assessed. Here we ignore the potential risk of respondent burden and refusals.

To summarize, while EHC methods and time diary methods have some distinct advantages over some measurement alternatives, using an EHC or a time diary should be carefully matched to the domain of interest. Clearly a panel may be preferred to recall, even with a well-designed EHC, but an initial EHC in a panel may provide valuable timeline data prior to the start of a panel. An EHC may also be valuable for interim information between panel waves to obtain a more complete picture of the temporal ordering of activities. Time diaries, too, have strengths and weaknesses. While they appear to give relatively unbiased reports of activities, they can be regarded as giving a small sample of the days in the life of a respondent. Seldom are more than two daily diaries for a given individual collected in national samples. For many rather usual activities of the respondent these may simply not have been activities on the two sampled days or the duration of the time in those activities may have been somewhat uncharacteristic.

Notes

1. As noted by Belli and Callegaro (Chapter 3), the EHC approach has been referred to by a variety of names, including, for example, life history calendar; my preference is to use EHC throughout this chapter.
2. For a study of youth based on ESM see Schneider and Stevenson (1999).
3. Or consider a second secondary (tertiary) activity.
4. Includes the code "myself."
5. For example, the diary data from CDS show greater TV time for children with mothers who work longer market hours at low wages; TV appears to play the role of a low-cost babysitter.
6. In CDS the goal of understanding the extent and impact of media exposure motivated the media content gathered in Column D.

Acknowledgment

I am grateful to NSF(SES 0094942), NIA (AG019802) and NICHD (HD033474) for financial support.

References

Abraham, K. G. (2005). *Beyond the market: Designing nonmarket accounts for the United States*. Washington, DC: National Academy Press.

Belli, R. F., Shay, W. P., & Stafford, F. P. (2001). Event history calendar and question list survey interviewing methods: A direct comparison. *Public Opinion Quarterly, 65*, 45–74.

Belli, R. F., Smith, L., Andreski, P. M., & Agrawal, S. (2007). Methodological comparison between CATI event history calendar and standardized conventional questionnaire instruments. *Public Opinion Quarterly, 71*, 603–622.

Bittman, M., & Wacjman, J. (2000). The rush hour: The character of leisure time and gender equity. *Social Forces, 79*, 165–189.

Csikszentmihalyi, M., & Csikszentmihalyi, I. S. (1988). *Optimal experience: Psychological studies in flow of consciousness*. Cambridge, UK: Cambridge University Press.

Csikszentmihalyi, M., & Larson, R. (1992). Validity and reliability of the experience sampling method. In M. W. de Vries (Ed.), *The experience of psychopathology:*

Investigating mental disorders in their natural settings (pp. 43–57). Cambridge, UK: Cambridge University Press.

Freedman, D., Thornton, A., Camburn, D., Alwin, D., Young-DeMarco, L. (1988). The life history calendar: A technique for collecting retrospective data. In C. C. Clogg (Ed.), *Sociological methodology* (Vol. 18, pp. 37–68). San Francisco: Jossey-Bass.

Gershuny, J. (2000). *Changing times: Work and leisure in postindustrial society.* Oxford, UK: Oxford University Press.

Gershuny, J., & Fisher, K. (2008). *Multinational Time Use Study.* Data archive available from University of Oxford, Centre for Time Use Research Web site: http://www .timeuse.org/mtus/

Grafova, I. B., & Stafford, F. P. (2008, January). *Persistent smokers and the wage gap* (Working Paper). Ann Arbor: University of Michigan, Department of Economics.

Hallberg, D., & Klevmarken, N. A. (2001). Time for children: A study of parents' time allocation. *Journal of Population Economics, 16,* 205–226.

Hill, D. (1985). The implications of home production and inventory adjustment processes for the time-of-day demand for electricity. In F. T. Juster & F. P. Stafford (Eds.), *Time, goods, and well-being* (pp. 493–513). Ann Arbor: University of Michigan, Institute for Social Research.

Hill, M. (1985). Investments of time in houses and durables. In F. T. Juster & F. P. Stafford (Eds.), *Time, goods, and well-being* (pp. 205–243). Ann Arbor: University of Michigan, Institute for Social Research.

Hofferth, S. (1999). *Family reading to young children: Social desirability and cultural biases in reporting.* Paper presented at the National Research Council Workshop on Measurement and Research on Time Use, Committee on National Statistics, Washington, DC.

Hofferth, S., & Sandberg, J. (2001). How American children spend their time. *Journal of Marriage and the Family, 63,* 295–308.

Jacobsen, J. P., & Kooreman, P. (2005). Timing constraints and the allocation of time: The effects of changing shopping hours regulations in The Netherlands. In D. S. Hamermesh & G. A. Pfann (Eds.), *The economics of time use* (pp. 19–42). Amsterdam: Elsevier Science.

Juster, F. T. (1985). The validity and quality of time use estimates obtained from recall diaries. In F. T. Juster & F. P. Stafford (Eds.), *Time, goods, and well-being* (pp. 63–91). Ann Arbor: University of Michigan, Institute for Social Research.

Juster, F. T., Ono, H., & Stafford, F. P. (2003). Alternative approaches to the measurement of time use. *Sociological Methodology, 33,* 19–54.

Juster, F. T., & Stafford, F. P. (1991). The allocation of time: Empirical findings, behavioral models, and problems of measurement. *Journal of Economic Literature, 29,* 471–522.

Kalton, G. (1985). Sample design issues in time diary studies. In F. T. Juster & F. P. Stafford (Eds.), *Time, goods, and well-being* (pp. 93–112). Ann Arbor: University of Michigan, Institute for Social Research.

Michelson, W. (2005). Time use: *Expanding the explanatory power of the social sciences.* Boulder, CO: Paradigm.

Patrick, D. L., Cheadle, A., Thompson, D. C., Diehr, P., Koepsell, T., & Kinne, S. (1994). The validity of self-reported smoking: A review and meta-analysis. *American Journal of Public Health, 84,* 1086–1093.

Robinson, J. P. (1985). The validity and reliability of diaries versus alternative time use measures. In F. T. Juster & F. P. Stafford (Eds.), *Time, goods, and well-being* (pp. 33–62). Ann Arbor: University of Michigan, Institute for Social Research.

Schneider, B. L., & Stevenson, D. (1999). *The ambitious generation*. New Haven, CT: Yale University Press.

Stafford, F. P. (1987). Organizational theory and the nature of jobs. *Journal of Institutional and Theoretical Economics, 143,* 519–536.

Stafford, F. P., & Sundström, M. (1996). Time out for child care: Signalling and earnings rebound effects for men and women. *Labour, 10,* 609–629.

Stafford, F. P., & Yeung, J. (2005). The distribution of children's developmental resources. In D. S. Hamermesh & G. A. Pfann (Eds.), *The economics of time use* (pp. 51–84). Amsterdam: Elsevier Science.

Stewart, J. (2004). *What do male nonworkers do?* (Working Paper #371). Washington, DC: U.S. Department of Labor, Bureau of Labor Statistics.

Szlai, A. (1972). Design specifications for the surveys. In A. Szlai (Ed.), *The use of time* (pp. 31–41). The Hague, the Netherlands: Mouton.

Timmer, S. G., O'Brien, K., & Eccles, J. (1985). How children use time. In F. T. Juster & F. P. Stafford (Eds.), *Time, goods, and well-being* (pp. 353–382). Ann Arbor: University of Michigan, Institute for Social Research.

Wilson, C. (2006). Reliability of sequence-alignment analysis of social processes: Monte Carlo tests of ClustalG software. *Environment and Planning, 38*(1), 187–204.

Wright, J. C., Huston, A. C., Vandewater, E. A., Bickham, D. S., Scantlin, R. M., Kotler, J. A., et al. (2001). American children's use of electronic media in 1997: A national survey. *Journal of Applied Developmental Psychology, 22,* 31–47.

3

The Emergence of Calendar Interviewing

A Theoretical and Empirical Rationale

Robert F. Belli and Mario Callegaro

Introduction

The overarching goal of any scientific data collection is to acquire valid information. In the arena of survey interviewing, acquiring valid data is dependent on the extent to which information provided by respondents matches an underlying true state of affairs. Assessments of the meaning of "what is truth" are always difficult (O'Muircheartaigh, 1997), but in principle, seeking factual data (as opposed to opinions or subjective judgments) through respondent reports has an objective truth criterion inherent in those conditions of experience that constitute the target of the questions being posed. Hence, the goal of acquiring valid factual data through survey interviewing translates into reducing the degree of difference between what is being reported and what exists or retrospectively has existed in objective conditions of experience.

In the history of survey interviewing, two main approaches have emerged in the collection of retrospective reports. By far the most prevalent approach has been the use of standardized interviewing techniques, which seeks to standardize the wording of questions so as to maximize reliability, and hence, validity. The second approach has been referred to by a variety of names including life history calendar and event history calendar (EHC), but for purposes of simplicity we will usually refer to this approach as calendar interviewing. In calendar interviewing, the acquisition of valid retrospective reports is assumed to depend on a flexible use of language to encourage respondents to remember the interrelationships of events that have occurred in their autobiographical past.

Standardized survey interviewing emerged from the increasing desire to conduct quantitative research (Fowler & Mangione, 1990), and its rise as the most prevalent and accepted form of survey interviewing for the collection of quantitative data has been a gradual historical process (Beatty, 1995; O'Muircheartaigh, 1997). Before the advent of statistical methods to analyze quantitative data, researchers generally relied on qualitative approaches to gain insight on topics of interest (Kirk & Miller, 1986). Qualitative research depends on in-depth flexible interviewing conducted by substantive experts, and usually with a small number of participants. Although qualitative researchers gain insights on the behavior of larger populations through this in-depth interviewing approach that provides rich information, they cannot directly draw quantitative inferences from samples to populations. With the advancement of inferential statistics, researchers were able to draw quantitative inferences to populations, but using inferential statistical methods requires the surveying of large samples, usually in the hundreds or thousands. Standardized interviewing methodology grew in prevalence as a means to ensure consistency in interviewing while using professional interviewers as a cost-containment practice, as the expense of collecting quantitative data using substantive experts as interviewers is prohibitive with large numbers of participants.

In the first introduction of calendar-based interviewing techniques to the scientific community, Balán, Browning, Jelin, and Litzler (1969) were also seeking a methodology to collect quantitative data with professional interviewers, while concentrating on the retrospective reporting of selected life course events. Prior to their innovative approach, researchers who were interested in examining life histories relied on qualitative approaches in which only a few individuals were extensively interviewed (e.g., Thomas & Znaniecki, 1958), or on quantitative approaches in which the areas of the life course that were examined were heavily restricted by topic and by collecting information on only part of the life span. Balán et al. interviewed 1,640 men in Monterrey, Mexico, on entire life course migratory, educational, partnering, parenting, health, and labor histories. Of especial interest was outlining a procedure by which life course responses could be entered into computer data files for purposes of statistical analyses. A number of studies adopting similar calendar interviewing approaches were to follow.

Because for the past several decades standardized survey interviewing has been considered as the sine qua non of collecting valid survey data by the vast majority of survey methodologists (Beatty, 1995; Fowler & Mangione, 1990; Viterna & Maynard, 2002), the theoretical rationale and empirical findings that support the use of calendar interviewing in the collection of retrospective reports has often been overlooked. The purpose of this chapter is to highlight the advantages of calendar interviewing by, first, comparing the methodologies of standardized and calendar interviewing; second, by reviewing empirical results in data quality that have emerged in studies, including those that have contrasted standardized and calendar interviewing methods; and third, by pointing to substantive studies in which calendar interviewing has been used.

A Comparison of Standardized and Calendar Interviewing Methodologies

In their description of standardized interviewing[1] as the best practice for survey interviewing, Fowler and Mangione (1990) advocate a methodology in which interviewers are to read exactly the questions and response options that are scripted in advance by the survey researchers. In addition, they are to probe as necessary, only when necessary, and always nondirectively, leaving all of the interpretation of question intent entirely to the respondent. Although different survey organizations implement standardized interviewing in slightly different ways, especially with regard to how nondirective probing is defined, the basic methodological practices as advocated by Fowler and Mangione are almost universally appreciated if not always exactly followed (Viterna & Maynard, 2002). The aim of standardization is to produce a survey instrument in which all of the variance in responses is due only to differences in the experiences (or attitudes) of the respondents. This aim is based on the idea that via the interviewer, who follows a standardized protocol, the survey researcher is providing a consistent tool by which to measure respondent variance, much like a ruler that is divided up into standard units (such as inches or centimeters) is able to accurately measure the variance that exists in objects of different lengths. Standardized interviewing hinges on the assumption that any problems of language and interaction between interviewers and respondents are the result of poorly written and inadequately pretested questions.

In more recent years, a number of criticisms have been levied against standardized interviewing. The most universally understood criticism is that standardization is an ideal that can never be completely achieved largely because the intricacies of language that are based on tacit, commonsense knowledge will always introduce variance of meaning (Schaeffer & Maynard, 2002). Yet, despite this criticism, standardization is seen as the best way to ensure validity. Some critiques, however, seemingly approach a conclusion that standardization, in and of itself, may be a threat to validity. Suchman and Jordan (1990) observed that attempts to write perfect standardized questions that could apply to every possible respondent circumstance were not possible, and that such attempts ran the risk of increasing misunderstanding, not alleviating it.

Schober and Conrad (1997) challenged the idea that using the same words is equivalent to providing consistent meaning, and offered evidence that conversational variability increases the understanding of intended meanings. Their results hinge on the realization that language has natural mechanisms that promote the repair of misunderstandings and that these mechanisms are stifled by attempts to create the same standardized wordings for everyone.

In an examination of standardized interviewers, a number of researchers (Belli, Lepkowski, & Kabeto, 2001; Dykema, Lepkowski, & Blixt, 1997; Ongena, 2005) have found that interviewers often violate standardized interviewing techniques in practice. According to Houtkoop-Steenstra (2000), these violations are the result of survey researchers placing interviewers in an impossible situation. On one hand, interviewers are to convey to respondents only the intended meanings of the survey researchers; "interviewers do not mean anything." On the other hand, interviewers must simultaneously be meaningful people who are responsive to their respondents by listening, thinking, and by expressing an awareness of the social world that they share with their respondents. At times, interviewers find themselves in a position in which they must explain their reading of questions as written by someone else, and in so doing, they distance themselves from any ownership or interest in the questions in and of themselves (see especially Houtkoop-Steenstra, 2000, but also Belli & Chardoul, 1997). The extent to which violations of standardization impact data quality is still uncertain, perhaps because at times violations may improve validity as well as endanger it.

In developing their innovative calendar interviewing approach designed to collect life course retrospective reports, Balán et al. (1969) recognized that maximizing the validity of data would be best accomplished by allowing flexible interviewing. Interviewers were allowed to provide their own precise wording to questions, and to choose which specific questions were asked and when. Interviewing flexibility is a key characteristic of calendar interviewing that distinguishes it from standardized interviewing. The promotion of flexibility in calendar interviewing does not mean that interviewers are free to ask anything about the life course as expert qualitative interviewers would do in collecting life stories (Atkinson, 1998; Tagg, 1985). In the calendar methodology, separate timelines for each of the areas or domains of interest to the survey researcher are depicted (e.g., migration, labor), with each timeline divided into the same units that correspond to the primary units of analysis within the instrument, whether these units are calendar years/ages in years (Balán et al., 1969), months (Freedman, Thornton, Camburn, Alwin, & Young-DeMarco, 1988), or thirds-of-a-month (Belli, Shay, & Stafford, 2001). Specific data elements to be collected within each area and unit of analysis are defined in advance, and may include names (e.g., employer names), categorical entries (e.g., rural, town, city), or numeric information (e.g., average rate of pay). Hence, interviewers are constrained to ask questions that satisfy the objectives of the calendar instrument that are defined by the survey researcher in advance. By collecting information on periods of stability (e.g., working for the same employer for a number of years), and the timing of transitions (e.g., change in work from one employer to another in a specific calendar year), survey researchers gain quantitative data for purposes of analyses. Although calendar-based interviewing can be used in quantitative research, other researchers have seen the benefits of its use in qualitative research as well (Martyn & Belli, 2002; Martyn & Martin, 2003; see also Martyn, Chapter 5, this volume).

Because the calendar approach is sensitive to "objective differences in the life histories themselves" (Balán et al., 1969, p. 107), and because participants would differ in which types of life experiences would be most memorable, Balán et al. advocated the calendar approach as an interviewing methodology in which the more memorable events would serve as cues to help remember other life events, hence the need for flexible interviewing. With remarkable prescience of the conclusions made by experts in autobiographical memory years later (Barsalou, 1988; Belli, 1998; Conway, 1996), Balán et al. noted the value of encouraging respondents to sequence the occurrences of events within each separate area or domain of the life history, but in addition to relate any changes in one domain to sequences that occurred in another. Belli and colleagues (Belli, 1998; Belli, Shay, & Stafford, 2001; Belli, Smith, Andreski, & Agrawal, 2007) have termed these interviewing approaches as encouraging sequential and parallel retrieval strategies, respectively. In sequential retrieval, respondents report on the sequences of periods of stabilities and transitions within the same life course domain, such as reporting the names of employers, and which employers occurred earlier and later in time. To assist in the remembering of the timing of transitions, such as stopping work for one employer and starting work for another, parallel retrieval encourages respondents to remember nearly contemporaneous events that happened within other domains, such as whether an occupational transition occurred contemporaneously with a residential change. Any gaps that are observed in domain timelines can then be queried and negotiated between interviewers and respondents using sequential and parallel retrieval strategies in order to complete the entry. Balán et al. recognized that thinking "about several areas of one's life for a given time period strengthened . . . the recall for any one of them," that "by moving back and forth among the areas the respondent often was able to give a more complete account than otherwise" (p. 110). These researchers saw the calendar approach as a cooperative effort between interviewers and respondents, and one in which rapport is built between them.

Similar interviewing and retrieval processes are likely engendered in time diary interviews (see Stafford, Chapter 2, this volume). Specifically, time diaries are instruments in which interviewers encourage sequential retrieval among respondents who use temporal and physical location cues to determine what they were doing, and when, while retrieving events that had happened across the 24 hours of the day before the interview. Because for many people a given day is driven by routines with regard to temporal clock-time governing activities and locations, the sequential retrieval is benefited more strongly in time diary interviews in comparison to calendar interviews by time tagging, that is, by remembering the specific times in which events occurred. A form of parallel retrieval may also occur in time diary interviews, in which respondents may remember performing more than one activity simultaneously the day before.

Survey methodologists who concentrate on the issue of standardized survey interviewing and validity have documented problems that standardization imposes on the quality of retrospective reports. Although in face-to-face interviewing, a static calendar is recommended for viewing as an aid to recall (Sudman & Bradburn, 1982), there is no direct attempt to encourage sequential or parallel retrieval strategies (Belli, 1998). The basic strategy in standardized interviewing is to ask "How many" questions within a predefined reference period, whether these are queries for behavioral frequencies (e.g., "How many times have you moved since January 1, 2005") or for durations (e.g., "How much work did you miss in 2001 because you were unemployed and looking for work?"). In some ways, asking about durations may approach using a sequential retrieval strategy as the respondent may begin to remember periods of stability (Belli, Lee, Stafford, & Chou, 2004). However, there typically is no attempt to string sequences of these periods together, or to determine which of these periods occurred before or after the other, in a full implementation of sequential retrieval strategies. With regard to asking for behavioral frequencies, researchers (Burton & Blair, 1991; Conrad, Brown, & Cashman, 1998; Menon, 1993) have noted that respondents will implement a variety of retrieval strategies, with enumeration (recalling and counting within a reference period) and rate estimation being the primary ones, but depending on the length of the reference period, and the regularity, frequency, and distinctiveness of events, which strategy is used, whether a combination of strategies is used, and the accuracy of the behavioral frequency reports, will all vary. Note that the calendar approach need not directly ask for behavioral frequencies; instead, the number of transitions that are reported can become summed for any desired reference period during analyses. Moreover, because standardized survey questionnaires will segment topical areas into different sections, there is never an attempt to encourage parallel retrieval strategies within their design. By encouraging both conversational flexibility and the use of effective retrieval cues inherent in the structure of autobiographical knowledge, calendar interviewing has been hypothesized to promote high-quality retrospective reports.

In addition to incorporating more effective retrieval strategies in comparison to standardized interviewing, calendar interviewing also benefits from increased respondent motivation and conversational interaction. The motivation arises from the use of effective retrieval cues, which rewards difficult retrieval attempts, and this motivation in and of itself promotes better recall through increased effort (Cannell, Miller, & Oksenberg, 1981). In addition, it may be more difficult to satisfice in calendar interviewing (Callegaro, Yu, Cheng, Liao, & Belli, 2005). When faced with a standardized questionnaire, respondents have been shown to satisfice (Krosnick, 1991) by providing plausible answers instead of working hard to provide the most accurate answers. Satisficing respondents do not try to understand the question fully, but rather understand just enough to form a plausible answer. They also do not fully retrieve all the available information from memory but often only the minimum necessary on which to base an answer. Because calendar interviewing encourages coherence and precision in reporting what happened and when, and because conversational flexibility and effective retrieval cues enhance the motivation, engagement, and interest of the respondents, optimizing strategies are encouraged (Krosnick, Narayan, & Smith, 1996). Evidence in support of these claims has been provided by Belli et al. (2004). Although increased rapport between interviewers and respondents, as measured by laughter, digressions, and emotive expression, is associated with poorer quality retrospective reporting in standardized interviewing, increased rapport has no detrimental association with response quality in calendar interviews. In standardized interviewing, rapport is often seen as encouraging satisficing as the interviewer and respondent are likely engaging in mutual strategies to complete the questionnaire with a minimum of effort (Houtkoop-Steenstra, 2000). With calendar interviewing, however, rapport may simply be a byproduct of conversational engagement, and hence, will not adversely affect respondents' attempts to answer questions well.

Calendar Interviewing and the Quality of Retrospective Reports

Several studies have confirmed that calendar interviewing provides retrospective reports of reasonably good quality. In a test-retest design, Engel, Keifer, Thompson, and Zahm (2001) interviewed participants 8–14 months apart about their lifetime employment. The calendar design incorporated icons representing transitions in different domains to facilitate the interviewing of farm workers who often were illiterate or partially literate. The intercalendar agreement was moderate to high across all periods for certain crops, for location, and for agricultural work in general. Agreement for job counts was high for certain crops, for example, .93 for apple-related work.

Other work has used prior reports from interviews conducted years earlier as validation data. Freedman and colleagues (1988) compared EHC data with validation data collected from the same respondents 5 years earlier. The percentage of agreement between the data was in the range of 87% to 95% for reports of birth events, marital status, school attendance, and employment status. Caspi et al. (1996) found more than 90% agreement of data reported in the same month 3 years earlier for living arrangements, cohabitation, schooling, employment, and job training. Using reports collected 15 years earlier as validation, Lin, Ensel, and Lai (1997) examined the correspondence of calendar reports with these earlier reports for 10 life event categories including marital changes, births, residential moves, education, employment, deaths, financial/ legal work, health, sexual difficulties, arguments with partner or spouse, and changes in social activities and recreation. They found that 25% of respondents made no recall errors in any of the 10 categories and another quarter made recall errors in only one of the 10 categories. Only 8% of participants made recall errors in 5 or more categories. Implementing a computerized calendar, Belli, James, Van Hoewyk, and Alcser (see Chapter 13, this volume) found fair to excellent agreement with reports collected up to 14 years earlier for smoking, employment status, church and organizational membership, and presence or absence of indoor plumbing, among a primarily working-class cohort of African American adults. Their results demonstrated the feasibility of using computerized calendars for life course research across a variety of population groups.

The most convincing evidence that favors the use of calendar interviewing in the collection of retrospective reports is studies that have contrasted calendar and standardized interviewing methods. When compared to standardized interviewing, calendar interviewing has usually demonstrated better data quality for retrospective reports by increasing precision in the placement of events in time, by reducing the underreporting of behavioral frequencies, and by providing better estimates of the duration of events. Similar results have also been found with time diaries, in that data collected from time diaries have provided better estimates of population characteristics in comparison to "stylized" standardized interviewing questions (Csikszentmihalyi & Larson, 1992; Juster, 1985; Robinson, 1985).

Engel, Keifer, and Zahm (2001) interviewed respondents with a standardized questionnaire in a first round of interviewing, and then in a second round conducted 8–10 months later, interviewed these same individuals with an icon-based paper-and-pencil calendar instrument. They found that an icon/calendar-based questionnaire significantly increased the reported number of lifetime jobs and amount of work time when contrasted with reports in a traditional conventional questionnaire among a cohort of migrant farm workers. More recently, and again in face-to-face interviewing while using paper-and-pencil instruments with a life course reference period, with a quasi-experimental design Yoshihama, Gillespie, Hammock, Belli, and Tolman (2005) found that calendar interviewing improved the quality of reports of intimate partner violence (IPV) as revealed by a higher number of reports of IPV that were experienced at earlier ages. Specifically, the calendar interviews elicited more reports of lifetime experiences of intimate partner abuse (93%–96%) than the standardized format (61%–64%). Most important, the calendar interviews eliminated an artifactual age-cohort effect that had been observed in the standardized interviews. In a split-ballot experimental design, van der Vaart (2004) applied a paper-and-pencil timeline methodology in face-to-face interviews, and found that the calendar-based timeline methodology improved the retrospective reporting of the number, starting date, and types of educational courses taken 4 to 8 years previously in comparison to a standardized interviewing condition in which a timeline was not used, particularly for less salient events. In comparing the sizes of a seam bias between waves of a panel survey, the Panel Study of Income Dynamics (PSID), Callegaro and Belli (2007) found significant reduction in the seam bias between waves that followed the adoption of an EHC interviewing methodology in comparison to the earlier implementation of a standardized interviewing approach.

In their implementation of two studies, Belli and colleagues have been the first researchers to directly compare calendar and standardized interviewing in split-ballot experimental designs. In their work, both interviewers and respondents are randomly assigned to parallel standardized and calendar instruments. In both studies, interviews were administered via telephone to respondents from the PSID. Reports collected from the same respondents during earlier waves of the PSID were used as validation data. In the first study, both the standardized and calendar designs involved paper-and-pencil instruments, and the comparative questions focused on a reference period that had occurred approximately 1 to 2 years previously. Belli, Shay, and Stafford (2001) demonstrated that calendar reports had significantly higher correspondence with the validation data for reported number of moves, annual income, number of weeks unemployed, and number of weeks missing work resulting from personal illness or the illness of another in comparison to retrospective reports collected by the standardized instrument. However, follow-up work with additional outcome measures (Belli & Stafford, 2006) has shown better correspondence in standardized interviews with reports of aid to dependent children, an entitlement. In the second study, Belli et al. (2007) collected retrospective reports with a reference period of up to 30 years, this time using computerized instruments for both standardized and calendar designs. The quality of reports on social and economic variables of residential, marriage, cohabitation, and labor history (employment and unemployment) was assessed. The computerized calendar demonstrated better overall data quality for cohabitation and labor histories; no difference was found for residence change and the standardized questionnaire showed better data only for marriage history.

The few instances in which standardized interviewing has shown advantages over the calendar implementation in the studies by Belli and colleagues have been instructive regarding the situations in which calendar interviewing is likely to be most effective. These instances should also not be overemphasized as considerably more variables demonstrated advantages with calendar interviewing. With the 2-year reference period calendar, the retrospective reporting of entitlements did not incorporate the consistency checks that were part of the collection of labor histories, in which both sequential and parallel cueing was emphasized. With regard to reports of marriage history in the life course calendar, the standardized questionnaire first asked respondents how many times they were married, whereas the calendar first asked for the names of married partners. Most likely, information regarding the number of marriages one has had resides in memory as an autobiographical fact that is easily reported (Brewer, 1986); evidence did indicate that respondents in the calendar condition failed to report all of the names of individuals to whom they had been married. Note that such autobiographical facts are likely to exist for a few variables and only for the entire life course, and that the "how many" strategy in asking for frequencies with defined reference periods will not lead to access to this type of prestored information. In addition, designers of calendar life course instruments should be vigilant to incorporate queries that will assist in the reporting of autobiographical facts; Freedman et al. (1988) did appropriately ask for the number of times respondents were married in the implementation of their life history calendar.

In terms of methodological results from both of the studies conducted by Belli and colleagues, the length of the interviews in the life course study was 10% longer (6 more minutes for a nearly hour-long interview) in the calendar interviews in comparison to the standardized interviewing condition, whereas no differences in terms of interview length were observed in the 2-year reference period study. In both studies, interviewers preferred the calendar instruments when measured in terms of respondents' cooperation, motivation, ability to understand and respond to questions, and in terms of the interviewers' own enjoyment and ease of administration in comparison to the standardized interviews. Interviewers' preferences may have resulted partly from being able to play a meaningful role by being able to provide their own question wordings and thereby take some degree of ownership in the questions that were eventually asked.

The Emergence of Calendar Interviewing

Calendar interviewing methodology has been applied to different fields of research, nationally and internationally, in both interviewer-administered and in self-administered forms. Based on the innovative work of Balán et al. (1969), who designed and administered the first calendar questionnaire (see above), researchers at Johns Hopkins University (Blum, Karweit, & Sørensen, 1969) conducted the first calendar survey in the United States. Several calendar studies followed, including a study that focused on later life outcomes for adolescent mothers (Furstenberg, Brooks-Gunn, & Morgan, 1987), and other unpublished studies reported by Freedman et al. (1988).

The article by Freedman et al. (1988) has been particularly influential in promoting calendar-based interviewing as it nicely details the data collection methodology underlying the approach. Their study was also the first to provide validation data on the quality of retrospective reports that result from calendar interviewing. Freedman et al. also highlight the usefulness of high-quality retrospective reports in lieu of the time and expense with regard to prospective panel studies. As demonstrated by Freedman et al., calendar interviewing produces rich life course data that highlight the interdependence among trajectories and transitions within life histories. It is from statistically analyzing the correlations among various domains in the life course with regard to the timing of periods of stability and points of transitions that life course researchers are able to draw inferences regarding how earlier life course events impact those that occur in later life (Elder, 1985).

Calendar interviewing has been applied to many fields, sometimes with specific terminology. Demographers have used calendar interviewing to study mainly reproductive and contraceptive history. The methodologies have been named *AGEVEN* (Antoine, Bry, & Diouf, 1987), *life history calendar* (Rosero-Bixby & Oberle, 1989), *women's health study calendar* (Wingo, Ory, Layde, & Lee, 1988), or *life events calendar* (Hunter et al., 1997). The Demographic and Health Surveys (DHS) program uses a calendar-aided questionnaire to record pregnancies and contraceptive use. (See also Strickler, Magnani, McCann, Brown, & Rice, 1997.)

At times, calendar-aided questionnaires are used in criminology research. The *crime calendar,* developed by Horney and Marshall (1991), departs somewhat from the Freedman et al. (1988) approach and has been employed in many studies of inmates (Horney, 2001; Li & MacKenzie, 2003). Very similar calendar questionnaires have been used by Eitle, Gunkel, and Van Gundy (2004) to study male gang membership and by Byrne and Trew (2005), who explored offenders' accounts. Victimization research uses life history calendars; one example is the Netherlands Survey on Criminality and Law Enforcement (Blokland & Nieuwbeerta, 2005; Witterbrood & Nieuwbeerta, 2000). Yoshihama used a life history calendar to study victims of domestic violence (Yoshihama, Clum, Crampton, & Gillespie, 2002; Yoshihama, Hammock, & Horrocks, 2006; see also Yoshihama, Chapter 8, this volume).

There are many examples of sociological studies employing the life history calendar methodology of Freedman et al. (Barber, 2004; Cress, McPherson, & Rotolo, 1997; Cunningham & Thornton, 2005; Munch, McPherson, & Smith-Lovin, 1997; Parrado & Zenteno, 2002). Sometimes the methodology is named *life events matrix* (Whitbeck, Hoyt, & Yoder, 1999). William Axinn and colleagues (Axinn, Barber, & Ghimire, 1997; Thornton, Axinn, & Hill, 1992) applied a life history calendar, called *neighborhood history calendar,* to a population that does not use an ordinary calendar to mark timing in its daily life. Nursing research using life history calendar examples are found in Youngblut and Brooten (1999) and in Youngblut et al. (2001). Recently, even military studies employed life event history calendars to study cohorts of soldiers' wellness across the years (Parker et al., 2002; Parker et al., 2001).

The questionnaire developed originally by Nurco, Bonito, Lerner, and Balter (1975) and then called *status sheet* by McGlothin, Anglin, and Wilson (1977) has been used to study drug and alcohol abuse (Chou, Hser, & Anglin, 1996). It is also called *natural history interview* (Hser, Anglin, Grella, Longshore, & Prendergast, 1997). Alcohol abuse has also been studied using the *Timeline FollowBack* technique developed by Sobell and Sobell (1992, 2003; see also Agrawal et al., Chapter 4, this volume) and with the *alcohol lifetime drinking history* (Skinner & Sheu, 1982).

Stress is measured with a calendar methodology where the life events are grouped into categories of life changes, for example, changes in marital status, residence, and education. An early example is the study by Horowitz, Schaefer, Hirito, Wilner, and Levin (1977) where the methodology is called *life event questionnaire.* Other examples are the studies by Lin and colleagues (1997), and Ensel, Peek, Lin, and Lai (1996). More recently Van Gundy (2002) studied stress in young adulthood using the Miami Dade sample (J. Turner & Andres, 2002). Another recent example is the study by H. Turner and Muller (2004).

The *life chart interview* has been used to study the course of psychopathology (Chen, Eaton, Gallo, Nestadt, & Crum, 2000; Lyketsos, Nestadt, Cwi, Heithoff, & Eaton, 1994). Landmark events are recorded first (residence, marital and occupational status). Then psychopathology events are recorded using a rating scale. An instrument that shares some similarity with the previous one is the National Institute of Mental Health *Life Chart Method*™ (Leverich & Post, 1998, 2002a, 2002b) for recurrent affective illness. The instrument collects comorbidities and psychosocial stressors with a rating of severity. A life event section provides an impact rating of landmark events (e.g., conflict at work) that can have a positive or negative impact on the psychosocial stressors. The instrument can be used in prospective or retrospective form and also in clinician or self-administered form (Leverich & Post, 1998).

In the majority of studies, calendar data collection is interviewer administered, either face to face or on the phone. There has been little work that has compared which of these modes produces better data, however. Visually depicting the calendar to respondents ought to assist in recall, assuming that the depiction is effective in illustrating visual cues (Belli, 1998). Surprisingly, Freedman et al. (1988) found no differences in the quality of data provided by face-to-face in comparison to telephone modes. In more recent work, Callegaro et al. (2005) examined the retrospective reporting of hospitalization events for a 2-year reference period. Notably, these authors found that visually viewing the calendar improved reporting accuracy in comparison to a condition that simulated a telephone mode, with these advantages appearing for events that happened more remotely in time.

In addition, there are two examples of a self-administered calendar data collection instrument. Due to the sensitivity of the topic, Martyn and Martin (2003; see also Martyn, Chapter 5, this volume) decided to use a modified self-administered calendar to investigate sexual activity in adolescent girls. A step-by-step guide explained how to complete the instrument. The adolescent respondents were asked to record significant life events such as starting high school, parents' divorce, substance use, rape, forced sex, or running away from home. After this contextual information, the adolescent girls were asked to record information about sexual partners, sexual activity, and contraceptive use. The data collected demonstrate good face validity and construct validity. Mortimer and Johnson (1998) mailed a 12-month calendar instrument to a cohort of high school graduates in order to record various activities during the previous year, such as work, schooling, military service, living arrangements, and parenthood.

The data obtained by a calendar interviewer are generally recorded by the interviewer on a paper calendar. There is, however, increased usage of computerized calendar methodology. In this case, the software assists the interviewer in entering the data, and the program can also perform consistency checks and give appropriate feedback (Belli, 2000; Kite & Soh, 2004). Examples of studies using computerized calendar interviewing are found in Belli et al. (2007), Callegaro et al. (2005), Kelly, Mosher, Duffer, and Kinsey (1997), and Pebley (2004).

Uses of Calendar Interviewing

Researchers who initially advocated calendar interviewing approaches concentrated primarily on its value in cross-sectional studies whereby longitudinal life course data could be collected inexpensively and expeditiously in comparison to panel designs (Freedman et al., 1988). The focus had been exclusively on quantitative research. Recognizing that panel designs also have a retrospective component with participants remembering back upon life events that happened since the prior wave, using calendar methods as a bridge between waves has been initiated by the PSID (Belli, 2003; McGonagle & Schoeni, 2006). Another use has been to supplement ongoing panel studies with retrospective histories collected by the calendar methodology (James, Van Hoewyk et al., 2006; Mortimer & Johnson, 1999). Because of the different needs to which calendar interviewing has been applied, researchers have incorporated reference periods of different lengths, ranging from months, to several years, up to the life course. Care must be taken to ensure that the units of the calendar are appropriate to the reference period. Units must increase in size for reference periods of increasing length, as seeking greater levels of detail regarding when transitions occur becomes more burdensome for respondents (and interviewers) as reference periods increase in length. With longer reference periods, it also becomes more difficult to depict fine units because of their increasing number. For a 2-year reference period, Belli, Shay, and Stafford (2001) used a calendar with one third of a month as a basic unit; with a 10-year reference period, Freedman et al. (1988) used a month as a unit. Using years as units is appropriate for life course reference periods (Belli et al., 2007), although finer units, such as months, can be probed once specific years have been established (Blum et al., 1969).

Although we have argued for and have highlighted empirical studies regarding the advantages in data quality that calendar interviewing provides in comparison to standardized interviewing in the collection of retrospective reports, we are not making claims that standardized interviewing ought to be abandoned altogether. At the very least, standardized interviewing approaches are advisable when the aim is the collection of contemporaneous information (in contrast to retrospective reports), although permitting more conversational approaches will also be advantageous in promoting clarity of meaning of important study concepts (Conrad & Schober, 2000; Schober & Conrad, 1997). Because many surveys include a number of questions that collect both contemporaneous and retrospective events and opinions, mixed methods that integrate standardized and calendar approaches can be especially appealing.

As noted above, calendar data collection methodologies were derived from the quantitative tradition in social sciences. They were designed in order to collect rich life histories while simultaneously limiting points of inquiry to those domains of the life course that would be most predictive regarding the important causes and consequences that govern the life course. Results using calendar techniques have been informative. As one example, Yoshihama et al. (2006; see also Yoshihama, Chapter 8, this volume) have found that among an at-risk population of women, experiencing intimate partner violence is predictive of later-life health problems but receipt of welfare is not. As another example, James, Fowler-Brown, Raghunathan, and Van Hoewyk (2006; see also Belli,

James, Van Hoewyk, & Alcser, Chapter 13, this volume) found that childhood socioeconomic position, as measured via a computerized calendar instrument, was predictive of adult obesity among a cohort of African American women. These examples illustrate that life course calendar interviewing has its place among quantitative data collection methodologies in the social and health sciences.

But the appeal of calendar interviewing methodologies also extends to qualitative approaches. The flexible nature of calendar data collection, and the ability to review important life events as a whole, can be especially appealing for qualitative researchers who want to use a semistructured data collection approach that has considerable potential to provide detailed insights. In a unique combination of methodologies, Martyn (Chapter 5, this volume) first asks adolescent girls to complete a self-administered calendar that especially focuses on intimate and sexual relationships. In a follow-up interview, the responses to the calendar are used to gain insights into the reasons underlying risky sexual behavior, potentially assisting the participants to seek a reduction in such risky behavior. Although the calendar approach has been used far more often in quantitative research, researchers who are mostly interested in drawing qualitative insights should consider calendar methods in the conduct of their research.

Conclusion

Calendar interviewing and data collection produce retrospective reports of high quality that have been successfully examined in the pursuit of a wide range of scientific questions. Calendar approaches have been administered in different modes (face to face, telephone, self-administered, paper and pencil, computer assisted), and with a wide range of reference periods that have included months, several years, and up to the entire life course. Calendar interviewing methods have also been shown to be feasible, not uncommon, and implemented with a variety of populations, including individuals who are low in literacy or who come from cultures that are not accustomed to linear time. Methodological work has shown that interviewing times between calendar and standardized interviews are comparable, that participants do not view calendar interviews as burdensome, and that interviewers prefer calendar to standardized interviews. Visually viewing an EHC may have advantages in data quality beyond those advantages observed in a telephone mode. Finally, attesting to the overall flexibility of the approach, calendar methods are applicable to both quantitative and qualitative pursuits. There can be no doubt that they can, and should, assume an ever-increasing prevalence in life course research.

Note

1. The term *standardized interviewing* is used throughout this paper. This method of interviewing has also been referred to as using a *question-list* instrument or as implementing a *conventional questionnaire.*

Acknowledgment

The writing of this chapter has been supported by NIH Grant 5R01AG/HD17977-05.

References

Antoine, P., Bry, X., & Diouf, P. D. (1987). The "AGEVEN" record: A tool for the collection of retrospective data. *Survey Methodology, 13,* 163–171.

Atkinson, R. (1998). *The life story interview.* Thousand Oaks, CA: Sage.

Axinn, W. G., Barber, J. S., & Ghimire, D. J. (1997). The neighborhood history calendar: A data collection method designed for dynamic multilevel modeling. *Sociological Methodology, 27,* 355–392.

Balán, J., Browning, H. L., Jelin, E., & Litzler, L. (1969). A computerized approach to the processing and analysis of life histories obtained in sample surveys. *Behavioral Science, 14,* 105–114.

Barber, J. (2004). Community social context and individualistic attitudes toward marriage. *Social Psychology Quarterly, 67,* 236–256.

Barsalou, L. W. (1988). The content and organization of autobiographical memories. In U. Niesser & E. Winograd (Eds.), *Remembering reconsidered: Ecological and traditional approaches to the study of memory* (pp. 193–243). New York: Cambridge University Press.

Beatty, P. (1995). Understanding the standardized/non-standardized interviewing controversy. *Journal of Official Statistics, 11,* 147–160.

Belli, R. F. (1998). The structure of autobiographical memory and the event history calendar: Potential improvements in the quality of retrospective reports in surveys. *Memory, 6,* 383–406.

Belli, R. F. (2000). Computerized event history calendar methods: Facilitating autobiographical recall. In *Proceedings of the Section on Survey Research Methods* (pp. 471–475). Alexandria, VA: American Statistical Association.

Belli, R. F. (2003). *The integration of a computer assisted interviewing event history calendar in the Panel Study of Income Dynamics.* Retrieved June 2006, from http://psidonline.isr.umich.edu/data/Documentation/Fam/2003/EHCManuscript.pdf

Belli, R. F., & Chardoul, S. A. (1997, May). *The digression of survey actors in a face-to-face health interview.* Paper presented at the 52nd annual conference of the American Association for Public Opinion Research, Norfolk, VA.

Belli, R. F., Lee, E. H., Stafford, F. P., & Chou, C.-H. (2004). Calendar and question list survey methods: Association between interviewer behaviors and data quality. *Journal of Official Statistics, 20,* 185–218.

Belli, R. F., Lepkowski, J. M., & Kabeto, M. U. (2001). The respective roles of cognitive processing difficulty and conversational rapport on the accuracy of retrospective reports of doctor's office visits. In M. L. Cynamon & R. A. Kulka (Eds.), *Seventh Conference on Health Survey Research Methods* (DHHS Publication No. [PHS] 01–1013, pp. 197–203). Hyattsville, MD: Government Printing Office.

Belli, R. F., Shay, W. L., & Stafford, F. P. (2001). Event history calendars and question list surveys: A direct comparison of interviewing methods. *Public Opinion Quarterly, 65*, 45–74.

Belli, R. F., Smith, L., Andreski, P. M., & Agrawal, S. (2007). Methodological comparison between CATI event history calendar and standardized conventional questionnaire instruments. *Public Opinion Quarterly, 71*, 603–622.

Belli, R. F., & Stafford, F. P. (2006, May 18–21). *When does the event history calendar improve the reporting of what happened?* Paper presented at the 61st annual conference of the American Association for Public Opinion Research, Montreal.

Blokland, A. A. J., & Nieuwbeerta, P. (2005). The effects of life circumstances on longitudinal trajectories of offending. *Criminology, 43*, 1203–1240.

Blum, Z. D., Karweit, N. L., & Sørensen, A. (1969). *A method for the collection and analysis of retrospective life histories* (No. 48). Baltimore, MD: Johns Hopkins University.

Brewer, W. F. (1986). What is autobiographical memory? In D. C. Rubin (Ed.), *Autobiographical memory* (pp. 25–49). Cambridge, UK: Cambridge University Press.

Burton, S., & Blair, E. (1991). Task conditions, response formulation processes, and response accuracy for behavioral frequency questions in surveys. *Public Opinion Quarterly, 55*, 50–79.

Byrne, C. F., & Trew, K. F. (2005). Crime orientations, social relations and involvement in crime: Patterns emerging from offenders' accounts. *Howard Journal of Criminal Justice, 44*, 185–205.

Callegaro, M., & Belli, R. F. (2007, December 5–6). *Impact of event history calendar on seam effect in the PSID: Lessons for SIPP.* Paper presented at the Event History Calendar Method Conference, U.S. Census Bureau, Suitland, MD.

Callegaro, M., Yu, M., Cheng, F.-W., Liao, D., & Belli, R. F. (2005). Comparison of computerized event history calendar and question-list interviewing methods: A two year hospitalization history study. In *2004 Proceedings of the American Statistical Association, 59th annual conference of the American Association for Public Opinion Research (AAPOR)* (CD-ROM) (pp. 4746–4753). Alexandria, VA: American Statistical Association.

Cannell, C. F., Miller, P. V., & Oksenberg, L. (1981). Research on interviewing techniques. *Sociological Methodology, 12*, 389–437.

Caspi, A., Moffitt, T. E., Arland, T., Freedman, D., Amell, J. W., Harrington, H., et al. (1996). The life history calendar: A research and clinical assessment method for collecting retrospective event-history data. *International Journal of Methods in Psychiatric Research, 6*, 101–114.

Chen, L.-S., Eaton, W. W., Gallo, J. J., Nestadt, G., & Crum, R. M. (2000). Empirical examination of current depression categories in a population-based study: Symptoms, course, and risk factors. *American Journal of Psychiatry, 157*, 573–580.

Chou, C.-H., Hser, Y.-I., & Anglin, D. M. (1996). Pattern reliability of narcotics addicts' self reported data: A confirmatory assessment of construct validity and consistency. *Substance Use & Misuse, 31*, 1189–1216.

Conrad, F. G., Brown, N. R., & Cashman, E. R. (1998). Strategies for estimating behavioral frequency in survey interviews. *Memory, 6,* 339–366.

Conrad, F. G., & Schober, M. F. (2000). Clarifying question meaning in a household telephone survey. *Public Opinion Quarterly, 64,* 1–28.

Conway, M. A. (1996). Autobiographical knowledge and autobiographical memories. In D. C. Rubin (Ed.), *Remembering our past: Studies in autobiographical memory* (pp. 67–93). New York: Cambridge University Press.

Cress, D. M., McPherson, M. J., & Rotolo, T. (1997). Competition and commitment in voluntary memberships: The paradox of persistence and participation. *Sociological Perspectives, 40,* 61–79.

Csikszentmihalyi, M., & Larson, R. (1992). Validity and reliability of the experience sampling method. In M. W. de Vries (Ed.), *The experience of psychopathology: Investigating mental disorders in their natural settings* (pp. 43–57). Cambridge, UK: Cambridge University Press.

Cunningham, M., & Thornton, A. (2005). The influence of union transitions on white adults' attitudes toward cohabitation. *Journal of Marriage and Family, 67,* 710–720.

Dykema, J., Lepkowski, J. M., & Blixt, S. (1997). The effect of interviewer and respondent behavior on data quality: An analysis of interaction coding in a validation study. In L. Lyberg, P. Biemer, M. Collins, E. de Leeuw, C. Dippo, N. Schwarz, & D. Trewin (Eds.), *Survey measurement and process quality* (pp. 287–310). New York: John Wiley.

Eitle, D., Gunkel, S., & Van Gundy, K. (2004). Cumulative exposure to stressful life events and male gang membership. *Journal of Criminal Justice, 32,* 95–111.

Elder, G. H., Jr. (1985). Life course dynamics. In G. H. Elder, Jr. (Ed.), *Life course dynamics: Trajectories and transitions, 1968–1980* (pp. 23–49). Ithaca, NY: Cornell University Press.

Engel, L. S., Keifer, M. C., Thompson, M. L., & Zahm, S. H. (2001). Test-retest reliability of an icon/calendar-based questionnaire used to assess occupational history. *American Journal of Industrial Medicine, 40,* 512–522.

Engel, L. S., Keifer, M. C., & Zahm, S. H. (2001). Comparison of traditional questionnaire with an icon/calendar-based questionnaire to assess occupational history. *American Journal of Industrial Medicine, 40,* 502–511.

Ensel, W. M., Peek, M. K., Lin, N., & Lai, G. W.-F. (1996). Stress in the life course: A life history approach. *Journal of Aging and Health, 8,* 389–416.

Fowler, F. J., & Mangione, T. W. (1990). *Standardized survey interviewing: Minimizing interviewer-related error.* Newbury Park, CA: Sage.

Freedman, D., Thornton, A., Camburn, D., Alwin, D., & Young-DeMarco, L. (1988). The life history calendar: A technique for collecting retrospective data. In C. C. Clogg (Ed.), *Sociological methodology* (Vol. 18, pp. 37–68). San Francisco: Jossey-Bass.

Furstenberg, F. F. J., Brooks-Gunn, J., & Morgan, P. S. (1987). *Adolescent mothers in later life.* New York: Cambridge University Press.

Horney, J. (2001). Criminal events and criminal careers: An integrative approach to the study of violence. In R. F. Meier, L. W. Kennedy, & V. F. Sacco (Eds.), *The process and structure of crime: Criminal events and crime analysis* (pp. 141–167). New Brunswick, NJ: Transaction Publishers.

Horney, J., & Marshall, I. H. (1991). Measuring lambda through self-reports. *Criminology, 29,* 471–495.

Horowitz, M., Schaefer, C., Hirito, D., Wilner, N., & Levin, B. (1977). Life event questionnaires for measuring presumptive stress. *Psychosomatic Medicine, 39,* 413–431.

Houtkoop-Steenstra, H. (2000). *Interaction and the standardized survey interview: The living questionnaire.* Cambridge, UK: Cambridge University Press.

Hser, Y.-I., Anglin, D. M., Grella, C., Longshore, D., & Prendergast, M. L. (1997). Drug treatment careers: A conceptual framework and existing research findings. *Journal of Substance Abuse and Treatment, 14,* 543–558.

Hunter, D. J., Manson, J. E., Colditz, G. A., Chasan-Taber, L., Troy, L., Stampfer, M., et al. (1997). Reproducibility of oral contraceptive history and validity of hormone composition reported in a cohort of US women. *Contraception, 56,* 373–378.

James, S. A., Fowler-Brown, A. G., Raghunathan, T. E., & Van Hoewyk, J. (2006). Life-course socioeconomic position and obesity in African American women: The Pitt County Study. *American Journal of Public Health, 96,* 554–560.

James, S. A., Van Hoewyk, J., Williams, D. R., Raghunathan, T. E., Belli, R. F., & Strogatz, D. S. (2006). Life-course socioeconomic position and hypertension in African American men: The Pitt County Study. *American Journal of Public Health, 96,* 812–817.

Juster, F. T. (1985). The validity and quality of time use estimates obtained from recall diaries. In F. T. Juster & F. P. Stafford (Eds.), *Time, goods, and well-being* (pp. 63–91). Ann Arbor: University of Michigan, Institute for Social Research.

Kelly, J. E., Mosher, W. D., Duffer, A. P. J., & Kinsey, S. H. (1997). Plan and operation of the 1995 National Survey of Family Growth. *Vital and Health Statistics, 36,* 1–98.

Kirk, J., & Miller, M. L. (1986). *Reliability and validity in qualitative research.* Newbury Park, CA: Sage.

Kite, J., & Soh, L.-K. (2004). An online survey framework using the life events calendar. Retrieved June 2006, from http://cse.unl.edu/facdb/csefacdb/downloader.php?area=TechReportArchive&file=TR-UNL-CSE-2004-0011.pdf

Krosnick, J. A. (1991). Response strategies for coping with the cognitive demands of attitude measures in surveys. *Applied Cognitive Psychology, 5,* 213–236.

Krosnick, J. A., Narayan, S., & Smith, W. R. (1996). Satisficing in surveys: Initial evidence. In M. T. Braverman & J. K. Slater (Eds.), *New directions for evaluation: Advances in survey research* (Vol. 70, pp. 29–44). San Francisco: Jossey-Bass.

Leverich, G. S., & Post, R. M. (1998). Charting the course of bipolar illness and its response to treatment. *Medscape Psychiatry & Mental Health eJournal, 3.* Retrieved June 5, 2008, from http://www.medscape.com/viewpublication/125_toc? vol=3&iss=3

Leverich, G. S., & Post, R. M. (2002a). *The NIMH Life Chart Manual™ for recurrent affective illness: The LCM™. Clinician retrospective.* Bethesda, MD: NIMH.

Leverich, G. S., & Post, R. M. (2002b). *The NIMH Life Chart Manual™ for recurrent affective illness: The LCM™. Prospective life chart ratings/clinician.* Bethesda, MD: NIMH.

Li, S. D., & MacKenzie, D. L. (2003). The gendered effects of adult social bonds on the criminal activities of probationers. *Criminal Justice Review, 28,* 278–298.

Lin, N., Ensel, W. M., & Lai, G. W.-F. (1997). Construction and use of the life history calendar: Reliability and validity of the recall data. In I. H. Gotlib & B. Wheaton (Eds.), *Stress and adversity over the life course: Trajectories and turning points* (pp. 249–272). Cambridge, UK: Cambridge University Press.

Lyketsos, C. G., Nestadt, G., Cwi, J., Heithoff, K., & Eaton, W. W. (1994). The life chart interview: A standardized method to describe the course of psychopathology. *International Journal of Methods in Psychiatric Research, 4,* 143–155.

Martyn, K. K., & Belli, R. F. (2002). Retrospective data collection using event history calendars. *Nursing Research, 51,* 270–274.

Martyn, K. K., & Martin, R. (2003). Adolescent sexual risk assessment. *Journal of Midwifery & Women's Health, 40,* 213–219.

McGlothin, W. H., Anglin, D. M., & Wilson, B. D. (1977). *An evaluation of the California Civil Addict Program.* Rockville, MD: Department of Health, Education, and Welfare; Public Health Service Alcohol, Drug Abuse, and Mental Health Administration; Public Institute of Drug Abuse.

McGonagle, K. A., & Schoeni, R. F. (2006). The Panel Study of Income Dynamics: Overview & summary of scientific contributions after nearly 40 years. Retrieved June 2006, from http://psidonline.isr.umich.edu/Publications/Papers/montrealv5.pdf

Menon, G. (1993). The effects of accessibility of information in memory on judgments of behavioral frequencies. *Journal of Consumer Research, 20,* 431–440.

Mortimer, J. T., & Johnson, M. K. (1998). Adolescent part-time work and educational achievement. In K. Borman & B. Schneider (Eds.), *The adolescent years: Social influences and educational challenges* (*97th Yearbook of the National Society for the Study of Education, Pt. I,* pp. 183–206). Chicago: University of Chicago Press.

Mortimer, J. T., & Johnson, M. K. (1999). Adolescent part-time work and postsecondary transition pathways in the United States. In W. R. Heinz (Ed.), *From education to work: Cross-national perspectives* (pp. 111–148). Cambridge, UK: Cambridge University Press.

Munch, A., McPherson, M. J., & Smith-Lovin, L. (1997). Gender, children, and social contact: The effects of childrearing for men and women. *American Sociological Review, 62,* 509–520.

Nurco, D. N., Bonito, A. J., Lerner, M., & Balter, M. B. (1975). Studying addicts over time: Methodology and preliminary findings. *American Journal of Drug & Alcohol Abuse, 2,* 183–196.

O'Muircheartaigh, C. (1997). Measurement errors in surveys: A historical perspective. In L. E. Lyberg, P. P. Biemer, M. Collins, E. de Leeuw, N. Schwarz, & D. Trewin (Eds.), *Survey measurement and process quality* (pp. 1–25). New York: John Wiley.

Ongena, Y. (2005). *Interviewer and respondent interaction in survey interviews.* Amsterdam: Vrije Universiteit.

Parker, M. W., Call, V. R. A., Toseland, R., Vaitkus, M., Roff, L., & Martin, J. A. (2002). Employed women and their aging family convoys: A life course model of parent care assessment and intervention. *Journal of Gerontological Social Work, 40,* 101–121.

Parker, M. W., Fuller, G. F., Koening, H. G., Bellis, J. M., Vaitkus, M. A., Barko, W. F., et al. (2001). Soldier and family wellness across the life course: A developmental model of successful aging, spirituality, and health promotion, Pt. II. *Military Medicine, 166,* 561–570.

Parrado, E. A., & Zenteno, R. M. (2002). Gender differences in union formation in Mexico: Evidence from marital search models. *Journal of Marriage and the Family, 64,* 756–773.

Pebley, A. R. (2004). EHC user's guide. Retrieved June 2006, from http:// www.lasurvey .rand.org//EHC%20Users%20Guide%20final.pdf

Robinson, J. P. (1985). The validity and reliability of diaries versus alternative time use measures. In F. T. Juster & F. P. Stafford (Eds.), *Time, goods, and well-being* (pp. 33–62). Ann Arbor: University of Michigan, Institute for Social Research.

Rosero-Bixby, L., & Oberle, M. W. (1989). Fertility change in Costa Rica 1960–84: Analysis of retrospective lifetime reproductive histories. *Journal of Biosocial Science, 21,* 419–432.

Schaeffer, N. C., & Maynard, D. W. (2002). Occasions for intervention: Interactional resources for comprehension in standardized survey interviewing. In D. W. Maynard, H. Houtkoop-Steenstra, N. C. Schaeffer, & J. van der Zouwen (Eds.), *Standardization and tacit knowledge: Interaction and practice in the survey interview* (pp. 261–280). New York: John Wiley.

Schober, M. F., & Conrad, F. G. (1997). Does conversational interviewing reduce survey measurement error? *Public Opinion Quarterly, 61,* 576–602.

Skinner, H. A., & Sheu, W.-J. (1982). Reliability of alcohol use indices: The Lifetime Drinking History and the MAST. *Journal of Studies on Alcohol, 43,* 1157–1170.

Sobell, L. C., & Sobell, M. B. (1992). Timeline follow-back: A technique for assessing self-reported alcohol consumption. In R. Z. Litten & J. P. Allen (Eds.), *Measuring alcohol consumption: Psychosocial and biochemical methods* (pp. 41–72). Totowa, NJ: Humana Press.

Sobell, L. C., & Sobell, M. B. (2003). Alcohol consumption measures. In J. P. Allen & V. B. Wilson (Eds.), *Assessing alcohol problems: A guide for clinicians and researchers* (2nd ed., pp. 75–99). Bethesda, MD: National Institute of Health.

Strickler, J. A., Magnani, R. J., McCann, G. H., Brown, L. F., & Rice, J. C. (1997). The reliability of reporting of contraceptive behaviors in DHS calendar data: Evidence from Morocco. *Studies in Family Planning, 28,* 44–53.

Suchman, L., & Jordan, B. (1990). Interactional troubles in face-to-face survey interviews. *Journal of the American Statistical Association, 85,* 232–241.

Sudman, S., & Bradburn, N. M. (1982). *Asking questions.* San Francisco: Jossey-Bass.

Tagg, S. K. (1985). Life history interviews and their interpretation. In M. Brenner, J. Brown, & D. Canter (Eds.), *The research interview: Uses and approaches* (pp. 163–199). London: Academic Press.

Thomas, W. I., & Znaniecki, F. (1958). *The Polish peasant in Europe and America.* New York: Dover.

Thornton, A., Axinn, W. G., & Hill, D. H. (1992). Reciprocal effects of religiosity, cohabitation, and marriage. *American Journal of Sociology, 98,* 628–651.

Turner, H. A., & Muller, P. A. (2004). Long-term effects of child corporal punishment on depressive symptoms in young adults: Potential moderators and mediators. *Journal of Family Issues, 25,* 761–782.

Turner, J. R., & Andres, G. G. (2002). Psychiatric and substance use disorders in South Florida: Racial/ethnic and gender contrasts in a young adult cohort. *Archives of General Psychiatry, 59,* 43–50.

van der Vaart, W. (2004). The time line as a device to enhance recall in a standardized research interview: A split ballot study. *Journal of Official Statistics, 20,* 301–317.

Van Gundy, K. (2002). Gender, the assertion of autonomy, and the stress process in young adulthood. *Social Psychology Quarterly, 65,* 346–363.

Viterna, J., & Maynard, D. W. (2002). How uniform is standardization? Variation within and across survey centers regarding protocols for interviewing. In D. W. Maynard, H. Houtkoop-Steenstra, N. C. Schaeffer, & J. van der Zouwen (Eds.), *Standardization and tacit knowledge: Interaction and practice in the survey interview* (pp. 365–397). New York: John Wiley.

Whitbeck, L. B., Hoyt, D. R., & Yoder, K. A. (1999). A risk-amplification model of victimization and depressive symptoms among runaway and homeless adolescents. *American Journal of Community Psychology, 27,* 273–296.

Wingo, P. A., Ory, H. W., Layde, P. M., & Lee, N. C. (1988). The evaluation of the data collection process for a multicenter, population-based, case-control design. *American Journal of Epidemiology, 128,* 206–217.

Witterbrood, K., & Nieuwbeerta, P. (2000). Criminal victimization during one's life course: The effects of previous victimization and patterns of routine activities. *Journal of Research in Crime and Delinquency, 37,* 91–122.

Yoshihama, M., Clum, K., Crampton, A., & Gillespie, B. (2002). Measuring the lifetime experience of domestic violence: Applications of the life history calendar method. *Violence and Victims, 17,* 297–317.

Yoshihama, M., Gillespie, B., Hammock, A. C., Belli, R. F., & Tolman, R. M. (2005). Does the life history calendar method facilitate the recall of intimate partner violence? Comparison of two methods of data collection. *Social Work Research, 29,* 151–163.

Yoshihama, M., Hammock, A. C., & Horrocks, J. (2006). Intimate partner violence, welfare receipt, and health status of low-income African American women: A lifecourse analysis. *American Journal of Community Psychology, 37,* 95–109.

Youngblut, J. M., & Brooten, D. (1999). Alternate child care, history of hospitalization, and preschool child behavior. *Nursing Research, 48,* 29–34.

Youngblut, J. M., Brooten, D., Singer, L. T., Standing, T., Lee, H., & Rodgers, W. L. (2001). Effects of maternal employment and prematurity on child outcomes in single parent families. *Nursing Research, 50,* 346–355.

Further Thoughts on Part I

As discussed in Chapter 1, both time diary and calendar methods are valuable tools in the collection of life course data. Yet to our knowledge, only one study, the Panel Study of Income Dynamics (PSID) (see http://psidon line.isr.umich.edu/), uses both methods. The PSID implements a 2-year reference period computerized event history calendar to serve as a bridge between waves of the core telephone interviews, and has recently administered a health history calendar to collect the child health histories of the respondents, which, to this point, had been missing from the panel data series. In addition, as part of the PSID, the Child Development Supplement (CDS) implements a time diary to collect information of the time use of the children of respondents. The time diary data, when combined with the core PSID data, have permitted an examination of life course issues such as the associations of children's time spent with parents as a function of parental employment and education (Sandberg & Hofferth, 2001; Yeung, Sandberg, Davis-Kean, & Hofferth, 2001). Hence, the value of time diary data can be especially enhanced when combined with longitudinal data collected within a panel study or collected from the administration of a life course calendar.

To researchers who are contemplating data collection using calendar and/or time diary methods, there are a number of methodological challenges that would need to be solved. With the calendar, considerations must focus on determining the number of domains of interest, their ordering in the calendar, the length of the time period, and the size of the time units. With the time diary, which day or days will be targeted, when interviews will take place, and what time of day the diary will start are issues that would need to be solved. Because people's time use varies depending on the day of the week, time diary data collections must ensure a representative collection of days. Some researchers may opt not to use either calendars or time diaries, preferring instead a more traditional standardized interviewing approach. Ultimately, such considerations require an in-depth assessment of the methodological strengths and weaknesses of different data collection options, and the substantive purposes to which these methods, and the resulting data analyses, will be employed.

References

Sandberg, J. F., & Hofferth, S. L. (2001). Changes in children's time with parents: United States. 1981–1997. *Demography, 38,* 423–436.

Yeung, W. J., Sandberg, J. F., Davis-Kean, P. E., & Hofferth, S. L. (2001). Children's time-use with fathers in intact families. *Journal of Marriage and the Family, 63,* 136–154.

PART II

Variations in the Collection and Application of Calendar, Diary, and Time Use Data

These four chapters illustrate that calendar and time diary methods have been applied to different areas for both scientific and clinical purposes. The Timeline Followback method (Agrawal, Sobell, & Sobell, Chapter 4) is among the most celebrated calendar interviewing methods. It has been used primarily to measure individual histories of substance use for both scientific and clinical purposes, including for the guiding of intervention programs. In another use of calendar interviewing for clinical purposes, Martyn (Chapter 5) illustrates the application to the measurement of the temporal contextualization of health risk behaviors. She concentrates on adolescents and discusses that with this age group, a self-administered calendar instrument appears to assist members of this population to reveal aspects of their personal lives that they would be more uncomfortable revealing in the presence of others. Wethington and Almeida (Chapter 6) use diary methods in the study of the impact of daily stressors on well-being, and argue that the findings from the data collection method that they developed—the Daily Inventory of Stressful Events—are able to contribute to multiple disciplines, including those pertaining to research on the life course. Their work with daily stressors illustrates the application of these methods in a more basic or scientific research setting. In the final chapter, Phipps and Vernon (Chapter 7) describe the American Time Use Study, an application of time diary methods to a national probability sample that collects data that are very informative to both researchers and policymakers who wish to develop a firmer understanding of how Americans use their time, and the value of such time use to individuals and society.

This small sample of studies illustrates not only variability in the substantive purposes of calendar and diary methods, but also shows variations in the modes of data collection, including both interviewer-administered face to face (Agrawal et al., Chapter 4), interviewer-administered telephone (Wethington & Almeida, Chapter 6, and Phipps & Vernon, Chapter 7), and self-administered modes (Martyn, Chapter 5). The chapter by Martyn is noteworthy in that although the bulk of research that uses calendar methods focuses on answering quantitative issues, her work uses calendar data primarily qualitatively. Also, echoing a theme introduced by Stafford (Chapter 2), both small-scale investigator (Martyn, Chapter 5) and large infrastructure data collections (Phipps & Vernon, Chapter 7) are illustrated.

4

The Timeline Followback

A Scientifically and Clinically Useful Tool for Assessing Substance Use

Sangeeta Agrawal, Mark B. Sobell, and Linda Carter Sobell

Introduction

The Timeline Followback (TLFB) was developed three decades ago as an assessment instrument for obtaining retrospective daily estimates of alcohol consumption using a calendar format. Although the TLFB was originally developed as a research tool for use with alcohol abusers, it has since been adapted for use in clinical settings and extended to assess illicit drug use (Fals-Stewart, O'Farrell, Freitas, McFarlin, & Rutigliano, 2000), tobacco use (Brown, Burgess, Sales, Evans, & Miller, 1998), gambling (Weinstock, Whelan, & Meyers, 2004), sexual behavior (Weinhardt et al., 1998), domestic violence (Fals-Stewart, Birchler, & Kelley, 2003), and food intake (Bardone, Krahn, Goodman, & Searles, 2000). The TLFB has also been extensively evaluated with a wide range of clinical and nonclinical populations and has met criteria for inclusion in the American Psychiatric Association's *Textbook of Psychiatric Measures* (American Psychiatric Association, in press) and the National Institute on Alcohol Abuse and Alcoholism's guidebook, *Assessing Alcohol Problems* (Allen & Columbus, 1995; Allen & Wilson, 2003). The TLFB has been shown in more than three dozen published studies to have good psychometric characteristics across several types of behaviors (Sobell et al., 2008).

In the early 1970s, when the TLFB was first developed, it filled a need related to assessing moderate drinking outcomes (Sobell & Sobell, 1973). Prior to then, treatment outcomes had been dichotomously portrayed as either sober (abstinent) or drunk (drinking), or as improved, same, or worse (Sobell & Sobell, 1992). Forty years ago, drinking behavior was assessed using primarily Quantity–Frequency measures. Such measures asked respondents to report the average number of days per week that they drank, and the average number of alcoholic drinks they consumed on such days. Although such data were acceptable for large survey studies, they did not allow for the assessment of individuals pursuing a reduced drinking goal. The TLFB, in contrast, asked respondents to reconstruct their day-by-day drinking over a specified interval using Standard Drinks as a common metric. This chapter describes where the TLFB fits among other drinking measures, summarizes psychometric evaluations of the TLFB, and discusses its utility as a clinical and research tool.

TLFB: A Measure of Drinking

The main way of gathering retrospective drinking data has been by self-reports. Although urban legend has it that individuals with alcohol problems give false reports of their substance use, many studies have found that when data are gathered under appropriate conditions (i.e., assurance of confidentiality, interviewed in a research or clinical setting, when drug and alcohol free), self-reports are more accurate, more complete, and less expensive and invasive than other sources of data (Babor, Steinberg, Anton, & Del Boca, 2000; Del Boca & Darkes, 2003; Sobell & Sobell, 1975). Although this chapter does not present a review of studies on the validity of self-reports, the TLFB was used in many such studies. When conditions for valid data collection are not possible, the recommendation is to use multiple assessment measures and to base conclusions on a convergence of measures (Sobell & Sobell, 1980, 1992).

As reviewed in detail elsewhere (Sobell & Sobell, 2003), four major methods have been used for obtaining self-reports of drinking: Quantity–Frequency methods, Lifetime Drinking History methods, Concurrent Recall methods, and Daily Estimation methods. Examples of each of these methods and references are shown in Table 3 in the review article by Sobell and Sobell (2003). As mentioned earlier, QF methods ask respondents to estimate the average number of drinking days over a certain period and then to estimate the average number of drinks consumed per drinking day. Summary drinking variables are then calculated as the product of those measures (e.g., average number of drinks per week). Quantity–Frequency (QF) measures are most useful in survey studies where time is at a premium and detailed information about drinking is not necessary. When assessing clinical populations, however,

QF methods have a serious drawback in that they cannot capture sporadic heavy drinking days and are not sensitive to infrequent drinkers who consume large amounts when drinking. Although methodological refinements have been made to some QF methods to better capture more detailed drinking data (Sobell & Sobell, 2003), such refinements have required additional questions, and thus lose the advantage of being quick and easy to administer.

Lifetime Drinking History (LDH) methods (Russell et al., 1998; Skinner & Sheu, 1982) use a QF methodology but collect data over the life course or a long interval. For example, the LDH developed by Skinner (Skinner & Sheu, 1982) asks respondents to report their drinking in discrete identifiable time periods with transitions between periods reflecting major changes in alcohol use. Respondents report their alcohol use for each period using a QF format. The major strength of LDH methods is that they are the only method that provides a picture of lifetime drinking. Yet because LDH methods are basically QF methods applied to long intervals, they suffer from the same weakness that plagues QF measures (i.e., that they are insensitive to sporadic or unpatterned drinking).

Concurrent Recall (CR) methods are used to collect prospective data. CR methods, commonly referred to as self-monitoring, are designed to gather reports of the behavior close to the time when the behavior occurs (e.g., same day, multiple times during a day). These methods ask respondents to record their behavior on logs or collect real-time data using automated speech recognition technologies or small personalized computers (Korotitsch & Nelson-Gray, 1999; Menon & Yorkston, 2000; Neal et al., 2006). The strength of CR methods is that there are fewer memory problems because the behavior is recorded immediately or shortly after it occurs (Sobell & Sobell, 2003). Moreover, because data can be summarized daily, the measure obtained is essentially identical to measures obtained with retrospective daily estimation methods. This is a very useful feature when data are collected for the periods prior to and after treatment using daily estimation methods, as the result is a running record, using the same metric, of a person's drinking before, during, and following treatment. The weakness of CR methods is that some individuals do not comply with instructions and fail to record their behavior when it occurs. In such cases daily estimation methods can provide an alternative source of data (i.e., respondents reconstruct the data retrospectively). Also, because CR methods by definition record data when the behavior occurs, such methods cannot be used to obtain retrospective reports, which are essential in most clinical settings and research studies.

The final method, Daily Estimation (DE), is the main focus of this chapter. The most studied DE method is the TLFB (Timeline Followback). As described earlier, the TLFB asks respondents to report their drinking retrospectively, day by day, for a designated interval. Because alcoholic beverages vary in their alcohol concentration, drinks are reported using a Standard Drink format. Standard

Drinks equates the amount of absolute alcohol consumed in different types of alcoholic beverages. Figure 4.1 is an example of a Standard Drink conversion card showing what amounts of different beverages contain equivalent amounts of alcohol. DE methods are most useful in research studies where relatively precise estimates of drinking are needed, especially when a complete picture of the distribution of drinking days (i.e., high- and low-risk drinking days) is required. The strength of this method is that it provides a continuous picture of drinking at all levels of alcohol use for all days of a specified interval. This strength also underlies the clinical utility of the method, as a completed calendar serves as an excellent vehicle for discussion of a client's drinking.

Administration of the TLFB

The TLFB can be administered by an interviewer using a paper-and-pencil format, self-administered, administered by computer, administered by telephone, and administered by therapists and researchers. It has been used with a variety of populations between the ages of 14 and 75 years and across a range of drinker groups from normal drinkers, to problem drinkers, to severely dependent alcohol abusers, including those with dual disorders. As mentioned earlier, the TLFB has also been used to collect data for a variety of addictive and nonaddictive behaviors. In addition, the TLFB has been translated into several languages (e.g., Spanish, German, French, Japanese, Swedish, Polish, Russian). The average time to administer the TLFB depends on the needed time frame. For example, a 90-day TLFB typically takes about 5 to 10 minutes to complete, while a 360-day TLFB will take about 20 to 30 minutes.

The TLFB has been evaluated for time windows ranging from 7 days up to 24 months. To collect drinking data more accurately and to assist recall over the designated time frame, the TLFB method uses several memory aids. Giving respondents a printed or computerized calendar with key dates and events such as holidays listed, as appears in the sample calendar shown in Figure 4.2, provides a temporal framework for more easily recalling events and drinking patterns. For example, there may have been a period of consecutive nondrinking days linked to a particular day that provides an anchor for the report. Remembering when anchor points occur, such as an illness, birthday, or arrest, helps facilitate recall of drinking.

Another way to facilitate recall when using the TLFB in an interview format is to use a boundary exaggeration technique to help respondents better specify their reports. For example, when respondents are asked how many beers they drank and they say "a lot," the interviewer then asks, "Does a lot mean 3 beers or 25 beers?" Such a technique gives the respondent permission to report large amounts of drinking, and in our experience leads to a more

What Is a Standard Drink?

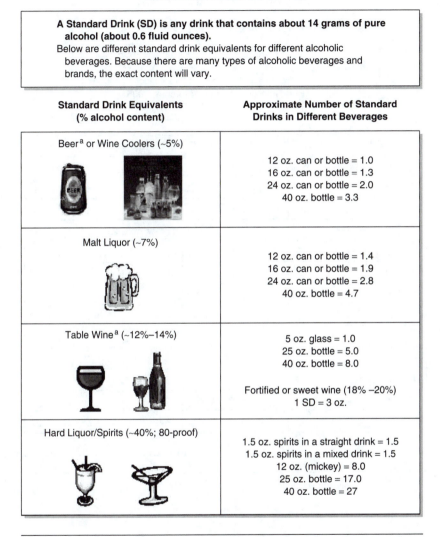

> **A Standard Drink (SD) is any drink that contains about 14 grams of pure alcohol (about 0.6 fluid ounces).**
> Below are different standard drink equivalents for different alcoholic beverages. Because there are many types of alcoholic beverages and brands, the exact content will vary.

Standard Drink Equivalents (% alcohol content)	Approximate Number of Standard Drinks in Different Beverages
Beer[a] or Wine Coolers (~5%)	12 oz. can or bottle = 1.0 16 oz. can or bottle = 1.3 24 oz. can or bottle = 2.0 40 oz. bottle = 3.3
Malt Liquor (~7%)	12 oz. can or bottle = 1.4 16 oz. can or bottle = 1.9 24 oz. can or bottle = 2.8 40 oz. bottle = 4.7
Table Wine[a] (~12%–14%)	5 oz. glass = 1.0 25 oz. bottle = 5.0 40 oz. bottle = 8.0 Fortified or sweet wine (18% –20%) 1 SD = 3 oz.
Hard Liquor/Spirits (~40%; 80-proof)	1.5 oz. spirits in a straight drink = 1.5 1.5 oz. spirits in a mixed drink = 1.5 12 oz. (mickey) = 8.0 25 oz. bottle = 17.0 40 oz. bottle = 27

Figure 4.1   Example of a Standard Drink Conversion Card

a. For light beer or light wine, Standard Drinks (SD) are calculated in terms of a ratio (e.g., 12 oz. of 2.5% light beer = 0.5 SDs; 12 oz. of 4% light beer = 0.8 SDs).

specific response such as, "No, not 25, it's more like 10 or 12 beers." In other words, when respondents offer nonspecific answers they can be easily prompted to provide more specific answers.

Complete the Following Information

Number of days to gather information: 90 days

Start Date (Day 1):   January 1, 2005
                          MO   DY   YR

End Date (Yesterday):   March 4, 2005
                            MO   DY   YR

2005	SUN		MON		TUES		WED		THURS		FRI		SAT	
									1 *New Year's Day*	2	2	8	3	9
J	4	6	5	5	6	0	7	0	8	12	9	6	10	10
A	11	0	12	0	13	0	14	0	15	0	16	0	17	0
N	18	0	19 *M. Luther King*	0	20	0	21	0	22	0	23	0	24	0
	25	0	26	0	27	0	28	0	29	0	30	20	31	18
F	1	13	2	0	3	0	4	0	5	0	6	16	7	12
E	8	2	9	0	10	0	11	0	12	0	13	0	14 *Valentine's*	4
B	15	4	16 *Pres. Day*	0	17	0	18	0	19	3	20	5	21	9
	22	0	23	0	24	0	25	0	26	0	27	21	28	8
M	1	0	2	0	3	0	4	0	5	0	6	12	7	11
A	8	0	9	0	10	0	11	0	12	0	13	0	14	0
R	15	0	16	0	17 *St. Patrick's Day*	0	18	0	19	0	20	0	21	0
	22	0	23	22	24	18	25	21	26	22	27	12	28	27
	29	23	30	12	31	25	1	14	2	25	3	0	4	0

Figure 4.2   Sample Timeline Followback Calendar

Respondents would typically be asked to complete the TLFB using instructions like the following:

> In order to get a picture of what your (insert target behavior) was like over the past _____ days, we would like you to complete a calendar as shown below. We recognize you won't have perfect recall, and that is okay, just provide your best estimate of your behavior. Our purpose in doing this is to get a sense of how frequently you engaged in (insert target behavior, e.g., drinking, gambling, cocaine use). It is important that you put a number in for each day, including 0's for days when you did not engage in (insert target behavior).

There is no optimum time interval over which TLFB data should be gathered. Because the time frame can vary from 1 to 24 months and data collection is a laborious process, careful consideration should be given to determining the minimum necessary reporting interval given the nature of the respondents and the type of information being sought. Until recently there had been a lack of research on the issue of what TLFB time window provides a representative picture of drinking. However, Vakili, Sobell, Sobell, Simco, and Agrawal (2008) used TLFB reports from a sample of 825 problem drinkers to examine how representative TLFB reports of annual drinking would have been if they had been estimated by extrapolating from a shorter time window. It was concluded that if the need was limited to aggregate reports (e.g., mean number of drinking days, mean drinks per drinking day) and large samples were used, data collected for a one-month interval would provide an acceptable estimate of overall annual drinking. However, when examining individual cases (e.g., in clinical assessments) or looking at small samples or when known events or seasonal variability in reporting could make a one-month report unrepresentative of the previous year, data should be collected for a minimum of 3 months because for individual cases large deviations from annual patterns can occur with shorter timeline windows.

Psychometric Characteristics of the TLFB

In terms of psychometric characteristics, the TLFB has been evaluated for test-retest reliability (stability), concurrent validity (e.g., compared with collaterals, official records, biochemical tests such as breath and liver function tests), and construct validity (e.g., compared with substance use assessment instruments such as the Alcohol Use Disorders Identification Test or the Drug Abuse Screening Test). Because these findings have been reviewed elsewhere (Sobell et al., 2008; Sobell & Sobell, 1992, 2000, 2003) they will be only summarized here. Temporal reliability has been found to be high for aggregate measures such as percentage of days drinking, but less strong for individual day-by-day comparisons. Numerous studies have used the TLFB as the main self-report measure in studies comparing self-reports with reports from collateral informants (e.g., significant others) and found that when self-reports are gathered under conditions conducive to validity, respondents typically report more drinking than is reported for them by their respective collaterals (Babor et al., 2000; Connors & Maisto, 2003; Kedia & Perry, 2005).

Few studies have examined the validity of self-reports of events (e.g., hospitalizations) as compared to official records, but as with collateral reports, typically events are reported validly and sometimes more events are reported by self-report than by records (Anglin, Hser, & Chou, 1993;

Hoffmann & Ninonuevo, 1994; Sobell, Sobell, & Samuels, 1974). Similarly, when TLFB self-reports of drinking were compared to liver function tests that can be elevated due to recent heavy drinking, only about a third of self-identified problem drinkers had abnormal blood test results (Babor et al., 2000; Sobell, Agrawal, & Sobell, 1999). Furthermore, other studies have shown that self-reports identify more alcohol abusers than liver function tests (Conigrave, Davies, Haber, & Whitfield, 2003). Similarly, research supports the validity of self-reports of drug use when collected under conditions conducive to valid reporting (Calhoun et al., 2000; Darke, 1998; O'Farrell, Fals-Stewart, & Murphy, 2003; Secades-Villa & Fernandez-Hermida, 2003). In summary, several studies have demonstrated that self-reports are generally a useful and accurate source of substance use data.

A methodological concern about all detailed retrospective methods, including the TLFB, is whether respondents might simply report a redundant pattern of use rather than reporting variability in their drinking. For example, a respondent wishing to quickly fill out a 12-month TLFB might report the same weekly pattern for all 52 weeks. Sobell et al. (2003) examined this question using 12-month TLFB reports from 825 problem drinkers and found little evidence of routinized reporting. In fact, only 1.8% (15 of 825) filled in the TLFB with the same number of drinks for each day on the one-year calendar (which possibly could have reflected actual drinking), and 80.6% had 9 or fewer matching weeks in an entire year. This suggests that most respondents report variability in their drinking.

Clinical and Scientific Applications of the TLFB

A particular strength of the TLFB for scientific purposes, as compared to QF methods, is that TLFB data can be used to generate a multitude of dependent variables. A listing of some of the variables that can be produced from TLFB data appears in Table 4.1. The inherent flexibility of measurement (i.e., ability to produce an array of variables) is an analytic strength of the TLFB because the data can be used in a variety of longitudinal analyses, including profile and factor analyses. In addition to treatment outcome evaluations, TLFB data have many other statistical uses. For example, Epstein, Labouvie, McCrady, Swingle, and Wern (2004) used TLFB data empirically to categorize alcohol abusers' drinking patterns into binge, episodic, sporadic, and steady pattern groupings. Such profile categorizations can be further examined in terms of relationships to other pretreatment (e.g., dependence severity) and within-treatment (e.g., compliance) variables, in addition to other outcome variables (e.g., types of consequences).

Table 4.1   Some Examples of Dependent Variables That Can Be Generated From TLFB Data

---

- Frequency of drinking (% drinking days)
- Mean number of drinks per drinking day
- Mean number of drinks consumed per week
- Percentage of days drinking at various levels (e.g., 1–2 drinks per day)
- Variation in drinking (standard deviation of drinks/drinking day)
- Total number of drinks consumed
- Number of days until first drink or first heavy drinking day (for survival analyses)
- Quantitative categorization of drinking patterns (e.g., ratio of Friday–Sunday drinking to Monday–Thursday drinking; profiles based on pattern analysis)
- Length (days) of relapse or abstinence episodes
- Intensity (drinks/day) of relapse episodes
- Frequency distribution of drinking (% days drinking at particular levels)

Although the TLFB was developed to assess treatment outcomes, for several reasons it has come to be recognized as also having considerable clinical value. First, when examining TLFB pretreatment data, clinicians can get a quick and detailed picture of the magnitude and frequency of a client's drinking, including important changes, such as relapses, that have occurred over time. Second, a TLFB summary can be used as a basis to elicit client reports of important events ("On the calendar you filled out, it looks like about 6 weeks ago you had a week of unusually heavy drinking. Tell me a bit more about that.") as a prompt for further discussion. Third, if clients maintain a self-monitoring log of their alcohol use during treatment, comparison of within-treatment drinking with pretreatment drinking can help clients identify changes they have made. This, in turn, can be helpful to motivate further change, and should the client experience a bad day or two, having a continuous record of pretreatment and within-treatment drinking can be used as a relapse management strategy to set the heavy drinking episode in perspective and encourage the person to get back on track.

Two recent studies have investigated the effect of TLFB feedback on the drinking of college students. In a randomized controlled trial, Carey, Carey, Maisto, and Henson (2006) found that participation in a TLFB assessment reduced drinking in heavy drinkers, with the reduction sustained over 12 months of follow-up. LaBrie, Lamb, Pedersen, and Quinlan (2006) similarly evaluated TLFB feedback with college students who had violated school alcohol policy, except the feedback was combined with several other brief interventions all delivered in a single session. Students who received the intervention demonstrated significant reductions in drinking over 3 months of follow-up. Thus,

TLFB feedback seems to have value as an intervention as well as an assessment instrument.

Researchers and clinicians desiring to use the TLFB can download materials and instructions free of charge by going to http://www.nova.edu/gsc on the Internet and clicking on "online forms."

References

Allen, J. P., & Columbus, M. (1995). *Assessing alcohol problems: A guide for clinicians and researchers.* Rockville, MD: National Institute on Alcohol Abuse and Alcoholism.

Allen, J. P., & Wilson, V. (2003). *Assessing alcohol problems* (2nd ed.). Rockville, MD: National Institute on Alcohol Abuse and Alcoholism.

American Psychiatric Association. (in press). *Textbook of psychiatric measures.* Washington, DC: Author.

Anglin, D. M., Hser, Y. -I., & Chou, C. P. (1993). Reliability and validity of retrospective behavioral self-report by narcotics addicts. *Evaluation Review, 17,* 91–108.

Babor, T. F., Steinberg, K., Anton, R., & Del Boca, F. (2000). Talk is cheap: Measuring drinking outcomes in clinical trials. *Journal of Studies on Alcohol, 61*(1), 55–63.

Bardone, A. M., Krahn, D. D., Goodman, B. M., & Searles, J. S. (2000). Using interactive voice response technology and Timeline Follow-back methodology in studying binge eating and drinking behavior: Different answers to different forms of the same question? *Addictive Behaviors, 25*(1), 1–11.

Brown, R. A., Burgess, E. S., Sales, S. D., Evans, D. M., & Miller, I. W. (1998). Reliability and validity of a smoking Timeline Follow-Back interview. *Psychology of Addictive Behaviors, 12*(2), 101–112.

Calhoun, P. S., Sampson, W. S., Bosworth, H. B., Feldman, M. E., Kirby, A. C., Hertzberg, M. A., et al. (2000). Drug use and validity of substance use self-reports in veterans seeking help for posttraumatic stress disorder. *Journal of Consulting and Clinical Psychology, 68*(5), 923–927.

Carey, K., Carey, M., Maisto, S., & Henson, J. (2006). Brief motivational interventions for heavy college drinkers: A randomized controlled trial. *Journal of Consulting and Clinical Psychology, 74*(5), 943–954.

Conigrave, K. M., Davies, P., Haber, P., & Whitfield, J. B. (2003). Traditional markers of excessive alcohol use. *Addiction, 98*(s2), 31–43.

Connors, G. J., & Maisto, S. A. (2003). Drinking reports from collateral individuals. *Addiction, 98*(2), 21–29.

Darke, S. (1998). Self-report among injecting drug users: A review. *Drug and Alcohol Dependence, 51*(3), 253–263.

Del Boca, F. K., & Darkes, J. (2003). The validity of self-reports of alcohol consumption: State of the science and challenges for research. *Addiction, 98,* 1–12.

Epstein, E. E., Labouvie, E., McCrady, B. S., Swingle, J., & Wern, J. (2004). Development and validity of drinking pattern classification: Binge, episodic, sporadic, and steady drinkers in treatment for alcohol problems. *Addictive Behaviors, 29*(9), 1745–1761.

Fals-Stewart, W., Birchler, G. R., & Kelley, M. L. (2003). The Timeline Followback spousal violence interview to assess physical aggression between intimate partners: Reliability and validity. *Journal of Family Violence, 18*(3), 131–142.

Fals-Stewart, W., O'Farrell, T. J., Freitas, T. T., McFarlin, S. K., & Rutigliano, P. (2000). The Timeline Followback reports of psychoactive substance use by drug-abusing patients: Psychometric properties. *Journal of Consulting and Clinical Psychology, 68*(1), 134–144.

Hoffmann, N. G., & Ninonuevo, F. G. (1994). Concurrent validation of substance abusers' self-reports against collateral information: Percentage agreement vs. k vs. Yule's Y. *Alcoholism: Clinical and Experimental Research, 18,* 231–237.

Kedia, S., & Perry, S. W. (2005). Factors associated with client-collateral agreement in substance abuse post-treatment self-reports. *Additive Behaviors, 30*(6), 1086–1099.

Korotitsch, W. J., & Nelson-Gray, R. O. (1999). An overview of self-monitoring research in assessment and treatment. *Psychological Assessment, 11*(4), 415–425.

LaBrie, J. W., Lamb, T. F., Pedersen, E. R., & Quinlan, T. (2006). A group motivational interviewing intervention reduces drinking and alcohol-related consequences in adjudicated college students. *Journal of College Student Development, 47*(3), 267–280.

Menon, G., & Yorkston, E. A. (2000). The use of memory and contextual cues in the formation of behavioral frequency judgments. In A. A. Stone, J. S. Turkkan, C. A. Bachrach, J. B. Jobe, H. S. Kurtzman, & V. S. Cain (Eds.), *The science of self-report: Implications for research and practice* (pp. 63–79). Mahwah, NJ: Lawrence Erlbaum.

Neal, D. J., Fromme, K., Boca, F. K., Parks, K. A., King, L. P., Pardi, A. M., et al. (2006). Capturing the moment: Innovative approaches to daily alcohol assessment. *Alcoholism: Clinical and Experimental Research, 30*(2), 282–291.

O'Farrell, T. J., Fals-Stewart, W., & Murphy, M. (2003). Concurrent validity of a brief self-report Drug Use Frequency measure. *Addictive Behaviors, 28*(2), 327–337.

Russell, M., Peirce, R. S., Vana, J. E., Nochajski, T. H., Carosella, A. M., Muti, P., et al. (1998). Relations among alcohol consumption measures derived from the Cognitive Lifetime Drinking History. *Drug and Alcohol Review, 17*(4), 377–387.

Secades-Villa, R., & Fernandez-Hermida, J. R. (2003). The validity of self-reports in a follow-up study with drug addicts. *Addictive Behaviors, 28*(6), 1175–1182.

Skinner, H. A., & Sheu, W. -J. (1982). Reliability of alcohol use indices: The Lifetime Drinking History and the MAST. *Journal of Studies on Alcohol, 43,* 1157–1170.

Sobell, L. C., Agrawal, S., & Sobell, M. B. (1999). Utility of liver function tests for screening "alcohol abusers" who are not severely dependent on alcohol. *Substance Use & Misuse, 34*(12), 1723–1732.

Sobell, L. C., Agrawal, S., Sobell, M. B., Leo, G. I., Johnson-Young, L., Cunningham, J. A., et al. (2003). Comparison of a Quick Drinking Screen and Timeline Followback with alcohol abusers. *Journal of Studies on Alcohol, 64,* 858–861.

Sobell, L. C., Dum, M., Voluse, A., Sobell, M. B., Bierman, M., & Wacha, A. (2008). *Timeline Followback: A review of studies and their psychometric characteristics and clinical and research applications.* Manuscript submitted for publication.

Sobell, L. C., & Sobell, M. B. (1975). Outpatient alcoholics give valid self-reports. *Journal of Nervous and Mental Disease, 161,* 32–42.

Sobell, L. C., & Sobell, M. B. (1980). Convergent validity: An approach to increasing confidence in treatment outcome conclusions with alcohol and drug abusers. In L. C. Sobell, M. B. Sobell, & E. Ward (Eds.), *Evaluating alcohol and drug abuse treatment effectiveness: Recent advances* (pp. 177–185). Elmsford, NY: Pergamon.

Sobell, L. C., & Sobell, M. B. (1992). Timeline Followback: A technique for assessing self-reported alcohol consumption. In R. Z. Litten & J. Allen (Eds.), *Measuring alcohol consumption: Psychosocial and biological methods* (pp. 41–72). Totowa, NJ: Humana Press.

Sobell, L. C., & Sobell, M. B. (2000). Alcohol Timeline Followback (TLFB). In American Psychiatric Association (Ed.), *Handbook of psychiatric measures* (pp. 477–479). Washington, DC: American Psychiatric Association.

Sobell, L. C., & Sobell, M. B. (2003). Alcohol consumption measures. In J. P. Allen & V. Wilson (Eds.), *Assessing alcohol problems* (2nd ed., pp. 75–99). Rockville, MD: National Institute on Alcohol Abuse and Alcoholism.

Sobell, M. B., & Sobell, L. C. (1973). Alcoholics treated by individualized behavior therapy: One year treatment outcome. *Behaviour Research and Therapy, 11,* 599–618.

Sobell, M. B., Sobell, L. C., & Samuels, F. H. (1974). Validity of self-reports of alcohol-related arrests by alcoholics. *Quarterly Journal of Studies on Alcohol, 35,* 276–280.

Vakili, S., Sobell, L. C., Sobell, M. B., Simco, E. R., & Agrawal, S. (2008). *Using the Timeline Followback to determine time windows representative of annual alcohol consumption with alcohol abusers.* Manuscript submitted for publication.

Weinhardt, L. S., Carey, M. P., Maisto, S. A., Carey, K. B., Cohen, M. M., & Wickramasinghe, S. M. (1998). Reliability of the Timeline Followback sexual behavior interview. *Annals of Behavioral Medicine, 20*(1), 25–30.

Weinstock, J., Whelan, J. P., & Meyers, A. W. (2004). Behavioral assessment of gambling: An application of the Timeline Followback method. *Psychological Assessment, 16*(1), 72–80.

5

Adolescent Health Research and Clinical Assessment Using Self-Administered Event History Calendars

Kristy K. Martyn

Introduction

This chapter describes an adolescent self-administered event history calendar (EHC) that elicits temporally linked information on life context; shows inter-relationships, patterns, and risk behavior trends; and facilitates risk perception and tailored health communication. Adolescent risk behavior is influenced by life course development, contextual linkages, and dynamic changes over time. New approaches are needed in adolescent health research and health care to address the complex developmental and contextual factors influencing adolescent risk behavior. The EHC is an ideal method for retrospective data collection and clinical assessment of adolescent health risk and protection behavior patterns and context. This method has research and clinical implications for increasing adolescent risk perception and communication.

Research findings on self-administered EHCs used with 15- to 19-year-old adolescent females ($n = 73$) and nurse practitioners ($n = 7$) illustrate how a self-administered EHC can be used for research and clinical assessment. Detailed 6- to 10-year adolescent histories were obtained on the EHCs, including patterns of substance use and sexual activity progression and triggers for unintended sexual intercourse. Results indicated that the EHC method clearly and concisely shows contextualized adolescent health risk behavior assessments, visually similar to a family tree or genogram. After recording their risk and protective histories on the EHC, adolescents reported increased risk perception and greater safe sex intentions. Qualitative discussions of protective and risky sexual decision making were stimulated by adolescents' self-report of risk behavior in their own words and reflective responses on the EHCs. Both adolescents and nurse practitioners indicated that EHCs encouraged recall, report, and discussion of health risk behavior.

Adolescent EHC

The adolescent EHC elicits temporally linked information on the context of the adolescent's life, shows risk and protective interrelationships and risk behavior patterns, and facilitates risk perception and communication. The adolescent EHC described in this chapter was developed based on seminal life history calendar work (Freedman, Thornton, Camburn, Alwin, & Young-DeMarco, 1988) and qualitatively derived domains to facilitate qualitative interviews focused on sexual risk and avoidance behavior (Martyn & Belli, 2002). The adolescent EHC visually and concretely shows integrated adolescent health risk behaviors that are accessible to adolescents and provides a common frame of reference for adolescent–interviewer communication. When adolescents complete the EHC, they use step-by-step instructions, autobiographical memory cues, and retrieval cycles that both encourage reflection on their time-linked integrated risk history graph, and also prepare them to discuss their actual and potential risk behavior history with the interviewer.

Initially, the adolescent EHC was developed using contextual domains identified in adolescent pregnancy avoidance qualitative research with African American young women (Martyn & Hutchinson, 2001; Martyn, Hutchinson, & Martin, 2002) and further developed with African American, Caucasian, and Hispanic adolescent females (Martyn & Martin, 2003; Martyn, Reifsnider, & Murray, 2006). Research using this adolescent EHC has focused on qualitative research description of adolescent females' individual and family protective processes over time (Martyn, Darling-Fisher, Smrtka, Fernandez, & Martyn, 2006; Martyn, Reifsnider, Barry, Treviño, & Murray, 2006) and on clinical feasibility of adolescent sexual risk assessment (Martyn & Martin, 2003; Martyn, Reifsnider, & Murray, 2006).

The adolescent EHC collects 6- to 10-year (starting at 10 years old) history data on (1) life context such as significant events, influential relationships, activities, and goals; (2) health information including medical conditions, eating problems, and exposure to violence (e.g., abuse, rape); (3) risk behaviors such as smoking, alcohol and substance use (e.g., marijuana), and sexual risk (including partners [male or female]), sexual activity, and contraceptive use; and (4) health outcomes such as sexually transmitted infections and pregnancy. The EHC grid provides a standard set of timing cues in columns labeled by time unit (years), age, and grade in school, and a set of substantive cues in rows labeled by domains (e.g., significant events, family, friends, smoking, alcohol and substance use, and sexual activity) (see EHC template in Table 5.1). The adolescent EHC is designed to be completed by starting at the top of the EHC with less sensitive data and then proceeding down the EHC to more sensitive risk behavior data.

EHC Background

EHCs are structured but flexible approaches to retrospective data collection that increase recall of past events by using past experiences as memory cues. These cues provide context for retrieval of autobiographical memories, which are structured hierarchically and accessed by a series of retrieval cycles that assist individuals to reconstruct past events and experiences accurately and completely (Belli, 1998; Conway, 1996). When compared to traditional survey methods, EHCs improve data quality, use of retrieval cues, cognitive abilities, and conversational engagement (Belli, Lee, Stafford, & Chou, 2004). Documenting the role of EHCs in promoting accurate recall, Belli, Shay, and Stafford (2001) found that an EHC approach provided better quality data than a traditional standardized question-list methodology without a significant increase in interviewing time. More detailed data were obtained with the EHC method and a more interactive communication likely had occurred between the interviewer and respondent.

WHY A SELF-ADMINISTERED EHC?

In initial qualitative research using the adolescent EHC, adolescents ($n = 43$) were given the option to self-administer the EHC using a step-by-step instruction guide or to have an interviewer administer the EHC prior to interviews focused on sexual risk behaviors (Martyn, Hutchinson, & Martin, 2002; Martyn & Martin, 2003). Most (85.7%) of the adolescents chose to self-administer the EHC. When they completed the EHC themselves, the adolescents were able to report sexual risk behaviors without concerns about being embarrassed or hesitant to disclose sensitive data with direct questioning by an interviewer. Once these sensitive data were recorded, they reported that it was easier to discuss their risk behavior histories with the interviewers. The adolescents' EHC

Table 5.1   Event History Calendar Template

Year			
Age (years)			
School Grade			
Activities: 1. Church/Clubs/Sports 2. Duration (x–x)			
School/Work: 1. Grades/Job 2. Duration (x–x)			
Goals Significant Events: Celebration/Losses			
Family (Circle if live with)			
Friends			
Role Models			

Health Status:
Physical changes,
    safety, violence
    (fighting, abuse)			

Tobacco Use: 1. Type: CIG/SN/CW 2. Amount (#/day) 3. Duration (x–x)			
Substance Use: 1. Type: AL/MJ/IN/CN/IJ 2. Amount (#/day/month) 3. Duration (x–x)			
Partners: 1. Initials 2. Age 3. Duration (x–x) 4. Type: D/S/E/M/Sx			
Sexual Activity: 1. Partner initials 2. Duration x–x			

3. Type: K/P/O/A/V/FOR
4. Contraception:
  a. Type: C/OC/W/DP/N/R
  b. Duration (x–x)			

Pregnancies			
Sexually Transmitted Infections: (T/CH/H/GW/ GC/HIV/AIDS)			

SOURCE: Martyn, K. K., & Belli, R.F. (2002). Retrospective data collection using event history calendars. *Nursing Research, 51*(4), 270–274. Used with permission.

(x–x) = Duration (inclusive dates)

Tobacco Use: CIG = Cigarettes, SN = Snuff, CW= Chewing tobacco

Substance Use: AL = Alcohol, MJ = Marijuana, IN = Inhalants, CN = Cocaine, IJ = Injectable drugs

Partners: D = Dating, S = Going steady, E = Engaged, M = Married, Sx = Sexually active

Sexual Activity: K = Kissing, P = Petting, O = Oral sex, A = Anal sex, V = Vaginal sex, FOR = Forced sex

Contraceptives: C = Condoms, OC = Oral contraceptives/pills, W = Withdrawal/pulling out, DP = Depo-Provera/Depo shot, N = Norplant, R = Rhythm method/safe period

Sexually Transmitted Infections: T = Trichomonas, CH = Chlamydia, H = Herpes, GW = Genital Warts, GC = Gonorrhea, HIV/AIDS

data served as a frame of reference for in-depth qualitative discussions about the reasons they engaged in sexual risk behaviors, decision making, protective behavior, and future behavioral intentions. Both the processes of self-administration and enhancement of the interview provided opportunities to facilitate the adolescents' perception of personal risk. Increased personal risk perception is especially desirable with adolescents, as it can facilitate intention to and actual avoidance of risk behaviors with lifelong consequences.

EHC self-administration is efficient for the interviewer or clinician, and the participants themselves. When the participant self-administers the EHC, time requirements for interviewer or clinician are decreased. This is especially important in today's economic environment where research funds are limited and busy clinical practices demand more patients be seen in less time. In addition, when one-on-one interviews are not required, the EHC can be administered to groups of participants like large-scale surveys are administered, obtaining comprehensive data while saving time and money. The self-administered EHC is also time-efficient for the participant.

How to Self-Administer EHCs

As previously mentioned, EHCs can be self-administered in a variety of ways using a variety of types of instruction. The adolescent EHC data described in this chapter has been obtained by interviewers giving the adolescents the 8″ × 14″ paper EHC, a pencil, and an instruction guide. They explained the purpose of the EHC and asked the adolescents to complete the EHC using the step-by-step instruction guide. The instruction guide described here was designed to be used with the EHC in Table 5.1. The guide includes a brief orientation to the EHC format and explanation of the use of cues to help recall and reflect, and the specific data to be obtained (including examples of what information is being requested). The guide directs the adolescents to record responses to open-ended questions about their activities, employment, goals, and significant life events, such as starting high school, prom, parents' divorce, or running away from home. Data on activities identify opportunities for staying busy and connections with others, as well as risk for being home alone.

After recording this contextual information, the guide directs the adolescents to report their general health status, including physical changes (e.g., weight changes, eating problems), safety (e.g., safe driving), and exposure to violence (e.g., abuse, rape, fighting). Then the guide directs adolescents to report their substance and sexual risk behavior histories: (1) tobacco use history (cigarette smoking, snuff, chew; amount and duration: x–x); (2) substance use history (alcohol, marijuana, cocaine, and other drug use; amount and duration); and (3) partner (male or female), sexual activity, and contraceptive use using partner initials, symbols, and codes (see EHC in Table 5.1).

The EHC guide directs the adolescents to reflect on their responses as they self-administer the EHC. In the first paragraph of the guide, the adolescents are informed that the EHC can "help them to see their own behavior, relationships, and events" as they complete the EHC. At the end of the guide the adolescents are directed to look at their history as a whole and think about their risk behavior patterns (across rows) and links with other risk behavior, influences, and outcomes (down columns). They are informed that next they will look over and discuss their history with the interviewer. The adolescents' cognitive perspective regarding their risk behavior history is encouraged in the instruction guide and by the interviewer or clinician. During interviews, adolescent participants have reflected on precipitation and co-occurrence of events (e.g., having sex when they are under the influence of alcohol or drugs, or during less supervised times with no activities), specific patterns of smoking and substance use (e.g., progression from drinking alcohol 2–3 times/month to 2–3 times/week), number of and frequency of sexual partners, sexual activity (e.g., progression from kissing and petting, to oral sex, to vaginal sexual intercourse), and contraceptive use (e.g., condom use with one partner but not another).

How to Interview Using Self-Administered EHCs

Prior to using the EHCs, both the interviewers and clinicians received training. Research interviewers received 8 hours of training that included an orientation to condition procedures, history form and concepts, and a review of sample forms and condition-specific history guidelines. EHC practice sessions and role-play were used to build skills and experience. This training was adapted for the clinicians, who received one hour of training focused on using the EHC for risk behavior assessment.

An interview process was developed based on adolescent EHC work to date that includes the following procedures:

1. Prior to reviewing the EHC data with the adolescent, the interviewer or clinician reviews the EHC data focusing on risk behavior patterns and interrelationship of risk behaviors, contextual factors, and outcomes. For example, they note contextual risk factors (stopped activities; parents divorced; alcohol use by parent, sister, friends), risk behavior (increasing frequency and amount of alcohol use, partner older and uses alcohol, progression from oral sex to vaginal sex with inconsistent condom use), and risk behavior interrelationships (possible connections between contextual risk factors and risk behavior).

2. The interviewers or clinicians place the completed EHC so it is visible to both the adolescent and themselves so they can together review the adolescent's EHC risk behavior patterns and interrelationship of risk behaviors, contextual factors, and outcomes:

   a. The interviewer or clinician asks the adolescent, "What did you think of your calendar history?" to assess and build on the adolescent's cognitive appraisal of his or her EHC data.

   b. The interviewer or clinician and the adolescent start horizontal row-by-row review and communication about contextual factors beginning with top rows (e.g., activities, goals, significant events, people, general health), and proceeding left to right (past to present).

   c. Then horizontal review and communication about risk behaviors row by row (tobacco use, alcohol use, drug use, and sexual activity, including partners, contraception, pregnancies, and STIs—type of risk behavior, length of time engaged in risk behavior, amount/frequency, pattern/progression of risk behavior over time) and left to right (past to present)

   d. Then vertical column-by-column review of risk behavior interrelationships, contextual factors, and outcomes (triggers for risk behaviors, contextual influences on risk behaviors, interrelationship of different risk behaviors) from top to bottom. For example, the interviewer may point out, "When you were 14 years old I see that you were involved in church and playing soccer, started going with J, kissing and petting. Then at 15, you quit going to church and soccer, started going with your current boyfriend (2 years older), smoking cigarettes, drinking alcohol, and having oral sex. . . ."

3. As they review the EHC together, the interviewers or clinicians encourage adolescents' cognitive appraisal and communication about their risk behaviors, patterns over time, interrelationship of risk behaviors, contextual factors, and outcomes graphed on the EHC. For example, they may say, "It looks like this year you have had a lot of changes in your life and are doing some things that are harmful to your health. What do you think about your smoking, drinking, and having sex? Do you think they are related to each other or to being with your boyfriend?"

4. After discussing the EHC data, the interviewer or clinician and adolescent can use the next blank column on the left side of the EHC to record future plans and goals for protective behavior (e.g., plan to use condoms every time they have sexual intercourse). During follow-up interviews or clinical visits the EHC goals can be reviewed for progress and the adolescents can update their EHC data. The EHC can be used in this way to obtain integrated risk histories and plan for protective behaviors with adolescents over time.

WHY AN ADOLESCENT EHC?

A retrospective data collection tool that is contextually and temporally linked and visually shows interrelationships and patterns of behavior and influences is ideal for adolescent risk behavior research and clinical assessment. Theoretical constructs relevant to adolescent risk behavior, developmental contextualism, and cognitive development provide rationale for the adolescent EHC.

Developmental contextualism, the dynamic interaction that occurs between adolescents and various social entities, such as family, school, and the community, results in risk behavior or protection from risk behavior (Lerner & Miller, 1993; Rew, 2005). Adolescent risk behavior has been determined to be most detrimental when it starts early and occurs frequently (time linked), friends also take risks, parents are permissive or authoritative, and communities are poor and crowded (context linked) (Lerner & Galambos, 1998). The adolescent EHC collects this type of data and other determinants of adolescent risk behavior, such as family, school, religion, and community risk and protective factors (Blum, McNeely, & Nonnemaker, 2002; Jessor, 1991, 1998).

Although adolescent risk behavior changes over time and within context, most risk behavior research and clinical methods use self-report measures focused on select points in time (e.g., "the first time, last time, or in the last 30 days you had sexual intercourse, did you use a condom?") without connecting the question to potentially influential individuals (e.g., sexual partners, parents, friends) or interrelationships with other risk behaviors (e.g., heavy drinking and sexual activity; progression of smoking/alcohol use to drug use). In contrast, the EHC method collects time- and context-linked data necessary to address relevant adolescent risk behavior issues, such as (1) risk behaviors that start during adolescence often continue into adulthood with negative lifetime consequences (Centers for Disease Control [CDC], 2002; Grunbaum et al., 2002), (2) a complex network of risk and protective factors are determinants of adolescent risk behaviors (Blum et al., 2002; Jessor, 1991, 1998), and (3) adolescent risk behaviors are interrelated (Jessor & Jessor, 1977; Romer, 2003).

EHCs facilitated the recall and report of 15- to 19-year-old African American, Caucasian, and Hispanic girls' sexual behavior and co-occurrence of other health risks within context and over time (Martyn & Martin, 2003; Martyn, Reifsnider, & Murray, 2006). Table 5.2 illustrates this in a composite of EHC data reported by the participants in qualitative studies.

The right-hand column (2002, 16 years old) on this EHC shows co-occurrence of running away, getting drunk, and having unprotected sexual intercourse (a "one night stand" with Joe[1]). The last two rows (partner and sexual activity domains) show progression of sexual activity and partner relationships: At 14 years, this girl started dating Adam (kissing only); at 15, they were going steady (kissing and petting); and at 16, after she had unprotected sex with Joe, she started having protected sex with Adam. The middle rows during the 16th year also show that her friends had unprotected sex and her family life was disrupted when her stepfather moved out. This EHC shows the complexity of adolescent risk behavior; the progression and interrelationships of risk behaviors and risk factors.

Cognitive development during adolescence is relevant to the adolescents' ability to recall, report, discuss, and perceive their own potential for risk using the EHC. Traditionally, adolescent cognition has been thought to develop over time from concrete thinking to abstract thinking and problem solving (Piaget & Inhelder, 1958, 1969, 1973). Short- and long-term memory, the ability to organize thinking, and metacognition, the ability to think about one's own thinking, are also thought to develop during adolescence (Lerner, 2002; Steinberg, 1996).

Recent and emerging adolescent brain development research also has implications for adolescent risk behavior (Spano, 2003). New findings suggest changes occur between puberty and adulthood in parts of the brain that are responsible for judgment and self-awareness, and areas that integrate visual, auditory, and tactile signals are immature until 16 years of age (Giedd et al., 1999; National Institute of Mental Health, 2001).

The EHC format provides the adolescents with a concrete visual structure that allows them to view and reflect on their own risk and protective behaviors. The EHC method is not only appropriate for adolescent cognitive development, it may lend itself to enhancing adolescent cognitive appraisal. The adolescents can see their timeline interaction of risk behaviors on the EHC. Adolescents' cognitive appraisal of their risk behavior and interviewer–adolescent communication are facilitated by together viewing and discussing the adolescents' integrated risk history.

Table 5.2   Co-Occurrence of Risk Behavior

Year	2000	2001	2002
Age (years)	14	15	16
School Grade	9	10	11
Activities Church/Club/Sports	Youth group Choir x ⟶	Youth group Choir ⟶	Youth Gr –x Choir–x
Employment Job/Duration (x–x)	Babysitting	Fast Food	Grocery Store
Future Goals	Finish HS	College	Paramedic
Significant Events	Friend died Question God	Friend died	Ran away Got drunk 10/6
Health Status	? Depression Medication		Depression Medication
Family (Circle if live with)	Mom & Stepdad	⟶	Mom ⟶ Stepdad left
Friends/Role Model	Friends sex, no condoms	⟶	⟶
Partners 1. First name 2. Duration (x–x) 3. D/S/E/M/Sx	Met & dated Adam x–Dating ⟶	Adam Steady ⟶	Joe (sex one time) Adam —S—S/Sex ⟶
Sexual Activity 1. Partner name 2. Duration (x–x) 3. Type: K/P/O/A/V 4. Contraception: a. Type: C/OC/ W/DP b. Duration (x–x)	Adam x–Kissing ⟶	Adam Kissing/ ⟶ Petting	V – Sex 1st time, 10/6, w/Joe? (C) Condom V – Sex 2nd time w/Adam after Joe (OC) Pill

NOTE: Arrow (→) indicates ongoing duration until ending at x; question mark (?) indicates adolescent unsure of history; x indicates beginning and ending points or duration of event or behavior.

Partners: D = Dating, S = Going steady, E = Engaged, M = Married, Sx = Sexually active

Sexual Activity: K = Kissing, P = Petting, OC = Oral sex, A = Anal sex, V = Vaginal sex

Contraceptives: C = Condoms, OC = Oral contraceptives/pills, W = Withdrawal/pulling out, DP = Depo-Provera/Depo shot

WHY A CLINICAL EHC?

EHC methods, traditionally used for retrospective research data collection, have been recommended "as an assessment tool and as a therapeutic guide to identify events that are linked temporally to problem behavior" (Caspi et al., 1996, p. 113). Caspi and others suggested that clinicians and patients work together using an EHC to recognize mental health patterns and triggers for relapse, and to set future health goals. Martyn, Reifsnider, and Murray (2006) conducted a clinical feasibility study with 30 Hispanic girls between 15 and 19 years of age and two nurse practitioners (NP). The adolescents in this study were able to self-administer the EHC in 10–15 minutes (on average) and reported it was easy to use, and only 10% needed clarification of meaning or spelling of unfamiliar terms such as gonorrhea or *quinceañera* (Martyn, Reifsnider, & Murray, 2006). The clinicians in this study reported that the EHC was easy to use to identify risk behavior processes and contextual interrelationships, and they were able to do so in an average of 2 minutes (Martyn, Reifsnider, & Murray, 2006). The NPs identified all reports of sexual risk behavior history on the EHC (unprotected sexual intercourse, multiple partners, and progression of sexual activity over time). Content analysis indicated that only one report of nonsexual risk behavior (a report of physical fighting by a virgin) was missed.

The NPs using the adolescent EHC in this study suggested that the primary benefit of clinical use of EHCs is to enhance adolescents' awareness of their own risk behavior (Martyn, Reifsnider, & Murray, 2006). They reported that the EHC was a time-efficient way to understand the context of an adolescent's life and identify smoking, alcohol, marijuana, and unprotected intercourse and co-occurrence of alcohol and marijuana use with sexual intercourse. The NPs also indicated the EHC was a "good teaching tool" to "identify high risk behavior and help teens to see their own risk behavior" (Martyn, Reifsnider, & Murray, 2006, p. 24). The adolescent girls who completed the EHC also recognized benefits for clinical assessment. For example, one girl said the EHC "would be good to have and fill out, I think. Like if you're at a doctor, I'm sure your doctor would need to know something about you. And half of this is definitely not on my record. My whole life on paper" (Martyn & Martin, 2003, p. 216).

In studies using the adolescent EHC with female participants ($n = 73$) (Martyn, Hutchinson, & Martin, 2002; Martyn & Martin, 2003; Martyn, Reifsnider, & Murray, 2006), detailed contextualized 6- to 10-year sexual histories have been obtained on the EHCs, including patterns of sexual activity progression (from kissing, to petting, to oral sex and vaginal intercourse) and triggers for unintended sexual intercourse (lack of supervision and getting drunk). Discussions of protective and risky sexual decision making were also stimulated by adolescents' self-report of sexual risk behavior in their own words and reflective responses on the EHC. In addition, the adolescent girls reported that the calendars were easy to use and made it easier to remember and discuss sensitive issues with the nurses.

According to the interaction model of client health behavior (Cox, 1982, 2003), a clinical practice model, adolescents' risk behavior is determined by the fit between their unique characteristics or, as referred to in this model, "client singularity" (e.g., past risk behavior and cognitive appraisal) and clinician–adolescent risk communication. The clinician–adolescent use of the EHC provides this fit and facilitates adolescents' perception of their risk, which could result in negative attitudes about risk behavior, facilitate clinician–adolescent communication, and subsequently reduce risk behavior.

Through qualitative and quantitative research using the EHC with adolescent females, key findings indicated that the EHC method has potential to play a role in adolescent risk behavior reduction. Using the EHCs, the adolescent participants (1) disclosed personal contextual risk behavior histories, (2) demonstrated awareness of and self-reflection about their risk behavior, and (3) reported increased safe sex intentions and safe sex behavior trends.

First, disclosure of personal contextual risk behavior histories provides the client singularity data necessary for the clinician to tailor effective adolescent–clinician communication (Cox, 1982). Disclosure of what was most meaningful to the adolescents about their lives helps clinicians to understand this singularity. Such disclosure is seen in the description of an EHC completed by a 15-year-old girl in a qualitative research study (Martyn & Martin, 2003). The adolescent reported her boyfriend history in the partner domain (row) on the EHC, and although she was abstinent, she was most concerned about the five different boyfriends she had since she was 13. She reported that she had really liked Jim since she was 13 and would go steady with him and probably have sex with him if he asked her, but he was dating other girls. She dated other boys (Tom, Dick, Harry, and Bob), but broke up with them when they pressured her for sex. This EHC revealed history information essential to tailoring adolescent–clinician risk prevention communication. However, when adolescents report they are not sexually active, clinicians typically do not focus on relationships with boyfriends or partners, often a major area of concern for adolescents.

Second, adolescent self-reflection occurred while completing the EHC and during interview discussions about their EHC data. The EHC is "a facilitative tool to encourage greater depth and poignancy in fully developing the adolescent's cognitive appraisal; it serves as a focused point of departure to facilitate tailored adolescent-provider communication" (Cheryl Cox, personal communication, April 21, 2005). Adolescents have reported self-reflection and value judgments about their own risk behavior on the EHC. For example, adolescent EHC reports have included comments such as being in "rebellious stages," that they "started really liking boys," and "started thinking I was ready for sex." And at the time of the interview they have reported on the EHC realizations that they were "not ready for sex" and decisions to "use condoms" or "go back to school." This type of data indicated that the EHC method not only allowed for disclosure of adolescent self-reflection, but encouraged adolescents' perceptions of their own personal risks.

Participants in the EHC clinical feasibility study conducted by Martyn, Reifsnider, and Murray (2006) were asked a "think aloud" question about their EHC data that elicited perceptions about their own risk behavior. Girls with sexual activity and substance use pointed to onset of their risk behavior on their EHCs and said things like, "I really messed up right here," "I can see how my life changed right here, [when my sister's] friends introduced me to weed," and "I see where my life went bad, I'm going to start doing better" (p. 25). Girls who did not have risk behaviors talked about the protective influences in their lives. For example, they said that their families protected them and that they in turn owed it to their families to protect them (Martyn, Darling-Fisher et al., 2006).

Third, adolescents in an EHC clinical feasibility study conducted by Martyn, Reifsnider, and Murray (2006) reported increased safe sex intentions and safe sex behavior trends after completing the EHC. Adolescents who perceive personal susceptibility to risk are more likely to intend to and to actually avoid risk behaviors (Fishbein, 2003; Millstein, 2003). Compared to their initial interview immediately after completing the calendar, the adolescents were significantly more likely to report that they intended to abstain from sex or use condoms ($\chi^2 = 9.3$, $df = 1$, $p < .002$). Differences in adolescent reports of past 3-month sexual activity and condom use obtained at initial interview and at 3-month follow-up approached significance ($\chi^2 = 2.88$, $df = 1$, $p < .09$), indicating a trend toward decreased sexual activity and increased condom use. At the 3-month follow-up interview, the majority (68%) of the girls who reported sexual activity at initial interview reported abstinence or protected sex in the past 3 months since the initial interview. Other results confirmed the co-occurrence of risk behaviors. The majority of adolescents with history of smoking or alcohol or marijuana use (57%) surveyed at the 3-month follow-up reported no smoking, alcohol, or marijuana use in the past 30 days.

Reliability and Validity

The adolescent EHC was initially pilot tested in 2000 with female subjects who had participated in an adolescent pregnancy avoidance qualitative research study in 1995–1998 from which the EHC domains were derived

(Martyn & Hutchinson, 2001; Martyn, Hutchinson, & Martin, 2002). Content analysis revealed that the EHC family, sexual partner, sexual activity, and contraceptive retrospective data were consistent with interview data collected 2–5 years earlier. The EHC format and instructions were found to be straightforward and easily understandable.

The adolescent EHC data obtained in subsequent qualitative and quantitative studies showed good face validity (Martyn & Martin, 2003; Martyn, Reifsnider, & Murray, 2006). The EHC sexual activity domains (e.g., sexual partner, sexual activity, and contraception use) were all pertinent to adolescent sexual risk behavior. The participants reported only the types of sexual activity, contraception, or substance use included in the EHC domains. Association of variables predicted to be correlated with adolescent risk behavior and risk avoidance indicated construct validity (Cronbach, 1970). Fisher's exact tests were calculated to determine risk behavior, protective factors, and risk factor differences between participants who reported sexual activity and those who reported abstinence. The participants who reported sexual activity were more likely to report history of alcohol or drug use (65% and 23%, respectively, $p < .001$) and more than one type of risk behavior (65% and 0%, $p < .001$). While those who reported sexual abstinence were more likely to identify family (100% and 47%, $p < .001$) and school connections (100% and 53%, $p < .001$), sexually active girls were significantly more likely than the abstinent girls to report risk factors such as living in one-parent or nonfamily homes ($p < .01$), no adult role models ($p < .01$), no friends ($p < .05$), quitting school/repeating grades ($p < .01$), and no activities/sports ($p < .01$).

Conclusion

The temporal and contextual features inherent in the EHC support the use of self-administered EHCs for adolescent research and clinical practice. Determining patterns and interrelationships of adolescent risk behaviors within the context of family, friends, school, and community will help address gaps in the adolescent literature. Much of our current understanding of adolescent risk behavior is derived from national surveys such as the CDC Youth Risk Behavior Surveillance (YRBS) (CDC, 2006). The YRBS uses conventional questionnaires to survey high school students about risk behaviors (e.g., sexual activity, smoking, substance use), health behaviors (e.g., physical activity, nutrition), and context (e.g., family, school, religion). Large-scale surveys like the YRBS could be enhanced by using EHC methods to collect time- and context-linked risk behavior data. The EHC could be included to enhance recall and report of risk behaviors in a variety of ways. It could be used at the beginning of the survey to increase recall and link events by asking about contextual data (education, living arrangements, work), as it has been used in the National Survey of Family Growth (Mosher, 1998). Sections of the EHC could be inserted in the survey to supplement select items. For example, a sexual behavior YRBS question asks how many people the adolescent had sexual intercourse with during his or her life; an EHC sexual activity section could be inserted to collect data on the trajectory of partners. In addition, a complete EHC could be administered as an adjunct to the survey data collected to explore the developmental contextualism further. And if using the EHC does enhance adolescent self-awareness and risk perception, an additional benefit of this type of data collection may be the facilitating of reductions in adolescent risk behaviors.

Although research has indicated that understanding the context of adolescents' lives is essential to understanding adolescent health risk behavior (Resnick et al., 1997), and adolescents have reported that they want to discuss school, friends, activities, and personal topics with clinicians (Sydnor-Greenberg & Dokken, 2001), health risk assessment methods typically focus on an adolescent's risk behavior and not interrelationships or contextual factors. For example, the "gold standard" adolescent assessment method, the *Guidelines for Adolescent Preventive Services (GAPS)* (American Medical Association, 1997; Elster & Kuznets, 1994), does not provide a framework for risk assessment that shows interrelationships between risk behaviors, depicts patterns or trends of risk behavior, or includes social influences other than family and friends. Not included are contextual questions such as: Do you have unprotected sex when you have been drinking alcohol or using drugs?; or for adolescents who smoke cigarettes, Do you intend to use alcohol or marijuana? Social influences such as relationships with sexual partners or supportive relationships with school, church, or involvement in extracurricular activities or sports are equally important, but not included.

Integrated adolescent health risk assessment and communication can be achieved by the clinician and adolescent working together using the EHC to connect health risk behaviors to each other (e.g., heavy drinking, unprotected sex) and to other influences (e.g., unsupervised time, limited parental supervision); identify patterns of and triggers for risk behaviors (e.g., progression from kissing to petting to sexual intercourse); and ascertain the influence of family, partner, peers, teachers, coaches, and others on adolescent health risk behavior (Dryfoos, 1998; U.S. Department of Health and Human Services, 2000). Ultimately, through EHC methods, adolescents may be able to increase awareness of their own risk behavior and make decisions to decrease detrimental behaviors.

Self-administered EHCs are also convenient for research and practice. They can be mailed to research participants as Mortimer and Johnson (1998) did in a longitudinal study with high school graduates to collect data on the previous year's activities and family structure changes. Recently, a self-administered EHC was used as a self-reflection tool in a high school classroom education program on sexually transmitted infection prevention. For greater convenience, the adolescent EHC was revised to be used without the instruction guide by including focused questions in each domain section on the EHC. For example, in the sexual activity domain, adolescents were asked to "write any sexual activity they had, including: partner (use initials), duration (use x–x), type (use symbols), contraception including how often used." In the risky behavior domain, they were asked to "write any risky behavior they had (smoking, alcohol, drugs, others and to use symbols to show what and x–x for when)." Both male and female adolescents completed EHCs in this education program and results are being analyzed in ongoing research.

Intervention research studies focused on the use of the EHC for adolescent clinical assessment, risk perception, and health education are needed. These could be conducted as discrete interventions (e.g., clinical assessment and communication) or as part of risk behavior education and intervention programs in schools or community-based settings. Further evaluation of reliability and validity of the adolescent EHC is also needed.

Note

1. The names reported are pseudonyms.

Acknowledgment

Research support was received from an NIH/NINR P20 MESA Center for Health Disparities Pilot Study Grant, a University of Michigan Rackham Faculty Research Grant and Fellowship, and a National Organization of Nurse Practitioners Faculties Research Award.

References

American Medical Association. (1997). *Guidelines for adolescent preventive services (GAPS): Recommendations monograph.* Chicago: Author.

Belli, R. F. (1998). The structure of autobiographical memory and the event history calendar: Potential improvements in the quality of retrospective reports in surveys. *Memory, 6*(4), 383–406.

Belli, R. F., Lee, E. H., Stafford, F. P., & Chou, C.-H. (2004). Calendar and question-list survey methods: Association between interviewer behavior and data quality. *Journal of Official Statistics, 20,* 185–196.

Belli, R. F., Shay, W. L., & Stafford, F. P. (2001). Event history calendars and question list surveys: A direct comparison of interviewing methods. *Public Opinion Quarterly, 65,* 45–74.

Blum, R. W., McNeely, C., & Nonnemaker, J. (2002). Vulnerability, risk, and protection. *Journal of Adolescent Health, 31*(1, Suppl.), 28–39.

Caspi, A., Moffitt, T. E., Thornton, A., Freedman, D., Amell, J. W., Harrington, H., et al. (1996). The life history calendar: A research and clinical assessment method for collecting retrospective event-history data. *International Journal of Methods in Psychiatric Research, 6*(2), 101–114.

Centers for Disease Control and Prevention. (2002). *Youth Risk Behavior Surveillance System: 2001 information and results.* Retrieved May 19, 2008, from http://www.cdc.gov/nccdphp/dash/yrbs/index.htm

Conway, M. A. (1996). Autobiographical knowledge and autobiographical memories. In D. C. Rubin (Ed.), *Remembering our past: Studies in autobiographical memory* (pp. 67–93). New York: Cambridge University Press.

Cox, C. L. (1982). An interaction model of client health behavior: Theoretical prescription for nursing. *Advances in Nursing Science, 5,* 41–56.

Cox, C. L. (2003). A model of health behavior to guide studies of childhood cancer survivors. *Oncology Nursing Forum, 30*(5), E92–E99.

Cronbach, L. J. (1970). *Essentials of psychological testing* (3rd ed.). New York: Harper & Row.

Dryfoos, J. G. (1998). Thirty years in pursuit of the magic bullet. *Journal of Adolescent Health, 23,* 338–343.

Elster, A. B., & Kuznets, N. J. (1994). *AMA guidelines for adolescent preventive services (GAPS): Recommendations and rationale.* Baltimore: Williams & Wilkins.

Fishbein, M. (2003). Toward an understanding of the role of perceived risk in HIV prevention research. In D. Romer (Ed.), *Reducing adolescent risk: Toward an integrated approach* (pp. 49–55). Thousand Oaks, CA: Sage.

Freedman, D., Thornton, A., Camburn, D., Alwin, D., & Young-DeMarco, L. (1988). The life history calendar: A technique for collecting retrospective data. In C. C. Clogg (Ed.), *Sociological methodology* (Vol. 18, pp. 37–68). San Francisco: Jossey-Bass.

Giedd, J., Blumenthal, J., Jeffries, N., Castellanos, F., Liu, H., Zijdenbos, A., et al. (1999). Brain development during childhood and adolescence: A longitudinal MRI study. *Nature Neuroscience, 2*(10), 861–863.

Grunbaum, J. A., Kann, L., Kinchen, S. A., Williams, B., Ross, J. G., Lowry, R., et al. (2002). Youth risk behavior surveillance—United States, 2001. *Morbidity and Mortality Weekly Report, 51,* SS-04, 1–64.

Jessor, R. (1991). Risk behavior in adolescence: A psychological framework for understanding and action. *Journal of Adolescent Health, 12,* 597–605.

Jessor, R. (1993). Successful adolescent development among youth in high risk settings. *American Psychologist, 48,* 117–126.

Jessor, R. (1998). *New perspectives on adolescent risk behavior.* Cambridge, UK: Cambridge University Press.

Jessor, R., & Jessor, S. L. (1977). *Problem behavior and psychosocial development: A longitudinal study of youth.* New York: Academic Press.

Lerner, R. M. (2002). *Adolescence: Development, diversity, context, and application.* Upper Saddle River, NJ: Pearson Education.

Lerner, R. M., & Galambos, N. L. (1998). Adolescent development: Challenges and opportunities for research, programs, and policies. *Annual Review of Psychology, 49,* 413–446.

Lerner, R. M., & Miller, J. R. (1993). Integrating human development research and intervention for America's children: The Michigan State University model. *Journal of Applied Developmental Psychology, 14,* 347–364.

Martyn, K. K., & Belli, R. F. (2002). Retrospective data collection using event history calendars. *Nursing Research, 51,* 270–274.

Martyn, K. K., Darling-Fisher, C., Smrtka, J., Fernandez, D., & Martyn, D. H. (2006). Honoring family biculturalism: Avoidance of adolescent pregnancy among Latina girls in the United States. *Hispanic Health Care International, 4*(1), 15–26.

Martyn, K. K., & Hutchinson, S. A. (2001). Low-income African American adolescents who avoid pregnancy: Tough girls who rewrite negative scripts. *Qualitative Health Research, 11,* 238–256.

Martyn, K. K., Hutchinson, S. A., & Martin, J. H. (2002). Lucky girls: Unintentional avoidance of adolescent pregnancy among low-income African American females. *Journal for Specialists in Pediatric Nursing, 7*(4), 154–162.

Martyn, K. K., & Martin, R. (2003). Adolescent sexual risk assessment. *Journal of Midwifery and Women's Health, 8,* 213–219.

Martyn, K. K., Reifsnider, E., Barry, M. G., Treviño, M., & Murray, A. (2006). Protective processes of Latina adolescents. *Hispanic Health Care International, 4*(2), 111–124.

Martyn, K. K., Reifsnider, E., & Murray, A. (2006). Improving adolescent sexual risk assessment with event history calendars: A feasibility study. *Journal of Pediatric Health Care, 20*(1), 19–26.

Millstein, S. G. (2003). Risk perception: Construct development, links to theory, correlates, and manifestations. In D. Romer (Ed.), *Reducing adolescent risk: Toward an integrated approach* (pp. 35–43). Thousand Oaks, CA: Sage.

Mortimer, J. T., & Johnson, M. K. (1998). New perspectives on adolescent work and the transition to adulthood. In R. Jessor (Ed.), *New perspectives on adolescent risk behavior* (pp. 425–496). New York: Cambridge University Press.

Mosher, W. D. (1998). Design and operation of the 1995 National Survey of Family Growth. *Family Planning Perspective, 30*(1), 43–46.

National Institute of Mental Health. (2001). *Teenage brain: A work in progress.* Retrieved May 19, 2008, from http://www.nimh.nih.gov/publicat/teenbrain.cfm

Piaget, J., & Inhelder, B. (1958). *The growth of logical thinking.* New York: Basic Books.

Piaget, J., & Inhelder, B. (1969). *The psychology of the child.* New York: Basic Books.

Piaget, J., & Inhelder, B. (1973). *Memory and intelligence.* New York: Basic Books.

Resnick, M. D., Bearman, P. S., Blum, R. W., Bauman, K. E., Harris, K. M., Jones, J., et al. (1997). Protecting adolescents from harm: Findings from the National Longitudinal Study of Adolescent Health. *Journal of the American Medical Association, 278,* 823–832.

Rew, L. (2005). *Adolescent health: A multidisciplinary approach to theory, research, and intervention.* Thousand Oaks, CA: Sage.

Romer, D. (2003). *Reducing adolescent risk: Toward an integrated approach.* Thousand Oaks, CA: Sage.

Spano, S. (2003). Adolescent brain development. *Youth Studies Australia, 22,* 36–38.

Steinberg, L. (1996). *Adolescence* (4th ed.). New York: McGraw-Hill.

Sydnor-Greenberg, N., & Dokken, D. I. (2001). Communication in healthcare: Thoughts on the child's perspectives. *Journal of Child and Family Nursing, 4,* 225–230.

U.S. Department of Health and Human Services, Public Health Service. (2000). *Healthy People 2010: Understanding and improving health.* Washington, DC: Author.

6

Assessment of Stressor Exposure Using Telephone Diaries

The Daily Inventory of Stressful Events

Elaine Wethington and David M. Almeida

Introduction

People exposed to major or persistent stressors in their social environments, whether major life events such as divorce or daily stressors such as juggling conflicting work responsibilities, are also more likely to suffer worse health. Although it has been accepted for some time in the research literature that stressor exposure is associated with poorer physical and mental health, it has been harder to establish with precision how much objective features and events in the social environment contribute to poorer health. The difficulty is that comparatively few studies have estimated the relative contribution of objective stressor exposure in comparison to the contributions of individual differences in personal characteristics that affect the severity of reaction to stressors (i.e., stress reactivity). In this chapter, we describe a new and innovative daily event assessment method, the Daily Inventory of Stressful Events (DISE) (Almeida, Wethington, & Kessler, 2002), which is designed to examine the contributions of daily stressor exposure and individual differences in reactivity to health and well-being.

Most of the research literature in psychology, and a great deal in other fields as well, has focused on individual differences that contribute to stressor reactivity. *Stressor reactivity* is the likelihood that an individual will show emotional or physical reactions to stressors (Almeida, 2005; Bolger & Zuckerman, 1995). The critical question addressed in this extensive literature is why some people rather than others are more "reactive" to stressors (e.g., Suls & Martin, 2005). Reactivity has been measured on the daily level as mood and physical symptoms (e.g., headaches) in response to exposure to stressors.

We agree that individual differences that contribute to stress reactivity constitute an exciting field of inquiry. However, to address the role of individual differences in the stress process researchers also require equally valid and reliable measures of stressor exposure. Differential reactivity to stressors should be assessed in relationship to differential exposure to stressors. Encountering stressors is not simply a matter of chance or bad luck; rather, differences in stressor exposure more often emerge from individual sociodemographic, psychosocial, and situational factors (e.g., Pearlin, 1999; Wheaton, 1999). Over the long term, exposure to chronic, persistent stressors is associated with the deterioration of physical and mental health (e.g., Wheaton & Clarke, 2003). There are features of the daily environment that pose risks to well-being, such as demanding work conditions, financial pressures, and work–family conflict. A question of considerable interest is whether some groups more than others bear a larger burden of chronic stressor exposure, thereby contributing to societal health inequalities (e.g., Pearlin, Schieman, Fazio, & Meersman, 2005). The answer to this question requires comprehensive, reliable, and valid measures of stressor exposure that are relevant to the experiences of diverse groups.

The development of the DISE was also shaped by concerns about self-report bias in measurement of daily stressors. An assumption underlying daily stressor measures is that they capture objective differences in the stressors themselves. Yet the typical measure of daily stressors asks for self-report of an event and the event's severity to assess objective exposure and objective differences between stressors. The reliance on self-reports means that hassle measures could be biased. Self-report of stressor severity may be confounded with the correlates of stressor appraisal—personality, mood at the time of recall, and history of exposure to stressors. Thus individual differences may be associated with self-reports of stressor exposure as well as with reactivity to stressors.

To address these demands for comprehensiveness, reliability, and validity, the DISE adopted several innovations in daily event measurement. To ensure comprehensiveness and validity, the DISE was developed using samples representative of the U.S. population. In order to reduce one type of self-report bias, the DISE includes a system of *investigator ratings* to assess the severity of stressor exposure on a daily basis, as well as respondent ratings of severity. In order to access representative population samples and implement investigator ratings of stressor exposure, the DISE is designed to be administered over the telephone.

Measuring Daily Stressor Exposure

A typical study of daily stressors (or events) uses a self-administered checklist consisting of a number of common occurrences that are believed to be associated with variations in mood or physical health symptoms. Several methodological concerns have been raised about daily checklist measures. First, there is evidence that memory for daily events may be imperfect. Recall of minor events decays after only a few hours (Stone, Kessler, & Haythornthwaite, 1991). Second, individual differences in what constitutes evaluation of something as a stressor—stressor *appraisal*—may affect the tendency to report an incident as a stressor. The consequence of such individual differences in appraisal is that appraisal and the putative "objective" report of a stressor are confounded (McQuaid et al., 1992). Third, to ensure adequate response, the daily diary questionnaire must be relatively brief. Brevity increases compliance but may reduce comprehensiveness (Herbert & Cohen, 1996).

Two important techniques for assessing daily experiences have been developed that address the methodological problems in self-report daily stressor measures, the experience sampling method (ESM) (Csikszentmihalyi & Larson, 1987) and the Day Reconstruction Method (DRM) (Kahneman, Krueger, Schkade, Schwarz, & Stone, 2004; see also Schwarz, Kahneman, & Xu, Chapter 9, this volume). Both of these methods have been designed to reduce or eliminate measurement bias caused by memory decay, appraisal bias, and lack of checklist comprehensiveness. The ESM requires respondents to report their activities and mood whenever they are randomly signaled by the investigator, thus reducing or eliminating memory decay and recall bias caused by subsequent appraisal. The DRM, rather than recording responses to random signals, uses a next day recall method to classify the day into distinct episodes of activity and to assess mood during those episodes.

In our view, ESM and DRM are interesting complements to measurements of daily events rather than substitutes for it. One major difference between daily events measures like the DISE and the ESM and DRM measures is that the latter capture routine activities of daily life while the DISE is intended to capture more out-of-the-ordinary occurrences that lead to variations in mood and physical symptoms. Events of interest to daily stress researchers may not be frequent or common enough to be represented in random samplings of respondents' days or recall of distinct episodes of activities in those days (the DRM). For example, Almeida and colleagues (2002) found in a national sample that arguments with a boss take place on 0.7% of days. An argument with the boss, which may put a job at stake, can be a very threatening event. And an argument would not necessarily occur at the time of a random beep during the workday (ESM) or be recalled as a distinct activity episode (DRM).

Another major difference between methods is that the ESM and the DRM target a different type of experience variability than daily events methods. DRM and ESM capture within-day variability typically across activities (DRM) or time of day. The DISE approach captures variability across stressful situations, between persons of different groups, or within persons over a period of time. Capturing situational variability is vital to elucidating how stressors trigger adaptation. Dohrenwend (2006) has detailed how situational variability is poorly measured by the traditional events checklist approach (e.g., McQuaid et al., 1992). A case in point is that not all arguments are the same. They vary in content, objective threat (shouting versus physical violence), and appraised meaning. The method we have developed, the DISE, is designed to capture intracategory variability across situations for events such as arguments. DISE methods make it possible to examine how such situational variability predicts adaptation responses, including the potential for tracking situational variability in physiological response (see Miller, Chen, & Zhou, 2007).

Development of the DISE

The DISE method was designed to measure exposure to daily stressors in a national sample of Americans. The respondents to the national study (NSDE; National Study of Daily Experiences) were 1,031 adults (562 women, 469 men), all of whom had previously taken part in the Midlife in the United States Survey (MIDUS), a nationally representative survey of 3,032 people aged 25–74 in 1995–1996 (Mroczek & Kolarz, 1998). Respondents to the NSDE were randomly selected from the MIDUS sample, with a response rate of 83%.

Over the course of 8 consecutive evenings, respondents completed short telephone interviews about their daily experiences. On the final evening of interviewing, respondents also answered additional questions about the previous week. The interviews took about 15 minutes to complete. Data collection activities spanned an entire year (March 1996 to April 1997) and consisted of 40 separate "flights" of interviews with each flight representing 8 days of interviews from approximately 38 respondents. The flights began on different days of the week to control for possible confounding between day of the week (Monday) and day of the study (first). Respondents completed an average of seven of the eight interviews ($M = 7.22$ days).

THE DISE METHOD

Daily stressors were assessed using the semistructured DISE (Almeida, 1998, 2005). The inventory consisted of a set of seven stem questions asking whether certain types of daily stressors had occurred in the past 24 hours, along with a set of interviewer guidelines for probing affirmative responses to rate stressor content, severity, and threat. The seven stem questions were derived from a series of pilot test interviews conducted by the investigators. The aim of the pilot test interviews was to reduce the number of stem questions to a number that was small enough to reduce respondent burden and increase compliance, but also comprehensive enough to encompass most daily stressors (Herbert & Cohen, 1996). The seven stem questions asked about arguments and disagreements, instances of avoided arguments, events at work or school, events at home, instances of discrimination, events that occurred to close friends or relatives, and an open-ended question about "anything else." It is important to note that in order to communicate that we were interested in somewhat out-of-the-ordinary situations several of the questions included the phrase "that most people would consider stressful." Thus appraisal of something as "stressful" was included in the question, although we attempted to guide respondents' replies by using a normative probing technique.

After obtaining an affirmative response to a stem question, the interviewer was instructed to probe to elicit a short narrative description of the stressor. The suggested probes were aimed at descriptive information that could be used to code the topic or content of the situation, who was involved, and how long the situation lasted. The open-ended information for each reported stressor was tape-recorded and then transcribed and coded to rate different aspects of "threat." The coders were graduate students who received 10 hours of initial training in investigator rating methods. We held 2-hour meetings every week to check accuracy, review training, and resolve any discrepancies in rating. New coders who joined the project had to demonstrate interrater reliability equal to that of experienced coders before they were allowed to begin coding.

After the narrative was obtained, the interviewer then asked the respondent to rate (appraise) the "stressfulness" of the situation, as not at all, not very, somewhat, or very stressful. For each event rated as "somewhat" or "very stressful," the respondents also were asked a series of structured questions that assessed primary appraisal of the stressors. These questions assessed what was perceived to be at risk in the situation, such as disruption to daily routine, financial situation, physical health or safety, plans for the future, others' health or well-being, and views about oneself. These dimensions of primary appraisal were based on the work of Lazarus and Folkman (1984) although the structured probes we used did not exhaust the possibilities for assessing primary appraisal.

THE INVESTIGATOR RATING METHOD

A unique aspect of the DISE was the implementation of investigator ratings of threat for each stressor, in addition to self-reported estimation of severity. To our knowledge, we were the first group of researchers to apply investigator rating methods to the study of daily stressors. Monroe and Kelly (1995) recommended coupling an investigator or "panel" approach to rating reports of stressors with the Lazarus and Folkman (1984) self-rated appraisal approach to assessing stressor severity. Event threat ratings assigned by an expert panel (e.g., Brown & Harris, 1978) enable researchers to compare self-reported ratings of stressor severity, which are confounded by stressor appraisal, to ratings based on established objective criteria. One of us (Wethington) was trained in investigator rating methods by George W. Brown and Tirril O. Harris, who pioneered the investigator-rated, or panel, method in the Life Events and Difficulties Schedule (LEDS; Brown & Harris, 1978). Investigator ratings are typically used in studies assessing major life events and difficulties.

We believed that adapting investigator ratings could lead to major innovations in the study of daily stressors. First, the main purpose of investigator rating methods is to estimate severity of the impact of a stressor independently from the respondent's report of severity, which may be confounded with individual differences in appraisal (Wethington, Brown, & Kessler, 1995). Second, investigator rating methods, based on the objective features reported about an event, make it possible to distinguish an objective occurrence (e.g., an argument with a spouse) from an affective response to a stressor (e.g., crying or feeling sad). Some early measures of daily stressors included affective reactions in event checklists (e.g., Dohrenwend, Dohrenwend, Dodson, & Shrout, 1984). Third, investigator ratings reduce the problem of intracategory variability (as described earlier) (Dohrenwend, 2006). Occurrences can be classified by severity, content, and type of threat using standardized criteria. Fourth, investigator ratings also make it possible to determine which affirmative responses to event questions are unique and distinct from other responses and which responses are duplicates (e.g., Kessler & Wethington, 1991). This eliminates another source of imprecision in the estimation of accumulated stress exposure over a period of time.

An investigator rating is a set of expert judgments based on an event narrative. The event narrative is self-report, but it is structured by questions asked by an interviewer who has been trained to probe for circumstances that are associated with an event of a particular type being on average more or less severe in its impact. The objective features that affect the severity rating of different types of events have been catalogued into dictionaries by the teams that have developed investigator ratings (e.g., LEDS; Brown & Harris, 1978); these features are given different weight in the calculation of probable "severity" of a situation. Use of an established dictionary documenting previous panel judgments enables an investigator to rate which experiences meet theoretically established thresholds of severity rather than to rely on the respondent's interpretation or response to a set of questions.

DEVELOPING DISE INVESTIGATOR RATINGS

Several challenges emerged in adapting investigator ratings to a study of daily events. First and foremost, existing dictionaries of events could not be used for rating severity because they are focused on events that meet high thresholds of severity, far above those typically considered as daily stressors. This is important because minor events that occur on a daily basis are likely to have a fleeting impact on mood, and severity ratings and classifications from existing investigator ratings methods could not be adopted uncritically. Taking a sick dog to the veterinarian during rush hour is a stressful situation for a short time, but its impact on the future is very different from having a spouse suffer a major heart attack. Second, the number of events generated by a study of the size of the National Study of Daily Experiences required logistical and training innovations. Investigator rating methods are typically used only in samples of less than 200 because of concerns about the expense of training and retraining to maintain consistency and reliability (Wethington et al., 1995).

Our strategy was to develop ratings over time in response to accumulated knowledge of what constituted the universe of stressful experiences reported in interviews. Key elements of investigator rating were selected from those used in the LEDS (Brown & Harris, 1978): classification (or topic) of the stressor, focus of the stressor (self, other, or a combination), and "contextual threat." Three dimensions of threat rated in the LEDS were included in the DISE: *loss* of a possession, person, or important idea, or more generally, a perceived deficit; *danger,* which was defined as the anticipation of future negative occurrence; and *disappointment,* defined as something not turning out as expected. In addition to these three dimensions, two other dimensions of threat emerged from the accumulation of daily event narratives, *frustration* (events and their outcomes out of the respondent's control) and *opportunity* (a chance for a positive outcome if action is taken). These five dimensions of threat were rated as present or not present for each event. In addition, objective severity or overall threat was rated based on the degree and duration of the unpleasantness and disruption created for the respondent by the situation. Ratings ranged from 1, a minor or trivial annoyance, to 4, a severely disruptive situation.

A training manual was developed based on the Structured Life Event Interview (SLI) (Wethington et al., 1995) interviewing and coding manual, a more structured version of the LEDS, and it was used as the basis for interviewer training. Consistent with methods used by Brown and associates, the manual was continuously updated with event and rating examples. The final dictionary consisted of nearly 4000 entries stored in a searchable database. Along with the updated manual, the investigators and coders constructed a rating dictionary, classifying events by content, focus, threat, and severity. Coders met weekly for interrater reliability checks, to resolve difficult coding cases, and for retraining.

SPECIFIC DISE RATINGS AND THEIR RELIABILITY

Table 6.1 presents a description of DISE measures of stressor content, focus, threat, severity, and primary appraisal. The first two measures in Table 6.1 assess the objective nature of the stressor. Each stressor was initially placed into a *content classification* that combined the broad classification (e.g., argument) with specific content or topic of the stressor (e.g., housework). (A pilot study of a national sample of 1,006 adults was initially conducted to generate the content classification list of daily stressors common to adults in the United States.) Another characteristic of daily stressors was *focus of involvement.* Focus refers to whether other individuals were involved in the stressors and, if so, what their relation was to the respondent (Brown & Harris, 1978).

The remaining measures in Table 6.1 assess the meaning of the stressor for the respondent. *Threat dimensions* were the investigator-rated stressful implications for the respondent. *Objective severity* ratings are the investigator ratings. The final two DISE measures were obtained from the respondents' own ratings. These included the respondents' perceived or *subjective severity* of stressor and reports on seven *primary appraisal domains* (i.e., the degree of risk the stressor posed in various areas of life).

The guidelines for assigning ratings are provided in an interview and coding manual (Almeida, 1998, 2005). This dictionary can be searched and cross-referenced by any of the DISE measures. The interrater reliability for DISE ratings ranged from good to excellent (see Table 6.1). Approximately 20% of the events in the study were independently rated by two coders. The interrater reliability ranged from .66 to .95 across all of the ratings. The ratings for specific content of the stressor had the lowest agreement across coders partially because there were 54 possible code categories.

Table 6.2 presents sample dictionary entries for three of these stressors. The first column shows the respondent's verbatim description of the stressor. The second column lists the broad and specific content, ratings for the focus of involvement and the relationship of the person if others were involved in the stressor, objective severity rating, subjective severity rating (which may differ), and the respondent's primary appraisal ratings. Higher numbers represent higher severity and greater perceived disruption. The overall pattern of correlations between ratings indicates a modest degree of independence between the severity ratings, threat dimensions, and appraisal domains. Only 3 of the 36 correlations between ratings were above .30. Coders' ratings of severity were only moderately associated with the respondents' subjective ratings of severity ($r = .36$, $p < .05$), indicating that these two measures are not redundant.

Table 6.1   Description and Interrater Coding Reliability of DISE Measures

Coding Category	Description	Interrater Reliability
Content classification	Stressful events are categorized into one of 7 broad classifications and 54 specific subclassifications. Specific classifications: interpersonal tensions (21 subclasses), work/school (9), home (9), finances (3), health/accidents (5), network events (7), and miscellaneous events (9).	Broad classification .90 Specific classification .66
Focus of involvement	Focus of involvement refers to who was involved in the event: *respondent*, *other*, and *joint*.	.88
Threat dimensions	Threat dimensions describe the implications of the event for the respondent. *Loss* is the occurrence of a deficit. *Danger* is the risk of a future negative occurrence. *Disappointment* occurs when something does not turn out as the respondent had expected. *Frustration* occurs when the respondent has little or no control over the events. *Opportunity* is a chance for positive outcome.	.74
Objective severity	The objective assessment of the severity of an event refers to the degree and duration of disruption and/or unpleasantness created for the respondent. *(1 = low severity, a minor or trivial annoyance, 2 = medium severity, 3 = high severity, 4 = extreme severity, a severely disruptive event)*	.61
Subjective severity	The subjective assessment of severity is the respondent's assessment of the degree of stressfulness involved in the event. *(1 = not at all stressful, 2 = a little, 3 = somewhat, 4 = very stressful)*	Not coded by raters

(Continued)

Table 6.1 (Continued)

Coding Category	Description	Interrater Reliability
Primary appraisal domains	Primary appraisal domains refer to the respondent's report of how much the following areas were at risk or at stake in the situation: (1) disruption of routine, (2) finances, (3) how respondent feels about self, (4) how others feel about respondent, (5) health or safety, (6) well-being of one close to respondent, (7) future plans. *(1 = not at all, 2 = a little, 3 = some, 4 = a lot)*	Not coded by raters

Prevalence of Daily Stressors

A major goal of the NSDE was to provide estimates of the prevalence of daily stressors among different groups. Respondents reported experiencing at least one stressful event on 39.4% of study days and multiple stressful events on 10.4% of study days. Table 6.3 provides a breakdown by various stressor categories. Although the most common stressors for both men and women were interpersonal arguments and tensions, accounting for half of all reported stressors, gender differences were evident. Women were more likely to report stressors that happened within a network of relatives or close friends and men were more likely to report paid work stressors, such as technical breakdowns, that were not interpersonal in nature (Almeida et al., 2002). Within the primary appraisal domains, stressors that risked the way respondents felt about themselves tended also to be perceived as a risk for the way others felt about them. Stressors that posed a risk to respondents' financial plans were related to respondents' plans for the future. Of the stressors, roughly 30% involved some sort of loss, nearly 37% posed danger, and 27% caused frustration. On average, the respondents subjectively rated stressors as having medium severity, whereas objective coders rated the stressors as posing low severity. The most common type of perceived threat posed by daily stressors was a disruption to the respondent's daily routine as compared to the other domains of life (e.g., finances, health, and safety).

The DISE categories significantly predicted physical symptoms and psychological distress (Almeida et al., 2002). Multilevel models revealed that the

Table 6.2   Examples of Daily Stressors and Coding Using the DISE Instrument

Stressor Description	DISE Ratings and Codes

"I was helping open and close the store so I had to get up this morning, get my son ready, drag him to work, pick up somebody who didn't have a car, pick them up, take them to work, open the store, make sure they were okay, take him back for kindergarten, drop him off at the bus, go back to work, pick him up from the bus, run to swimming lessons for 45 minutes and then go back to work to close the store. I think that's a little bit stressful." (R. had to open and close the store because the manager that usually does it was on jury duty.) "I feel good about myself for being able to get it all done today."	*Broad Classification:* Work
	Specific Classification: Time Pressure
	Focus: Self
	Objective Severity: 2
	Subjective Severity: 2
	Self-Rated Primary Appraisal Domains
	   Disrupting Daily Routine: 3
	   Finances: 3
	   Way You Feel About Self: 1
	   Way Others Feel About You: 1
	   Physical Health/Safety: 1
	   Health/Well-Being of Close Other: 3
	   Plans for Future: 1

"I had a problem with an employee. And also today she called and had cancelled something I had ordered three months ago and now I have to start running and searching and waiting for something. It was a big disappointment. It wasn't an argument, it was her fear that she had ordered the wrong thing and she didn't want to go through the stress and stuff. Nor did I obviously. Both of us. Since she had doubts that she had done the right thing, she cancelled the order. So, it was very stressful for me."	*Broad Classification:* Interpersonal Tension
	Specific Classification: Job Procedures
	Focus: Joint/Coworker
	Objective Severity: 3
	Subjective Severity: 1
	Self-Rated Primary Appraisal Domains
	   Disrupting Daily Routine: 4
	   Finances: 4
	   Way You Feel About Self: 4
	   Way Others Feel About You: 3
	   Physical Health/Safety: 4
	   Health/Well-Being of Close Other: 1
	   Plans for Future: 4

"It was regarding my mom. It's just that she was supposed to be picked up by a family member, and they didn't pick her up and didn't bother to call me. My mother is 86, so that's why it was stressful for me."	*Broad Classification:* Network
	Specific Classification: Family Responsibility
	Focus: Other/Parent
	Objective Severity: 2
	Subjective Severity: 4
	Self-Rated Primary Appraisal Domains
	   Disrupting Daily Routine: 3
	   Finances: 1
	   Way You Feel About Self: 3
	   Way Others Feel About You: 3
	   Physical Health/Safety: 1
	   Health/Well-Being of Close Other: 4
	   Plans for Future: 3

Table 6.3   Description of NSDE Measures of Stressor Content, Focus, Threat, Severity, and Primary Appraisal

Variables	Total (N = 1,031)
Broad Classification (% Events)[a]	
Interpersonal tensions	50.0
Work/school	13.2
Home	8.2
Health/accidents	2.2
Network[b]	15.4
Miscellaneous[c]	3.5
Threat Dimensions (% Events)	
Loss	29.7
Danger	36.2
Disappointment	4.2
Frustration	27.4
Opportunity	2.3
Stressor Severity (Mean)[d]	
Objective severity	1.3
Subjective severity	2.7
Primary Appraisal Domains (Mean)[e]	
Disrupting daily routine	2.3
Financial situation	1.3
Way feel about self	1.5
Way others feel about you	1.4
Physical health or safety	1.3
Health/well-being of someone you care about	1.5
Plans for the future	1.4

a. Seven percent of events could not be placed into categories of the coding scheme.

b. Events that happen to others.

c. Miscellaneous events include traffic, weather, news, public speaking, and financial events not elsewhere classified.

d. Range: 1–4 (not at all stressful to very stressful).

e. Range: 1–4 (no risk to a lot of risk).

entire set of DISE stressor variables accounted for 17% of the within-person variance in physical symptoms and 31% of the within-person variance in psychological distress. Specific types of daily stressors such as interpersonal and network stressors (i.e., events that occur to close others) were unique predictors of both physical symptoms and psychological distress. In addition, both objective severity and subjective severity measures predicted physical symptoms and distress. Individuals who had a greater proportion of stressors that posed higher severity, loss, or danger reported more symptoms and psychological distress. Furthermore, stressors appraised as disrupting daily routines or posing risk to physical health and safety were also shown to be unique predictors of symptoms and mood.

Research Potential of the DISE

Use of the DISE in research on daily stress processes has the potential to contribute to multiple disciplines, including (but not limited to) the sociology of the life course and life span psychology, health and developmental psychology, and study of the contribution of genes and the environment to health and well-being. We briefly illustrate this potential with findings of published studies using the National Survey of Daily Experiences.

For example, findings documenting age differences in objective and subjective characteristics of daily stressors (Almeida & Horn, 2004; Birdett, Fingerman, & Almeida, 2005) are relevant to life course sociology and life span psychology. Young (25–39 years) and middle-aged (40–59 years) individuals report a greater daily frequency of experiencing at least one stressor and multiple stressors than do older individuals (60–74 years), consistent with previous research documenting that older adults tend to experience fewer life events and daily stressors. Young and midlife adults also perceive their stressors as more severe, as more likely to affect how others feel about them, and to experience a greater proportion of overloads and stressors that cause disruption to their daily routines than older adults. The age-related patterns reflect the varying demands of life across the life course from social roles. Subsequent analyses used multilevel modeling to assess age differences in reactivity to daily stressors. Overall, younger adults were more emotionally reactive to interpersonal tensions and older adults were more reactive to network stressors, again reflective of varying life course demands.

Another series of studies has assessed the interconnections among socioeconomic status, stress, and physical and mental health by specifying differential exposure and reactivity models (Almeida, Neupert, Banks, & Serido, 2005; Almeida, Serido, & McDonald, 2006; Grzywacz, Almeida, Neupert, & Ettner, 2004). Consistent with the broad literature describing socioeconomic inequalities in physical and mental health, the results of these analyses indicate that on any given day, better-educated adults report fewer physical symptoms and less psychological distress. In contrast to previous studies, however, stress exposure increases with greater levels of education. Analyses using multilevel models indicate that differences in severity and stressor appraisal accounted for education differences in physical health symptoms.

In a different set of analyses we found a stronger association between daily stress and negative affect for persons high on neuroticism compared to those low on this trait (Mroczek & Almeida, 2004). This association was stronger for older individuals. This finding suggests that older people high in neuroticism may be particularly sensitive to daily stressors. Some have hypothesized that neuroticism, and the constant elevated levels of negative affect that accompany this trait may, over a lifetime, lead to dysregulated emotion in older adulthood (Kendler, Thornton, & Gardner, 2001). Our results are consistent with this hypothesis, as we found that older adults who are high in neuroticism are more emotionally reactive to daily stressors than younger adults.

Another line of work has examined the accumulation and linkages between different types of stressors over time (Serido, Almeida, & Wethington, 2004). Although they may share a common etiology, we found that reports of persistent, chronic stressors at work or at home and daily stressors related to those domains are distinct types of stressors with unique effects on psychological distress. Also of note was that on days when stressors occurred, those who also previously reported chronic stressors were more likely to experience psychological distress.

A supplemental data collection to the NSDE, a MIDUS subsample of 240 twin pairs, has made it possible to examine the behavioral genetics of daily stress processes. One set of papers has focused on daily and weekly levels of negative affect, as well as intraindividual variability in daily affect (Neiss & Almeida, 2004). Genetic and environmental influences on exposure to daily stressors have also been investigated (Charles & Almeida, 2007). Both genetic and environmental effects account for the variance in stressor occurrence, whereas shared family and environmental effects account for the variance in perceived severity of these stressors.

Performance of the DISE in Comparison to Self-Administered Daily Diary Methods

The previous sections describe the flexible ways in which the DISE can be used to address a number of questions related to the relationship of daily stressors to well-being. However, we have not yet addressed an important methodological question: Is the DISE a significant improvement over self-administered checklist daily diary methods? To explore this final question, we present a series of analyses comparing the DISE to the Detroit Area Study Life Experiences study (DAS) (Bolger, DeLongis, Kessler, & Schilling, 1989). The DAS was a 6-week self-administered diary study of married couples in the Detroit area in 1986. Respondents responded daily to a checklist of 22 stressor items, primarily representing work and family.

Table 6.4 presents the first comparison, the percentage of days that stressors were reported in each diary mode. The first column reports findings from the total DISE sample, the second findings from the subset of the DISE that is comparable to DAS respondents (all married couples; comparable age range), the third column the DAS, and the fourth column statistical tests of differences between the restricted DISE sample and the DAS. A major limitation of this comparison is that question texts differ.

In general, DISE respondents reported significantly fewer stressors than comparable respondents in the DAS, except for arguments and tensions. One interpretation of this difference is that asking fewer questions results in reporting fewer events. Consistent with this interpretation is that DISE estimates also include arguments that were avoided, presumably increasing the total reported. A second interpretation is that a combination of fewer questions and investigator rating reduces counting the same event twice and eliminates counting events that are affective reactions rather than objective occurrences. Consistent with this interpretation is that respondents to the DISE reported a lower percentage of days with any stressors (42.4% vs. 68.2%, $t = -13.5$, $p < .01$) and fewer days with multiple stressors (11.1% vs. 31.7%, $t = -12.6$, $p < .01$). Both explanations for the differences between the two modes probably have validity.

A question that immediately follows is whether the DISE sacrifices predictive power by evoking fewer event reports. The answer to this question is: probably not. The evidence for our conclusion is that relatively few respondents volunteered reports of other types of stressors not covered by the seven daily

Table 6.4   Comparison of the Prevalence of Daily Stressors: DISE Versus DAS

| | Daily Stressors (% Days) | | | |
	DISE (Total Sample)	DISE (Restricted)[a]	DAS	DISE-DAS (t)
Interpersonal tensions	22.8	24.6	23.8	0.5
Home	8.3	8.8	32.4	−13.9**
Work/school	9.9	11.9	27.7	−9.2**
Network	6.0	5.3	20.8	−10.8**
Other stressors	5.4	5.7	9.3	−3.4**
Any stressors	39.4	42.4	68.2	−13.5**
Multiple stressors	9.8	11.1	31.7	−12.6**

a. Restricted sample that matches demographic characteristics of the DAS sample.
**$p < .01$

event questions. Stressors were reported in response to the "other stressor" question on only 1.7% of study days. There is additional evidence that the DISE did not sacrifice predictive power in relationship to daily symptoms. Table 6.5 presents a second comparison between the DISE and the DAS: correlations between daily stressors and physical health symptoms. The correlations between "any stressors" and symptoms and "multiple stressors" and symptoms do not differ significantly between the two samples. In regard to specific types of stressors, the correlation between arguments and symptoms is significantly lower in the DAS, while the correlation between network stressors and symptoms is lower in the DISE. Otherwise, differences are not statistically significant.

This comparison, however, is not definitive because there is no way to estimate which of the methods produces a truer picture of the prevalence and impact of daily stressors on well-being. The DISE telephone-based approach, however, provided several advantages. The first advantage is that telephone interviewing with a limited number of questions appears to have produced a reasonably comprehensive estimate of the prevalence of daily stressors with a minimal number of questions. The limited time frame of the DISE and telephone administration may reduce respondent burden. Respondents were called at times convenient to their schedules and the average interview was only about 15 minutes. In addition, the use of telephone interviewing reduces instances of missing data because there is more control over reporting.

We hoped that telephone interviewing, the smaller number of questions, and the shorter time frame would also reduce fall-off in reports of daily stressors

Table 6.5   Correlations Between Daily Stressors and Physical Health Symptoms: DISE Versus DAS

	Physical Health Symptoms (% Days)			
	DISE (Total Sample)	DISE (Restricted[a])	DAS	DISE DAS (z)
Interpersonal tensions	0.23*	0.27*	0.13*	1.97*
Home	0.16*	0.17*	0.30*	−1.86
Work/school	0.08	0.08	−.03	1.48
Network	0.17*	0.15*	0.31*	2.04*
Other stressors	0.15*	0.16*	0.07	1.22
Any stressors	0.28*	0.31*	0.29*	0.29
Multiple stressors	0.21*	0.23*	0.28*	−0.73

a. Restricted sample that matches demographic characteristics of the DAS sample.

*$p < .05$

over the contact period. We found that fall-off was less than that reported in the self-administered DAS study but remained significant over the 8-day period. In other words, the method reduces fall-off but does not eliminate it completely (Almeida et al., 2002).

Conclusion

The NSDE was the first study of its kind to estimate the prevalence of daily stressors in the United States. We believe that its measurement innovations and the rich data it has produced are important contributions to the study of daily stressor exposure.

MEASUREMENT INNOVATIONS

It is important to note that the DISE estimates a lower prevalence of daily stressors than checklist studies (see Bolger et al., 1989). However, the discrepancy in estimated prevalence may be explained by two useful features of the interview method. The DISE measure applies objective criteria to counting a report as an event. Indeed, 5% of reports of daily stressors in the NSDE failed to reach the objective event threshold. The DISE method applies rating methods that address the problem of intracategory variability in the assessment of stressor exposure (Dohrenwend, 2006). The DISE also reduces instances of double reporting of stressors. These two issues have been significant methodological problems in the measurement of stressors. The DISE method also reduces significant sources of respondent burden. In addition, the telephone method made it logistically possible to collect data on daily stressors from a national sample.

The major benefit of the DISE method, however, is that we obtained detailed information regarding both objective characteristics of daily stressors as well as multiple measures of subjective appraisal. This combination produces a more comprehensive picture of the types of stressors that people experience than the standard daily diary design. It is important, however, to balance methodological innovations against limitations of the DISE. Although the DISE method may be less burdensome for respondents, it is more burdensome for the investigator than the checklist method. The self-administered checklist method is probably still more desirable for smaller scale, exploratory studies. Some groups may also be very hard to reach by telephone. For example, caregivers of relatives with Alzheimer's might find even a 15-minute phone call too disruptive. A significant number of low-income Americans do not have ready access to phones. In addition, some research questions may require the use of diaries over longer periods of time, and daily telephone contact may be hard to maintain for more than one week.

The DISE method reduces, but does not eliminate, confounding between reports that a stressor occurred and stressor appraisal. The method relies on self-reports that something stressful has occurred. In addition, some stem questions contain the word *stressful*, which contributes to this concern. The DISE method also reduces, but does not eliminate, fall-off in the reports of stressors over the course of a study. People still learn that if they say "no," the interview will be shorter.

The DISE method also does not alleviate other concerns about event reporting. We have no way of determining whether some people fabricate or exaggerate reports of daily stressors. Female respondents report significantly more daily stressors. The narrative method may have capitalized on women's tendency to describe occurrences in more detail. These concerns, however, apply to all methods of assessing stressors through naturalistic, self-report methods.

THEORETICAL INNOVATIONS

Perhaps the most valuable feature of diary methods is the ability to assess *within-person* processes. This represents a shift from assessing mean levels of stressor and well-being between individuals to charting the day-to-day fluctuations in stress and well-being within an individual. Stress is a process that occurs within the individual, and research designs need to reflect this. For example, instead of asking whether individuals with high levels of work stress experience more distress than individuals with less stressful jobs, a researcher can ask whether a worker experiences more distress on days when she has too many deadlines (or is reprimanded) compared to days when her work has been stressor-free. This within-person analytic approach allows the researcher to rule out temporally stable personality and environmental variables as third variable explanations for the relationship between stressors and well-being. In addition, the intensive longitudinal aspect of the daily diary design permits a temporal examination of how stressors are associated with changes in well-being from one day to the next. By establishing within-person associations between varying daily stressors and well-being through time, researchers can more precisely establish the short-term effects of concrete daily experiences (Bolger, Davis, & Rafaeli, 2003; Larson & Almeida, 1999). In contrast, the Day Reconstruction Method (DRM) focuses on activity episodes, rather than on occurrences that may affect well-being, and has not yet been applied to a within-person analysis of changes in well-being over the course of time.

The DISE also pioneered several innovations that provide new ways to look at the relationship between daily stressors and health outcomes. The DISE addresses head-on the problem of intracategory variability, the fact that individual experiences reported in response to close-ended event checklist questions are highly variable in terms of severity and type of threat (Dohrenwend,

2006). One exciting area of research is that the method allows for more concrete specification of the health and physiological consequences of different types of daily stressors, depending on the type of threat they pose (see Miller et al., 2007). Daily stressors posing the threats of loss or danger may be more likely to result in sad or depressed mood. Daily stressors that involve frustration may be more likely to produce physical or psychological fatigue. As well, daily stressors that pose "opportunity" may be more likely to produce more positive mood, or may buffer the impact of negative daily stressors. We also believe that the DISE method can contribute to the study of stressor proliferation across roles and domains of life, such as work and family, and over time in people's lives.

References

Almeida, D. M. (1998). *Daily Inventory of Stressful Events (DISE) expert coding manual.* Tucson, AZ: University of Arizona, Division of Family Studies and Human Development.

Almeida, D. M. (2005). Resilience and vulnerability to daily stressors assessed via diary methods. *Current Directions in Psychological Science, 14,* 64–68.

Almeida, D. M., & Horn, M. C. (2004). Is daily life more stressful during middle adulthood? In O. G. Brim, C. D. Ryff, & R. C. Kessler (Eds.), *How healthy are we? A national study of well-being at midlife* (pp. 425–451). Chicago: University of Chicago Press.

Almeida, D. M., Neupert, S. D., Banks, S. R., & Serido, J. (2005). Do daily stress processes account for socioeconomic health disparities? [Special issue]. *Journals of Gerontology, Series B: Psychological and Social Sciences, 60B,* 34–39.

Almeida, D. M., Serido, J., & McDonald, D. A. (2006). Does the daily life of baby boomers differ by cohort timing? In S. Whitbourne & S. L. Willis (Eds.), *The baby boomers grown up: Contemporary perspectives on midlife.* Mahwah, NJ: Lawrence Erlbaum.

Almeida, D. M., Wethington, E., & Kessler, R. C. (2002). The Daily Inventory of Stressful Events (DISE): An investigator-based approach for measuring daily stressors. *Assessment, 9,* 41–55.

Birdett, K. S., Fingerman, K. L., & Almeida, D. M. (2005). Age differences in exposure and reactions to interpersonal tensions: A daily diary study. *Psychology and Aging, 20,* 330–340.

Bolger, N., Davis, A., & Rafaeli, E. (2003). Diary methods: Capturing life as it is lived. *Annual Review of Psychology, 54,* 579–616.

Bolger, N., DeLongis, A., Kessler, R. C., & Schilling, E. (1989). Effects of daily stress on negative mood. *Journal of Personality and Social Psychology, 57,* 808–818.

Bolger, N., & Zuckerman, A. (1995). A framework for studying personality in the stress process. *Journal of Personality and Social Psychology, 69,* 890–902.

Brown, G. W., & Harris, T. O. (1978). *Social origins of depression: A study of psychiatric disorder in women.* New York: Free Press.

Charles, S. T., & Almeida, D. M. (2007). Genetic and environmental effects on daily life stressors: More evidence for greater variation in later life. *Psychology and Aging, 22,* 331–340.

Csikszentmihalyi, M., & Larson, R. (1987). Validity and reliability of experience sampling method. *Journal of Nervous and Mental Disease, 175*, 526–536.

Dohrenwend, B. P. (2006). Inventorying stressful life events as risk factors for psychopathology: Toward resolution of the problem of intracategory variability. *Psychological Bulletin, 132*, 477–495.

Dohrenwend, B. S., Dohrenwend, B. P., Dodson, M., & Shrout, P. E. (1984). Symptoms, hassles, social supports, and life events: Problem of confounded measures. *Journal of Abnormal Psychology, 93*, 222–230.

Grzywacz, J. G., Almeida, D. M., Neupert, S. D., & Ettner, S. L. (2004). Socioeconomic status and health: A micro-level analysis of exposure and vulnerability to daily stressors. *Journal of Health and Social Behavior, 45*, 1–16.

Herbert, T. B., & Cohen, S. (1996). Measurement issues in research on psychosocial stress. In H. B. Kaplan (Ed.), *Psychosocial stress: Perspectives on structure, theory, life-course, and methods* (pp. 295–332). New York: Academic Press.

Kahneman, D., Krueger, A., Schkade, D., Schwarz, N., & Stone, A. (2004). A survey method for characterizing daily life experience: The Day Reconstruction Method. *Science, 306*, 1776–1780.

Kendler, K. W., Thornton, L. M., & Gardner, C. O. (2001). Genetic risk, number of previous depressive episodes, and stressful events in predicting onset of major depression. *American Journal of Psychiatry, 158*, 582–586.

Kessler, R. C., & Wethington, E. (1991). The reliability of life event reports in a community survey. *Psychological Medicine, 21*, 723–738.

Larson, R. W., & Almeida, D. M. (1999). Emotional transmission in the daily lives of families: A new paradigm for studying family process. *Journal of Marriage and Family, 61*, 5–20.

Lazarus, R. S., & Folkman, S. (1984). *Stress, coping, and appraisal.* New York: Springer.

McQuaid, J., Monroe, S. M., Roberts, J. R., Johnson, S. L., Garamoni, G. L., Kupfer, D. J., et al. (1992). Toward the standardization of life stress assessment: Definitional discrepancies and inconsistencies in methods. *Stress Medicine, 8*, 47–56.

Miller, G. E., Chen, E., & Zhou, E. S. (2007). If it goes up, must it come down? Chronic stress and the hypothalamic-pituitary-adrenocortical axis in humans. *Psychological Bulletin, 133*, 25–45.

Monroe, S. M., & Kelly, J. M. (1995). Measurement of stress appraisal. In S. Cohen, R. C. Kessler, & L. U. Gordon (Eds.), *Measuring stress: A guide for health and social scientists* (pp. 122–147). New York: Oxford University Press.

Mroczek, D. K., & Almeida, D. M. (2004). The effect of daily stress, personality and age on daily negative affect. *Journal of Personality, 72*, 355–378.

Mroczek, D. K., & Kolarz, C. M. (1998). The effect of age on positive and negative affect: A developmental perspective on happiness. *Journal of Personality and Social Psychology, 75*, 1333–1349.

Neiss, M., & Almeida, D. M. (2004). Age differences in the heritability of mean and intraindividual variation of psychological distress. *Gerontology, 50*, 22–27.

Pearlin, L. I. (1999). The stress concept revisited. In C. Aneshensel & J. C. Phelan (Eds.), *Handbook of the sociology of mental health* (pp. 395–415). New York: Kluwer Academic/Plenum.

Pearlin, L. I., Schieman, S., Fazio, E. M., & Meersman, S. C. (2005). Stress, health and life course: Some conceptual perspectives. *Journal of Health and Social Behavior, 46*, 205–219.

Serido, J., Almeida, D. M., & Wethington, E. (2004). Chronic stressors and daily hassles: Unique and interactive relationships with psychological distress. *Journal of Health and Social Behavior, 45,* 17–33.

Stone, A. A., Kessler, R. C., & Haythornthwaite, J. A. (1991). Measuring daily events and experiences: Methodological considerations. *Journal of Personality, 46,* 892–906.

Suls, J., & Martin, R. (2005). The daily life of the garden-variety neurotic: Reactivity, stressor exposure, mood spillover, and maladaptive coping. *Journal of Personality, 73,* 1485–1501.

Wethington, E., Brown, G. W., & Kessler, R. C. (1995). Interview measurement of stressful life events. In S. Cohen, R. C. Kessler, & L. U. Gordon (Eds.), *Measuring stress: A guide for health and social scientists* (pp. 59–79). New York: Oxford University Press.

Wheaton, B. (1999). Social stress. In C. Aneshensel & J. C. Phelan (Eds.), *Handbook of the sociology of mental health* (pp. 277–300). New York: Kluwer Academic/Plenum.

Wheaton, B., & Clarke, P. (2003). Space meets time: Integrating temporal and contextual influences on mental health in early adulthood. *American Sociological Review, 68,* 680–706.

7

Twenty-Four Hours

An Overview of the Recall Diary Method and Data Quality in the American Time Use Survey

Polly A. Phipps and Margaret K. Vernon

Introduction

This chapter focuses on issues regarding the methodology and data quality inherent to the American Time Use Survey (ATUS). The ATUS is the first federally funded, ongoing, and nationally representative time use survey ever undertaken in the United States. The survey is sponsored by the U.S. Bureau of Labor Statistics (BLS), and data are collected by the U.S. Census Bureau. Since 2003, annual estimates of the amounts of time people spend in activities such as paid work, child care, volunteering, and socializing have been available and are posted for public consumption on the BLS Web site, along with public use microdata files.[1]

We first describe the development process that led to the ATUS, outline analytical uses of the data, and provide an overview of the ATUS methodology. Second, we focus on current methodological issues that affect data quality, including measurement error associated with the diary instrument, computer-assisted telephone interviewing, and lack of secondary activities (activities

AUTHORS' NOTE: The views expressed here are those of the authors and do not necessarily represent the policies of the Bureau of Labor Statistics.

done while doing something else); and nonresponse error associated with the sampling design and response burden. While time diaries are considered a tried-and-true method, there is ample literature documenting survey error and trade-offs in different designs (National Academy of Sciences, 2000; Robinson, 1985, 1999). Also, there are methodological issues that are relatively unexplored, such as understanding respondents' cognitive processes when completing time diaries. We focus on both measurement and nonresponse error, describe current research that has assessed ATUS data quality, and suggest future research that could benefit and perhaps improve the ATUS.

ATUS Development Process

The United States has a long history of collecting data on time use, ranging from time-budget clocks collected by the Department of Agriculture in the 1920s and 1930s to measure the time use of homemakers (Stinson, 1999), to a rich history of time use diary surveys carried out at the University of Michigan beginning in the 1960s and at the University of Maryland beginning in the 1980s (Juster & Stafford, 1985; Robinson, 1999). In many countries, however, central statistical agencies conduct recurring time diary studies of their population: examples are Australia, Canada, Finland, Germany, Japan, Korea, New Zealand, the Netherlands, Norway, and Sweden, among others (Harvey & Pentland, 1999).

The BLS first began to consider the idea of carrying out a time use survey in 1991 when Congress introduced a bill that called for the Bureau to conduct surveys to measure the amount of time spent on "unremunerated" or unpaid work in the United States and to place a monetary value on such work.[2] While exploring the idea of conducting a time use survey, the BLS began to realize the extent of federally sponsored time use surveys in other countries, and that the international statistics community considered a U.S. time use survey an important statistical effort.

Launching a new federal survey is a major undertaking, requiring extensive design, testing, and funding approval (see Horrigan & Herz, 2004, for a detailed review of the ATUS development process). After initial design and development research, BLS undertook a time use feasibility test in 1997, presenting the results at a conference cosponsored by BLS and the MacArthur Network on Family and the Economy. In 1998, BLS put together a detailed plan for collecting time use data, forming the foundation for the ATUS methodology and funding proposal. The BLS simultaneously attended the 1999 National Academies workshop on the feasibility of collecting time use data, which helped to narrow and refine both methodological issues and analytical goals (National Academy of Sciences, 2000). In December of 2000 the survey received approval and funding, and a BLS–Census Bureau team was formed to address management oversight, sampling and weighting, computerized instrument development, activity coding, and operations. Between December 2000 and January 2003, when data collection began, BLS undertook further pretesting, a field test, a dress rehearsal, and a prefielding period to resolve remaining problems.

Analytical Uses

While the ATUS was first considered as a way to measure and place a value on unremunerated work, many other analytical uses have since been brought to BLS's attention (Frazis & Stewart, 2004, 2007; Hamermesh, Frazis, & Stewart, 2005; Horrigan & Herz, 2004; Joyce & Stewart, 1999). Time diary data can be used across a wide range of disciplines to look at hours spent in paid work and productive nonmarket work, such as housework and child care. Work is just one of a number of major activities captured by time diaries; others include education, consumer purchases and services, eating and drinking, socializing and leisure, sports and exercise, personal care, religious participation, civic obligations, volunteering, and travel.

Time use data can be used to analyze the distribution and timing of activities over the course of a day, such as sleep, work, household, consumption, and leisure activities. Figure 7.1 shows that work activities claim most of the morning and afternoon hours of employed persons during the workweek, with household and consumer activities peaking in the early evening, and leisure and sports activities continuing into the late evening. Further detail on leisure time is displayed in Figure 7.2, showing that on average, a little over 5 hours a day is spent in leisure time, with television watching making up the greatest share of leisure hours.

Many researchers are interested in comparing time use between different groups, such as time spent in child care between men and women. Time use information that is collected on an ongoing basis, as the ATUS data are, allows for across-time comparisons. For example, the data might be used to assess changes in commuting time over several years. Researchers are interested in using time use data as a measure of quality of life, for example, looking at free time or leisure time, as well as time spent with friends and family, as indicators of well-being. In addition, sleep researchers use the data to assess amount of time spent sleeping and when sleeping takes place. Time use data can be used to estimate the amount of time allocated to learning, such as time spent in class or in educational pursuits. There are also diverse users of time use data ranging from academia and government to business and legal communities. For example, both health and market researchers are interested in finding out how

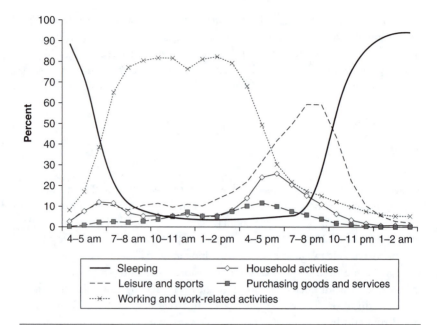

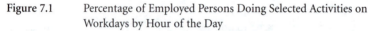

Figure 7.1   Percentage of Employed Persons Doing Selected Activities on
Workdays by Hour of the Day

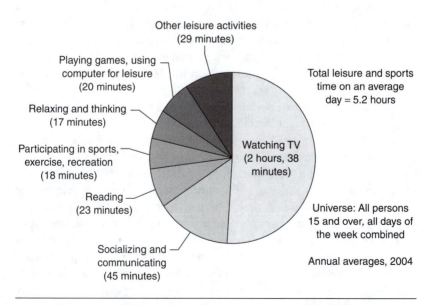

Figure 7.2   Average Hours per Day, Leisure and Sports Activities

much time people spend eating, and where eating takes place. The opportunity to analyze where activities take place in the latter example illustrates one of the unique features of time diary data, the collection of the activity location. Finally, lawyers are interested in using time use data to estimate the economic damages in personal injury and wrongful death cases. These are a few examples of how the ATUS data are being used, and there are almost certainly many more uses.[3]

Overview of ATUS Methodology

Data collection for the ATUS occurs continuously on nearly every day of the calendar year. The sample size per year is approximately 24,000. The sample is nationally representative, and includes an oversample of Hispanic and black households, as well as households with children, in order to improve the reliability of the estimates for those groups. One person is randomly selected from each sample household to participate in the ATUS; selected persons are also assigned a specific day of the week about which to report. Response rates averaged 57% in 2005,[4] resulting in approximately 13,000 completed interviews. The ATUS interview is a computer-assisted telephone interview (CATI) that takes, on average, about 20 minutes to complete.[5] During the interview, the preselected household member reports about his or her time use during the 24-hour period of the day before the interview. Interviewers use a set of scripted open-ended questions in tandem with conversational interviewing techniques[6] to walk respondents chronologically through the 24-hour day, collecting information about time spent in activities beginning at 4:00 a.m. on the previous day up until 4:00 a.m. of the interview day. The interviewer uses precoded categories to record commonly reported activities, and for other activities, he or she types the verbatim responses in the activity lines of the diary grid, as seen in Figure 7.3. For each activity reported, the interviewer asks how long the activity took, recorded either as a duration or with start and stop times. Respondents are also asked questions about who was in the room with them (if at their own or another's home) or who accompanied them (if traveling or away from home) and where each activity took place, which are recorded using precoded categories.[7] There are some exceptions to the "who" and "where" rules: "who" and "where" information is not collected for certain personal activities (such as sleeping or grooming), nor is "who" information collected when respondents report working or attending high school. After completing this sequence of questions on an activity, interviewers prompt respondents for the next activity by asking them what they did next.

Although the 24-hour recall diary is a fairly standard way to collect time use data, there are methodological challenges, including some that are unique

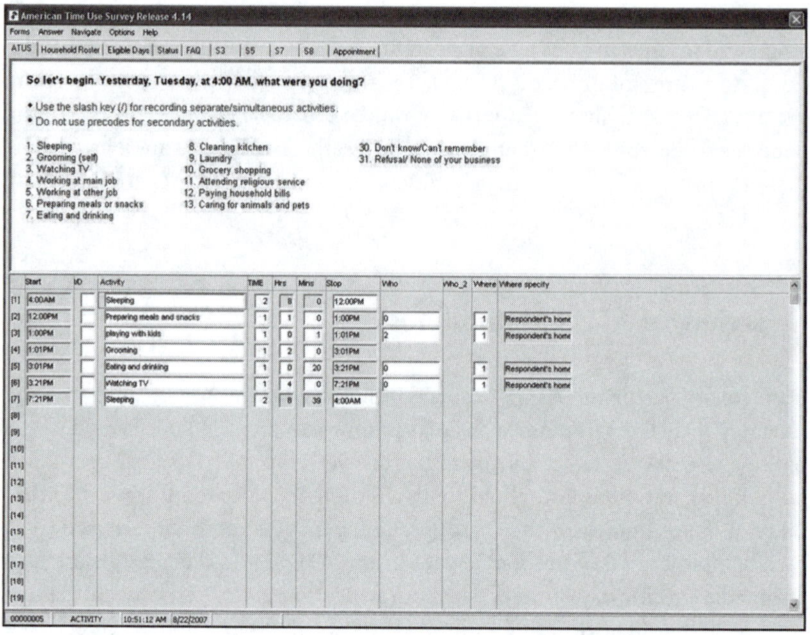

Figure 7.3   ATUS Computer-Assisted Telephone Interview, First Diary Screen

to the ATUS. We highlight some of these challenging issues, such as instrument design, computer-assisted telephone interviewing technology, and sample design, that impact the data quality of time use estimates.

Instrument Design

Survey cost and data quality considerations led BLS to decide upon a 24-hour recall diary to be used in tandem with computer-assisted telephone interviewing. In North America, time use information has been collected extensively through the use of the 24-hour recall diary method. The 24-hour recall instrument was used in 1975–1976 and 1981–1982 at the University of Michigan; in 1985, 1992–1994, 1995, and 1997–1998 at the University of Maryland; and in 1992 and 1998 at Statistics Canada. While there is some consensus that a personal interview combined with a leave-behind paper diary covering more than one day is the "Mercedes" of time diary survey administration (National Academy of Sciences, 2000), the 24-hour recall diary has been shown to produce good data with much lower costs (approximately 3 to 1; Juster, 1986). Robinson's (1985) studies of reliability and validity of the 24-hour recall diary, conducted in the 1970s, found no systematic bias associated with the method when comparing it to paper diaries or activities respondents reported during a random hour of their diary day or when a pager was activated; nor did Juster (1986) in a comparison of husband and wife diaries. However, Robinson identified several problems, such as under- and overreporting, including the underreporting of activities with short time frames.

In the 1990s, the use of cognitive interviews became commonplace to assess respondents' comprehension of questions and ability to recall, judge, and communicate answers (Willis, 2004). While the 24-hour recall diary allows the respondent to describe his or her activities chronologically in an open-ended manner, little research had been conducted on the cognitive processes that respondents use to reconstruct their prior day. BLS and Westat researchers planning tests of the diary instrument were concerned about possible variation in data quality associated with differences in how respondents interpret "activities," the effects of highly salient activities, routine activities, and schemata (or everyday activities) on recall; and heuristic or rule-of-thumb strategies for estimating activity duration (Forsythe, 1997b).

Cognitive interviewing was carried out as part of the 1997 feasibility test to see how respondents interpreted "activities," and what strategies were used to recall events. Findings from the 33 cognitive interviews indicated that participants recalled activities and time durations more easily when their activities and times were atypical and/or when they had an appointment or time commitment. Some participants used a visualization technique as part of the recall process, while others used a decomposition strategy—recalling a larger block of time or major activity to set time boundaries, then recalling what happened during the time period. While participants who lived by the clock reported by the clock, others had difficulty identifying starting and stopping times, and reported time durations instead. To assist comprehension and recall, a checklist of common activities was tested, but was found less successful than general probes such as simply asking if participants did anything else during the time period. In the actual feasibility field test, a standard 24-hour recall instrument with no probes for additional activities was tested against an "enhanced" recall instrument. The enhanced instrument included probes asking respondents whether they did something else during the time period, and if so, whether they stopped their initial activity to do the additional activity. The average number of activities and time accounted for were higher under the enhanced version, particularly for nonmarket work (Forsythe, 1997a), as the enhanced recall instrument elicited secondary activities (activities done while doing something else). However, concern about respondent burden, and the complexity involved in programming the computer software to collect additional activity time durations ultimately led to a decision not to attempt to collect secondary activities (Horrigan & Herz, 2004). Since the feasibility test, BLS has not conducted further research on respondent comprehension, recall, judgment, and communication associated with the questions used in the 24-hour recall diary. The computerized instrument, however, as well as interviewer instructions, has undergone numerous revisions since the ATUS has been in the field, based on the interviewer feedback about respondents' reactions and concerns that BLS obtains during regularly scheduled focus groups, debriefings, and refresher training sessions. Nonetheless, further research on understanding respondents' cognitive processes as they complete the 24-hour recall diary questions could aid in developing additional instrument and interviewer interventions to assist respondents in their task and further reduce measurement error.

Computer-Assisted Telephone Interviews

Compared to a paper diary, using a computer-assisted telephone instrument (CATI) as the mode of data collection and having interviewers verbally walk the respondent through his or her 24-hour time diary presents both data quality advantages and disadvantages. A major advantage of 24-hour telephone recall using a CATI system is consistency and control in how data are collected. CATI allows for interviewer monitoring to make certain that interviews are being conducted in a uniform manner. The survey task is the same, presenting the same challenges, for every respondent. When a paper diary is issued and respondents are asked to fill it out, there is more uncertainty about how and when respondents might choose to fill out the diary. Some respondents might fill out the diary as they go through their day while others might choose to fill it out at the end of the day, or even several days later, depending on the survey design.

While the 24-hour recall method utilizing CATI allows for more control, recalling activities that one did the previous day could be a more challenging task than filling out a diary as one goes through the day. Robinson's (1985) finding that leave-behind paper diaries elicited about 5% to 10% more activities than recall interviews could suggest that recalling activities that one did the day before and cataloging the activities orally is a more cognitively difficult task than recording activities in writing. Alternatively, it has been documented that within a survey, telephone interviews often take less time than other modes of administration, such as face-to-face interviews (McGrath, 2005). This could be because there is less chitchat on the phone compared with an in-person interview or because people simply don't want to stay on the phone as long as they would talk with an in-person interviewer or take to fill out a paper diary. Based on these findings, it might be expected that there would be fewer activities reported in a telephone diary task compared with an alternative mode. To examine this assumption, the ATUS conducted an experiment to assess whether having respondents fill out a paper diary in advance of the telephone interview would improve data quality, such as the number of activities collected, variety of activities[8] reported, and time estimates. The results of the test showed that there were no differences in the mean number of activities or types of activities reported or in the reporting of rounded time estimates between people who completed and did not complete an advance diary (National Opinion Research Center, 2002).

Another major advantage of using a telephone interview is that interviewers can probe for and record the level of detail of activities needed to code the data properly. ATUS has a set of 15 precoded commonly reported activities that interviewers select from (shown in Figure 7.3), and they record actual activities verbatim when the activity does not clearly fit into a precoded category. The ATUS uses a three-tiered activity classification system that allows for very detailed coding of diary activities (Shelley, 2005). ATUS interviewers are trained in both interviewing and coding, so they know both how to record activities to make the coding task more reliable and when to probe for more detail, such as when a respondent reports an ambiguous or vague activity. This helps data quality in several ways. First, if interviewers were not present to probe for the appropriate level of detail, there would be higher levels of incorrectly coded or uncodable activity data in the diary. For example, in the ATUS coding scheme, grocery shopping is differentiated from other types of shopping. If interviewers were not present to find out what type of shopping took place, respondents might provide the diary entry "shopping," which would be coded as "shopping, not otherwise classified," providing less precise data for analysis purposes. In addition to obtaining more accurate and codable data, using trained interviewers allows for more consistency and reliability in how data are both collected and coded. For example, trained interviewers prompt and probe for level of detail in a more consistent way than data would be gathered if each respondent personally wrote his or her own time diary. In addition to recording data, all interviewers code interviews. Interviewers do not code diary data they themselves collect, but code other interviewers' diaries. In fact, each completed diary is coded separately by two different interviewers. If there is any inconsistency in how an activity is coded, the diary goes to an adjudicator who resolves the difference between the two codes. Thus, reliability checks are built in to make sure that the interviewers are collecting data consistently and with the appropriate level of detail. Having all interviewers trained and participating in both data collection and coding most probably leads to greater accuracy, consistency, and reliability in the data. Future research, such as an observational study of interviewer practices and coding reliability research, would help to verify the potential advantages of the ATUS operational methods.

In addition to interviewers being trained in recording and coding data, they are also trained in conversational interviewing techniques, which allows for checks to be built into the interview. Interviewers are trained to insert conversational data checks in several ways. First, though interviewers move forward in time through the instrument, they are trained to check back about timing of activities. For example, after a respondent says that he or she ate dinner for an hour, the interviewer might check back, "That brings us up to 7:00 p.m., does that sound about right?" This type of time check helps respondents to stay "on track" when remembering their day's activities and double checks with respondents on the sequence and timing of activities. The CATI instrument is flexible and accommodates changes, additions, and deletions of activities and times.

In addition to time checks, interviewers are trained to confirm an activity or activity length at any time in the interview if a respondent says something that doesn't make sense. There are also required checks built into the instrument asking about work breaks; activities other than work, school, or sleep lasting longer than 2 hours; and sleep lasting more than 10 hours. Often these checks reframe activities for respondents, helping them to catch mistakes in reporting and provide logical and coherent time data.

Finally, interviewers are trained to use one of several techniques to facilitate recall when respondents have difficulty remembering what activity they did next. One such technique is called working backwards. If a respondent can't remember what he or she did right after lunch, interviewers will ask, "Alright, what is the next thing you remember doing (and what time did that take place)?" Interviewers will then prompt respondents and try to jog their memories by saying, "You finished eating lunch at 1:00 and you can remember sitting down to watch Oprah at 4:00. Can you think of what you did in between?" This working backwards technique will often help respondents to fill in the gaps. Interviewers are also trained in visualization techniques. For example, they might ask respondents to picture where they were in order to facilitate recall. Following with the previous example, an interviewer might say, "You said that you went into the family room to watch Oprah at 4:00. Can you picture where you were right before you walked into the family room?" Although visualization is less commonly used by interviewers than working backwards, this technique does help respondents to remember forgotten activities. ATUS regularly conducts interviewer debriefings to determine how conversational interviewing and recall techniques are used and to develop refresher training and/or revise interviewer instructions accordingly. Further research to evaluate how conversational interviewing and specific recall techniques are used by interviewers and whether the techniques are successful in helping respondents reconstruct their day would provide important information on ATUS procedures and data quality.

Secondary Activities

Closely related to the telephone collection method, the automated instrument used to collect and synthesize data over the phone also plays a role in data quality. A drawback to using the current CATI instrument is that it cannot be configured to collect the duration of secondary or simultaneous activities (Horrigan & Herz, 2004). While the activity itself can be collected, time durations are programmed to correspond to a 24-hour time period, with no overlapping times. In contrast, time use studies that use leave-behind paper diaries and allow people to record primary and secondary activities find that people are often engaged in two or more activities at any given time (Robinson, 1985). If an ATUS respondent reports that he or she was working on the computer and listening to the radio, interviewers are trained to ask, "Which was your main activity?" Both activities are recorded (with the primary/main activity recorded first), but only the main activity is subsequently coded and output in the data, so the information about the secondary activity is lost. In other cases information on secondary activities is never captured at all, as the respondent is unlikely to offer the information, and there is no interviewer probe for additional activities. This may affect data quality for several reasons. First, without the systematic collection and coding of secondary or even tertiary activities, it is impossible to capture the full complexity and diversity of activities that humans engage in during a 24-hour day. When only primary activities are captured, 24-hours' worth of time is accounted for, but the *number* of activities that a person engages in is underestimated. Thus ATUS data do not provide a complete picture of the total number and different types of activities people engage in throughout the day, or of how people combine different activities at any given time. One such area of research that could be very interesting, for example, would be to learn more about how people engage themselves on their commutes to work. Some people might use this time to catch up on phone calls, to read or listen to music, or even sleep or eat breakfast.

The absence of secondary activities is less problematic for estimates produced for activities that are always done and coded as main or primary activities. For example, travel is always coded as a primary activity in the ATUS. Therefore, the travel that people engage in and the amounts of time in a 24-hour day that people spend traveling are well captured by the ATUS. The ATUS estimate for time spent in travel has been shown to be a valid measure. Bose and Sharp (2005) found that estimates for time spent in travel produced by the ATUS and the Bureau of Transportation Statistics are very similar. Work is another activity usually coded as a main activity. Frazis and Stewart (2004) compared estimates of respondents' hours worked from ATUS time diaries to Current Population Survey (CPS) estimates and found that they were quite similar, when usual hours were controlled for, and the respondent's diary day falls inside the CPS reference week.

While certain types of activities, such as travel and work, that are done as primary activities are well captured by the ATUS, activities that are done frequently as secondary activities are not. One such activity we highlight that is of importance to the Bureau of Labor Statistics is child care. As was mentioned in the introduction, the ATUS was originally conceived as a way to place a value on nonmarket work. Accurately capturing time spent in child care is essential to this task. Yet much of the child care activity that caregivers engage in is often done as a secondary activity. Parents, guardians, and caregivers are likely to "keep an eye" on children and be responsible for them while engaging in primary activities such as traveling for errands, cleaning around the house, and even while doing personal care activities such as showering or dressing.

In order to improve estimates of the total amount of time spent in secondary child care, the ATUS cognitively tested questions measuring supervision of children and added a summary question that follows the main time diary section of the interview (Schwartz, 2001). The summary question asks, "During any part of the day yesterday was a child who is 12 years old or younger in your care?"[9] If the response is yes, the interviewer checks a box next to the relevant primary activity to indicate that a child was being cared for, capturing passive secondary child care that occurred while the respondent was doing something else as a main activity. In 2003, this secondary child care question increased estimates of total time spent in child care by approximately 1.75 hours per day for the population.[10]

The secondary child care summary question was not designed to capture active secondary child care. Because the ATUS does not collect information on active secondary child care, the survey cannot provide information on specific active child care that takes place as a secondary activity. For example, reading and talking with children is of critical importance to children's academic and social development. If talking with one's child took place as a secondary activity (which one might assume would happen quite often), and was captured as secondary care, analysts would not be able to break apart how much time parents are spending doing this activity with children. Furthermore, Fisher (2005) suggested that time spent reading with children often occurs during travel; for example, reading in the car, on the train, or on the bus. Since travel is always coded as a primary activity in the ATUS, this reading activity would be captured as "care" and would not be separated from other types of more passive care such as "keeping an eye on" a child. These examples make the point that while the summary question method does increase time estimates of child care, the rough level of care captured does not allow for more refined analyses of the type of care being provided. Given the complexity of collecting child and parental activities and time, other studies have taken an alternative measurement approach. For example, the Child Development Supplement of the Panel Study of Income Dynamics at the University of Michigan collected time diary data from children and/or their caregivers to produce estimates of time children spend interacting with caregivers (Stafford & Yeung, 2005).

Bianchi, Wight, and Raley (2005) compared secondary child care estimates from the ATUS (which uses the summary question measure) to the 2000 National Survey of Parents (NSP), which uses a probe asking, "What else were you doing?" to collect secondary in addition to primary activities. They found that there are large differences in time estimates of secondary care using these two different methods. For example, they report that the 2000 NSP picked up about 0.4 hours per day of secondary child care for fathers, while the 2003 ATUS picked up about 4.5 hours per day for fathers. As already noted, however, the ATUS question wording for child care is broader than typical definitions. The "in your care" language is designed to pick up on indirect or passive child care—or times when care or assistance could have been given—rather than more active types of care. It seems that when people report secondary activities using the "what else were you doing" probe they typically think of more active types of care. Recent work by Allard, Bianchi, Stewart, and Wight (2006) confirms this distinction. They compare the ATUS and NSP on three measures of child care and find that the surveys produce similar estimates of primary child care and time spent with children, the latter a broad measure calculated using the "who were you with" question asked of ATUS and NSP respondents for each primary activity. To measure secondary child care, the authors compare time estimates from the NSP secondary activity question "what else were you doing" to the ATUS "in your care" summary question, excluding primary child care, and times when the respondent and all children are asleep. Their results and conclusions indicate that the surveys are very different in regard to secondary child care. The ATUS is more consistent with a passive-care concept, capturing 5.8 hours per day of secondary child care compared to eight-tenths of one hour per day in the NSP, a measure more consistent with an activity-based concept.

While the ATUS has made substantial efforts to capture time spent in secondary child care, there may be other activities of interest that are being underrepresented because they are often done as secondary activities. For example, the Economic Research Service sponsored new questions that were added to the ATUS in October of 2005 that capture secondary eating and drinking, or eating and drinking that takes place while the respondent is doing something else. Preliminary data suggest that the questions designed to capture secondary eating and drinking are increasing the number of episodes of eating and drinking reported, and increasing estimates for the amount of time spent eating and drinking. Other activities, such as watching TV, listening to the radio, talking on the telephone, talking with a spouse or other family members, and cuddling family pets, also may be underrepresented. Thus, the operational limitation of using a CATI instrument that does not capture secondary activities impacts data quality in two ways. First, people often engage in more than one activity at any given time, so the instrument fails to capture the full complexity of human behavior. Second, certain *types* of activities that often take place as secondary activities are undercounted and underrepresented more than other types of activities, affecting the frequency counts and time estimates of such activities.

Sample Design Methodology

The ATUS uses a household population–based sample to provide estimates on how the U.S. population uses its time. Respondents are age 15 and older. The ATUS sample is selected from households that have completed their eighth and final Current Population Survey (CPS) interview. Households become eligible for selection into the ATUS sample 2 months after their final CPS interview. The CPS is a BLS-sponsored monthly panel survey that collects information about employment, unemployment, and household composition. Drawing the sample from CPS households is a very efficient way to select a scientific sample because the demographic, employment, and contact information of respondents is already known. It also decreases respondent burden because the ATUS can update household composition and selected demographic and employment information rather than collect it for the first time. In addition, the use of the CPS as a sampling frame reduces sampling costs. While drawing the ATUS sample from CPS households does decrease respondent burden and allows for an efficiently selected sample, this method is not without its liabilities.

RESPONSE RATE AND BURDEN

First, to be selected into the ATUS sample, the household must have completed the final CPS interview (wave 8). Wave 8 on average has the highest response rate of the eight CPS panels: 93.2% in 2004. However, the approximately 6.8% of sample members who refuse the CPS interview or are not able to be contacted have no chance of being selected for the ATUS sample. This could be a source of error, including bias. For example, Dixon and Tucker (2000) found multiunit housing structures; some demographic groups, including males and persons of black race; people enrolled in school; and those with higher than usual hours worked were associated with higher CPS nonresponse. How this might affect the ATUS sample has not yet been examined.

Second, the ATUS has a lower than desired response rate, ranging from an average of 56% to 58% per year over the first 3 years of production.[11] Of the 44% nonresponse in 2003,[12] the types of nonresponse outcomes, from highest to lowest are: refusals (19.3%); unknown eligibility due to an incorrect or unconfirmed telephone number (9.9%); inability to contact respondents on the designated day (7.3%); and other noninterviews, including language barriers and health issues (7.2%; O'Neill & Dixon, 2005).[13] In 2004, the ATUS recontacted a subset of respondents and nonrespondents to discuss why they did or did not choose to participate in the ATUS (O'Neill & Sincavage, 2004). Of this subset, approximately 32% of nonrespondents and 81% of respondents participated in the recontact survey. The main reason nonrespondents gave for not participating in the ATUS was their previous CPS participation. Both nonrespondents and respondents reported that they felt that they were doing more than their "fair share" and that they were tired of the Census Bureau calling them. ATUS nonrespondents also stated several other reasons for not participating, however; survey fatigue was by far the most often stated reason. Thus, drawing the sample from CPS households increases sample efficiency and decreases survey costs, including a reduced interview length, but has a tendency to overburden and fatigue some persons who are selected to participate in both the CPS and ATUS.

Other features of the sampling design also contribute to nonresponse. In particular, the ATUS randomly selects one person from a household and preelects a designated day of the week for which that person is to report.[14] This design ensures the sample is representative and all days of the week are equally represented.[15] However, designating one person means that if the person is unavailable, an alternative person in the household cannot complete the survey as a proxy respondent, as is the practice in the CPS. In addition, when the designated person is busy on the assigned reporting day, he or she either might be more difficult to contact or may refuse to participate. For example, if the designated reporting day is a Thursday, and the respondent is out of the house working all day and then goes to a class in the evening, he or she would be very difficult to contact. The ATUS sample stays in rotation for 8 weeks, so a person assigned to report on a Thursday would be contacted every Thursday for 8 weeks in a row.[16] However, if this person is out of the house every Thursday, he or she would be difficult to contact on any Thursday. Selecting a designated person and assigning a day of the week helps to ensure a representative sample, but contributes to both noncontact and refusal to participate in the ATUS.

Potential problems in contacting the selected respondent and obtaining a high response rate were identified as early as the 1997 feasibility test (Levin, 1997). In response, BLS put a great deal of effort into field testing alternative advance contact methods, number of eligible interviewing days, advance interview scheduling, 4- versus 8-week data collection duration, telephone versus in-person interviews, and incentives. The procedures with the highest return on investment were adopted (within budget constraints), including use of priority mail for advance contact, an 8-week data collection period, and incentives for households without a telephone number (Piskurich, Nelson, & Herz, 2001). Based on informational gaps and reasons for participation identified in the 2004 survey of respondents and nonrespondents, BLS added an "Information for

Respondents" link to its Web site and introduced revised advance materials. Further research on survey sample design—including the role that increasing cell phone use might be playing with regard to noncontact—and field procedures is now under way to identify interventions that could reduce nonresponse.

EFFECTS OF NONRESPONSE

Relatively low response rates of approximately 56%–58% have raised concern that there might be bias in the time use estimates. Two studies have been undertaken to assess nonresponse bias. O'Neill and Dixon (2005) found that several demographic characteristics including race, age, marital status, and presence of relatives in the household were related to the probability of being unable to contact a sample member, or for the sample member to directly refuse to participate. But their findings showed little evidence of bias across time use categories. Using CPS data and propensity scoring to model who among the actual respondents looked most like nonrespondents, they found that the modeled nonrespondents spent less time in household activities and more time in personal care and religious activities. The category of personal care (sleeping, showering, grooming, and personal/private activities) showed the biggest evidence of bias; however, the difference was still relatively small, approximately 12 minutes out of a total of 12 hours. The second study, by Abraham, Maitland, and Bianchi (2005), found a number of similar factors were related to the probability of participating in the survey, such as age, race, education, marital status, hours worked by the respondent and his or her spouse, ages of children in the household, presence of other adults in the household, home ownership, and urbanicity. However, when Abraham and colleagues constructed new weights based on response propensities and compared the time use estimates to those produced using BLS standard weights, there were only minimal differences. Both of these studies have congruent findings that suggest that despite nonrandom nonresponse, the estimates show little evidence of bias due to nonresponse. Abraham and colleagues are planning further research using ATUS telephone call history data to compare time use estimates of difficult and easy to contact respondents.

Conclusion

The BLS has accomplished much in bringing the ATUS to implementation, building on the hard work and successes of the time use research community, and filling a major void in U.S. national statistics. The ATUS is now in the 7th year of data collection. Yearly time use estimates are published by BLS, and there is an active community of analysts using the data for both substantive and methodological research.

The current ATUS methodology impacts data quality in a variety of ways. The 24-hour diary is considered a tried-and-true method, allowing respondents to report their daily activities in a relatively open-ended way. Yet relatively little research has been conducted on how respondents understand and structure the 24-hour recall diary task, the strategies they use to recall activities and times, how they judge the adequacy of a response and communicate it to the interviewer, and how interviewers shape the interaction. Computer-assisted telephone interviewing provides consistency in how activities are reported compared with a paper diary that individuals fill out at their leisure. It is also much less expensive than an in-person interview. However, the current CATI program doesn't allow for collection of time durations for secondary activities, reducing the accuracy of time estimates for activity categories often done as secondary activities.

Sample design methodology also impacts data quality in different ways. A sample drawn from the CPS helps keep costs down and lessens burden in the form of a shorter interview, but increases nonresponse due to respondent fatigue. Randomly selecting one person from a household and interviewing him or her on a designated day ensures representation of the sample and days of the week, but also contributes to survey nonresponse. Yet, even with lower than desired response rates, studies conducted so far have not found bias associated with nonresponse.

As with most surveys, many methodological decisions and trade-offs were made when designing the ATUS. Options were carefully considered: Studies and tests were conducted, experts and users were consulted, and quality and cost issues were weighed. With the survey solidly in place, evaluation of current methodology with an eye to quality improvement is under way at BLS. The ATUS presents numerous opportunities for further assessment of data quality, including additional research on respondent cognitive processes, respondent–interviewer interaction, coding reliability, measurement of secondary activities, sample design and nonresponse, respondent burden, and nonresponse bias.

Notes

1. Available at http://www.bls.gov/tus.

2. The bill was not enacted. National economic accounts have not included non-market production (e.g., domestic activity, child care, shopping, and education), a component of total productive activity. A major conference was held in 1994 on the Measurement and Valuation of Unpaid Work (see Statistics Canada, 1994). In addition, the 1995 Beijing Women's Conference called for the collection of time use data to measure nonmarket production (Harvey & Pentland, 1999).

3. For many examples of how time use data are used, see presentations and posters from the ATUS Early Use Conference at the University of Maryland, http://www.atususers.umd.edu/papers/atusconference/index.shtml.

4. Based on American Association for Public Opinion Research Response Rate 2 calculations (AAPOR, 2006).

5. This includes the time to complete the ATUS as well as a temporary module on secondary eating and drinking added to the survey in 2005; the module adds an average of 5 minutes.

6. Conversationally flexible interviewing techniques allow interviewers to engage in more ordinary conversation during the interview and deviate from the structured script to assure respondent understanding of questions (Schober & Conrad, 1997). See section on Computer Assisted Telephone Interviewing for detail on specific techniques.

7. There are 22 "Who" categories (e.g., alone, spouse, household child, friends). There are 26 "Where" categories that are associated with either a place (e.g., home, workplace) or mode of transportation (e.g., bus). See the ATUS User's Guide (Bureau of Labor Statistics, 2006) for further detail.

8. The types of activities were tested using the first tier or aggregate level coding scheme. In addition, there was no difference between the conditions in the rounding of time periods.

9. This wording slightly varies if there are children under 12 living in the household, but the "in your care" concept is the same.

10. The population includes persons aged 15 and up. A small percentage of secondary child care time is imputed.

11. The expected response rate for the ATUS was approximately 70% (Horrigan & Herz, 2004).

12. O'Neill and Dixon calculate nonresponse outcomes using data that have undergone final editing and processing. During the processing, completed cases with poor quality data are moved into the nonresponse category, lowering final annual average response rates by 1% to 3%.

13. BLS considers CPS households that have moved as ineligible for the ATUS, and thus, are not considered nonrespondents. Abraham, Maitland, and Bianchi (2005) suggest that these households should be considered as "non-contacts."

14. See Stewart (2002) for an assessment of contact strategies, including designated and convenient day contacts and field periods, potential activity bias, and recommendations for the ATUS procedures.

15. The ATUS sample is split between weekdays and weekends. Approximately 50% of the sample is selected to report for a specific weekday (10% for each day), and 50% for a weekend day (25% each on Saturday and Sunday).

16. A field experiment tested whether substitution of days increased response rates (Piskurich, Nelson, & Herz, 2001). The findings indicated that response rates are equivalent after eight attempts whether or not substitution was used. Since substitution tended to increase reporting for Wednesdays, and reduce reporting on Fridays, ATUS adopted the eight attempts rather than a substitution procedure.

References

Abraham, K., Maitland, A., & Bianchi, S. (2005). *Nonresponse in the American Time Use Survey: Who is missing from the data and how much does it matter?* University of Maryland, ATUS Early Results Conference. Retrieved from http://www.atususers .umd.edu/papers/atusconference/index.shtml

Allard, M. D., Bianchi, S., Stewart, J., & Wight, V. (2006). *Measuring time spent in child-care: Can the American Time Use Survey be compared to earlier U.S. time-use urveys?* Washington, DC: Bureau of Labor Statistics.

American Association for Public Opinion Research. (2006). *Standard definitions—Final dispositions of case codes and outcome rates for surveys.* Retrieved from http://www.aapor.org/pdfs/standarddefs_4.pdf

Bianchi, S., Wight, V., & Raley, S. (2005). *Maternal employment and family caregiving: Rethinking time with children in the ATUS.* Retrieved May 21, 2008, from University of Maryland, ATUS Early Results Conference Web site: http://www.atususers.umd.edu/papers/atusconference/index.shtml

Bose, J., & Sharp, J. (2005). *Measurement of travel behavior in a trip-based survey versus a time use survey.* Retrieved May 21, 2008, from University of Maryland, ATUS Early Results Conference Web site: http://www.atususers.umd.edu/papers/atusconference/index.shtml

Bureau of Labor Statistics. (2006). *American Time Use Survey user's guide.* Retrieved from http://www.bls.gov/tus/atususersguide.pdf

Dixon, J., & Tucker, C. (2000, May). *Modeling household and interviewer nonresponse rates from household and regional characteristics.* Paper presented at the Annual Meeting of the American Association for Public Opinion Research, Portland, OR.

Fisher, K. (2005, November). *Examining the dynamics of childcare using the American Time-Use Survey and USA heritage time use data sets.* Paper presented at the 2005 International Association for Time Use Research Conference, Halifax, Canada.

Forsythe, B. (1997a, November). *Assessing data quality: How well did our approach work?* Paper presented at the Conference on Time Use, Non-Market Work and Family Well-Being. Washington, DC: Bureau of Labor Statistics and MacArthur Network on the Family and the Economy.

Forsythe, B. (1997b). *Cognitive laboratory research plan for collecting time use data.* Washington, DC: Bureau of Labor Statistics, Office of Survey Methods Research.

Frazis, H., & Stewart, J. (2004). What can time-use data tell us about hours of work? *Monthly Labor Review, 127,* 3–9.

Frazis, H., & Stewart, J. (2007). Where does time go? Concepts and measurement in the American Time Use Survey. In E. R. Berndt & C. R. Hulten (Eds.), *Hard-to-measure goods and services: Essays in honor of Zvi Griliches* (National Bureau of Economic Research Studies in Income and Wealth, Vol. 67). Chicago: University of Chicago Press.

Hamermesh, D. S., Frazis, H., & Stewart, J. (2005). Data watch: The American Time Use Survey. *Journal of Economic Perspectives, 19,* 221–232.

Harvey, A. S. (2003). Guidelines for Time Use Data Collection. *Social Indicators Research, 30,* 197–228.

Harvey, A. S., & Pentland, W. E. (1999). Time use research. In W. E. Pentland, A. S. Harvey, M. P. Lawton, & M. A. McColl (Eds.), *Time use research in the social sciences* (pp. 3–14). New York: Kluwer Academic/Plenum.

Horrigan, M., & Herz, D. (2004). Planning, designing, and executing the BLS American Time-Use Survey. *Monthly Labor Review, 127,* 3–19.

Joyce, M., & Stewart, J. (1999). What can we learn from time use data? *Monthly Labor Review, 122,* 3–6.

Juster, F. T. (1986). Response errors in the measurement of time use. *Journal of the American Statistical Association, 81,* 390–402.

Juster, F. T., & Stafford, F. P. (Eds.). (1985). *Time, goods, and well-being.* Ann Arbor: University of Michigan, Institute for Social Research.

Levin, K. (1997, November). *Administrative details and costs: An assessment of feasibility.* Paper presented at the Conference on Time Use, Non-market Work and Family Well-Being. Washington, DC: Bureau of Labor Statistics and MacArthur Network on the Family and the Economy.

McGrath, D. E. (2005). Comparison of data obtained by telephone versus personal visit response in the U.S. Consumer Expenditures Survey. *2005 Proceedings of the American Statistical Association,* Survey Research Methods Section. Alexandria, VA: American Statistical Association.

National Academy of Sciences. (2000). *Time-use measurement and research: Report of a workshop.* Washington, DC: National Academy Press.

National Opinion Research Center. (2002). *Pretesting of the Advance Diary for the American Time Use Survey.* Washington, DC: Bureau of Labor Statistics, Office of Employment and Unemployment Statistics.

O'Neill, G., & Sincavage, J. (2004). *Response Analysis Survey: A qualitative look at response and nonresponse in the American Time Use Survey.* http://www.bls.gov/tus/home.htm

O'Neill, G., & Dixon, J. (2005). Nonresponse bias in the American Time Use Survey. *Proceedings of the American Statistical Association,* Survey Research Methods Section. Alexandria, VA: American Statistical Association.

Piskurich, K., Nelson, D. V., & Herz, D. E. (2001 May). *Maximizing respondent contact in the American Time Use Survey.* Paper presented at the Annual Meeting of the American Association for Public Opinion Research, Montreal, Canada.

Robinson, J. P. (1985). The validity and reliability of diaries versus alternative time use measures. In F. T. Juster & F. P. Stafford (Eds.), *Time, goods, and wellbeing* (pp. 33–62). Ann Arbor: University of Michigan, Institute for Social Research.

Robinson, J. P. (1999). The time-diary method: Structures and uses. In W. E. Pentland, A. S. Harvey, M. P. Lawton, & M. A. McColl (Eds.), *Time use research in the social sciences* (pp. 47–87). New York: Kluwer Academic/Plenum.

Schober, M. F., & Conrad, F. G. (1997). Does conversational interviewing reduce survey measurement error? *Public Opinion Quarterly, 61,* 576–602.

Schwartz, L. K. (2001). *Minding the children: Understanding how recall and conceptual interpretations influence responses to a time-use summary question.* Retrieved from http://www.bls.gov/tus/home.htm

Schwartz, L. K. (2002). The American Time Use Survey: Cognitive pretesting. *Monthly Labor Review, 125,* 34–44.

Shelley, K. (2005). Developing the American Time Use Survey activity classification system. *Monthly Labor Review, 128,* 3–15.

Stafford, F., & Yeung, J. (2005). The distribution of children's developmental resources. In D. S. Hamermesh & G. A. Pfann (Eds.), *The economics of time use* (pp. 289–313). Amsterdam: Elsevier.

Statistics Canada. (1994). *International Conference on the Measurement and Valuation of Unpaid Work: Proceedings.* Ottawa, Ontario, Canada: Author.

Stewart, J. (2002). Assessing the bias associated with alternative contact strategies in telephone time-use surveys. *Survey Methodology, 28,* 157–168.

Stinson, L. (1999). Measuring how people spend their time: A time-use survey design. *Monthly Labor Review, 122,* 12–19.

Willis, G. (2004). *Cognitive interviewing: A tool for improving questionnaire design.* Thousand Oaks, CA: Sage.

Further Thoughts on Part II

As noted by Stafford (Chapter 2), both small-scale investigator and large infrastructure data collections have proven valuable in answering scientific questions concerning life course dynamics. Given the limited funds of small-scale investigations, paper-and-pencil calendar and time diary instruments are more likely to be implemented than computerized versions, with the work by Martyn (Chapter 5) a case in point (but also see Yoshihama, Chapter 8, and Roberts and Mulvey, Chapter 9). When calendar and time diary instruments are self-administered, there are also benefits to using paper-and-pencil instruments to avoid problems that arise from variability that will exist in the computer skills among respondents (see Martyn, Chapter 5; Schwarz, Kahneman, & Xu, Chapter 9; and Rowan, Camburn, & Correnti, Chapter 10). When seeking to design paper-and-pencil calendar and time diary instruments, formatting is critical to facilitate both administration and data recording. Although such formatting is not trivial for time diaries, calendars require more attention due to the complexity associated with varying lengths of reference periods, temporal units, the manner in which trajectories and transitions are to be recorded, and the inclusion of multiple domain timelines.

As noted by Belli and Callegaro (Chapter 3), Freedman, Thornton, Camburn, Alwin, and Young-DeMarco (1988) is an especially valuable resource on how to design a paper-and-pencil calendar and includes details on how to use symbols and lines to record events that vary in length of time. However, using Freedman et al.'s design as a basis for one's own instrument is limited to calendars in which the reference period is fixed (e.g., past 10 years or past 2 years) and, hence, will not correspond well if one's interest is to collect data across respondents' life spans among respondents who vary in age. Axinn, Pearce, and Ghimire (1999) deal directly with these situations. Their solution is to pre-enter calendar years, and to have respondents' ages entered by hand. This design necessitates permitting respondents to start entering data at that point in the middle of the calendar that corresponds to date of birth, requiring the placement of domain names on the right side of the calendar. Axinn et al. also discuss how to incorporate a number of timing cues, including calendar year and culturally salient landmarks, and strategies for varying the smallest time unit so that the first events of any type are recorded at a finer level than any remaining transitions.

As observed by Belli and Callegaro (Chapter 3), although calendar interviewing had been initially, and is currently, designed for quantitative analyses, the clinical applications of Agrawal, Sobell, and Sobell (Chapter 4) and Martyn (Chapter 5) point to the possibility of using calendar data collection for purposes of qualitative analyses. That the flexible nature of calendar interviewing permits the application of both types of analytic tools should be considered as a strength, not as a weakness. Axinn and Pearce (2006), themselves advocates of calendar interviewing, argue that the qualitative/quantitative distinction is, at best, vague. Although at times the distinction has been based on the number of respondents who have been interviewed, the distinction is probably best conveyed by whether the analysis is based on numbers (quantitative) or verbal expressions (qualitative). Even here, the distinction is not clear cut, as the goal of content analyses is to code and score verbal behaviors quantitatively, and using a mix of quantitative and qualitative analyses provides the richest scientific insights. Curiously, qualitative approaches have been a mainstay of seeking to determine the quality of quantitative standardized survey questions (e.g., Willis, 2005), and largely qualitative approaches are providing valuable information regarding the interactions between interviewers and respondents in calendar data collections that will lead to improvements in calendar interviewing (see Dijkstra, Smit, & Ongena, Chapter 15, and Belli & Stafford, Chapter 17).

References

Axinn, W. G., & Pearce, L. D. (2006). *Mixed method data collection strategies.* New York: Cambridge University Press.

Axinn, W. G., Pearce, L. D., & Ghimire, D. (1999). Innovations in life history calendar applications. *Social Science Research, 28,* 243–264.

Freedman, D., Thornton, A., Camburn, D., Alwin, D., Young-DeMarco, L. (1988). The life history calendar: A technique for collecting retrospective data. In C. C. Clogg (Ed.), *Sociological methodology* (Vol. 18, pp. 37–68). San Francisco: Jossey-Bass.

Willis, G. B. (2005). *Cognitive interviewing: A tool for improving questionnaire design.* Thousand Oaks, CA: Sage.

PART III

Data Quality Assessments of
Calendar and Diary Instruments

A s Stafford (Chapter 2) has observed, assessments of data quality for calendar and time diary instruments involve a comparison of some type (see also Alwin, Chapter 16). Oftentimes, a "gold standard" is identified. For example, researchers may seek the level of concordance of calendar retrospective reports with the reports from these same respondents that were collected when the events were originally taking place as the "gold standard" (e.g., see Freedman, Thornton, Camburn, Alwin, & Young-DeMarco, 1988). Data collected via calendar or time diary instruments may also be compared to data collected via more conventional standardized questionnaire design methods with an evaluation of which of these approaches provides better quality data, at times by determining which method reveals higher concordance rates with a "gold standard" (e.g., see Belli, Smith, Andreski, & Agrawal, 2007). The calendar method known as the Timeline Followback (see Agrawal, Sobell, & Sobell, Chapter 4), which has concentrated mainly on the collection of substance use histories, has been subjected to an extensive program that reveals sound psychometric properties, including comparisons to assess concurrent and construct validity.

The chapters in Part III extend assessments of data quality into time diary methods, other methods to measure time use besides diaries, and additional calendar applications. Yoshihama (Chapter 8) finds that in comparison to conventional standardized question-list (Q-list) approaches, calendar interviewing about exposure to intimate partner violence (IPV) led to women reporting more exposure to IPV and having experienced violence at earlier ages, indicating that calendar interviews attenuated the recall difficulty that is typically associated with conventional questionnaires. In measuring affective states, Schwarz, Kahneman, and Yu (Chapter 9) found that their time diary Day Reconstruction Method (DRM) shows excellent convergence with more costly in situ experience sampling methods. However, both DRM and experience sampling methods diverge from global reports of affect and predictions of affective experience; whereas the former are able to capture the affect associated with experiences as they are happening, the latter are governed by inferences based on expectations. Rowan, Camburn, and Correnti (Chapter 10) presented teachers with self-administered daily checklists to report on their teaching activities, and found that these logs provided best convergence with observations made by trained observers for grosser levels of detail and more frequently occurring items, and that teacher logs reduced the overreporting of desirable teaching behavior in comparison to annual survey reports. Perhaps by testing the limits of calendar methods by interviewing respondents with chaotic life histories, that is, respondents with known histories of substance use, violence, and involvement in the mental health system, Roberts and Mulvey (Chapter 11) generally found low concordance with contemporaneous reports collected 6 to 45 months previously from these same respondents on the same 6-month period. Although not using a time diary method, Hurd and Rohwedder (Chapter 12) find that reports of time use with conventional self-administered questions that target activities that had occurred in the past week or month converge well with time diary reports by showing nearly identical mean levels across a number of different activities, and that these reports also reveal plausible patterns of activity by demographic group. Finally, Belli, James, Van Hoewyk, and Alcser (Chapter 13) implement a computerized calendar interviewer administered instrument in a cohort of African American respondents to measure histories of substance use, labor histories, wealth, and organizational membership. They find reasonably good concordance with contemporaneous annual measures from these same participants collected 8 and 13 years previously. In addition to examining data quality, several chapters offer substantive conclusions on causes and consequences based on the collected data. Yoshihama (Chapter 8) concludes that the high-quality retrospective reports collected via calendar interviewing reveal that exposure to IPV leads to compromised health outcomes; Rowan et al. (Chapter 10) observe that teacher logs reveal considerable variance in what is taught by teachers after controlling for grade level, and that differing teaching methods do impact on student performance; and Belli et al. (Chapter 13) show that negative social relationships and socioeconomic deprivation during childhood are variously associated with later life health conditions or behaviors such as obesity, hypertension, and cigarette smoking.

References

Belli, R. F., Smith, L., Andreski, P. M., & Agrawal, S. (2007). Methodological comparison between CATI event history calendar and standardized conventional questionnaire instruments. *Public Opinion Quarterly, 71,* 603–622.

Freedman, D., Thornton, A., Camburn, D., Alwin, D., & Young-DeMarco, L. (1988). The life history calendar: A technique for collecting retrospective data. In C. C. Clogg (Ed.), *Sociological methodology* (Vol. 18, pp. 37–68). San Francisco: Jossey-Bass.

8

Application of the Life History Calendar Approach

Understanding Women's Experiences of Intimate Partner Violence Over the Life Course

Mieko Yoshihama

Introduction

Violence perpetrated by intimate partners (intimate partner violence,[1] IPV hereafter) is prevalent across all national, racial, cultural, class, and educational boundaries, and has both acute and long-lasting health consequences on women's well-being (Heise, Ellsberg, & Gottemoeller, 1999; World Health Organization, 2005). Due to the underreporting that is common in survey research, the high lifetime prevalence rates (21%–31% in the United States, for example; see Collins et al., 1999; Straus & Gelles, 1990; Tjaden & Thoennes, 2000) may be an underestimation. IPV accounts for approximately 1,400 deaths annually in the United States alone (U.S. Federal Bureau of Investigation, 2007). Social costs of IPV are enormous, including those of health care, criminal legal response, social services, shelters, and other assistance programs (Centers for Disease Control and Prevention [CDC], 2003). The high prevalence of IPV and its serious health and social costs require urgent investigation to develop effective social policies and programs.

Although any victimization can have serious and long-lasting negative impacts on the victims, IPV has several characteristics that are likely to complicate and intensify its effects, such as its recurrent nature and its tendency to occur in private. These characteristics also pose considerable methodological challenges to researchers who seek to understand the relationship between IPV and its impact on women's well-being over the women's life course.

In this chapter, I will first examine the aspects of IPV that require methodological innovations in order to enhance our understanding of women's experiences of IPV over the life course, followed by an investigation of possible recall problems in previous studies of IPV, including my own study. Both of them have led to the application of the life history calendar (LHC) method (Freedman, Thornton, Camburn, Alwin, & Young-DeMarco, 1988). Subsequently, I will discuss efforts to apply the LHC method to community-based studies of IPV, their results, and lessons learned.

Methodological Challenges

RECURRENT EPISODES AND MULTIPLE PERPETRATORS

Because an intimate partner has ongoing access to the woman, IPV is often recurrent and can last for a considerable portion of the woman's life. Recurrence can be episodic (with varying interval lengths) or ongoing (e.g., every day or week). It is also possible (and quite common) that a woman is abused by more than one partner at different periods over her life course. Also possible is that a woman is abused by multiple persons at the same time, such as her husband and his parent. A previous partner can continue to abuse the woman even after physical and/or legal separation; in some cases, an ex-partner may reappear in the woman's life after a period of no contact. In considering these various possibilities of multiple victimizations over a woman's life course, gaining valid and reliable information about lifetime IPV can be challenging but is crucial in order to understand the cumulative effect of IPV on women's well-being.

TEMPORARY SHIFTING, MUTUALLY MODIFYING IPV, ITS CONSEQUENCES, AND WOMEN'S HEALTH OVER TIME

Because intimate partners share residence, finances, and intimacy, among other things, IPV is likely to trigger a chain of secondary stressors, such as physical, mental, and reproductive health problems and income decline, which may directly or indirectly affect women's well-being. For example, IPV may lead a woman to quit her job, whether it is due to health problems resulting from IPV or because her abusive partner demands that she quit. This may in turn lead to loss of health insurance, which reduces access to health care, thereby exacerbating or prolonging the health consequence of IPV. An abusive partner may intentionally isolate a woman from her social network, or a woman may withdraw socially because of stigma and/or fear of others discovering her IPV experiences. She may also face gossip by community members or may be shunned by the social network that she previously had enjoyed. Diminished social network and support are likely to result in lower well-being.

As these examples illustrate, there are numerous pathways in which IPV precipitates other life events causing stress and strains, which in turn compromise women's well-being. The relations among these variables are reciprocal and mutually reinforcing over time. Just as IPV is recurrent, these stressors and strains also recur over time. To better understand such pathways, researchers must obtain temporal sequences of these events in multiple interrelated life domains. Such a life course approach examining trajectories of women's experiences is critically needed.

WOMEN'S SELF-REPORT AS THE SOLE DATA SOURCE

IPV often occurs in private, which makes it extremely difficult to obtain collateral reports to verify the self-report of IPV. In addition to the absence of witnesses, the social stigma associated with IPV discourages one from reporting victimization or perpetration in survey research. This social stigma also discourages victims from reporting IPV to outside agencies, such as law enforcement and health care. As a consequence, the records of IPV cases reported to outside agencies are not suitable as collateral information. In the absence of witnesses, one way to verify individuals' experiences of IPV is to observe them 24 hours a day for a certain period of time. Such observation would affect how people behave, which challenges the data validity. Moreover, ethical concerns and practical difficulties make such observation infeasible.

One potential witness who could verify the self-report of the victim—the perpetrator—does not prove to be a valid source of data. Research suggests that individuals are likely to underreport their own acts of IPV perpetration (Browning & Dutton, 1986; Szinovacz & Egley, 1995). Further, even in the unlikely event that the perpetrator's reports were valid and reliable, because, as discussed previously, woman are often abused by multiple partners, tracking down all of the partners to verify her report poses considerable logistic challenges. Besides, contacting abusive partners threatens the safety of the woman and violates a fundamental principle of research—to do no harm. In considering limitations of other data sources, women's self-reports are the sole data source in most cases when researchers are interested in women's experiences of IPV over the life course.

Empirical data exist to support the use of women's self-report of IPV experiences. Social desirability responding is not associated with women's self-reports of IPV victimization experiences (Arias & Beach, 1987; Dutton & Hemphill,

1992). People are not likely to fabricate the experience of IPV, a highly undesirable event; and thus self-report of IPV is likely to reflect actual occurrence. As discussed below, however, self-report may be incomplete and/or inaccurate.

Recall Difficulties

In addition to the above described methodological challenges, there is another major challenge that confronts researchers of IPV: the respondent's recall ability. (In fact, this challenge confronts research of almost any topic; it is not limited to IPV.) Research has found that the quality of conventionally collected self-report data declines as the length of the recall period increases (Rubin & Wenzel, 1996; Thompson, Skowronski, Steen, Larsen, & Betz, 1996; Wagenaar, 1986). Thus, in studies of women's IPV experiences over their life course, incomplete and/or inaccurate recall on the part of respondents is likely to compromise the validity of the data.

Nevertheless, when assessing women's lifetime IPV experiences, researchers have made little, if any, attempt to enhance the respondents' recall. Without incorporating specific strategies to assist respondents' recall ability, researchers customarily use existing measures of IPV, which were originally developed for a shorter recall window. Not surprisingly, results from previous studies appear to have underestimated women's lifetime IPV experiences, especially among middle-aged and older respondents. For example, in most previous studies, either a smaller proportion of middle-aged and older women reported ever having experienced IPV than their younger counterparts (Smith, 1990) or the proportion of women reporting ever having experienced IPV was fairly constant across age groups (Colten, 1998; Lloyd & Taluc, 1997; Neff, Holamon, & Schluter, 1995). Although cohort effects are plausible, the analysis of three national surveys conducted in 1975, 1985, and 1992 with similar methodologies (Straus, 1995) provides little evidence for systematic cohort effects that could explain the lower rate of lifetime IPV victimization among older respondents (see Yoshihama & Gillespie, 2002, for more detail).

One of my own investigations assessed women's lifetime IPV experiences using a set of behavior-specific questions and also found a lower rate among middle-aged women than among their younger counterparts. As shown in Figure 8.1, the report of IPV experience pattern varied significantly by age group (log rank $\chi^2 = 58.8$, $df = 2$, $p < 0.0001$), with women in their 30s and 40s significantly less likely to report IPV experiences than women aged 30 or under. In addition, women in their 30s and 40s tended to report the first IPV to have taken place later than did younger women, suggesting that middle-aged women were less likely to report IPV that took place in their remote past (see Yoshihama & Gillespie, 2002, for more detail). These findings, which appeared to suggest that middle-aged respondents might have underreported their IPV experiences due to recall difficulty, have led to the effort to develop research methodologies to enhance respondents' recall ability, which will be described in the remainder of this chapter.

The recall difficulty is not limited to studies of IPV. Researchers of various fields have addressed the respondents' recall problem through various memory-priming procedures and question formats (Kessler & Wethington, 1991; Knäuper, Cannell, Schwarz, Bruce, & Kessler, 1999; Wittchen, 1994; Wittchen et al., 1989). The LHC method, one systematic methodological attempt to enhance the respondents' recall, has been successfully applied to studies of various topics (Axinn, Pearce, & Ghimire, 1997; Caspi et al., 1996; Ensel, Peek, Lin, & Lai, 1996; Freedman et al., 1988; Kominski, 1990). Recognizing the need for similar methodological improvements in the field of IPV research, I chose

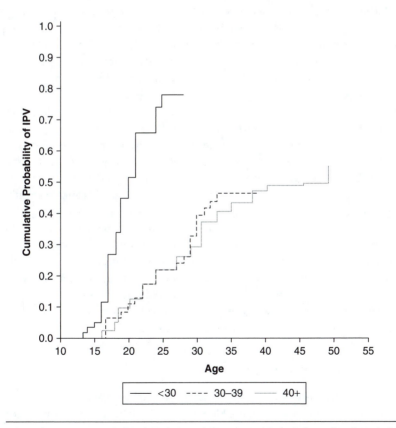

Figure 8.1   Cumulative Probability of Intimate Partner Violence (IPV) Over the Life Course by Age Group

to apply the LHC method to a study of IPV as one effective way to enhance respondents' recall.

Application of the LHC Method to Research on IPV and Well-Being

INSTRUMENT DEVELOPMENT

Building upon previous LHC studies and our own pilot tests, and aided by expert consultation, we developed a calendar instrument and accompanying semistructured interview guide (detail is described in Yoshihama, Clum, Crampton, & Gillespie, 2002). The interview guide included instructions for each section, such as section objectives, an introductory statement to read, and suggested probes, as well as coding, recording, and skip instructions.

The LHC instrument developed for this study includes a horizontal axis to represent time units (one year), while the vertical axis lists domains of life events (see "Assessment of IPV" for specific domains included) that were believed to serve as memory cues for experiences of IPV—the focus of the study. Underneath these domains on the vertical axis, the questions pertaining to IPV, its consequences (e.g., injury), and sources of help-seeking (e.g., the police) were listed. As in other LHC instruments, we placed more memorable and/or easily recalled life domains, such as births of children, before the IPV-related questions, so that the former could serve as memory cues for the latter. In determining the order of domains, we also considered the relative sensitivity of the questions; to help facilitate the development of rapport between the respondent and the interviewer, we placed life domains considered to be less threatening and/or sensitive (e.g., births of children) before more sensitive questions (e.g., abortions).

Reflecting the study goals of examining women's experiences of IPV and well-being over the life course, our examination covered a period starting from the age at which the respondent began dating, which is generally during the teenage years, resulting in a recall period of more than 40 years for some respondents. Considering the relatively long recall period and difficulty and fatigue that respondents would experience in trying to recall a smaller time unit, we chose one year as the time unit for this study.[2]

INTERVIEW ADMINISTRATION

Using these instruments, we conducted a study of IPV and health in the spring of 2000 with a sample of 42 low-income women aged 18–54 who were randomly selected from a list of welfare recipients in an urban country in a Midwestern state (see Yoshihama, Gillespie, Hammock, Belli, & Tolman, 2005, for more detail). Respondents were interviewed twice, 2 to 4 weeks apart, and the interviews were tape recorded with permission from the respondent.

Two female interviewers were recruited for this study from a pool of trained interviewers at a survey institute of the author's university. They participated in 1.5 days of training prior to the beginning of data collection, and one half-day midcourse training after the data collection began. The project staff reviewed the audiotape and the calendar instrument for the first five interviews completed by each interviewer, and they provided detailed feedback both verbally and in writing. Conference calls were held regularly to discuss and troubleshoot interview administration. A clinical social worker was available for the interviewers and respondents to provide consultation and assistance in dealing with distress and other emotional difficulties they might experience during the study period.

ASSESSMENT OF IPV

After obtaining consent, the interviewer conducted a face-to-face interview. Prior to the questions pertaining to IPV, respondents were asked to report the occurrence and timing of their experiences in the following life domains: residence (residential moves), schools attended, work history, financial difficulties (receipt of public assistance), relationship history (e.g., partners' initials or first name; relationship duration; timing of cohabitation, marriage, separation, and divorce), and births of children and pregnancies. In addition, respondents were asked to report memorable and significant events in their lives other than those events in the preselected domains (respondent-generated landmarks, hereinafter).

Subsequently, respondents were asked about their experiences of IPV. The assessment of IPV experiences used a set of 22 behavior-specific questions, which included physical violence (12 items), sexual violence (2 items), and threats/harassment (8 items). These items were adopted from the existing scales and a previous study (Straus, 1990; Tolman & Rosen, 2001). For each intimate partner the respondent mentioned in the previous section of the interview, she was asked whether she had experienced each of the 22 types of IPV, and if yes, the interviewer probed for the years in which she experienced a given type of IPV. Subsequently, the respondents were asked about the consequences of IPV (e.g., injury sustained) as well as help-seeking behaviors (e.g., medical care, contact with the police, and a protection order).

THE PERCEIVED EFFECTIVENESS OF LHC INTERVIEWS

Taped interviews revealed that both the respondent and the interviewer used the calendar actively, and often spontaneously. Recording the timing of personally experienced events on the calendar instrument in plain view of the respondent provided a situational context for the respondent to ascertain whether a particular event in question took place and, if yes, when (e.g., before or after the occurrence of the event already recorded on the calendar). In addition, the visual representation helped the respondent, as well as the interviewer, identify discrepancies in the time sequence of events: For example, one respondent reported a pregnancy during a period in which no intimate relationship was reported.

At the end of the interview, respondents were asked to rate the degree to which they thought the LHC method was effective on a 5-point Likert-type scale ranging from 1, "not at all," to 5, "extremely." Overall, respondents rated the LHC as effective in both the first and the second interviews ($M = 3.8$ and 4.0, respectively). Neither the respondents' age nor the interview length was significantly associated with their perceived effectiveness of the LHC. Respondents also rated on the same 5-point scale how difficult it was to recall events in specific domains ("difficulty ratings") and how helpful events in specific domains were in remembering IPV experiences ("helpfulness ratings").

In general, respondents' assessments show low degrees of difficulty in recalling events in the preselected domains (range 1.1–2.1), indicating "slight" difficulty or lower. The following domains had relatively higher difficulty ratings than others: the timing of intimate relationships (1.9–2.1), work history (1.5–1.6), and residence (1.6). Somewhat to our surprise, among the lowest was the perceived difficulty of remembering IPV experiences (1.1–1.2). The respondents' age was not significantly associated with the perceived difficulty in any domain. Not surprisingly, however, the interview length was positively associated with difficulty ratings in several domains, such as work history and the timing of intimate relationships. With respect to helpfulness ratings, residence and names/initials of partners received relatively higher ratings (> 3). Respondent-generated landmarks also had high helpfulness ratings (> 3). There was no significant relationship between the interview length and helpfulness ratings in any domain.

Using the same 5-point scale, the interviewers also rated the perceived effectiveness of the LHC, as well as their perceptions of the given respondent's reaction to the LHC interview, such as the degree to which she appeared interested, serious about recalling events, confused, and tired. The interviewers' overall rating of the effectiveness of the LHC was 3.1 ($SD = 1.1$) at first interview, and 2.6 ($SD = 1.0$) at second interview. Neither rating was associated with the interview length or the respondents' age. The interviewers' assessments indicate that the respondents were interested in the LHC interview and made serious efforts to recall events during the interview (> 3.5 ratings). On average, the interviewers felt that respondents were less than "slightly" confused or frustrated (mean ratings 1.4–1.9). Although the interviewers in general considered the LHC interview administration not so difficult (mean rating 1.9–2.1), the longer the interview, the more difficult they considered the interview administration.

RELIABILITY AND VALIDITY

Reliability

We assessed the reproducibility of respondents' reports of various aspects of IPV between the first and second interviews, such as the number of lifetime abusive partners; whether they reported physical violence, sexual violence, and threats/harassment; and the age at first IPV. A test-retest correlation for the number of lifetime abusive partners was high ($r = .80$), as was test-retest agreement on whether the respondent reported having experienced IPV; percentage agreement ranged from 80% for sexual violence to 95% for physical violence (κ range .53–.71). The test-retest correlation for the age at first partner physical violence was $r = .92$; correlation was somewhat lower for sexual violence ($r = .59$) and for threats/harassment ($r = .62$).

We conducted additional analyses of the reliability of reports of IPV that took place *in the distant past.* We first assessed the reproducibility in respondents' reports of the duration of IPV in their first intimate relationship (the reported number of years in which the respondent experienced violence[3]). The test-retest reliability for the number of years in which the respondents experienced partners' physical or sexual violence or both (physical/sexual violence, hereinafter) was high ($r = .88$, $p < .0001$; 85% agreement). The test-retest reliability was also high for more ambiguous events and threats/harassment ($r = .70$, $p < .0001$; 80% agreement).

We also assessed the test-retest reliability of reports of event sequence, such as whether the respondent reported consistently the relative sequence of the first episode of IPV in relation to the first receipt of welfare benefits or the first full-time employment. High agreement was found between the first and second interviews; the respondent reliably reported that the first physical/sexual violence had occurred before the first receipt of welfare ($\kappa = .61$, 85% agreement) and before the first full-time employment ($\kappa = .50$, 81% agreement).

Furthermore, we assessed the test-retest reliability of the reported number of IPV types respondents experienced in their first relationship—distant past. The respondents consistently reported the number of IPV types experienced *within a given relationship* ($r = .62$, $p = .0004$ for physical/sexual violence; $r = .81$, $p = .0003$ for threats/harassment) between the two interviews. In addition, they reliably reported the number of physical/sexual violence types (75% agreement) and of threats/harassment (83% agreement) experienced *in each year of their first relationship.*

Validity

The construct validity was assessed by examining the degree to which the respondents' reports of IPV were associated with those variables theoretically and/or empirically linked with IPV. Women with a history of childhood physical abuse reported a significantly larger number of lifetime abusive partners (3.6) than did those without such history (2.1; $t = 3.1$, $p = .002$), consistent with social learning theory and previous studies (Arata, 2002; Messman & Long, 1996). In addition, women with a history of IPV reported a higher level of health problems than those without such a history. The levels of health problems were also positively correlated with several indicators of the severity of IPV (e.g., medical care sought due to IPV, restraining order obtained, and contact with the police).

Collectively, these results indicate that when interviewed with the LHC method, women's retrospective reports of the occurrence, timing, duration, and the relative severity of IPV over the course of women's lives are highly reliable, and that women can reliably report the temporal sequence of different types of events. A particularly encouraging finding is that the reliability was high for reports of events in the remote past, as well as nondiscrete events such as threats/harassments.

DIRECT COMPARISON OF DATA FROM LHC INTERVIEWS VERSUS STRUCTURED INTERVIEWS

We compared the report of partners' physical/sexual violence obtained in this study to that obtained in another study that used a sample randomly selected from the same sampling frame.[4] This comparison study (Mothers' Well-Being Study, MWS[5]) used the same set of 22 behavior-specific questions to assess IPV[6] in a structured interview. Using the methods of survival analysis, we calculated and plotted a cumulative incidence function (CIF) (at age t, the CIF value represents the probability that physical/sexual violence occurred at or before age t) for the LHC sample and the MWS comparison sample. In addition, we estimated the age at which 50% of the women would experience partners' physical/sexual violence (median age of victimization) for each sample. The women in the LHC sample were more likely to report the experience of partners' physical/sexual violence than the women in the MWS comparison sample (log rank $\chi^2 = 27.62$, $df = 1$, $p < .0001$). The women in the LHC sample tended to report that the first IPV occurred at a younger age than the women in the MWS comparison sample. In fact, the median age at the first IPV for the LHC sample (18.5) was 3.5 years younger than that of the MWS comparison sample (22.0). Even after controlling for the respondents' sociodemographic characteristics, the LHC method elicited more reports of lifetime partners' IPV (see Yoshihama et al., 2005, for more detail).

Although the LHC and MWS samples were comparable with respect to age, education, mother's education, and current welfare receipt status, they differed on the proportion of women who were cohabiting with a partner at interview (32.5% in the LHC sample and 14.8% in the MWS sample). In the above described comparison, the cohabitation status at interview was not controlled because it is not constant across adult years. In this study, however, we also found that a smaller proportion of women cohabiting with a partner (15%) reported recent IPV than did those who were not cohabiting with a partner at interview (41%) ($p = .11$). Given this association, IPV reports would have been lower among the LHC sample that had a higher proportion of women cohabiting with a partner at interview. In light of the opposite finding of higher IPV reports among the LHC sample, the difference in the IPV report appears to reflect the degree to which the LHC facilitated the respondents' recall, not the measured sample differences.

Nevertheless, we cannot rule out the possibility that sample differences in other unmeasured and/or uncontrolled characteristics might have contributed to the differences in reported IPV. Thus, we conducted further analysis. Using the Kaplan-Meier estimator, we estimated and compared the distributions of the age at the first IPV episode across three age groups (<30, 30–39, and 40+ at interview) within both the LHC sample and MWS comparison samples. Among women in the MWS comparison sample, their report of IPV (Figure 8.2) varied significantly across age groups (log rank $\chi^2 = 8.49$, $df = 2$, $p = .01$); women in the oldest age group reported less and later IPV than the youngest age group. This is consistent with previous studies of similar low-income single mothers (Yoshihama, Tolman, & Gillespie, 2004) and Japanese American women (see Figure 8.1 as well as Yoshihama & Gillespie, 2002, both of which were based on the same data set of a random sample of women of Japanese descent in Los Angeles). In contrast, when interviewed with the LHC method, older women reported no less IPV than younger women (log rank $\chi^2 = 0.71$, $df = 2$, $p = .70$). As the three virtually identical lines in Figure 8.3 show, women across all age groups in the LHC sample reported similar patterns of IPV experiences. These results held up even after controlling for other variables. The results of this additional analysis suggest that the use of LHC attenuated the recall difficulty encountered by middle-aged women, providing further support for the effectiveness of the LHC method.

Collectively, results of a series of comparisons between LHC and MWS studies suggest that the LHC facilitated the respondents' recall. It is true that several alternative explanations may be plausible; however, none of them, alone or together, appear to account for the high IPV reports obtained via an LHC interview compared to a structured interview that did not include specific memory-enhancing strategies. One alternative explanation is the difference in sample characteristics, such as cohabitation status. As discussed previously,

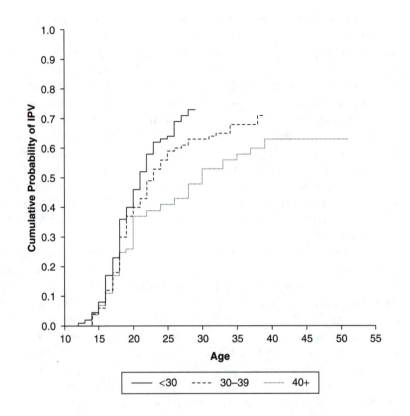

Figure 8.2   Cumulative Probability of Intimate Partner Violence (IPV) Reported
by Low-Income African American Single Mothers, by Age Group:
The Mothers' Well-Being Study (MWS) Comparison Sample

SOURCE: Yoshihama et al. (2005). Copyright 2005, National Association of Social Workers, Inc.,
Social Work Research. Used with permission.

however, observed differences in IPV report between the two samples were in
the opposite direction from that suggested by the difference in cohabitation
status. Additional alternative explanations involve differences in data collection
methods other than the inclusion of the LHC methodology. Such differences
revolve around the order of domains (e.g., what questions were asked before
IPV-related questions) and the order of questions within a domain (e.g., the
location of the question about the age at first IPV). Although each of these differences could have affected the respondents' recall ability differently, it is
unlikely that the order of questions or domains could have resulted in the large
differences observed (see Yoshihama et al., 2005, for more detail).

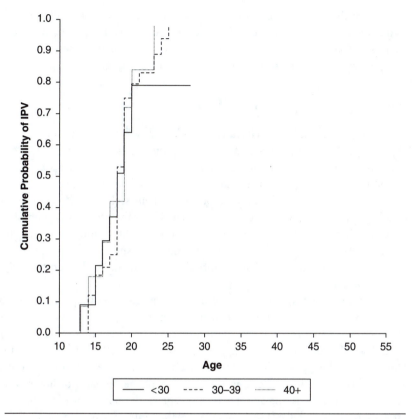

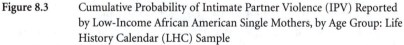

Figure 8.3   Cumulative Probability of Intimate Partner Violence (IPV) Reported by Low-Income African American Single Mothers, by Age Group: Life History Calendar (LHC) Sample

SOURCE: Yoshihama et al. (2005). Copyright 2005, National Association of Social Workers, Inc., Social Work Research. Used with permission.

Lessons Learned and Future Directions

Many respondents in this study had frequent residential moves and interruptions in their schooling and employment history, which was likely to have protracted the interview administration. However, an encouraging finding is that the interview length was not associated with the respondents' or the interviewers' perceptions of the effectiveness of the LHC. The psychometric assessments and the comparisons of the data from this LHC study to those obtained from the comparison study are encouraging indications of successful application of the LHC method.

Nevertheless, the process of applying the LHC method to the current study of IPV was not without difficulties. We have encountered various challenges and made attempts to resolve them. In the remaining section of the chapter, we will discuss some of our on-the-spot learning.

THE INTERVIEW LENGTH

The average length of LHC interview administration was 56 minutes ($SD = 24.3$, range 23–140) in the first interview and 55 minutes ($SD = 28.1$, range 15–145) for the second interview. (A similar study of IPV and women's well-being recently conducted in Japan lasted longer than 100 minutes. This study included much more detailed questions about help-seeking.) Although many studies of IPV also involved lengthy interviews, long interviews pose a physical and emotional burden. They also may discourage participation in general, particularly for people with busy schedules, thereby resulting in a low response rate and/or selection bias. Thus, effort should be made to shorten the LHC interview length.

For those respondents who are older, have relocated frequently, and/or have had many changes in jobs or schools, completing the questions in these life domains can require a long period of time, and they (and interviewers) could be exhausted before reaching the questions about IPV—the study's main focus. Thus, the types of life domains must be carefully selected. For our study, we used two principal criteria in the selection of the domains of life experiences: (1) whether asking about events in a given domain is likely to enhance the respondent's recall of the events that are the central focus of the study—for our study, IPV episodes and well-being, and (2) whether events in a given domain are associated with the occurrence and timing of events that are the central focus of the study. If the latter is true, asking about those events could contribute to model building—for example, through inclusion in a multivariate analysis as covariates. These criteria worked well for the most part. However, determining which domains met the first criterion was difficult (as is discussed in more detail below under "Balance Between Idiosyncratic Recall Approaches and Standardization").

In addition, the level of details to obtain within a given domain must also be determined carefully. For example, for some respondents, it was difficult or took an extremely long time to remember the name of a city or street in the Residence section. The name of a city/street was not central to the investigation. Besides, if the respondent does not remember the name of a city or street, such unmemorable information is not likely to serve as a memory cue for that person. Thus, we decided to ask for memorable aspects of the respondent's residence (e.g., yellow house, a house with a chimney) when the name of the city/street was not available. Because the relocation may be related to IPV (e.g., women relocate to flee from IPV and/or post divorce), whether the respondent relocated or the number of residential moves within a given year (or other time unit used in a given study) may be the level of detail needed. It is this balance between eliciting detailed information so that it could serve as a memory cue and not spending too much time and energy in this process that must be struck. As more studies are conducted using the LHC method, it is hoped that increased empirical data will be available to determine what types of information enhance the recall of IPV (or other topics of researchers' interest). Such information will help construct an LHC interview schedule with a parsimonious set of effective memory cues.

BALANCE BETWEEN IDIOSYNCRATIC
RECALL APPROACHES AND STANDARDIZATION

In most LHC studies, including ours, researchers select a predetermined set of life domains to prime the respondents' memory. Although people in general remember past events better when they are anchored to other memorable experiences, it is unlikely that a particular set of memory cues works for everyone or for every type of event. The high helpfulness ratings of respondent-generated landmarks as memory cues described earlier illustrate the usefulness of idiosyncratic memory cues. Thus, one inherent challenge of LHC studies is striking a balance between certain degrees of standardization and allowing for idiosyncratic recall pathways.

The taped interviews and debriefing with the interviewers reveal that respondents used a variety of recall approaches across different life domains. For some respondents, it was easier to report events in some domains chronologically forward (from the remote past to present); however, for others, backward chronological order (from the present to the remote past) was preferable. The preference of forward versus backward chronology was not necessarily a function of individual preference. The same respondent used both forward and backward approaches depending on the life domains. In addition, in reporting IPV experiences, those who experienced episodic IPV tended to prefer reporting types of IPV experienced in a given episode (vertical move on the calendar instrument where the types of IPV were listed across rows) to reporting the years in which they experienced a particular type of IPV (horizontal move on the calendar instrument where the time units were listed across columns). Our experience indicates that allowing for flexibility of recall approaches (such as forward, backward, vertical, and horizontal movements) is important in order to capitalize on the memory-priming ability of a calendar— the principal strength of the LHC method.

THE EFFECT OF LHC INTERVIEW ADMINISTRATION
ON THE INTERVIEWER AND RESPONDENT

Although the interviewers' ratings of difficulty in interview administration were low ("slightly" or lower), their lower ratings of overall effectiveness of the LHC (2.6–3.1) than respondents' ratings (3.8–4.0) may reflect the difficulty of conducting this type of interview. The emotional effect of conducting LHC interviews about IPV (and other sensitive topics) on the interviewers deserves mention. In anticipation of strong emotional reactions in some respondents and interviewers, we arranged for a clinical social worker throughout the duration of the study. The project staff held conference calls regularly to debrief with interviewers. The two interviewers who worked on this study had extensive experience, including working on other studies of IPV. One of the interviewers experienced a considerable degree of emotional difficulty and used assistance from the clinical social worker.

In a similar LHC study of IPV recently conducted in Japan, interviewers also expressed strong emotional reactions. Three out of the six interviewers in the study in Japan had varying degrees of experience assisting women who have experienced IPV. All interviewers expressed emotional effects from listening to the stories of respondents. During more than one debriefing session, those interviewers who worked with abused women mentioned that listening to the women's stories of IPV affected them more in this LHC study than in the assistance setting. As we explored collectively, we identified several possible reasons for their heightened reaction. One possible reason was the different function that listening to the life course IPV experiences serves. Although it is common for a worker to listen to women's stories of lifelong IPV experiences, interviews in the assistance setting tend to focus on the woman's current and recent abuse and on what action she can or should take (e.g., whether she is eligible for public assistance, how to apply for a protection order). In contrast, in LHC interviews, the focus was on eliciting and recording the life course IPV experiences, which made the interviewers pay much closer attention to the duration and extent of IPV experiences. Another difference identified was the visualization of long duration and recurrence of IPV over the women's life course in the LHC study. For example, if a respondent reported that she had experienced a particular type of IPV (e.g., slap, forced sex) throughout her marriage, the interviewer would draw a line across the columns to represent the duration of the marriage. If the marriage lasted for a long period of time, a long line was drawn across the calendar instrument. The impact of seeing a single long line alone can be enormous. The effect is intensified when the respondent experienced many types of IPV for a long period of time, which involved drawing multiple long lines. Watching those lines throughout the interview reminded the interviewers of the long duration of IPV, making them ponder on the degree of pain and suffering the respondents have experienced.

The stronger emotional impact experienced by interviewers points to the need for developing measures to debrief and assist the interviewers during the study administration. By extension, the emotional impact of participating in an LHC interview on the part of the respondents should not be minimized. The research protocol and interviewer training must address these risks and incorporate sufficient measures to link respondents to assistance programs.

Conclusion

The life history calendar (LHC) has been used successfully in studies of a wide range of topics with various population groups with respect to age, gender, race/ethnicity, and language (Axinn et al., 1997; Caspi et al., 1996; Ensel et al., 1996; Freedman et al., 1988). While our study and the work of other researchers provide empirical support for the reliability of retrospective reports obtained using the LHC method, there is an inherent limitation of a retrospective design. The best way to minimize recall bias is to use a longitudinal, prospective design; however, longitudinal, prospective studies are costly, require long study periods, and are likely to suffer from sample attrition and the attendant selection biases. The high prevalence of IPV and its serious consequences require urgent investigation while waiting for long-term prospective studies currently under way or proposed. This view is consistent with that of other researchers of psychiatric epidemiology:

> As the NCS [National Comorbidity Survey] revealed alarmingly high rates of untreated symptoms among the general population, we must expedite the search for antecedents to these problems; interventions simply cannot wait for long-term prospective and experimental studies to advance our understanding of developmental psychopathology. Although retrospective reports have limitations . . . such data nonetheless constitute an invaluable supplement to more time- and cost-intensive methods. (Kessler, Mroczek, & Belli, 1999, pp. 277–278)

The LHC method is a highly promising approach to enhancing the quality of retrospective data. Another advantage of the LHC is that events in many life domains (e.g., birth of a child, change in SES) not only can serve as memory cues for IPV experiences, but also represent factors correlated with IPV and/or health in women. In other words, the LHC method by design obtains information on both the occurrence and timing of IPV and events that affect IPV-health relationships. An additional and important advantage of using the LHC method is the wide range of analysis possibilities. For example, assessment of whether (and when) a particular event occurred in each time unit (one year in our study) resulted in a matrixlike data structure, with multiple observations for each respondent. This type of data permits longitudinal analysis. Capitalizing on this feature of LHC data, we recently assessed the relative temporal sequence of IPV experiences and receipt of welfare benefits using techniques of longitudinal analysis (Yoshihama, Hammock, & Horrocks, 2006).

Although the association among IPV, welfare receipt, and health status has been well established, little is known about the temporal sequencing of these events. In this study, the life course data obtained using the LHC method permitted longitudinal analyses of whether previous IPV experience was associated with subsequent welfare receipt, whether past welfare receipt was associated with subsequent IPV, and whether compromised health status was associated with cumulative IPV, cumulative welfare receipt, or both. Controlling for relevant factors, this study found that prior IPV experience, but not previous welfare receipt, increased the probability of women's receiving welfare benefits in a given year. Cumulative IPV, but not cumulative welfare receipt, was associated with health problems in the current or past year. These findings suggest that IPV leads women to turn to welfare assistance, and that compromised physical and mental health due to past cumulative IPV interferes with women's gainful employment.

As seen in this example, LHC data offer opportunities to analyze the relationships among various types of life events and temporary shifting life conditions beyond correlational analyses. This possibility is believed to enhance not only data quality but also social policies and programs to be developed from (enhanced) empirical data. This is particularly true for studies of IPV, whose devastating consequences call for urgent action.

Notes

1. Also referred to as *domestic violence.*
2. The LHC study does not necessarily have to cover the respondent's lifetime as a reference period and can be used in a study that covers a shorter reference period (e.g., the past 12 months or since the last data collection in a panel study). If a shorter reference period is used, smaller time units, such as months or weeks, can be used.
3. As done by other researchers (Riddle & Aponte, 1999; Wittchen et al., 1989), we assessed percentage of agreement by allowing plus or minus one.
4. Both groups of respondents were randomly selected from a list of individuals receiving welfare in an urban county in a Midwestern state.
5. The Mothers' Well-Being Study (MWS) was aimed at assessing the prevalence and comorbidity of psychiatric disorders, physical disabilities, and IPV among low-income single mothers receiving welfare, and examining the relationship of these issues to employment. For purposes of comparability, to have a racially and demographically comparable comparison sample for the present investigation, we selected a subsample of 359 women from the 668 MWS respondents who identified themselves as African American and resided in the same county as the LHC sample.

6. In the LHC study, in response to suggestions made by the participants of the pretest, two additional questions were asked about IPV other than the 22 preidentified types. However, comparison of the reported rates of IPV between the LHC and MWS sample was limited to the original 22 types of IPV. Because these additional questions were asked after the same set of 22 types of IPV, reports of additional types of IPV were unlikely to have served as cues for any of the 22 preidentified types of IPV.

References

Arata, C. M. (2002). Child sexual abuse and sexual revictimization. *Clinical Psychology-Science and Practice, 9,* 135–164.

Arias, I., & Beach, S. (1987). Validity of self-reports of marital violence. *Journal of Family Violence, 2,* 139–149.

Axinn, W. G., Pearce, L. D., & Ghimire, D. (1997). *Innovations in life history calendar applications.* Unpublished manuscript, Population Research Institute, Pennsylvania State University, University Park, Pennsylvania.

Browning, J., & Dutton, D. (1986). Assessment of wife assault with the Conflict Tactics Scale: Using couple data to quantify the differential reporting effect. *Journal of Marriage and the Family, 48,* 375–378.

Caspi, A., Moffitt, T. E., Thornton, A., Freedman, D., Amell, J. W., Harrington, H., Smeijers, J., & Silva, P. A. (1996). The life history calendar: A research and clinical assessment method for collecting retrospective event-history data. *International Journal of Methods in Psychiatric Research, 6,* 101–114.

Centers for Disease Control and Prevention. (2003). *Costs of intimate partner violence against women in the United States.* Atlanta, GA: Author.

Collins, K. S., Schoen, C., Joseph, S., Duchon, L., Simantov, E., & Yellowitz, M. (1999). *Health concerns across a woman's lifespan: The Commonwealth Fund 1998 Survey of Women's Health.* New York: Commonwealth Fund.

Colten, M. E. (1998). *Unpublished data analysis of the domestic violence among Massachusetts AFDC recipients.* Unpublished manuscript. Center for Survey Research, University of Massachusetts, Boston.

Dutton, D. G., & Hemphill, K. J. (1992). Patterns of socially desirable responding among perpetrators and victims of wife assault. *Violence and Victims, 7,* 29–39.

Ensel, W. M., Peek, M. K., Lin, N., & Lai, G. (1996). Stress in the lifecourse: A life history approach. *Journal of Aging and Health, 8,* 389–416.

Freedman, D., Thornton, A., Camburn, D., Alwin, D., & Young-DeMarco, L. (1988). The life history calendar: A technique for collecting retrospective data. In C. C. Clogg (Ed.), *Sociological methodology* (pp. 37–68). San Francisco: Jossey-Bass.

Heise, L., Ellsberg, M., & Gottemoeller, M. (1999). Ending violence against women. *Population Reports, 27,* 1–43.

Kessler, R. C., Mroczek, D. K., & Belli, R. F. (1999). Retrospective adult assessment in child psychopathology. In D. Shaffer, C. P. Lucas, & J. E. Richters (Eds.), *Diagnostic assessment in child and adolescent psychopathology* (pp. 256–284). New York: Guilford.

Kessler, R. C., & Wethington, E. (1991). The reliability of life event reports in a community survey. *Psychological Medicine, 21,* 723–738.

Knäuper, B., Cannell, C. F., Schwarz, N., Bruce, M. L., & Kessler, R. (1999). Improving accuracy of major depression age-of-onset reports in the U.S. National

Comorbidity Survey. *International Journal of Methods in Psychiatric Research, 8*, 39–48.

Kominski, R. (1990). The SIPP event history calendar: Aiding respondents in the dating of longitudinal events. In American Statistical Association, Survey Research Methods Section (Ed.), *Proceedings of the section on survey research methods* (pp. 553–558). Alexandria, VA: American Statistical Association.

Lloyd, S., & Taluc, N. (1997). *Unpublished data analysis of the effects of violence on work and family project.* Unpublished manuscript. Northwestern University, Joint Center for Poverty Research.

Messman, T. L., & Long, P. J. (1996). Child sexual abuse and its relationship to revictimization in adult women: A review. *Clinical Psychology Review, 16*, 397–420.

Neff, J., Holamon, B., & Schluter, T. (1995). Spousal violence among Anglos, blacks, and Mexican Americans: The role of demographic variables, psychosocial predictors, and alcohol consumption. *Journal of Family Violence, 10*, 1–21.

Riddle, K. P., & Aponte, J. F. (1999). The Comprehensive Childhood Maltreatment Inventory: Early development and reliability analyses. *Child Abuse & Neglect, 23*, 1103–1115.

Rubin, D. C., & Wenzel, A. E. (1996). One hundred years of forgetting: A quantitative description of retention. *Psychological Review, 103*, 734–760.

Smith, M. D. (1990). Sociodemographic risk factors in wife abuse: Results from a survey of Toronto women. *Canadian Journal of Sociology, 15*, 39–58.

Straus, M. A. (1990). The Conflict Tactics Scale and its critics: An evaluation and new data on validity and reliability. In M. A. Straus & R. J. Gelles (Eds.), *Physical violence in American families: Risk factors and adaptations to violence in 8,145 families* (pp. 49–73). New Brunswick, NJ: Transaction Press.

Straus, M. A. (1995). Trends in cultural norms and rates of partner violence: An update to 1992. In S. M. Stith & M. A. Straus (Eds.), *Understanding partner violence: Prevalence, causes, consequences, and solutions* (pp. 30–33). Minneapolis, MN: National Council of Family Relations.

Straus, M. A., & Gelles, R. J. (1990). *Physical violence in American families: Risk factors and adaptations to violence in 8,145 families.* New Brunswick, NJ: Transaction Publications.

Szinovacz, M. E., & Egley, L. C. (1995). Comparing one-partner and couple data on sensitive marital behaviors: The case of marital violence. *Journal of Marriage and the Family, 57*, 995–1010.

Thompson, C. P., Skowronski, J. J., Steen, F., Larsen, S. F., & Betz, A. L. (1996). *Autobiographical memory: Remembering what and remembering when.* Mahwah, NJ: Lawrence Erlbaum.

Tjaden, P., & Thoennes, N. (2000). *Extent, nature, and consequences of intimate partner violence: Findings from the National Violence Against Women Survey.* Washington, DC: U.S. Department of Justice, Office of Justice Programs, National Institute of Justice.

Tolman, R. M., & Rosen, D. (2001). Domestic violence in the lives of women receiving welfare: Mental health, substance dependence and economic well-being. *Violence Against Women, 7*, 141–158.

U.S. Federal Bureau of Investigation. (2007). *Crimes in the United States 2006: Uniform crime reports.* Washington, DC: U.S. Department of Justice.

Wagenaar, W. A. (1986). My memory: A study of autobiographical memory over six years. *Cognitive Psychology, 18*, 225–252.

Wittchen, H.-U. (1994). Reliability and validity studies of the WHO—Composite International Diagnostic Interview (CIDI): A critical review. *Journal of Psychiatric Research, 28,* 57–84.

Wittchen, H.-U., Burke, J. D., Semler, G., Pfister, H., Von Cranach, M., & Zaudig, M. (1989). Recall and dating of psychiatric symptoms: Test-retest reliability of time-related symptom questions in a standardized psychiatric interview. *Archives of General Psychiatry, 46,* 437–443.

World Health Organization. (2005). *WHO Multi-Country Study on Women's Health and Domestic Violence against Women: Summary report of initial results on prevalence, health outcomes and women's responses.* Geneva, Switzerland: Author.

Yoshihama, M., Clum, K., Crampton, A., & Gillespie, B. (2002). Measuring the lifetime experience of domestic violence: Application of the life history calendar method. *Violence and Victims, 17,* 297–317.

Yoshihama, M., & Gillespie, B. (2002). Age adjustment and recall bias in the analysis of domestic violence data: Methodological improvement through the application of survival analysis methods. *Journal of Family Violence, 17,* 199–221.

Yoshihama, M., Gillespie, B., Hammock, A. C., Belli, R. F., & Tolman, R. (2005). Does the life history calendar method facilitate the recall of domestic violence victimization? Comparison of two methods of data collection. *Social Work Research, 29,* 151–163.

Yoshihama, M., Hammock, A. C., & Horrocks, J. (2006). Intimate partner violence, welfare receipt, and health status of low-income African American women: A life-course analysis. American *Journal of Community Psychology, 37,* 95–109.

Yoshihama, M., Tolman, R. M., & Gillespie, B. (2004). *Age adjusted probabilities, risk and protective factors of partner abuse among low-income single mothers.* Unpublished manuscript. University of Michigan, School of Social Work.

9

Global and Episodic Reports of Hedonic Experience

Norbert Schwarz, Daniel Kahneman, and Jing Xu

Introduction

Most people would agree that a life filled with pleasant activities is preferable to a life filled with unpleasant ones. As Juster (1985) noted, "An important ingredient in the production and distribution of well-being is the set of satisfactions generated by activities themselves" (p. 333). As the contributions to this volume illustrate, life events may change a person's mix of activities and the time allocated to them. If this is a good or bad thing in terms of the person's quality of life depends, in part, on whether the activities are experienced as pleasant or unpleasant. The integral of experienced enjoyment and misery over time provides an indicator of well-being that addresses this issue (Kahneman, 1999). To compute it, we need two sources of data: (1) time use data that bear on the allocation of time to activities and (2) data that indicate the extent to which a given activity is enjoyable. While most contributions to this volume address the former component, this chapter is concerned primarily with the latter: How do we determine if people enjoy what they do?

One answer, usually favored by economists, is to rely on people's choices. Presumably, they know what is good for them and reveal their preferences in their choice of activities. A second answer, usually favored by psychologists and social scientists, is to ask for self-reports of enjoyment. Such reports may take one of three forms. First, we may ask respondents to provide global reports of how much they generally enjoy an activity, for example, along a rating scale from "dislike very much" to "enjoy a great deal." This is the strategy used by Juster and colleagues (e.g., Juster & Stafford, 1985; Robinson, 1977) in their pioneering studies of Americans' use of time. Second, we may assess people's hedonic experience in situ, using methods of momentary data capture, like experience sampling (e.g., Stone, Shiffman, & DeVries, 1999). For reasons discussed below, these concurrent reports set the gold standard for assessing hedonic experience, but the associated high cost and respondent burden render experience sampling unsuitable for large-scale studies. As a compromise, we may, third, collect retrospective reports of respondents' feelings during a recent specific instance of the activity. The Day Reconstruction Method (DRM) (Kahneman, Krueger, Schkade, Schwarz, & Stone, 2004a) provides a technique for doing so and has been shown to capture much of the information provided by experience sampling, while being suitable for large samples.

As we will illustrate, which of these measurement strategies we use may profoundly affect at which conclusions we arrive. In general, choices and global reports of "usual" enjoyment are likely to show good convergence—but may fail to capture what people actually experience in situ. Conversely, concurrent and retrospective episodic reports also show good convergence and capture actual hedonic experience—but may fail to predict people's choices and behaviors.

The chapter is organized as follows. We first review psychological research into self-reports of emotions, paying attention to the different sources of information that respondents draw on when providing concurrent and retrospective episodic or global reports of hedonic experience. Next, we introduce the Day Reconstruction Method and a close variant, the Event Reconstruction Method. Both are designed to collect retrospective episodic reports about a recent specific instance of an activity. Subsequently, we report on studies that compare global and episodic reports of hedonic experience and highlight how these reports diverge in a reliable and theoretically predicted manner. The chapter concludes with a discussion of the methodological implications.

Reporting on One's Feelings: Concurrent, Episodic, and Global Reports

Numerous studies have documented profound discrepancies between people's concurrent and retrospective reports of emotional experience (e.g., Gilbert & Ebert, 2002; Kahneman, 1994; Loewenstein & Adler, 1995; for a comprehensive review see Robinson & Clore, 2002). To conceptualize the underlying processes, Robinson and Clore proposed an accessibility model of emotion report.

When people report on their *current* feelings, the feelings themselves are accessible to introspection, allowing for accurate reports on the basis of experiential information. But affective experiences are fleeting and not available to introspection once the feeling has dissipated. Accordingly, the opportunity to assess emotion reports based on experiential information is limited to methods of momentary data capture (Stone, Shiffman, Atienza, & Nebeling, 2007), like experience sampling (Stone et al., 1999). Once the feeling has dissipated, the affective experiences need to be reconstructed on the basis of episodic or semantic information. When the report pertains to a specific *recent episode*, people can draw on episodic memory, retrieving specific moments and details of the recent past. Such reports can often recover the actual experience with some accuracy, as indicated by convergence with concurrent reports (e.g., Kahneman et al., 2004a; Robinson & Clore, 2002; Stone et al., 2006). In contrast, *global* reports of past feelings are based on semantic knowledge. When asked how they "usually" feel during a particular activity, people draw on their general beliefs about the activity and its attributes to arrive at a report. The actual experience does not figure prominently in these global reports because the experience itself is no longer accessible to introspection, and episodic reconstruction is not used to answer a global question. Finally, as Xu and Schwarz (2007) noted, the same semantic knowledge serves as a basis for *predicting* future feelings, for which episodic information is not available to begin with. These hedonic predictions, in turn, often serve as a basis for behavioral *choice* (March, 1978).

This rationale predicts a systematic pattern of convergences and divergences in affect reports. First, concurrent reports and retrospective reports pertaining to specific recent episodes are likely to show good convergence, provided that the episode is sufficiently recent to allow detailed reinstantiation in episodic memory. Second, retrospective global reports of past feelings and predictions of future feelings are also likely to converge, given that both are based on the same semantic inputs. Hence, global memories are likely to "confirm" predictions. Third, choices are based on predicted hedonic consequences and are therefore usually consistent with predictions and global memories. Fourth, global retrospective reports as well as predictions and choices will, however, often diverge from concurrent and episodic reports, given that the different types of reports are based on different inputs. As a result, our expectations and global memories go hand in hand, but may fail to reflect what we actually experience moment to moment.

In addition, a large body of research into affective predictions shows that people's forecasts are usually more extreme than their experiences. Known as the "focusing illusion" (Schkade & Kahneman, 1997), this bias derives from a focus on core attributes of the activity at the expense of other information. Thus, Midwesterners who predict how happy they would be if they moved to

California may focus on the pleasant California climate, missing, for example, that they would still have to spend most of the day in an office cubicle. Predictions and choices as well as global retrospective reports are likely to be subject to such focusing effects. Hence, we may, fifth, expect that predictions and global retrospective reports overestimate the intensity of the experience, relative to concurrent and episodic reports.

Numerous findings are compatible with these predictions (see Loewenstein & Schkade, 1999; Robinson & Clore, 2002, for reviews). As an illustration, consider people's vacation experiences. Not surprisingly, people believe that vacations are highly enjoyable and this belief shapes their predictions and global memories, even when the actual experience was less rosy. Mitchell, Thompson, Peterson, and Cronk (1997) assessed prospective, concurrent, and retrospective reports of vacation enjoyment. They found that prospective reports converged with retrospective reports; however, both the predicted and remembered affect was more positive than the affect reported concurrently during the vacation. In a more detailed follow-up study, Wirtz, Kruger, Scollon, and Diener (2003) tracked college students before, during, and after their spring-break vacations and compared their predicted, concurrent, and remembered affect. They found that predicted and remembered experiences were more intense (i.e., more positive and more negative) than was actually the case, as reflected in concurrent reports collected during the vacation. However, the remembered experience best predicted the desire to repeat the vacation, illustrating that we learn from our memories rather than from our actual experiences. Our own research, reviewed below, will further highlight such discrepancies.

Methods for Assessing Episodic Reports

As the preceding discussion indicates, experience sampling methods are the gold standard for assessing people's affective experience. They can capture the experience in situ, while the person has access to the current feeling, and hence minimize problems of recall and inference. Yet their high cost and respondent burden limits their feasibility for large-scale studies. As an alternative, we may draw on episodic reports, provided the relevant episode is recent and can be reinstantiated in memory in sufficient detail. Two methods were developed for this purpose. The Day Reconstruction Method (DRM) is designed to capture the activities and experiences of the preceding day; this has the advantage of limiting reports to very recent episodes, which are recalled in the context of other episodes of the day. On the other hand, the focus on a single day renders it difficult to assess infrequent activities, which may not have occurred for a sufficient number of respondents. The Event Reconstruction Method (ERM) avoids this limitation by asking respondents to review the most recent episode of such activities. Next, we describe these methods and report selected findings bearing on their validity.

DAY RECONSTRUCTION METHOD

The DRM (Kahneman et al., 2004a, 2004b) is designed to collect data describing the experiences a person has on a given day, through a systematic reconstruction conducted on the following day. The DRM builds on the strengths of time-budget measurement (Juster & Stafford, 1985; Michelson, 2005; Robinson, 1977) and experience sampling (Stone et al., 1999), and employs techniques grounded in cognitive science.

Method

The DRM asks respondents to reconstruct the *previous* day by completing a structured self-administered questionnaire.[1] Respondents first reinstantiate the previous day into working memory by producing a short diary consisting of a sequence of episodes, usually covering the time from when they got up to when they went to bed. The format of this diary draws on insights from cognitive research with Event History Calendars (Belli, 1998) and facilitates retrieval from autobiographical memory through multiple pathways; its episodic reinstantiation format attenuates biases commonly observed in retrospective reports (Robinson & Clore, 2002; Schwarz & Oyserman, 2001; Schwarz & Sudman, 1994). Respondents' diary entries are confidential and the diary does not need to be returned to the researcher. This allows respondents to use idiosyncratic notes, including details they may not want to share.

Next, respondents receive a response form and are encouraged to draw on their confidential diary notes to answer a series of questions. These questions ask them to describe key features of each episode, including (1) when the episode began and ended, thus providing time use data; (2) what they were doing; (3) where they were; (4) whom they were interacting with; and (5) how they felt during that episode, assessed on multiple affect dimensions. The details of this response form can be tailored to the specific issues under study; only this form is returned to the researcher for analysis. For methodological reasons, it is important that respondents complete the diary before they are aware of the specific content of the later questions about each episode. Early knowledge of these questions may affect the reconstruction of the previous day and may introduce selection biases. The DRM can be administered individually or in group settings, and respondents can report on a complete day in 45 to 75 minutes.

In sum, the DRM provides a joint assessment of activities and subjective experiences, including information about the duration of each experience that can be used for duration-weighted analyses. Compared to experience sampling, the DRM has the advantage of covering a full day, which experience sampling can provide only through very dense sampling schemes with accompanying high respondent burden. Compared to global reports of daily experiences, the DRM has the advantage of lower susceptibility to retrospective reporting biases.

Findings and Correspondence With Experience Sampling

Kahneman and colleagues (2004a) report illustrative findings based on a sample of 909 employed women in Texas. Table 9.1 shows the time spent in selected activities and in different social interactions along with their affective quality.

DRM reports have been validated against experience sampling data obtained from other samples (Kahneman et al., 2004a; Stone et al., 2006). These analyses showed that the DRM captures changes in affect over the course of the day that closely correspond to the changes captured by experience sampling. Importantly, these diurnal patterns are not obvious to respondents and often contradict respondents' own beliefs, indicating that these episodic reports of affect are not derived from general semantic knowledge. Figure 9.1 shows two examples.

EVENT RECONSTRUCTION METHOD

Although infrequent activities are more likely to be captured by the full-day coverage of the DRM than by experience sampling, the usefulness of the DRM is limited when only a few respondents engage in an activity on a given day. The ERM addresses this shortcoming by extending the time frame beyond a single day; it asks respondents to reinstantiate the "most recent" episode of the activity in memory and then proceeds as described above for the DRM. Note that this method provides information about the affective experience associated with an activity, but does not provide time use data.

Comparisons of ERM and DRM reports indicate that the ERM can capture the same information as the DRM, provided that the last episode is indeed recent. Figure 9.2 provides an example of this correspondence. We hasten to add, however, that recalling episodes in the context of preceding episodes (as done in the DRM) is preferable over the more isolated recall of episodes in the ERM. Moreover, we currently know little about how "recent" is recent enough for an accurate report; the time that can elapse without negative consequences for data quality is likely to depend on the memorability of the specific episode. Once sufficient time passes, episodic information will no longer be accessible. In this case, respondents will turn to general semantic knowledge to arrive at an answer, as they do for global reports, thus undermining the goal of episodic reporting. These methodological issues await further research.

Table 9.1   Mean Affect by Situation

Positive affect is the average of happy, warm/friendly, enjoying myself. Negative affect is the average of frustrated/annoyed, depressed/blue, hassled/pushed around, angry/hostile, worried/anxious, criticized/put down. For each situation, the table shows the mean ratings on affect descriptors, the average amount of time all respondents spent in the situation, and the proportion of respondents reporting at least one episode of each type. Episodes for which the respondent reported multiple activities or interaction partners were included in each of the corresponding computations.

	Mean Affect Rating					Mean Hours/Day	Proportion of Sample Reporting
	Positive	Negative	Competent	Impatient	Tired		
Activities							
Intimate relations	5.10	0.36	4.57	0.74	3.09	0.2	0.11
Socializing	4.59	0.57	4.32	1.20	2.33	2.3	0.65
Relaxing	4.42	0.51	4.05	0.84	3.44	2.2	0.77
Pray/worship/ meditate	4.35	0.59	4.45	1.04	2.95	0.4	0.23
Eating	4.34	0.59	4.12	0.95	2.55	2.2	0.94
Exercising	4.31	0.5	4.26	1.58	2.42	0.2	0.16
Watching TV	4.19	0.58	3.95	1.02	3.54	2.2	0.75
Shopping	3.95	0.74	4.26	2.08	2.66	0.4	0.3
Preparing food	3.93	0.69	4.2	1.54	3.11	1.1	0.62
On the phone	3.92	0.85	4.35	1.92	2.92	2.5	0.61
Napping	3.87	0.6	3.26	0.91	4.3	0.9	0.43
Taking care of my children	3.86	0.91	4.19	1.95	3.56	1.1	0.36
Computer/e-mail/Internet	3.81	0.8	4.57	1.93	2.62	1.9	0.47
Housework	3.73	0.77	4.23	2.11	3.4	1.1	0.49

(Continued)

Table 9.1 (Continued)

	Mean Affect Rating						Mean Hours/Day	Proportion of Sample Reporting
	Positive	Negative	Competent	Impatient	Tired			
Working	3.62	0.97	4.45	2.7	2.42		6.9	1.00
Commuting	3.45	0.89	4.09	2.6	2.75		1.6	0.87
Interaction partners								
Friends	4.36	0.67	4.37	1.61	2.59		2.6	0.65
Relatives	4.17	0.8	4.17	1.7	3.06		1.00	0.38
Spouse/significant others	4.11	0.79	4.1	1.53	3.46		2.7	0.62
Children	4.04	0.75	4.13	1.65	3.4		2.3	0.53
Clients/customers	3.79	0.95	4.65	2.59	2.33		4.5	0.74
Coworkers	3.76	0.92	4.43	2.44	2.35		5.7	0.93
Boss	3.52	1.09	4.48	2.82	2.44		2.4	0.52
Alone	3.41	0.69	3.76	1.73	3.12		3.4	0.9
Duration-weighted mean	3.89	0.84	4.31	2.09	2.9			
% time > 0	97%	66%	90%	59%	76%			

SOURCE: Kahneman, D., Krueger, A. B., Schkade, D., Schwarz, N., & Stone, A. A. (2004). A survey method for characterizing daily life experience: The Day Reconstruction Method (DRM). *Science, 306*, 1776–1780. Reprinted by permission.

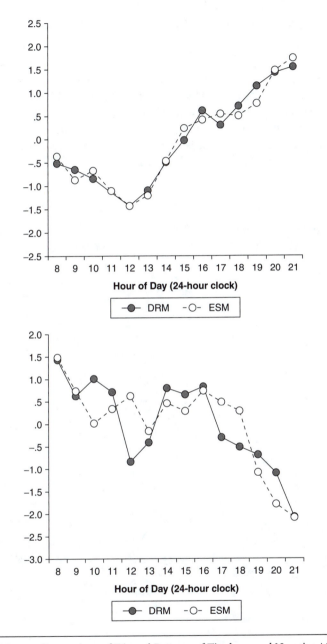

Figure 9.1   Comparison of Diurnal Patterns of Tiredness and Negative Affect for DRM and Experience Sampling Studies

SOURCE: Kahneman, D., Krueger, A. B., Schkade, D., Schwarz, N., & Stone, A. A. (2004). A survey method for characterizing daily life experience: The Day Reconstruction Method (DRM). *Science, 306,* 1776–1780. Reprinted by permission.

NOTE: The top panel shows reported tiredness and the bottom panel reported negative affect; points are standard scores computed across hourly averages within each sample.

The Divergence of Global and Episodic Reports

As expected on theoretical grounds, we observed in several studies that global and episodic retrospective reports of hedonic experience diverge in systematic ways. Moreover, predictions of hedonic experience show close correspondence with global retrospective reports, but neither predictions nor global retrospective reports seem to capture what people actually experience. We first review two selected examples and discuss the underlying processes; subsequently, we turn to their methodological implications.

HOW MUCH DO PEOPLE ENJOY BEING WITH THEIR KIDS?

In 1975, Juster and his colleagues asked American survey respondents to rate 28 activities from "dislike very much" (0) to "enjoy a great deal" (10).

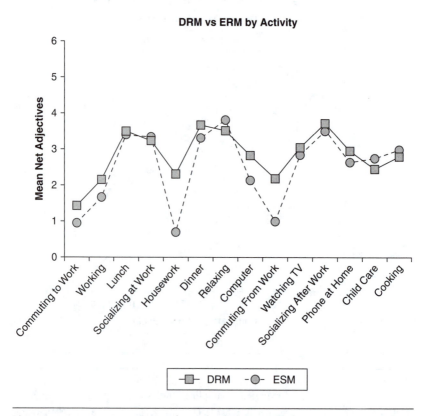

Figure 9.2   Correspondence of DRM and ERM Reports

NOTE: Shown is net affect (difference between positive and negative affect terms) by activity.

They observed that activities with one's children consistently topped the list (ranks 1–4), whereas grocery shopping and cleaning the house were reported as least enjoyable (ranks 27 and 28, respectively; Juster, 1985, p. 336). Later surveys replicated these rankings with minor variations (Juster, 1985), mostly due to changes in the activities listed, and a conceptual replication in Sweden (Flood, 1997) yielded similar results. Despite these high rankings of child-related activities, several studies indicate that parents' marital satisfaction drops when children arrive, reaches a lifetime low when the children are teenagers, and recovers after the children leave the house (for a review see Argyle, 1999). Are the children a more mixed pleasure than global reports of enjoyment convey? As shown in Table 9.1, DRM data from 909 employed women in Texas suggest so (Kahneman et al., 2004a). In episodic reports of affective experience, taking care of one's children ranks just above the least enjoyable activities of working, housework, and commuting; data from other samples replicated this pattern.

Several processes contribute to this theoretically predicted divergence. First, global judgments of enjoyment are based on general beliefs ("I enjoy my kids"), which are often supported by belief-consistent memories of great vividness (like fond memories of shared activities). Yet many mundane episodes on a given day are less enjoyable than the episodes that make for fond memories. Second, activities are organized in memory by their focal features. Attempts to recall memories pertaining to one's interactions with the children will therefore result in an overrepresentation of child-focused activities, at the expense of numerous other episodes of the day in which the children were present. The DRM avoids many of these problems of selective recall and provides a fuller assessment of the affective impact of children throughout the day. Our findings suggest that part of the reason that children seem more enjoyable in general than on any given day is simply that parents do not consider the full range of child-related time use when providing global reports. Finally, global reports are subject to higher social desirability pressures than episodic reports. A parent who reports, "I don't enjoy spending time with my children" is clearly a bad parent; but noting that "They were a pain last night" is perfectly legitimate. Hence, episodic reports of hedonic experience, as collected in the DRM and ERM, are likely to attenuate the influence of social desirability and self-presentation concerns.

DOES IT FEEL BETTER TO DRIVE A LUXURY CAR?

Findings from other domains of hedonic experience show similar divergences, as a series of studies into drivers' enjoyment of their cars illustrates (Xu & Schwarz, 2007). Not surprisingly, people expect that driving a luxury car is more enjoyable than driving an economy car. When undergraduates were asked to predict how they would feel while driving a BMW, a Honda Accord, or a Ford Escort, they expected that positive feelings (e.g., happy, thrilled) increase, and negative feelings (e.g., depressed, frustrated) decrease, with the value of the car. The first panel of Figure 9.3a shows the reported positive affect as an example. The students' expectations are consistent with drivers' global reports of how they feel driving their cars. Specifically, in the global reporting conditions, we asked university faculty and staff (second panel of Figure 9.3a) and participants in a Web survey (third panel) which car they drive (brand, model, and year) and how they generally feel while driving their car, using the affect scales along which students made their predictions. In both samples, the Blue Book value of the car was a significant predictor of the drivers' reported emotions. Figure 9.3a shows the mean estimated positive affect scores corresponding to the Blue Book values of a BMW, Accord, or Ford Escort. Apparently, the students' predictions of drivers' feelings were right on target.

Episodic reports of the drivers' experience, however, paint a different picture. We asked university faculty and staff assigned to the episodic reporting condition to recall their most recent commute (i.e., an episode from the same day) and to report how they felt during that specific episode of driving. In this case, the quality of the car driven, as indexed by its Blue Book value, was thoroughly unrelated to the drivers' affective experience. The first panel of Figure 9.3b shows the mean estimated positive affect scores corresponding to the Blue Book values of a BMW, Accord, or Ford Escort. Participants in the Web survey were asked to recall the last time they drove their car for 20 minutes or more and to indicate the nature of this trip before they reported how they felt during this specific episode of driving. Again, the quality of the car driven was unrelated to the drivers' affective experience. The second panel of Figure 9.3b shows the estimated mean positive affect scores.

The observed divergence of global and episodic reports is consistent with theoretical predictions. When asked to report how they usually feel while driving their car, drivers focus on attributes of the car to arrive at an answer. This is also what others do when asked to predict the driver's feelings, resulting in the observed convergence of undergraduates' predictions and drivers' global reports. In both cases, the positive attributes of luxury cars result in higher reports of expected or experienced positive affect. But while driving, something else is on the driver's mind and the attributes of the car make little difference, as reflected in drivers' episodic reports. Instead, the driver's feelings are a function of the purpose of the trip, and driving to dinner, for example, feels better than commuting to work. This logic suggests that the car should make a difference when the car is on the driver's mind, that is, in car-focused episodes. Empirically, this is the case. The respondents to the Web survey reported a small number of episodes that they categorized as "driving for fun." As

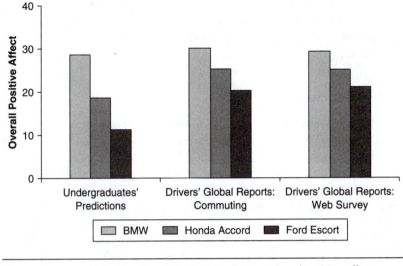

Figure 9.3a   Global Reports of Predicted and Remembered Positive Affect as a
Function of Car Type

SOURCE: Adapted from Xu & Schwarz (2007).

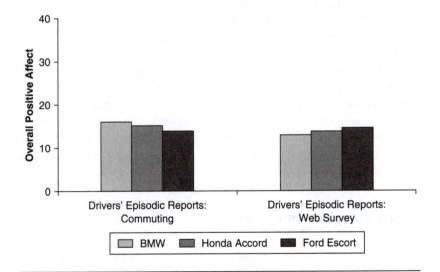

Figure 9.3b   Episodic Reports of Positive Affect as a Function of Car Type

SOURCE: Adapted from Xu & Schwarz (2007).

expected on theoretical grounds, the positive affect reported for these episodes increased with the Blue Book value of the car. By the same token, we would expect that new cars or stuttering old clunkers are likely to affect the driver's experience, given that they may be on the driver's mind while driving.

LIFE'S CIRCUMSTANCES

Our analysis further predicts that the objective circumstances of a person's life should figure more prominently in global evaluations than in the person's moment-to-moment affective experience. When asked, "How satisfied are you with your life as a whole?" people are likely to compare their own fortunes to others' (for a review see Schwarz & Strack, 1999). Variables like income, education, employment, or marriage are likely to come to mind and will figure relatively prominently in the assessment. However, these variables are unlikely to be on people's mind as they pursue their daily activities. Hence, their influence on moment-to-moment experiences is likely to be indirect and will depend mostly on whether these variables influence which activities people engage in. We may therefore expect that objective background variables are more closely related to satisfaction judgments than to moment-to-moment affective experience. Finally, global reports of affective experience should fall in between these extremes, reflecting that background variables may be considered in arriving at theory-driven global assessments of one's feelings.

The findings of a recent DRM study with 745 women in Columbus, Ohio, support these predictions (Kahneman, Krueger, Schkade, Schwarz, & Stone, 2006). These women reported their overall life satisfaction, estimated the percentage of time they spent in a good mood yesterday, and finally, completed a DRM for the preceding day. Figure 9.4 shows the correlation of income, marital status, years of education, and employment with these judgments. As expected, these objective circumstances of life were significantly correlated with satisfaction judgments but exerted a negligible influence on moment-to-moment affect. Again, however, global reports of affect in form of estimates of the percentage of time spent in a good mood again exaggerated the influence of background conditions.

Methodological Implications

The combination of time use data and indicators of hedonic experience provides a promising approach to characterizing subjective well-being. It holds particular promise for investigating the impact of life events, which may influence the allocation of time to activities as well as the affective experience associated with a given activity. While the measurement of time use has seen considerable methodological progress, less attention has been devoted to the

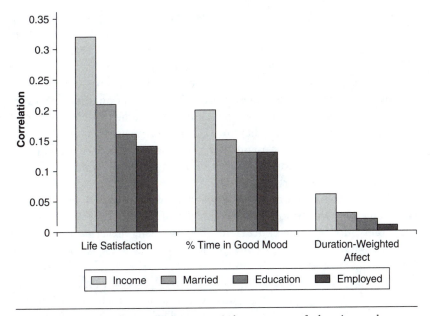

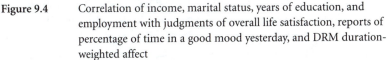

Figure 9.4   Correlation of income, marital status, years of education, and employment with judgments of overall life satisfaction, reports of percentage of time in a good mood yesterday, and DRM duration-weighted affect

SOURCE: Based on data reported in Kahneman, Krueger, Schkade, Schwarz, & Stone (2006).

assessment of the subjective experiences associated with activities. To date, time use surveys have relied exclusively on global reports of enjoyment (e.g., Flood, 1997; Juster, 1985). Such global reports seem to have high face validity because they usually converge with our own intuitions. Ironically, however, this convergence merely reflects that we, as observers, draw on the same general knowledge about the world as the respondents who report on their own lives, and hence arrive at similar rankings—as the convergence of students' predictions and drivers' global affect reports in the above car studies illustrates. When respondents' reports pertain to their affective experiences during a recent specific episode, or when affective experiences are assessed in situ, we often arrive at strikingly different conclusions about the hedonic value of activities.

The observed discrepancies reflect that feelings are fleeting and not well represented in memory (Robinson & Clore, 2002). Hence, respondents need to draw on episodic or semantic knowledge to arrive at a report. When the episode is sufficiently recent to allow a detailed reinstantiation in memory, episodic reports can provide relatively accurate information about affective experience, as indicated by the convergence of concurrent experience sampling reports and retrospective DRM reports (Kahneman et al., 2004a; Stone et al., 2006). When episodic knowledge is not accessible, or its reinstantiation not encouraged, respondents draw on general semantic knowledge to infer what their experience must have been. Such belief-driven reports approach the actual experience when the belief is correct, but diverge from the actual experience when it is not. At present, little is known about the variables that determine the accuracy of beliefs about one's own affective experiences. Moreover, the experience of major life events is probably associated with changes in relevant beliefs (Ubel, Loewenstein, Schwarz, & Smith, 2005), which provides a promising avenue for further research.

The reviewed findings have important methodological implications. Researchers who want to assess peoples' actual hedonic experiences should preferably do so with concurrent reports, using experience sampling methodologies (Stone et al., 1999). If this is not feasible, episodic reporting methods like the DRM or ERM provide a less burdensome alternative that can capture the experience with some accuracy, provided that the relevant episodes are recent. In contrast, global reports of affect are theory driven, not experience driven. They capture respondents' beliefs about their experience rather than the experience itself and are subject to pronounced focusing effects, as the reviewed studies illustrate. Finally, people's choices are based on their expected hedonic consequences. These expectations converge with global memories but often diverge from the actual experience. Hence, predictions, choices, and global memories are poor indicators of experience. Yet when people make behavioral decisions, global memories and expectations are likely to figure prominently in the information they consider. Ironically, this turns faulty indicators of experience into good predictors of future choices and behaviors (e.g., Wirtz et al., 2003).

Note

1. A sample instrument (titled "Day Reconstruction Method Documentation") and related papers are available at http://sitemaker.umich.edu/norbert.schwarz/day_ reconstruction_method.

Acknowledgment

We thank the William and Flora Hewlett Foundation and the National Institute of Aging (Grant AG024928) for supporting the reported research and the preparation of this chapter.

References

Argyle, M. (1999). Causes and correlates of happiness. In D. Kahneman, E. Diener, & N. Schwarz (Eds.), *Well-being: Foundations of hedonic psychology* (pp. 353–373). New York: Russell Sage.

Belli, R. (1998). The structure of autobiographical memory and the event history calendar: Potential improvements in the quality of retrospective reports in surveys. *Memory, 6,* 383–406.

Flood, L. (1997). *Household, market, and nonmarket activities. Procedures and codes for the 1993 time-use survey* (Vol. 6). Uppsala, Sweden: Uppsala University, Department of Economics.

Gilbert, D. T., & Ebert, J. E. (2002). Decisions and revisions: The affective forecasting of changeable outcomes. *Journal of Personality and Social Psychology, 82,* 503–514.

Juster, F. T. (1985). Preferences for work and leisure. In F. T. Juster & F. P. Stafford (Eds.), *Time, goods, and well-being* (pp. 331–351). Ann Arbor: University of Michigan, Institute for Social Research.

Juster, F. T., & Stafford, F. P. (Eds.). (1985). *Time, goods, and well-being.* Ann Arbor: University of Michigan, Institute for Social Research.

Kahneman, D. (1994). New challenges to the rationality assumption. *Journal of Institutional and Theoretical Economics, 150,* 18–36.

Kahneman, D. (1999). Objective happiness. In D. Kahneman, E. Diener, & N. Schwarz (Eds.), *Well-being: The foundations of hedonic psychology* (pp. 3–25). New York: Russell Sage.

Kahneman, D., Krueger, A. B., Schkade, D., Schwarz, N., & Stone, A. A. (2004a). A survey method for characterizing daily life experience: The Day Reconstruction Method (DRM). *Science, 306,* 1776–1780.

Kahneman, D., Krueger, A. B., Schkade, D., Schwarz, N., & Stone, A. A. (2004b). Toward national well-being accounts. *American Economic Review, 94,* 429–434.

Kahneman, D., Krueger, A., Schkade, D., Schwarz, N., & Stone, A. (2006). Would you be happier if you were richer? A focusing illusion. *Science, 312,* 1908–1910.

Loewenstein, G. F., & Adler, D. (1995). A bias in the prediction of tastes. *Economic Journal, 105,* 929–937.

Loewenstein, G. F., & Schkade, D. A. (1999). Wouldn't it be nice? Predicting future feelings. In D. Kahneman, E. Diener, & N. Schwarz (Eds.), *Well-being: Foundations of hedonic psychology* (pp. 85–105). New York: Russell Sage.

March, J. (1978). Bounded rationality, ambiguity, and the engineering of choice. *Bell Journal of Economics, 9,* 587–608.

Michelson, W. (2005). *Time-use: Expanding explanation in the social sciences.* Boulder, CO: Paradigm Publishers.

Mitchell, T. R., Thompson, L., Peterson, E., & Cronk, R. (1997). Temporal adjustments in the evaluation of events: The "rosy view." *Journal of Experimental Social Psychology, 33,* 421–448.

Robinson, J. P. (1977). *How Americans use time. A social-psychological analysis of everyday behavior.* New York: Praeger.

Robinson, M. D., & Clore, G. L. (2002). Belief and feeling: Evidence for an accessibility model of emotional self-report. *Psychological Bulletin, 128,* 934–960.

Schkade, D. A., & Kahneman, D. (1997). Does living in California make people happy? A focusing illusion in judgments of life satisfaction. *Psychological Science, 9,* 340–346.

Schwarz, N., & Oyserman, D. (2001). Asking questions about behavior: Cognition, communication and questionnaire construction. *American Journal of Evaluation, 22,* 127–160.

Schwarz, N., & Strack, F. (1999). Reports of subjective well-being: Judgmental processes and their methodological implications. In D. Kahneman, E. Diener, & N. Schwarz (Eds.), *Well-being: The foundations of hedonic psychology* (pp. 61–84). New York: Russell Sage.

Schwarz, N., & Sudman, S. (Eds.). (1994). *Autobiographical memory and the validity of retrospective reports.* New York: Springer Verlag.

Stone, A. A., Schwartz, J. E., Schwarz, N., Schkade, D., Krueger, A., & Kahneman, D. (2006). A population approach to the study of emotion: Diurnal rhythms of a working day examined with the Day Reconstruction Method (DRM). *Emotion, 6,* 139–149.

Stone, A. A., Shiffman, S. S., Atienza, A., & Nebeling, L. (Eds.). (2007). *The science of real-time data capture: Self-reports in health research.* New York: Oxford University Press.

Stone, A. A., Shiffman, S. S., & DeVries, M. W. (1999). Ecological momentary assessment. In D. Kahneman, E. Diener, & N. Schwarz (Eds.), *Well-being: The foundations of hedonic psychology* (pp. 26–39). New York: Russell Sage.

Ubel, P. A., Loewenstein, G., Schwarz, N., & Smith, D. (2005). Misimagining the unimaginable: The disability paradox and health care decision making. *Health Psychology, 24,* S57–S62.

Wirtz, D., Kruger, J., Scollon, C. N., & Diener, E. (2003). What to do on spring break? The role of predicted, on-line, and remembered experience in future choice. *Psychological Science, 14*(5), 520–524.

Xu, J., & Schwarz, N. (2007). *How do you feel while driving your car? Depends on how you think about it.* Unpublished manuscript.

10

Using Time Diaries to Study Instruction in Schools

Brian Rowan, Eric M. Camburn,
and Richard Correnti

Introduction

For more than 20 years, research on teaching has had two central aims: to gather descriptive data on classroom teaching under different conditions of practice and to estimate the effects of different teaching practices on student learning (Brophy & Good, 1986; Rowan, Correnti, & Miller, 2002). In studying these issues, educational researchers have generally used two strategies to gather data. The most common approach has been to send trained observers into classrooms to collect structured observational data and, more recently, to make video recordings of selected samples of lessons for later coding by experts. While these approaches are often viewed as the "gold standard" for classroom data collection, they are quite costly, and their use is typically confined to small-scale studies (exceptions, however, are found in the use of video recording of teaching in the Third International Mathematics and Science Study [Hiebert et al., 2005] and the use of classroom observations in some large-scale program evaluations commissioned by the U.S. Department of Education's Institute for Education Sciences).

A second approach to collecting instructional data has been used by the National Center for Education Statistics (NCES) since the 1980s. NCES large-sample surveys often include a small number of items on teacher surveys to measure teaching practices in U.S. schools (e.g., the Schools and Staffing

Survey, the National Assessment of Educational Progress, the Second and Third International Mathematics and Science Studies, the National Educational Longitudinal Studies of 1988 and 2002, the Early Childhood Longitudinal Study). Obviously, data from one-time surveys are less expensive to collect than observational or videotaped data, and are well suited for large-sample research. However, researchers have questioned the accuracy and validity of these data (Mayer, 1999; Mullens & Gayler, 1999).

This chapter discusses a third (less frequently used) approach to gathering data on classroom instruction—the use of teacher logs. In this chapter, we argue that teacher logs can be used in large-scale research on teaching and demonstrate that data from teacher logs can be used to investigate method-ological and substantive questions about classroom instruction. Our discussion focuses on data collected as part of the Study of Instructional Improvement (SII), conducted by the Institute for Social Research at the University of Michigan under contract with the Consortium for Policy Research in Education. SII collected data on approximately 150,000 reading/language arts and mathematics lessons carried out by approximately 2,000 teachers working in 115 high-poverty elementary schools during the 2000–2001 to 2003–2004 school years.[1]

The Problem

Classroom instruction is notoriously complex and difficult to measure (Jackson, 1990). Over the course of a 9-month academic year, the typical elementary school teacher will conduct 140 or more lessons in a given academic subject for the 20–30 students in her or his classroom, sometimes differentiating instruc-tional activities by student or subgroups of students. Moreover, during any given lesson, a teacher's instruction will typically unfold along many different dimen-sions. For example, a teacher will normally cover several content objectives at dif-ferent levels of cognitive demand during a single lesson in a subject like reading, working in several different behavior settings, using a variety of subject-specific instructional techniques. Although some features of classroom instruction are implemented repeatedly across the school year, many others are not, making instructional practice not only multidimensional, but also highly variable across days of the school year (Rogosa, Floden, & Willet, 1984).

Such complexity and variability present two problems for researchers. One problem occurs when survey researchers ask teachers to report on their teaching activities over an entire academic year in a survey administered near the end of that year—the most common data collection strategy in large-scale survey research. Here, teacher memory is the problem; in particular, the strong potential for inaccuracies in retrospective reports of the frequencies or rates at which particular teaching activities were undertaken (Smithson & Porter, 1994). Variability in teaching creates a different problem, mainly for researchers conducting observations or making video recordings of instruction. Here, the problem is generalizability, that is, obtaining a sample of teaching observations that can be generalized to the universe of teaching events that unfolded over a 9-month academic year. To the extent that teaching varies systematically across days of the school year, and especially if it involves many rare events, attempts to sample teaching activities adequately and discriminate reliably among different teachers' yearly patterns of instruction will require more in-class observations than all but the most well-funded studies can afford to collect.

These issues motivate our discussion of teacher logs. Logs (as typically administered) ask teachers to report on their instruction at the end of the school day, thus radically reducing the time period over which teachers must exercise recall. This, in turn, should increase teachers' reporting accuracy. Moreover, logs are really survey instruments, so they can be administered at a much lower unit cost than classroom observations or videotaping sessions, allowing data to be gathered on much larger samples of lessons, thereby improving the ability to generalize from a set of observations to the universe of teaching activities conducted over an entire academic year. Despite these advantages, logs are not without problems. As survey instruments, they are subject to errors in measurement due to social desirability, the response categories presented, and so on. Moreover, while frequent administration of logs can decrease coverage error and increase generalizability, these benefits come at the cost of increased respondent burden, which can increase survey nonresponse or lead to response bias if respondents develop time-saving (but inaccurate) patterns of filling out log surveys.

The purpose of this chapter is to discuss some of the lessons learned about these issues as a result of administering teacher logs to a large sample of teachers during the SII. We begin by discussing how the researchers conducting this study constructed the log, as well as the training procedures and incentives developed to increase response accuracy, minimize respondent burden, and improve response rates. We then discuss possible "survey errors" due to respondent and instrument error inherent in log-based measures of teaching (Groves, 1989). Here, we discuss how teachers' log responses compared to the reports of trained observers and to the responses teachers made about their instructional activities on an annual survey completed at the end of the year. Next, we discuss different measurement models that can be used with log data and show how multilevel statistical models can be used to understand better the psychometric properties of log-based measures. We conclude by discussing some of the main findings of our work about the nature of elementary school instruction and its consequences for student learning. Throughout the chapter we focus solely on the reading/language arts log developed as part of the SII.

Readers interested in the mathematics log developed for this study can consult Rowan, Harrison, and Hayes (2004).

Logs and Log Administration

The reading/language arts log administered as part of the SII was a paper-and-pencil survey instrument containing more than 100 items, mostly in checklist format, that teachers in first through fifth grades were asked to fill out at the end of a school day. In completing a log, teachers were instructed to report on the instruction provided to a single student in their reading class. To ensure an accurate record of teachers' overall patterns of teaching, teachers rotated log reports across a representative sample of eight students in their classes during three extended logging periods spaced evenly across the academic year. In this design, teachers who participated in all logging sessions with a complete roster of students would complete roughly 90 logs, or about 11 logs per student. However, because the elementary schools under study used many different instructional grouping arrangements for reading instruction, and because many students switched reading teachers midyear, the average teacher in the sample completed about 39 logs over the course of the year.

The main purpose of the log was to gather data on several dimensions of instruction. The opening (or "gateway") section asked teachers to report on the amount of time spent by a focal student on reading/language arts instruction on the reporting day, as well as the amount of emphasis given to each of the following topics: word analysis, concepts of print, oral or reading comprehension, vocabulary, writing, grammar, spelling, and research strategies. Then, if teachers checked that word analysis, comprehension, or writing was an emphasis for a student on a given day, teachers completed additional items (in the so-called back end of the log) about the specific content objectives that were taught to the student in that domain, the methods used to teach that content, and the tasks and materials the focal student engaged with that day.

Building on previous experience administering teacher logs for the Panel Study on Income Dynamics (Roth, Brooks-Gunn, & Linver, 2003), field staff conducting the SII designed field administration procedures intended both to improve the accuracy of teacher responses to log items and to ensure adequate response rates. To improve response accuracy, field staff from the Institute for Social Research conducted a 45-minute training session for teachers before the first logging period of the year. This session introduced teachers to the definitions of terms used in the log and taught teachers how to complete the log questionnaire. That session was followed by a suggested 2-hour home study period during which teachers were asked to study a glossary defining and illustrating the terms used in the log, and then by a one-hour, in-school, follow-up training session prior to the first logging period. Once logging began, teachers could call a toll-free phone number or ask local field staff to address any difficulties they were having with logging.

Also, an incentives plan was developed to increase teacher response rates. Using data on teachers' salaries nationwide, researchers calculated the average daily wage of teachers, and then offered payments to teachers based on the expectation that a single log would take about 5 minutes to complete. Rather than use piece rate incentives, teachers were paid at the end of each logging period in which they logged. The actual incentive was $150 per 6-week logging period if a teacher was logging for the full 8 students called for by the original design. In addition, field staff provided logging teachers with small gifts (coffee mugs, paper weights, pencils or pens) on a variable interval reinforcement schedule to motivate log completion further.

Overall, response rates for the reading/language arts log were quite high. About 90% of the teachers asked to log did so, and they completed 90% of the logs they were administered. Although teachers often struggled when they began logging, after about a week they typically completed the reading language arts log in about 5 minutes' time. Moreover, as the response rates demonstrate (and as teacher comments suggest), logging was not perceived as overly burdensome. Moreover, using logs was cost effective. A "back-of-the-envelope" calculation based on initial budgets and log administration data suggests a research cost of about $27.50 per log administered, far less than the cost of conducting a single classroom observation or videotaping session, although more expensive than administering an annual survey to teachers.

Sources of Survey Error in Logs

These results demonstrate that it is possible to administer instructional logs to large samples of teachers over a prolonged period of time, and to achieve high response rates in doing so. An important question, however, is whether the data gathered from logs is accurate. To examine this problem, we undertook several analyses to compare teachers' log reports to (a) log data collected by trained observers and (b) teachers' responses on an annual survey administered near the end of the academic year. From a "survey error" perspective (Groves, 1989), these analyses provide useful information about the different forms of measurement error that arise as different observers report on the same events and/or when different instruments are used to measure instruction as it unfolded over the course of a year.

LOGS VERSUS OBSERVATIONAL DATA

To examine observer bias in log use, we conducted a small study in eight public elementary schools where 31 teachers from various grades were pilot testing logging procedures. In the study, eight trained observers were sent two at a time into the classrooms of logging teachers on a given day during a 3-month period, during which time both teachers and observers completed logs. In this design, log reports for a single lesson were available from three individuals—two trained observers and a logging teacher. Using these data, Camburn and Barnes (2004, pp. 54–60) conducted a number of statistical analyses to examine rates of agreement among teachers and observers, and observers themselves. They also used qualitative data from teacher interviews, narrative observation records, and observer reports to examine sources of disagreement among the teachers and observers who recorded data on the same lesson.

Camburn and Barnes's (2004) statistical analysis focused on two types of teacher–observer agreement. The first, called a "gateway" match, occurred if and only if both teacher and observer completed the gateway section of the log so that both ended up in the same section of the back end of the log. Camburn and Barnes found that teachers and observers had appropriate gateway matches 81% of the time for instruction in word analysis, 90% of the time for reading comprehension instruction, and 87% of the time for writing instruction. A second type of match occurred at the back end of the log where teachers completed checklists describing the specific content objectives, teaching practices, and instructional tasks and materials used in teaching a focal topic. Here, two kinds of matches were possible: matches where both teachers and observers checked an item during a lesson (a 1-1 match), and cases where both teachers and observers did *not* check the item during the lesson (a 0-0 match). Considering both matches simultaneously, Camburn and Barnes found the probability of teachers and observers producing a match on any item in the back end of the log to be about .73. Yet since most items in the back end of the log were *not* checked during a given lesson, this high rate of matching resulted in part because 0–0 matches dominated the data set. Thus, Camburn and Barnes also examined the probability of 1-1 matches. Here, match rates were much lower—only .22 for teacher–observer matches and .41 for observer–observer matches. An important finding was that 1-1 match rates were much higher for items that were checked with highest mean frequencies in the data set (about .85 for the most frequently checked word analysis items, .77 for the most frequently checked comprehension items, and .75 for the most frequently checked writing items).

Using both match rate and qualitative data, Camburn and Barnes (2004) drew a number of conclusions about observer error in log surveys of instruction. First, the high match rates for gateway items and for frequently occurring items suggests that teacher logs are most accurate (a) when describing instruction at a grosser (rather than finer) level of detail, and (b) for describing frequent (rather than rare) instructional practices. In addition, Camburn and Barnes concluded from their analysis of qualitative data that both teachers and trained observers made fallible reports of instructional practice. Indeed, a common error for both teachers and observers resulted from improper application of the coding conventions enumerated in the log glossary. In comparison to trained observers, teachers' errors seemed to result when teachers overlooked quick, but routine, aspects of their teaching (e.g., correcting students' decoding errors as they read), while observer errors occurred when they were unable to see particular instructional acts, when particular instructional acts took place during very short lesson segments, or when observers misjudged teachers' intentions, particularly in terms of teachers' cognitive goals for students.

LOGS VERSUS ANNUAL QUESTIONNAIRES

Camburn and Han (2006) conducted an additional analysis comparing teachers' log reports to their reports of instruction on the teacher questionnaire administered near the end of each school year. Here, data were drawn from the responses of 1,535 teachers in Grades 1–5 who completed a reading/language arts log at least once during the SII and who also completed an annual questionnaire the year they logged. By design, 24 items included on the language arts log were also included on the annual questionnaire, and by design, the wording of these questions was made as similar as possible on both instruments (although response formats differed).

Camburn and Han (2006) examined the amount and sources of *divergence* in teachers' responses to these 24 items across the log and questionnaire. The most important finding was that teachers uniformly reported higher frequencies of engaging in teaching practices on the annual questionnaires versus the log. This is consistent with prior research on the correspondence between logs and questionnaires in educational settings (e.g., Burstein et al., 1995), but is inconsistent with research in other settings (e.g., Hoppe et al., 2000; Leigh, 2000; Leigh, Gillmore, & Morrison, 1998). Overall, the median difference in teachers' estimates of the frequency of teaching word analysis skills was about +7.3 days/month (or nearly 2 days/week) on the questionnaire versus the log, and about +4 days per month (or one day a week) for comprehension and writing. The general tendency to overreport was more pronounced for female teachers, African American teachers, more experienced teachers, and teachers who individualized instruction. These latter findings constitute another form of observer bias (i.e., bias due to the characteristics of the respondent).

Psychometric Properties of Log Data

In this section, we discuss various measurement and statistical models that can be used to analyze log data once collected. Here, we discuss two challenges present in log data. First, log data consist mostly of dichotomously scored items, requiring analysts to move from statistical and measurement models based on the normal distribution to statistical or measurement models appropriate for categorical data. Second, log data (as collected in the SII) are clustered, that is, hierarchically nested. In particular, daily observations from a single log are nested within students, students are nested within teachers, and teachers are nested within schools. As a result, analysis of log data requires analytic methods appropriate to clustered data.

MEASUREMENT MODELS FOR LOG DATA

The basic unit of instructional data collected during the SII was a single log filled out by a teacher on a given day. In what follows, we call this lowest unit of analysis a "lesson." Now, as teachers fill out the reading/language arts log, they have the potential to check more than 100 separate items describing many different dimensions of instruction. To some extent, researchers will take an analytic interest in single items checked during a lesson—for example, the number of minutes in any given day that a teacher taught reading/language arts, or whether or not the teacher focused on a particular topic, say word analysis, reading comprehension, or writing. If that is the case, no measurement model need be applied to the data.

Suppose, however, an analyst wants to combine more than one item from the log to form a multi-item scale for a single, unidimensional, latent trait. When the log items to be included in this scale are dichotomously scored (0,1), an obvious approach to building multi-item scales at the lesson level is item-response theory (IRT), a form of latent trait analysis especially suited to the analysis of dichotomous items (for an accessible discussion of IRT, see Embretson & Reise, 2000). As an example, Rowan, Camburn, and Correnti (2004) used an IRT model to create a measure of the "cognitive demand" (or skill difficulty) of reading comprehension lessons taught to third-grade students on any given day. The reading/language arts log contained 12 dichotomous items that were assumed to describe this latent dimension of reading instruction, where some items were theorized in advance to index reading skills taught at a low level of cognitive demand (e.g., activating prior knowledge, previewing and surveying text), others were assumed to index more cognitively demanding skills (e.g., summarizing details in the text, sequencing information or events in the text), and still others were assumed to index highly demanding skills (e.g., analyzing/evaluating text, examining literary techniques). With lessons as the unit of analysis, Rowan, Camburn, and Correnti (2004) used a one-parameter IRT model to construct a scale measuring the cognitive demand of reading instruction for each day in the data set. As expected, item difficulties from the estimated measurement model were in the theorized direction, the point biserial correlations of items to the total scale ranged from .56 to .28, and the scale had an estimated person reliability of .63.

In many cases, however, a data analyst might not be certain about the underlying traits being measured by some arbitrary (and possibly large) number of log items and would therefore want to explore the dimensionality of the data to reduce the number of dimensions measured to fewer than the number of items initially present in the data set. The most common tool used for this purpose is factor analysis. In most statistical software packages, however, the factor analysis subroutine requires a set of continuous observed variables and will yield incorrect results if the data are dichotomous, as with log data. One solution to this problem is to calculate the tetrachoric correlations between all item pairs and then factor analyze the resulting matrix as one would a matrix of Pearson correlations (using, e.g., SAS PROC FACTOR). An alternative is to use one of the available statistical packages specifically designed for binary factor analysis, such as TESTFAC. Both procedures provide factor scores for a given case on each latent trait identified by the model.

These factor analyses can be quite informative. As an example, we have been interested in how word analysis was taught in particular lessons. The back end of the log contains a set of nine items indexing two possibly distinct approaches to word analysis: four that index the strategy of sound blending, and five that index sound segmenting. A binary factor analysis showed that these items did in fact load on different dimensions, and as a result we now use separate scores to index how much a lesson focused on one or the other approach to word analysis. We have obtained similar results in the areas of reading comprehension and writing; for example, reducing 31 items from the reading section of the log to nine different, and theoretically meaningful, dimensions of comprehension instruction, and likewise for writing instruction. A problem, however, is that most of the scales resulting from these factor analyses contain only 3–4 items and have low reliabilities. It is worth noting, therefore, that many analysts will not be interested in constructing lesson-level measures of the sort just discussed and will instead simply want to aggregate data across lessons to the teacher level of analysis. Interestingly, although this procedure loses a great deal of information about how teaching practices vary over time for teachers, we have found that aggregation does little harm in terms of measurement. For example, when item-level responses are aggregated into percentages for teachers, we have found that most percentages are nearly normally distributed and that linear factor analytic scores derived from these aggregated variables correlate in the range of .85 to .95, with the measures built up from the lesson level before being aggregated across teachers.

GENERALIZABILITY ISSUES IN LOG DATA

Although it is interesting to build measures of teaching at the lesson level, log data (as collected in the SII) are highly clustered, with lesson-level measures nested within students, who are nested within teachers, who are nested within schools. In the early days of research on teaching, this kind of clustering presented formidable data analysis problems. Today, however, a number of statistical packages allow researchers to analyze clustered data, including hierarchical linear models (HLMs) (Raudenbush & Bryk, 2002) and SAS PROC MIXED. In this section, we discuss how clustered log data can be analyzed using HLM in order to determine how many logs are needed to discriminate patterns of teaching reliably across various objects of measurement (e.g., students, teachers, or schools).

To begin, consider a very simple case where logs have been used to record the number of minutes of reading instruction across multiple lessons in a sample of teachers. A simple two-level HLM for this continuous measure of teaching can be developed, where the level 1 model is $Y_{ij} = \beta_{0j} + e_{ij}$ and the level 2 model is $\beta_{0j} = \gamma_{00} + u_{0j}$. At level 1, Y_{ij} is the number of minutes in reading instruction for a lesson occurring on occasion i taught by teacher j. In the model, this outcome is seen as varying randomly around the mean number of minutes for the teacher (across all observed lessons), where e_{ij} is an error term assumed to be normally distributed with mean 0 and variance (σ^2). At level 2 of the model, the mean lesson time for teacher j (β_{0j}) is seen as varying around the grand mean in lesson time for the whole sample (γ_{00}), plus a random teacher effect (u_{0j}) assumed normally distributed with mean 0 and variance τ_{00}.

This simple model can be used to examine the question of how many logs must be administered in order to discriminate reliably among teachers in their patterns of instructional time allocations. It is well known, for example, that a researcher's ability to discriminate reliably among objects of measurement when measures are taken repeatedly is a function of three main factors: (1) the internal consistency of the measuring instrument, (2) the variance in "true score" measurements over time and across objects of measurement, and (3) the number of occasions on which measures are taken. If a single measurement tool is used, thereby controlling for errors of measurement, a simple expression describes the reliability with which we can measure β_{0j}, teachers' average lesson length. The formula is simply: $\alpha = \tau / [\tau + (\sigma^2/n_j)]$, where α is the reliability coefficient, τ is the variance among teachers in time allocations, σ^2 is the variance within teachers in time allocations, and n_j is the average number of observations of teachers. In general, the formula shows that reliability always increases as the number of observations increases. But, when variance among teachers (τ) is large, and variance across occasions (σ^2) is small, only a few occasions of measurement are needed to discriminate reliably among teachers. Alternatively, as variance among teachers becomes smaller and/or variance across occasions increases, more observations will be needed to discriminate reliably among teachers. An important point is that if researchers have data on teachers' time allocations at multiple time points, and if they conduct the simple variance decomposition just described, they can simply plug different values of n_j into the formula just above to see how many observations they might need in future studies to achieve some desired level of reliability.

Although we illustrated this point with a two-level HLM, similar analyses can be conducted with more complex models, say HLMs with three or more levels, or nonlinear HLMs where outcomes are dichotomous, count, or ordinal variables (for examples, see Raudenbush & Bryk, 2002, Chapter 10). In fact, we have conducted many such analyses in the course of our work (for one example, see Rowan, Camburn, & Correnti, 2004), and on the basis of these analyses we have reached some general conclusions. In general, we have found that for any given academic year, data from our logs cannot reliably discriminate among patterns of instruction experienced by students within the same classroom. As it turns out, this is not so much a result of inherent flaws in log data but rather occurs because the percentage of variance in instructional variables lying among students within classrooms is always tiny, while the percentage of variance in instruction lying within students over time is always very large. In fact, our data suggest that teachers do not differentiate reading instruction among students, leading to the lack of reliability in estimating differences among students in instruction received.

By contrast, we are able to discriminate patterns of instruction reliably among teachers within the same school, and patterns of instruction across schools. In three-level HLMs, for example, the variance components we get in analyses suggest that our ability to discriminate reliably among teaching practices at the teacher level increases rapidly as the number of logs administered per teacher goes from 1 to about 10, increases more slowly from about 10 to 20 administrations, and then increases very little thereafter. So, collecting about 20 logs per year from teachers seems sufficient if the measurement goal is to discriminate reliably among teachers. Note, however, that the actual reliability obtained with 20 observations will depend on a number of factors. For example, it is very difficult to discriminate reliably among teachers when teaching events are rare, when the practice of interest varies greatly within teachers over time but very little across teachers, and when the dependent measure is unreliably measured (making σ^2 larger). In these cases, maximum reliabilities at about 20 observations can be as low as .60 or .70.[2]

Finally, it is worth noting that a researcher's ability to discriminate reliably among schools in patterns of reading instruction depends not only on the number of logs administered, but also the number of teachers sampled within schools, where increasing the sample of teachers completing logs will markedly improve between-school reliabilities. For example, if we are attempting to estimate teacher-level means in teaching practices at a single grade level in an elementary school, we will typically have only 3–4 teachers, and our school-level parameter estimates will have much lower reliability (.30–.40) than if we look at patterns of teaching across all grade levels, where the presence of 15–20 teachers will produce school-level reliabilities on the order of .70–.80 in most cases. Increasing the number of logs per teacher also will increase the reliability of school-level parameter estimates, but within any sized sample of teachers, increasing the number of logs beyond about 20 has virtually no effect on the reliability of school-level parameter estimates.

Substantive Findings With Log Data

The nested data provided by logs have allowed researchers working on the SII to investigate variations in teaching practice at many different levels of analysis. In this section, we discuss what we have learned about variation in teaching across days of the week and year, about the extent and sources of variation in teaching practice among teachers within the same school, and about school-to-school variation in our sample. The most extensive treatment of these issues using log data from the SII is Correnti (2005).

We begin by illustrating how log data illuminate the daily and yearly rhythms of reading/language arts instruction in U.S. elementary schools. In general, log data from SII show that the frequency of reading/language arts lessons increases at a decelerating rate over the course of the academic year, reflecting a somewhat slow start and then the well-known November–April grind. Moreover, the frequency of lessons varies predictably across the school week. For example, reading/language arts lessons have been found to be less likely on Fridays and on days just before and after holidays. Overall, the logs suggest that when both a student and his or her teacher are present in school, the student has about an 85% chance of having a reading/language arts lesson on a given day, the remaining days being given over to test preparation, field trips, assemblies, and other activities.

The logs show that reading/language arts instruction also varies predictably across grades. In first grade, reading lessons lasted about 90 minutes; the amount of time given to the subject declined as students progressed through the grades, so that by fifth grade, the average reading/language arts lesson lasted only about 65 minutes in most schools. The content covered in reading/language arts and the level of cognitive demand of lessons also varied across grades. First-grade teachers typically devoted about 40% of their lessons to word analysis, but this dropped to about 20% in second grade, and then to below 10% in third grade and beyond. Meanwhile, the percentage of lessons devoted to reading comprehension and writing stayed about the same across grade levels—about 50% of lessons for reading comprehension and about 45% of lessons for writing, with the two subjects often taught together on the same day. However, while the amount of time devoted to these subjects stayed the same, the cognitive demand of lessons increased as students progressed through the grades. At higher grades, students tended to read and write longer and more complex texts, work on more demanding reading tasks, and engage in more planning and editing of their writing.

Despite these general trends, one of the most extraordinary findings from the SII was the large variation that exists in teaching practice—even among teachers working in the same school and teaching at the same grade. In first grade, for example, where there is nearly universal agreement among reading experts that a heavy focus should be placed on the teaching of word analysis skills, our analytic models suggest that it would be very common to find two first-grade teachers in the same school, one of whom focused on word analysis skills about one day a week and another who focused on this topic 4 days a week. Similarly large variations in teaching practice would be found across all content areas, with teachers in the same school at the same grade often varying by as much as 3–4 days a week in the percentages of lessons devoted to teaching reading and writing. Even more striking, we have found that very little of this variation is due to the average achievement levels of students in a classroom, or to variations in ethnic or socioeconomic composition, although there is a slight tendency for teachers with higher percentages of students with behavior problems to be less academically focused. Moreover, variables indexing teachers' professional preparation (e.g., professional degrees, number of courses in different subjects, years of experience, pedagogical knowledge) have only tiny effects on teaching practices. In many ways, this extreme variability in teaching signals that schools remain "loosely coupled" organizations where teachers have considerable autonomy and function largely as curriculum brokers (Meyer & Rowan, 1978; Porter, 1989).

There are nevertheless some hopeful findings in our studies of teaching. The SII was designed as a quasi-experiment that included groups of schools participating in three very different instructional reform programs, as well as a set of comparison schools not participating in these programs. One of the most striking findings of the study to date has been the extraordinarily large effects two of these reform programs had on the instruction occurring in schools. One of these programs, known as America's Choice (AC), was designed to foster a "literature-based" teaching regime that focused on writing as a means of improving students' reading comprehension. Analyses conducted by Correnti (2005) showed that teachers in AC schools were far more likely to engage in this form of instruction than teachers in comparison schools, the odds ratio being about 4 (for AC vs. comparison schools) for the likelihood that on any given day, a reading comprehension lesson would also

cover writing, and odds ratios ranging from 1.4 to 2.9 for other relevant indicators of this form of instruction. Similarly, the Success for All (SFA) program
was designed to foster "skill-based" reading instruction, that is, reading lessons
focused largely on basic reading comprehension skills. Analyses conducted by
Correnti (2005) show that teachers in SFA schools were far more likely to
engage in this form of instruction than were teachers in comparison schools,
the odds ratios ranging from 4.4 to 1.4 for SFA versus comparison schools on
items indexing this form of instruction. Finally, in analyses not yet published,
we are finding that these different forms of instruction produce gains in
students' measured reading comprehension, with skill-based reading instruction working better at the early grades (Rowan, Raudenbush, Correnti,
Schilling, & Johnson, 2005), and literature-based instruction working better at
later grades (Correnti, Rowan, & Camburn, 2003).

Conclusion

Overall, we have found that logs can be a cost-effective, reliable, valid way to
measure instruction and examine the causal effects of instruction on student
learning. Although the use of logs is more expensive than gathering data from
annual questionnaires, our discussion suggests that log data are far more trustworthy than annual questionnaire data. Moreover, our discussion suggests that
for many types of items—especially items measuring coarse-grained features of
instruction that occur frequently—logs can provide data that is nearly equivalent to what would be obtained by sending trained observers into classrooms.
The data presented here further suggest that for most study purposes, administration of somewhere around 20 logs (evenly spaced over the academic year)
should allow researchers to discriminate instructional practices reliably in the
area of reading/language arts across teachers and schools. Thus, using logs to
gather data on instruction is a far less expensive way to gather adequately sized
samples of reading instruction in large-scale studies as compared to the use of
observations. Finally, our analyses suggest that log data have strong construct
validity, as shown by the effects of intervention programs on teaching, and by
the effects of different kinds of teaching regimes on student learning. As a result,
we believe that logs are a viable method of data collection in large-scale research
on teaching and that the use of logs should be expanded in the future.

Notes

1. For a description of the aims and methods of this study, see http://www
.sii.soe.umich.edu.

2. In fact, we have found that more than 20 logs will be needed in the domain of mathematics instruction, largely because many teaching events in this domain are rare, and because there is a great deal of day-to-day variation in mathematics teaching. Moreover, even in data from the Study of Instructional Improvement, we often obtain reliabilities for teacher means in mathematics instruction well below the .70 mark discussed above.

Acknowledgment

The research reported here was supported by grants from the U.S. Department of Education to the Consortium for Policy Research in Education (CPRE) at the University of Pennsylvania (Grant No. OERI-R308A60003); the Center for the Study of Teaching and Policy at the University of Washington (Grant No. OERI-R308B70003); the National Science Foundation's Interagency Educational Research Initiative (Grants No. REC-9979863 & REC-0129421); the Atlantic Philanthropies, USA; and the William and Flora Hewlett Foundation.

References

Brophy, J. E., & Good, T. (1986). Teacher behavior and student achievement. In M. C. Wittrock (Ed.), *Handbook of research on teaching* (3rd ed., pp. 328–375). New York: Macmillan.

Burstein, L., McDonnell, L., Van Winkle, J., Ormseth, T., Mirocha, J., & Guiton, G. (1995). *Validating national curriculum indicators.* Santa Monica, CA: RAND.

Camburn, E., & Barnes, C. A. (2004). Assessing the validity of a language arts instruction log through triangulation. *Elementary School Journal, 105*(1), 49–74.

Camburn, E., & Han, S. W. (2006*). Factors affecting the validity of teachers' reports of instructional practice on annual surveys.* Madison: Wisconsin Center for Education Research.

Correnti, R. J. (2005). *Literacy instruction in CSR schools: Consequences of design specification on teacher practice.* Unpublished doctoral dissertation, University of Michigan.

Correnti, R. J., Rowan B., & Camburn, E. (2003, April). *Variation in 3rd grade literacy instruction and its relationship to student achievement among schools participating in Comprehensive School Reforms.* Paper presented at the annual meeting of the American Educational Research Association, Chicago.

Embretson, S. E., & Reise, S. P. (2000). *Item response theory for psychologists.* Mahwah, NJ: Lawrence Erlbaum.

Groves, R. M. (1989). Research on survey data quality. *Public Opinion Quarterly, 51,* part 2, S156–S172.

Hiebert, J., Stigler, J. W., Jacobs, J. K., Givvin, K. B., Garnier, H., Smith, M., et al. (2005). Mathematics teaching in the United States today (and tomorrow): Results from the TIMSS 1999 Video Study. *Educational Evaluation and Policy Analysis, 27*(2), 111–132.

Hoppe, M., Gillmore, M., Valadez, D., Civic, D., Hartway, J., & Morrison, D. (2000). The relative costs and benefits of telephone interviews versus self-administered diaries for daily data collection. *Evaluation Review, 24*(1), 102–116.

Jackson, P. W. (1990). *Life in classrooms*. New York: Teachers College Press.

Leigh, B. (2000). Using daily reports to measure drinking and drinking patterns. *Journal of Substance Abuse, 12*, 51–65.

Leigh, B., Gillmore, M., & Morrison, D. (1998). Comparison of diary and retrospective measures for recording alcohol consumption and sexual activity. *Journal of Clinical Epidemiology, 51*(2), 119–127.

Mayer, D. (1999). Measuring instructional practice: Can policymakers trust survey data? *Educational Evaluation and Policy Analysis, 21*(1), 29–45.

Meyer, J. W., & Rowan, B. (1978). The structure of educational organizations. In M. W. Meyer and Associates, *Organizations and environments*. San Francisco: Jossey-Bass.

Mullens, J. E., & Gayler, K. (1999). *Measuring classroom instructional processes: Using survey and case study field test results to improve item construction* (Working Paper No. 1999–08). Washington, DC: U.S. Department of Education, National Center for Education Statistics.

Porter, A. C. (1989). A curriculum out of balance: The case of elementary school mathematics. *Educational Researcher, 18*(5), 9–15.

Roth, J. R., Brooks-Gunn, J., & Linver, M. R. (2003). What happens during the school day? Time diaries from a national sample of teachers. *Teachers College Record, 105*(3), 317–343.

Raudenbush, S. W., & Bryk, A. S. (2002). *Hierarchical linear models: Applications and data analysis methods*. Thousand Oaks, CA: Sage.

Rogosa, D., Floden, R., & Willet, J. B. (1984). Assessing the stability of teacher behavior. *Journal of Educational Psychology, 76*(6), 1000–1027.

Rowan, B., Camburn, E., & Correnti, R. (2004). Using teacher logs to measure the enacted curriculum in large-scale surveys: Insights from the Study of Instructional Improvement. *Elementary School Journal, 105*, 75–102.

Rowan, B., Correnti, R., & Miller, R. (2002). What large-scale, survey research tells us about teacher effects on student achievement: Insights from the *Prospects* Study of Elementary Schools. *Teachers College Record, 104*(8), 1525–1567.

Rowan, B., Harrison, D. M., & Hayes, A. (2004). Using instructional logs to study mathematics curriculum and teaching in the early grades. *Elementary School Journal, 105*, 103–127.

Rowan, B., Raudenbush, S. W., Correnti, R., Schilling, S. G., & Johnson, C. (2005, May). *Studying "balance" in balanced literacy instruction: How different mixes of word analysis and text comprehension instruction affect first grade students' reading achievement*. Paper prepared for research seminar on learning from longitudinal data, National Center for Education Statistics.

Smithson, J., & Porter, A. (1994). *Measuring classroom practice: Lessons learned from efforts to describe the enacted curriculum—The Reform Up Close Study* (CPRE Research Report Series, No. 31). Madison: Wisconsin Center for Educational Research.

11

Reports of Life Events by Individuals at High Risk for Violence

Jennifer Roberts and Edward P. Mulvey

Introduction

Life events calendars (LECs) are fast becoming a regularly used and recognized method for data collection in the social sciences. Although differing in specific procedures depending on the researcher, the general approach involves asking an individual to reconstruct activities and events in specific realms of life (e.g., romance, employment) over a bounded recall period by making reference to a calendar of key events and other activities during that period (see, e.g., Horney, 2001). While the LEC approach has been used most broadly in research on life transitions, it is becoming increasingly popular in studies of antisocial behavior and developmental psychopathology (see, e.g., Caspi, Elder, & Bem, 1987; Horney, Osgood, & Marshall, 1995; LeBlanc & Loeber, 1998; Nagin, Farrington, & Moffitt, 1995). Most of the studies examining the efficacy of the LEC for providing accurate recall, however, have been done with normative, community-based samples (Belli, Shay, & Stafford, 2001; Caspi & Amell, 1994; Caspi et al., 1987; Freedman, Thornton, Camburn, Alwin, & Young-DeMarco, 1988).

The LEC is attractive for both theoretical and practical reasons. The approach has firm roots in the science of how people remember events and life situations (Belli, 1998; Bradburn, Rips, & Shevell, 1987), and capitalizes on these processes to generate accounts of past events. On a more practical level, it provides researchers with a richer set of data points. Instead of simply getting a summary measure of life changes over an extended recall period, the LEC places these changes at specific points in time. This richer set of ordered observations opens up the possibility of examining sequences of events, providing a much richer picture of potential causal mechanisms within individuals (Fals-Stewart, 2003; Mulvey et al., 2006).

The broader use of LECs to investigate antisocial behaviors with individuals who live generally disordered lifestyles (e.g., mentally ill, criminal populations) raises questions about the possible limits of this approach. The accuracy of the information obtained using the LEC approach is determined by an interaction of the capacities of the research participant, the situational characteristics of the interview, and the types of life changes being investigated. Each of these becomes important to consider for its potential effects when doing research on antisocial activities.

Obviously, there is limited value in having LEC information from a research participant with clearly impaired capacities to provide a cogent account about the sequential nature of past events (e.g., a person with brain damage, a child with developmentally delayed ability to construct narrative accounts), even though individuals like this may be able to provide adequate informed consent to participate in the research study. There are, however, subtler cases where the capacities of research participants, especially those likely to be involved in antisocial lifestyles, may distort the type of data obtained. Young adults with persistent offending careers and violent histories or individuals who were severely abused as children, for instance, may have subtle neurological deficits and/or personality characteristics that make accounts of past events less accurate regarding intentions and actions of others (Dodge & Rabiner, 2004; Lewis & Yeager, 2000; Moffitt, 1993). The extent of these more subtle distortions of capacity on recall, however, is a largely unexplored area.

The situational characteristics of the interview also play a role in determining the accuracy of the information obtained using the LEC approach. For example, the amount of time that has elapsed between the events being recalled and the interview can affect the ability to sequence events accurately, most often producing "telescoping," where particular types of events are placed closer in time than when they actually occurred. In addition, the current behavioral state of the research participant at the time of the interview can bias recall. Individuals who are either intoxicated at the time of the interview (Allen, 2004; Sobell & Sobell, 1990) or who are currently in a period of heavy drinking in their lives have been shown to overestimate the level or pattern of previous drinking (Collins, Graham, Hansen, & Johnson, 1985; Czarnecki, Russell, Cooper, & Salter, 1990; Lemmens, 1998).

The type of life change or event investigated can also have a notable influence on the accuracy of recall. The LEC approach is considered most accurate when it asks about changes in extended life circumstances, such as school enrollment or living situation, since these can often be tracked effectively by referring to other events in a person's life or to a particular point in the recall period (Belli, 1998; Caspi et al., 1996). Changes of this type alter the broader context of an individual's life and are more far-reaching in their impact on daily routines. Oftentimes, though, involvement in more general events (e.g., heavy drinking periods) are harder to recall, since the definitional and event-related boundaries of these periods are often more ambiguous. Without some memorable event, like a divorce, for example, it might be difficult for individuals to determine very accurately whether they had been drinking heavily in a particular month.

Recalling specific events and placing them in a LEC calendar often presents particular problems. Providing specific dates of events is often a difficult task for research participants, even in the context of a LEC interview. Events with very high salience that portend a shift in lifestyle (e.g., an alcoholic's first AA meeting) may be recalled with impressive accuracy; but other, less salient, more frequent events, even if they are of considerable interest to the researcher (e.g., domestic disputes), may not be recalled with equally impressive accuracy.

This chapter reports on the current state of our ongoing effort to explore the limits of the LEC method for obtaining data from individuals with histories of substance use, violence, and involvement with the mental health system. The sample of individuals examined in this study were originally interviewed weekly for 6 months about changes in various aspects of their lives as part of a study regarding the precursors to violence for persons involved with the mental health system. After their involvement with this original study, these individuals were relocated and reinterviewed using a LEC approach about life changes, starting with the period covered by the initial set of weekly interviews through the LEC interview date (i.e., 12 to 51 months total recall). Our previous work has examined the degree of concordance regarding reports of violence (discussed briefly below; see Roberts, Mulvey, Horney, Lewis, & Arter, 2005, for a more thorough discussion). The present study explores the concordance of reports regarding several other types of life changes (i.e., drinking, hospitalizations, living arrangements). The different topics examined represent different levels of event specificity, thus providing a view of the potential for LEC calendars to obtain certain types of recalled information within a sample of individuals with considerable clinical and policy interest.

Methodology

The sample for the current study was initially identified in the emergency room at Western Psychiatric Institute and Clinic (WPIC) for a study that involved weekly interviews within the community for 6 months ("Intensive Follow-Up of Violent Patients," funded by the National Institute of Mental Health [NIMH]; Edward Mulvey, Ph.D., and Charles W. Lidz, Ph.D., co-principal investigators; referred to as the "NIMH study" throughout). The sampling strategy identified individuals who were likely to be involved in repeated violence over the 6 months following their appearance in a psychiatric emergency room. The screening criteria for eligibility were stringent, with only 3% of those appearing for evaluation in the emergency room qualifying for participation (Skeem, Mulvey, Lidz, Gardner, & Schubert, 2002). Subjects were specifically recruited based upon a recent involvement in violence, high recent drinking and/or drug use, a young age (14–30 years old), and a high score (7 or greater) on the hostility scale of the Brief Symptom Inventory (Derogatis & Melisaratos, 1983). Individuals with moderate to profound mental retardation or a thought disorder were purposely excluded from the NIMH sample. Using diagnostic information in the charts, most of the NIMH subjects would be seen as having an affective disorder (76%), with almost half also having a co-occurring Axis I and substance abuse disorder (45%). For this NIMH study, 92% of the possible weekly interviews with subjects were completed, and 51% of the enrolled subjects completed 25 or 26 of their possible 26 interviews. Details of the approach taken in this study and the success of efforts to recruit and retain subjects are presented in Schubert, Mulvey, Lidz, Gardner, and Skeem (2005).

The data from the NIMH study have been useful for testing the association between changes in particular behaviors (e.g., drinking, symptoms) and the occurrence of violence. So far, analyses of these data have shown "bursts" of substance using and violent days in the lives of these individuals, a short-term association between alcohol use and violence, and a relationship between symptoms of hostility and violence (see Mulvey et al., 2006; Skeem et al., 2006). These findings have implications for focusing intervention efforts with individuals in the mental health system who are repeatedly involved in violent incidents.

For the current project using the LEC in a follow-up interview, we successfully recruited and interviewed 75 of the original 132 subjects for a LEC interview that was timed anywhere from 12 to 51 months following enrollment in the NIMH project. The majority of the LEC subjects were female (55%) and African American (53%), with the average subject being 23.5 years old at the time of the interview. We compared the LEC sample against those NIMH subjects who were not interviewed and found no statistically significant differences in diagnosis or demographics. The only statistically significant difference was the number of prior hospitalizations, with the LEC sample having more (LEC subjects, mean = 2.0; not interviewed, mean = 1.29).

Care was taken to ensure that the LEC sample was relatively evenly split in terms of the length of time from their original interview in the NIMH study: 12 to 24 months before (n = 22, 29.3%), more than 24 to 26 months before

($n = 25, 33.3\%$), and more than 36 months before ($n = 28, 37.3\%$). Due to time and resource constraints, we were not able to recruit all of the original subjects. However, every subject who was asked to participate in the LEC interview agreed to take part. Each subject provided informed consent. The subjects were told that the purpose of the interview was to see how well they could recall information they initially provided in the NIMH study. Subjects were allowed to choose the most comfortable location for the interview, and most (88%) were done in the subject's home.

LEC INTERVIEW METHODS

A paper calendar was placed in front of each of the subjects and numbered 1 through X (i.e., the full month prior to the current LEC interview). Month 1 was determined based upon the date of the subject's first NIMH interview. Thus the first 6 months on the LEC calendar corresponded to the 6 months of involvement with the original NIMH study. The paper calendar served as a visual cue to help structure recall for the subjects. On the left-hand side of the paper calendar were years with multiple dimensions listed under each year (e.g., where living, employment, violence). Across the top of the calendar were the names of each month. We also included a space in each month for the month number. The actual data were entered onto both the paper calendar and into a laptop computer by the interviewer during the session. Subjects were instructed to focus on the numbered months (referred to below as the calendar period) when answering questions. The questions in the life event calendar study were identical to those in the NIMH study except that the time unit was one month versus one week.

Before beginning the formal survey, the interviewer helped the subjects lay out important dates on the calendar (e.g., birthdays, holidays, any other major memorable event). We then started the structured interview with questions about extended events, inquiring about living arrangements, periods of incarceration, hospitalizations, marriages/intimate relationships, children/pregnancies, employment, and schooling during the calendar period. For the incarceration, hospitalization, pregnancy, and intimate partner events, respondents were asked global questions about the domain (e.g., "Was there any time during the calendar period that you were incarcerated?"). If they answered yes, the subjects then identified relevant months on the calendar. The remaining extended events were queried by first asking about the last month (month X) on the calendar (e.g., "In this last month, were you employed?"). The interviewer asked follow-up questions to determine months in which the event was different (e.g., not employed). This information about broad life changes provided context for the more general and specific events questions that followed.

We inquired about several general events, including routine activities (e.g., "In the last calendar month, how often did you go to bars, clubs, or pool halls?"), stressful periods, treatment involvement, and substance use (alcohol and drugs). The respondent was asked to characterize the occurrence of these behaviors at the monthly level by indicating times during the recall period when the pattern changed. In addition, we asked about several specific events, including arrests (e.g., "Were you arrested at any time during the calendar period?") and violence. For the violence questions we used a series of behavioral screening questions (e.g., "Were you involved in any situations where you threw an object, like a rock or a bottle, at someone else?"). If respondents answered yes to any of these questions, we then had them identify the months in which these events took place and the frequency of these events in each month.

Findings

To examine the utility of the LEC for aiding recall, we compared results from the LEC interview with those from the NIMH study. We believe the NIMH data provide an excellent source of comparison for our study for a number of reasons. First, the data were collected weekly, which minimized the likelihood of memory decay. Second, as stated above, the NIMH data are relatively complete. Third, we used a trained, bachelor's-level interviewer who had also worked on the NIMH study, for the current LEC study. Finally, the NIMH data provide recall about a number of events at differing levels of specificity. As a result, we can examine recall for five different events, ranging from the most specific type of recall (regarding involvement in violent incidents) to the recall of extended states (living arrangements).

Our analysis is limited to full months of data from the LEC study. Thus, the average subject had 5 full months of data in these analyses. In order to make the weekly NIMH data comparable to the monthly LEC data, the weekly accounts were aggregated up to the monthly level. We primarily used *kappa* statistics (or weighted *kappa* when appropriate) to examine the degree of concordance between the two methods. While this approach has been used successfully in the past in similar types of studies (Belli et al., 2001), this study is different because each subject supplies multiple months of data. *Kappa* statistics, however, assume that observations are independent, and analyses examining "person-months" in this chapter therefore violate this assumption. In these analyses, we present a global *kappa* statistic, realizing that it is not a strict measure of concordance, and then examine the concordance for each month independently (in which instance each person provides only a single observation). This allows us to present concordance in terms of the range of *kappa* values for the person-months (typically five values).

VIOLENCE

The current analyses build on the work we have done examining the degree of concordance between the LEC approach and the original NIMH study for specific violent events. While the current study examines more general and extended events, we feel a discussion of our previous results concerning the recall of violent events is in order (these results are reported in more detail in Roberts et al., 2005). This original work sets the stage and provides a context for the further analyses reported in this chapter.

For purposes of this research (and the original NIMH study), we characterized violent events as being serious or minor, in accord with previous research regarding self-reported violence of individuals with mental illness (Monahan et al., 2001; Mulvey et al., 2006). Serious violence was defined as an incident that resulted in visible injury to either party, sexual assault, or that involved a threat made with a weapon in hand. Minor violence was defined as any less serious incident involving a physical action (i.e., laying hands on another person) that fell below this threshold for serious violence. However, we specifically excluded incidents of child discipline, verbal threats alone, and incidents where our respondent was clearly the victim (e.g., the respondent was mugged). We wanted to examine the concordance of recall according to the timing of the violent events (the month in which they occurred) and the type of violent event (serious, minor, any).

We used the same series of screening questions when asking about violence in the LEC study as we did for the NIMH study. The screen lists a number of acts of violence that the respondent may have been involved in during the calendar period. If the research participant assents to a particular question, he or she is then asked to provide details about the incident, identify the month in which it took place, and the frequency with which it occurred (in that month).

We started our analysis broadly by examining whether subjects could identify a particular month as having any violent event (serious or minor). Table 11.1 shows these results. A comparison of the two methods reveals that slightly more than half of the 380 person-months (58.9%, $n = 224$ months) were reported identically. Viewing the off diagonals indicates that most of the disagreement came from underreporting of violence using the LEC approach. When examining serious violence, we did find that a greater percentage of person-months (76.1% [(276+12)/378]) were identically reported as having/not having a serious violent incident. However, there were still a substantial number of person-months ($n = 75$) that were categorized as a serious violence month in the NIMH study but not in the LEC study. The concordance for the minor violence was worse with 112 person-months characterized as having minor violence in the NIMH study but not in the LEC study.

Table 11.1 Summary of Findings for Concordance of NIMH Method and LEC

Dimension	Number	Percentage Agreement	Percentage Underreporting[a]	Percentage Overreporting[b]	Kappa Statistic	Range of Kappas
Violence						
Month by month						
• Any	380	58.95	37.37	3.68	.12	−.24 to .11
• Serious	378	76.19	19.84	3.97	.11	−08 to .22
• Minor	378	67.72	29.63	2.65	.02	−.10 to .18
Case						
• Any	75	50.67	49.33	0.00	.17	N/A
• Serious	75	66.67	29.33	0.00	.36	N/A
• Minor	75	33.33	66.67	4.00	.07	N/A
Drinking						
Month by month	350	63.14	17.14	19.71	.21	.12 to .32
Hospitalizations						
Month by month	2,341	91.71	6.53	1.75	.23	−.05 to .65
Case	75	62.67	33.33	4.00	.51*	N/A
Residence						
Month by month	369	86.99	7.86	5.15	.263	.12 to .41
Case	75	81.33	13.33	5.34	.392	N/A

a. Underreporting is defined according to the number of subjects who would have been classified as having done something in a given month (e.g., committed violence, drank alcohol) with the NIMH or WPIC data but not with the LEC data.

b. Overreporting is conversely defined according to the percentage of subjects who would have been classified as not having done something in a given month (e.g., committed violence, drank alcohol) with the NIMH or WPIC data but did do something according to the LEC data.

*Weighted *kappa* statistic.

We also examined whether a case (person) could be characterized as being violent/not violent using the two methods (i.e., did they report any violent incident during the overlapping 5-month period). We again started broadly by examining reports of any violence during the calendar period. This analysis shows that only 38 of the 75 subjects would have been characterized identically between the two methods (10 no violence reported, 28 violence reported). The remaining cases ($n = 37$) would have been characterized as violent using the NIMH weekly approach but not violent using the LEC approach. For minor violence only 25 of the 75 cases would have been identified identically between the two methods. The remaining 50 cases would have been classified as having minor violence using the NIMH approach but not having minor violence using the LEC approach. We did, however, see an improvement when looking at classification for serious violence. That is, 50 of the 75 cases would have been identically classified between the two methods, with 22 of the remaining 25 cases classified as having serious violence with the NIMH approach but not having serious violence with the LEC approach.

DRINKING

While the results from the violence data were not promising, we were uncertain whether this was due to the type of data being collected (specific event), the unique nature of our sample (person factor), or some combination of the two. In order to investigate this exact issue more fully, we next examined patterns of drinking during the calendar period. This was a challenge with this sample, given that one of the screening criteria for the NIMH study involved a recent history of heavy drinking or drug use. To accommodate to this reality, we instructed our interviewer to schedule interviews at times when the subject was more likely to be sober and to avoid any interviews with intoxicated subjects. While we believe subjects were sober at the time of the interviews, past research has found that people with alcohol addiction can present as sober when they are not (Sobell & Sobell, 1990).

The drinking questions were collected to provide a quantity–frequency measure. Subjects were first asked to identify whether they had drunk any alcohol in a given month. For the months noted as "drinking months," the subjects were asked to estimate the number of times they drank (frequency) during that month and the number of drinks they typically consumed when they did drink (quantity).

Our first analysis examines a broad measure of drinking; that is, whether the month can be characterized as a "drinking" or "not drinking" month. We excluded cases that had 8 or more days of missing data in the NIMH data. These results are presented in Table 11.1, which shows that 63.1% of the person-months (221/350) were reported identically between the two methods. The remaining 36.9% of the months were almost evenly split between under- and overreporting using the LEC method. The *kappa* statistic of .21 indicates a poor degree of concordance between the two methods. The *kappa* statistics for each month ranged from .12 to .32.

As mentioned previously, prior research has found that a subject's current level of drinking can influence recall of prior drinking (Collins et al., 1985; Czarnecki et al., 1990; Lemmens, 1998). As a result, we calculated a quantity × frequency (QF) measure for the most recent month in the LEC data and looked for the effect of this value on reporting. The QF measure was highly skewed, however, so we broke the subjects into tertiles on this measure to retain interpretability. We compared this QF tertile regarding recent drinking status against a QF tertile for the overlapping window period to determine the type of bias that might be introduced using the two different methods (i.e., those who over-reported their drinking using the LEC method compared to the NIMH method, those who accurately reported their drinking using the LEC method, and those who underreported their drinking using the LEC method). Those subjects who had the lowest QF rating in the last month were more likely to underreport their earlier drinking while those with the highest QF rating in the last month were more likely to overreport their earlier drinking. The difference however, was only marginally statistically significant ($\chi^2 = 8.91$; $p = .06$).

HOSPITALIZATION

Given the nature of our sample, it was appropriate to analyze the accuracy with which subjects reported mental health hospitalizations. We were able to obtain intake records from WPIC to determine which months and how many days in each month a person was hospitalized at this facility. These records are the same as those used for billing purposes, and as such, provide a valuable reference for the LEC data. For these analyses, we counted only overnight visits (a stay of at least one night) and we examined only stays in WPIC. Since we were examining stays that lasted at least one night, we considered this a general event, but not an extended change of life situation or a specific event. It should be noted, though, that the process itself of being admitted to a hospital could be viewed as a specific event often associated with a certain set of interpersonal interactions. What we were examining here, however, was whether someone recalled a series of events, from admission to discharge, that extended over a reasonably long time period.

We first examined whether a particular person-month could be classified as being a hospitalized/not hospitalized month on the LEC calendar and the hospital records (see Table 11.1). Since we were using hospital records for the entire period covered by the LEC calendar, we were able to examine concor-dance across the subject's entire calendar (approximately 12 to 51 months). Overwhelmingly, most of the person-months were reported identically between the two methods (91.7%). However, this is largely attributable to the fact that most person-months did not have a hospitalization. What is interesting to note is that only 36 of the "hospitalized" months were reported identically between the two methods. Conversely, 153 months were "hospitalized" months according to the WPIC records but "not hospitalized" according to the LEC data. In addition, 41 months were considered as "hospitalized" for the LEC study but "not hospitalized" in the WPIC records. The resulting *kappa* statistic of .23 indicates a poor degree of concordance between the two methods. *Kappas* for the individual months varied from –.0515 to .6474.

We also examined how accurately each subject reported the total number of months he or she was hospitalized for at least one night using the LEC. For this analysis, each subject was categorized as being hospitalized zero months, 1–2 months, or 3 or more months for both methods. There is an appreciable increase in accuracy of reporting when the data are examined in this way. Forty-seven of the 75 subjects (62.7%) reported the same total number of months hospitalized between the two methods. However, we also see underreporting using the LEC approach again, with 14 subjects having hospitalization months according to the WPIC data but not according to the LEC data. The resulting *kappa* statistic of .51 is considerably better. Similarly, we conducted a simple difference of means test to determine the amount of difference between the two methods regarding the number of months hospitalized for at least one night. According to the WPIC records, the average subject was hospitalized in 2.52 months, while in the LEC study, the average subject was hospitalized in 1.03 months ($t = 5.26$; $p < .001$).

LIVING ARRANGEMENTS

Our final analysis examines recall of an extended event. Prior research examining the validity of the LEC has found a substantial amount of agreement between weekly reports of living arrangements and those given during an LEC interview 3 years later (Caspi & Amell, 1994). Given the transient nature of our sample, it would be nearly impossible to pinpoint an exact location where our subjects had been at in any given month. It was quite common for our subjects to have a month where they were living with friends, living with a relative, and living on the streets. In order to account for this, we decided to examine the accuracy with which this sample could remember living in the community versus not living in the community.

To make the distinction, we operationalized "living in the community" as any time the subjects were living in a home (theirs or someone else's), shelter, supervised living arrangement or halfway house, cooperative apartment, or boarding/rooming house. "Not in the community" was operationalized as residing inpatient at a psychiatric hospital, nursing/rest home, or being incarcerated (jail). During the LEC interview, we instructed the subjects to categorize a month according to where they had lived 2 weeks or more. We made the NIMH data comparable by collapsing weekly reports to the corresponding monthly intervals.

Table 11.1 also shows the results of this analysis. Overwhelmingly, 87% of the subjects reported the months identically between the two methods [(309+12)/369]. This is again, however, largely driven by the fact that the bulk of the person-months were spent in the community. Also, there appeared to be underreporting of events associated with the LEC method. There were 41 months that were reported as being "not in the community" according to the NIMH data. However, 29 of these months were reported as being "in the community" in the LEC study. The resulting *kappa* statistic of .26 indicates a poor degree of concordance between these two methods. In addition to the month-by-month analysis, we also examined the cases over the entire reference period. If the respondents reported any month as being "not in the community," then the case was coded accordingly. Sixty-four of the 75 cases (81.33%) were coded identically between the LEC and NIMH approaches. This was again largely driven by the fact that most of the respondents had not spent any time out of the community during the window period. Like the previous analysis, most of the cases that were reported as being "not in the community" in the NIMH study were reported as being "in the community" in the LEC study (10 out of 17 cases).

Discussion

In the current study we were primarily concerned with understanding how the nature of the event (i.e., specific, general, extended) affected the accuracy of recall using two different methods covering the same time period. There are clearly some differences in how the individuals in this sample recalled these types of events. At the same time, though, the current study design does not provide totally clean estimates of the power of the effect of recalling different types of events. The screening criteria used to select individuals into the study could also have influenced research participants' abilities to recall different events. Because of this confabulation of sample characteristics and recall method, it is impossible to determine with clear certainty whether the observed levels of accuracy are the result of the methods tested or the sample used. Based on the results of this investigation, though, it seems clear that one task for the future is to find better ways to elicit information from special populations.

We fully expected to, and did, find different degrees of recall depending on the type of event examined. We found that the LEC method produced a significant amount of underreporting of violence in this sample compared to the NIMH method. We did find improvement in recall when inquiring about major violence (compared to minor violence), but the level of recall concordance was still unimpressive. While researchers typically think about specific, seemingly dramatic, events as being potentially more salient to subjects, this may not always be the case. In this sample, for example, the subjects reported 7.2 violent incidents on average over a 6-month period during the original

NIMH study (Skeem et al., 2002). This sample may be involved in violence to an extent that recalling one particular event is actually difficult. Simply put, what is salient to one population may not be to another.

To examine recall of general events, we analyzed data on drinking patterns and hospitalizations. Regarding drinking patterns, we found evidence of both under- and overreporting using the LEC method. For example, a substantial number of person-months were incorrectly identified as being "drinking/not drinking" by our subjects. The incorrect reporting fell almost evenly between over- and underreporting. In addition, our examination of the recall of the quantity and frequency of drinking showed a slight degree of overreporting using the LEC method. In order to examine this over- and underreporting issue, we analyzed how recent drinking affects recall of prior drinking, with some indication that recent drinking status did affect reporting. These results failed to achieve statistical significance ($p = .06$), but this may be an issue of statistical power.

The hospitalization findings were not much better. Subjects poorly recalled whether they were hospitalized for at least one night in a given month using the LEC method compared to the actual hospital records. This recall was drastically improved, however, when examining the total number of months that would be classified as a "hospitalization month" for each subject. Again, though, this level of concordance was not too impressive.

Our final set of analyses examined an extended event. We fully expected that subjects would be able to recall whether they had resided in the community (or not) for the majority of a particular month with a rather high degree of consistency. While the percentage agreement for the person-months was high, the *kappa* statistic was not. Prior research found that subjects' recall of living arrangements was excellent (Caspi & Amell, 1994). Sample differences likely explain at least part of the discrepancy in results. The research participants in the Caspi and Amell study were from a community sample, and the research participants in the current study were selected from an atypical group (individuals coming to a psychiatric emergency room). Our subjects' lives are markedly chaotic, with frequent moves around the community, often bouncing from one living arrangement to another. These moves are interspersed with occasional visits to mental health facilities or jails. While remembering extended events such as residence should be a relatively easy recall task for most research subjects, it may be more arduous for a sample like ours. Overall, we did see some improvement in concordance when research participants recalled general and extended events compared to specific events, despite the low level of concordance on the whole.

We believe that these generally low levels of concordance are the result of the nature of the sample, the nature of the events we inquired about, and potential telescoping. The individuals studied here live chaotic lives, marked by fairly regular substance use, bouts with symptoms of mental illness, and violence. Their life experiences may make consistent recall an extremely difficult task. Similarly, most of the events we examined in this chapter were factors in subject recruitment. This interaction between subject selection and events studied may have influenced subject recall and should be borne in mind when interpreting the results.

In addition, given that month 1 of our LEC calendar was month 1 of the NIMH study, we cannot rule out that telescoping may have had an effect. If research subjects typically push events into the more recent part of the recall period, then making the recall period of interest the most distant place in the past may stack the deck against people remembering accurately. Also, the start date for the calendar (month 1) was somewhat unconventional in that it did not correspond to the beginning of a calendar year. We have no way to examine this issue accurately with these data, but we cannot rule out the possibility that this influence may have dampened accuracy of recall.

Even in light of these design limitations, our research suggests that event factors do matter, and that person factors also matter a good bit, especially when dealing with those on the fringe of socially acceptable lifestyles. These results also beg the question of how methods might be improved when dealing with samples of this sort. There may be a few ways to achieve this goal.

Future LEC research with these populations should consider modifying the traditional calendar approach to better accommodate the regularities in the lives of these subjects. For example, these research subjects may require more assistance than usual when laying out their calendars for the reference period. It may be important to have at least two contacts with each subject. During the first, researchers could obtain informed consent, potentially gain access to relevant official records (e.g., hospital records, criminal histories) and/or a collateral subject, and leave a paper calendar with the subject to think about or fill in. In the time between the first and second contact, the researcher could consult with a collateral subject or the subject's official records to begin filling in relevant information on the LEC. During this same period, the primary subject could be instructed to think about a certain time period, consult any records, and begin filling in specified domains.

In addition, specifically orienting subjects to periods of related behaviors might be useful. Analyses conducted after the original data collection was completed revealed that violent events, for example, often occur as bursts of activity clustered in time, and that these specific events and other general events (periods of very heavy drinking/drug use) may be related to each other (see Mulvey et al., 2006). If interviewers can help subjects identify periods where they were "out of control," they may be able to gather more fine-grained information on distinct events within this bounded time period. Also, for the current study, we asked subjects to identify different violent acts they had been involved in. It may be that subjects could recall these events more fully if they used a different or additional initial orienting point, such as the co-participant in these violent incidents.

While we cannot definitively comment on the boundaries of the LEC for all antisocial groups, this research does suggest that the LEC does not guarantee accurate recall for all subjects. Indeed, the results here seem to indicate that considerable additional research is needed to understand the usefulness of the LEC with antisocial populations. To refine our methods, we need to know more about how recent involvement in antisocial activities, the demands of the recall situation, and the type of events being examined affect recall accuracy. Only then can we be confident that we are getting accurate data and are presenting accurate conclusions regarding questions of considerable theoretical and practical importance.

Acknowledgment

This study was supported by a grant from the National Consortium on Violence Research, a center funded by the National Science Foundation. The original data collection on this sample was supported by a grant from the National Institute of Mental Health (R01 MH40030-13). We want to thank Carol Schubert for her assistance in data management.

References

Allen, J. (2004). Assessment of alcohol problems: An overview. In J. Allen & V. Wilson (Eds.), *Assessing alcohol problems: A guide for clinicians and researchers* (pp. 1–11). Bethesda, MD: National Institute on Alcohol Abuse and Alcoholism.

Belli, R. F. (1998). The structure of autobiographical memory and the life history calendar: Potential improvements in the quality of retrospective reports in surveys. *Memory, 6,* 383–407.

Belli, R. F., Shay, W. L., & Stafford, F. P. (2001). Event history calendars and question list surveys: A direct comparison of interviewing methods. *Public Opinion Quarterly, 65,* 45–74.

Bradburn, N., Rips, L., & Shevell, S. (1987). Answering autobiographical questions: The impact of memory and inference on surveys. *Science, 236,* 157–161.

Caspi, A., & Amell, J. (1994). *The reliability of life history calendar data* (DPPP Technical Report No. 94–01). University of Wisconsin, Madison.

Caspi, A., Elder, G., & Bem, D. (1987). Moving against the world: Life-course patterns of explosive children. *Developmental Psychology, 23,* 308–313.

Caspi, A., Moffitt, T., Thornton, A., Freedman, D., Amell, J., Harrington, H., et al. (1996). The life-history calendar: A research and clinical assessment method for collecting retrospective event-history data. *International Journal of Methods in Psychiatric Research, 6,* 104–114.

Collins, L., Graham, J., Hansen, W., & Johnson, C. (1985). Agreement between retrospective accounts and earlier reported substance use. *Applied Psychological Measurement, 9,* 301–309.

Czarnecki, D., Russell, M., Cooper, M., & Salter, D. (1990). Five-year reliability of self-reported alcohol consumption. *Journal of Studies on Alcohol, 51,* 68–76.

Derogatis, L., & Melisaratos, N. (1983). The Brief Symptom Inventory: An introductory report. *Psychological Medicine 13,* 595–605.

Dodge, K., & Rabiner, D. (2004). Returning to roots: On social information processing and moral development. *Child Development, 75,* 1003–1008.

Fals-Stewart, W. (2003). The occurrence of partner physical aggression on days of alcohol consumption: A longitudinal diary study. *Journal of Consulting & Clinical Psychology,* 71, 41–52.

Freedman, D., Thornton, A., Camburn, D., Alwin, D., & Young-DeMarco, L. (1988). The life history calendar: A technique for collecting retrospective data. In C. C. Clogg (Ed.), *Sociological methodology* (Vol. 18, pp. 37–68). San Francisco: Jossey-Bass.

Horney, J. (2001). Criminal events and criminal careers: An integrative approach to the study of violence. In R. Meier, L. Kennedy, & V. Sacco (Eds.), *The process and structure of crime: Criminal events and crime analysis.* New Brunswick, NJ: Transaction Publishers.

Horney, J., Osgood, D. W., & Marshall, I. (1995). Criminal careers in the short term: Intra-individual variability in crime and its relation to local life circumstances. *American Sociological Review, 60,* 655–673.

LeBlanc, M., & Loeber, R. (1998). Developmental criminology updated. In M. Tonry (Ed.), *Crime and justice: A review of research* (Vol. 23, pp. 115–199). Chicago: University of Chicago Press.

Lemmens, P. (1998). Measuring lifetime drinking histories. *Alcoholism: Clinical and Experimental Research,* 22, 29s–36s.

Lewis, D., & Yeager, C. (2000). Diagnostic evaluation of the violent child and adolescent. *Child and Adolescent Psychiatric Clinics of North America, 9,* 815–839.

Moffitt, T. (1993). Adolescent-limited and life-course persistent antisocial behavior: A developmental taxonomy. *Psychological Review, 100,* 674–701.

Monahan, J., Steadman, H., Silver, E., Applebaum, P., Robbins, P., Mulvey, E., Roth, L., Grisso, T., & Banks, S. (2001). *Rethinking violence risk assessment: Mental disorder and the law.* New York: Oxford University Press.

Mulvey, E., Odgers, C., Skeem, J., Gardner, W., Schubert, C., & Lidz, C. (2006). Substance use and community violence among high risk psychiatric patients: A test of the relationship at the daily level. *Journal of Consulting and Clinical Psychology, 74,* 743–754.

Nagin, D., Farrington, D., & Moffitt, T. (1995). Life-course trajectories of different types of offenders. *Criminology, 33,* 111–137.

Roberts, J., Mulvey, E., Horney, J., Lewis, J., & Arter, M. (2005). A test of two methods of recall of violent events. *Journal of Quantitative Criminology, 21,* 175–193.

Schubert, C., Mulvey, E., Lidz, C., Gardner, W., & Skeem, J. (2005). Weekly community interviews with high-risk participants: Operational issues. *Journal of Interpersonal Violence, 20,* 632–646.

Skeem, J., Mulvey, E., Lidz, C., Gardner, W., & Schubert, C. (2002). Identifying psychiatric patients at risk for repeated involvement in violence: The next step toward intensive community treatment programs. *International Journal of Forensic Mental Health, 1,* 155–170.

Skeem, J., Schubert, C., Odgers, C., Mulvey, E., Gardner, W., & Lidz, C. (2006). Psychiatric symptoms and community violence among high-risk patients: A test of the relationship at the weekly level. *Journal of Consulting and Clinical Psychology.*

Sobell, L., & Sobell, M. (1990). Self-report issues in alcohol abuse: State of the art and future directions. *Behavioral Assessment, 12,* 77–90.

12

Time Use in the Older Population

Variations by Socioeconomic Status and Health

Michael D. Hurd and Susann Rohwedder

Introduction

This chapter uses time use data that are collected as part of the Health and Retirement Study (HRS), a large general-purpose panel survey that is representative of the U.S. population age 51 and over. Every 2 years the HRS interviews about 20,000 persons about a wide array of topics, covering economic status, physical and mental health, family relations and support, labor market status, and retirement planning.[1] The core HRS interview takes place in even years, such as 1998, 2000, 2002, and so on. In the odd years, beginning in 2001, the Consumption and Activities Mail Survey (CAMS) has been administered biennially to a random subsample of the HRS. CAMS collects recall information on time use and spending by means of a paper-and-pencil questionnaire. Wave 1 and wave 2 of CAMS sampled 5,000 respondents in 5,000 households who participated in the HRS 2000 survey. In a couple, the addressee is chosen at random. The same households are followed over time. The first wave of CAMS generated 3,866 responses; wave 2 received 3,254 responses.[2] The data for the third wave, administered in the fall of 2005, had not yet been released at the time of writing this chapter. Therefore we focus on the first two waves of CAMS.

The design of the time use section aims to produce population estimates of a wide range of activities that can be related to the rich cross-sectional and longitudinal background information collected in the HRS core interview on the same people. In addition, a group of researchers involved in the initial design of the time use section of CAMS was interested in patterns of social interaction at older ages. While one-day diaries might have been the best option to arrive at population estimates of certain activities, a longer reference period for each respondent is needed to capture a sufficiently representative set of activities from individuals' activities that can be related to other individual characteristics of the respondent. Also, to capture social interactions, a one-day snapshot is not sufficient. Diaries covering a week or more are likely to suffer from lack of compliance over such an extended period and yield low data quality. CAMS adopted a standardized, questionnaire-based format, asking respondents to recall how much time they spent on each of 31 activities. The reference period is either "over the *last week*" for activities that people tend to engage in more frequently, like sleeping, house cleaning, or walking; and for less frequent activities, like volunteer work or attending concerts or movies, the reference period is "over the *last month*." The questionnaire being paper and pencil, the respondent can take as much time as needed to retrieve the requested information. This is important, because the question format is unlikely to yield reasonable data quality in face-to-face or telephone interviews, where the presence of the interviewer tends to limit the amount of time respondents will take to reflect upon their answers. The advantage of the standardized format and its particular implementation is that time use data could be collected for a fairly large sample, at limited costs, and also respondent burden is contained at a level that can be accommodated in a general-purpose survey, such as the HRS. All three advantages played an important role in the design of the instrument.

The CAMS survey was somewhat experimental at the outset, but, as we show in this chapter, data quality appears to be good and descriptive statistics by covariates show very plausible patterns. Overall, CAMS appears to have been a success. Combined with the rich information, in cross-section and panel, that is available for the CAMS respondents, the CAMS data provide a unique resource to address a large set of research questions, in particular once the spouse's time use data are added in the 2005 CAMS.

In the next section we discuss the survey design. Following that we present empirical evidence on data quality and then provide descriptive statistics of time use among older populations, illustrating the richness of the HRS data and taking advantage of the large sample size.

Survey Instrument

The CAMS questionnaires were sent out in the fall of the respective survey year (2001, 2003, and 2005) to 5,000 respondents in 5,000 households.[3] The sample for CAMS wave 1 was drawn as a random sample of HRS respondents who participated in HRS 2000. CAMS wave 2 was administered to the same households. The third wave of CAMS included an additional refresher sample drawn from the newly added cohort of 51- to 56-year-old respondents to HRS 2004.

The first part of the questionnaire (Section A) asked about time use of the addressee; the second part (Section B) asked about spending of the household. Even if a household had two HRS respondents (addressee and spouse), time use information was collected from only one of them, that is, the addressee.[4] Figure 12.1 replicates the instructions for the time use section of the questionnaire and an example of the format in which time spent on activities is elicited.[5]

Section A:

In the first part of this questionnaire section, we ask you to estimate how much time you spent doing various activities during the last week. For each activity, please tell us the number of hours you spent doing that activity. If you haven't done that activity at all in the last week, then mark the "0 hours" box to the right. If you spent less than an hour doing an activity, tell us how much of an hour you did spend (such as ¾ or ½).

PLEASE NOTE:

- Sometimes people do more than one activity at a time -- for example, listening to music while preparing a meal. That is, one hour of listening to music while preparing a meal would count as one hour of listening to music and also one hour of preparing meals.
- Similarly, one behavior might represent more than one activity included in the list. For example, e-mailing friends is both using the computer and communicating with friends. Record that time for both of the activities.
- Please include the time you spent traveling to and from an activity when estimating the amount of time spent on that activity.
- We realize that last week might have been unusual, and that your answers may not reflect your typical activity patterns. It is important, however, to report the actual amount of time spent on each activity, rather than the usual amount.
- If you did not do an activity in the last week, please check the "0 hours" box.

	Hours spent last week		No time spent last week
A1. Watching programs or movies/videos on TV	―― hours last week	**OR**	☐ 0 hours
A2. Reading newspapers or magazines	―― hours last week	**OR**	☐ 0 hours

---

Figure 12.1   Survey Instructions to Respondents and Extract of Questionnaire

Following the format displayed in the text box, respondents were asked about a total of 31 time use categories in wave 1; wave 2 added two more categories. These cover the following life domains:

- Leisure activities (8 categories)
- Errands and duties around the home (10 categories)
- Exercise (2 categories)
- Socializing (6 categories)
- Working for pay
- Other activities (4 categories)

The number of categories in parentheses indicates the level of detail covered in the questionnaire for each domain.

Several elements from the instructions deserve attention from a methodological viewpoint: First, note that the instructions call for double counting of the same hours if respondents engage in more than one activity at the same time and also if respondents consider one and the same activity to fit more than one of the time use categories provided. This will lead to total hours in activities that add up to more than there are hours in a day or hours in a month for a considerable fraction of the sample. Both forms of double counting are encouraged as it is not always clear whether an activity represents two activities that could be reported separately, or whether one and the same activity fits two different categories in the questionnaire. For example, cooking with friends could be considered both cooking and socializing. The advantage of this method is that it leaves room for respondents to report secondary, tertiary, and potentially more activities, even though the *distinction* of primary activities and other activities is not observed by the researcher. At the same time, given the length of the recall period (one week or one month), secondary activities will suffer from higher underreporting than primary activities: While respondents may recall fairly well their main activities over the past week or month when giving it some thought, recalling what other activity they were engaging in at the same time adds another layer of difficulty.

Second, the instructions request information on "last week" or "last month" even if last week or last month was unusual. This may seem at odds with the objective of eliciting usual time use patterns of the respondent. However, to achieve high data quality in a paper-and-pencil survey, where there is no opportunity to ask questions of an interviewer, it is important to leave as little room for interpretation as possible about what respondents should report. Also, cognitively, the exercise of recalling activities from last week or last month is easier to perform than trying to assess "usual" hours of a certain activity. Even if, for some respondents, last week was not representative, it will simply add noise to the estimates, which can be overcome with a larger sample size.

Finally, notice that the question format does not include an explicit option for "don't know" or "refuse." The rationale for this is to avoid reminding respondents that nonresponse is a valid option for any single question. Of course, the cover page of the questionnaire stated clearly that respondents could always leave blank a question that they did not want to answer.

A limitation of the experimental design of CAMS is that it collects time use information from only one person in the household. This limits the extent to which one can study the sharing of tasks within the household, and over time whether certain activities are simply no longer done in the household or whether another household member has taken those over. CAMS 2005 remedies this limitation, but the data were not available as of the writing of this chapter.

Data Quality

In this section, we present empirical evidence for several indicators of data quality, such as unit response, item response, time to complete the questionnaire, and total hours of activities accounted for in CAMS.

UNIT RESPONSE

The raw response rates (i.e., not adjusted for mortality or undeliverable questionnaires) for CAMS waves 1 and 2 were 77.3% and 78.3%, respectively.[6] Because the CAMS sample was drawn as a random sample from respondents to HRS 2000, we have a lot of background information on both respondents and nonrespondents to the CAMS. Comparison of the characteristics of the two groups in cross-tabulations shows that response rates differ by age, self-reported health, education, marital status, race, income, and wealth.[7] We therefore apply weights in the analysis of time use patterns in the population presented in the descriptive statistics below.

ITEM RESPONSE RATES AND
TIME TO COMPLETE THE QUESTIONNAIRE

Item response rates to the time use questions in CAMS wave 1 were very high, and even slightly higher in wave 2. All are in the high 90% range. The activities with the lowest response rates, even though they are still in the mid-nineties, may have been considered sensitive to answer by some respondents: "physically showing affection for others through hugging and kissing" (94.8% and 95.3% in waves 1 and 2, respectively), "praying and meditating" (95.3% and 96.2%, respectively), and "treating or managing an existing medical condition of your own" (95.4% and 95.8%, respectively).

When analyzing the distribution of the number of missing items at the individual level by age and education we find that about 78% of the sample answered all categories, and 4.8% had missing values in four or more categories. As one might expect, the fraction of full reporters is lower at higher ages, while the fraction of full reporters is higher among those with higher levels of education.[8]

Data quality is likely to be related to the time the respondent dedicated to filling out the time use section of the questionnaire. At the end of the time use section, respondents were asked to estimate how long they took to complete that section. Based on these self-reports, average completion time was 15 minutes; the mode was 10 minutes. A closer look at the distribution of the self-reported completion time reveals that 6% of wave 1 respondents spent less than 5 minutes; about 4% spent 40 minutes or more. Introspection suggests that the relation between completion time and data quality follows an inverse U shape: too short a completion time implies that the person did not really try hard to remember the activities from last week or the last month; long completion times may indicate difficulties with the task (even though for some it may be extreme conscientiousness). This pattern is confirmed in the CAMS data. The study of the distribution of missing values by categories of time spent to complete the time use section shows that the fraction of full reporters first increases with completion time and then decreases.[9] The fraction missing four or more categories is highest for respondents who were particularly fast or particularly slow to complete the survey (10.0% and 11.7%, respectively, compared to 2.6% among those who took about the average time of 15–19 minutes). Response times also vary by age and education: Short response times are more prevalent among younger age groups, and respondents with high education are less likely to have extreme completion times, long or short.

TOTAL HOURS OF ACTIVITIES ACCOUNTED FOR IN CAMS

To compute total hours of recorded activities we need to make categories that are measured in hours "last week" comparable to those measured in hours "last month." We do so by multiplying the ones measured in hours "last week" by 4.3 to arrive at an estimate of hours "last month" for the same categories. Summing over all categories gives the total number of hours recorded over the last month. We consider two scenarios that differ in the treatment of missing values: In the first scenario we set all missing values to zero and report summary statistics for the entire sample. This necessarily leads to an underestimate. However, the resulting bias is quantitatively not very large because the rates of item nonresponse are so small in CAMS. In the second scenario we show statistics computed over only the sample of full reporters. The results are very similar, so we focus the discussion on the full sample. The average of total hours is remarkably close to the number of total hours that there are in a month, that is, 720 hours (30 × 24 = 720). For men the total is 681 and for women it is 731. Women report systematically a larger number of hours than men. Note that the survey instrument allows for double counting of hours either as a result of individuals engaging in multiple activities at the same time or as a result of certain activities fitting the description of more than one category asked about in CAMS. Therefore, we expect a wide distribution of hours around the mean, and, indeed, that is the case. For example, the maximum total monthly hours reported in the survey amounts to 4.4 times the number of hours there are in a month. Of course, some of the hours' dispersion could be the result of reporting error. In particular, extreme values tend to be generated when one or more activities reported with the reference period "last week" were entered with an unusually high value. Conversion into a monthly value by multiplying by 4.3 inflates such values by a noticeable factor. This is an inherent problem of combining items that operate on different time scales.

Overall, the distribution of reported hours is fairly symmetric (not shown). The medians are very close to the mean, and other quantiles also evidence symmetry. For example, at the 25th percentile, total hours are equivalent to about 0.8 months, and to 1.2 months at the 75th percentile.

For both men and women the total hours accounted for decline with age: For men (women) age 50–64 the total amounts to 715 (758) hours per month, while it is 636 (736) for those age 65–74. Among the oldest age group (75+) the total is about the same for men as in the next younger group, but for women the total drops further to 663 hours.

Totals also vary with education. They are lowest for individuals in the lowest education group (602 hours for men, 649 for women), and with a few exceptions they are higher the higher the level of education (714 hours in the highest education group for men, 758 for women in the highest education group).

COMPARISON OF CAMS TIME USE DATA WITH THE AMERICAN TIME USE SURVEY (ATUS)

As another indicator of data quality we compare summary statistics from CAMS to outside data. The only survey that collects comprehensive data on time use suitable for producing population estimates that are representative of the U.S. population is the American Time Use Survey (ATUS), conducted by the Bureau of Labor Statistics (BLS). It was first collected in 2003, which coincides with the second wave of CAMS. Comparisons with the ATUS are not without limitations because of differences in sampling, interview mode, and whether a diary is used to elicit time use information. The sampling frame for the ATUS is the pool of Current Population Survey (CPS) respondents;[10] interviews are conducted via computer-assisted telephone technology, and ATUS uses the diary method.[11] CAMS, on the other hand, has its sample drawn as a random sub-sample from the HRS 2000; it relies on paper-and-pencil questionnaires and asks respondents to recall how much time they spent on various activities either last week or last month. These sampling and methodological differences are bound to lead to some differences in the reported summary statistics. For example, the recall method in CAMS is expected to result in underestimates, because respondents are likely to forget some incidences of a certain activity over the last week or month. On the other hand, CAMS statistics include secondary activities, which ATUS does not. Table 12.1 shows the results for two age groups, by gender, for selected categories, including watching TV; reading; socializing and communicating; working for pay; telephone, mail, and e-mail; personal care activities; household activities (including purchasing goods and services); leisure and sports; and caring for and helping nonhousehold members. Overall, the summary statistics turn out to be fairly close to each other. ATUS records somewhat higher totals for time spent watching TV than CAMS (except for women age 55–64). The differences span between one third and about 1 hour per day. Note that ATUS includes in watching TV also related activities such as borrowing or returning a movie to the library, for example. The same observation applies to the slightly higher totals for working, where ATUS includes many work-related activities. CAMS shows higher totals for reading by about half an hour, and the statistics for telephone, mail, and e-mail show more time spent on this in CAMS as well. Here, the coding scheme in ATUS is likely to give rise to these differences by assigning various reading activities to other categories, and similarly for various communication activities.[12] For household activities, which we aggregated with purchasing goods and services, the differences are very small. In summary, we conclude that the time use information in CAMS and ATUS is quite closely comparable in spite of the many methodological differences.

Descriptive Statistics by Age, Education, Economic Status, and Health

In this section, we turn to analyzing the patterns of time use in a number of activities. From the 31 activities that were queried in CAMS we construct 12 aggregate categories: leisure, errands and housework, working for pay, personal care, exercise, socializing, helping others and volunteering, religious and spiritual activities, time at computer, sleeping, pet care, and managing finances.

CATEGORIES OF TIME USE BY AGE AND SEX

Table 12.2 presents the total number of hours per month spent in each of the 12 aggregated categories by age band for males and females. Not surprisingly,

Table 12.1   Comparison of CAMS and ATUS 2003 (Daily Hours)

	CAMS 2003			ATUS 2003		
	Men	Women	All	Men	Women	All
Watching TV						
55–64	2.76	2.75	2.76	3.06	2.53	n/a
65+	2.99	3.17	3.11	4.05	3.70	n/a
Reading						
55–64	1.08	1.18	1.14	0.43	0.55	n/a
65+	1.42	1.73	1.63	0.94	1.01	n/a
Socializing and Communicating						
55–64	0.83	1.09	0.98	0.63	0.78	n/a
65+	0.95	1.16	1.09	0.73	0.81	n/a
Working						
55–64	3.57	2.28	2.82	4.64	2.88	3.7
65+	0.87	0.51	0.63	1.20	0.43	0.77
Telephone, Mail, and E-Mail						
55–64	0.53	0.83	0.71	0.13	0.28	0.21
65+	0.56	0.85	0.76	0.16	0.36	0.27
Personal Care Activities						
55–64	8.31	8.61	8.48	8.93	9.31	9.13
65+	8.25	8.51	8.42	9.51	9.76	9.65
Household Activities, Including Purchasing Goods and Services						
55–64	2.47	3.55	3.10	2.47	3.81	3.18
65+	2.74	3.53	3.27	2.79	3.95	3.44
Leisure and Sports						
55–64	6.65	6.26	6.43	5.55	5.02	5.27
65+	7.01	7.27	7.19	7.52	6.88	7.16
Caring for and Helping Nonhousehold Members						
55–64	0.27	0.43	0.37	0.27	0.52	0.40
65+	0.30	0.33	0.32	0.31	0.31	0.31

SOURCE: Authors' calculations for CAMS; First Results News Release for ATUS 2003.

working for pay still plays an important role among the 50- to 64-year-olds, and much more so among men than among women. The amount of time spent working drops sharply with age.

On the other hand, errands and housework make up for many more hours among women at all ages. Taking the sum of hours worked for pay and errands and housework, one finds that it is the same for men and women age 50–64: about 180 hours per month. At older ages this sum is higher for women, however,

Table 12.2   CAMS Wave 1, Average Total Hours per Month, by Age, Category, and Sex (Weighted)

	Men				Women			
	All	*50–64*	*65–74*	*75+*	*All*	*50–64*	*65–74*	*75+*
Leisure	155.7	148.8	155.5	177.7	171.5	155.9	193.8	178.8
Errands and housework	68.6	65.1	72.0	74.5	108.4	106.2	117.7	101.3
Personal care	29.6	26.6	30.3	38.1	40.1	39.9	41.8	38.5
Exercise	40.6	39.9	42.1	40.3	28.9	30.3	29.6	25.1
Socializing	52.9	54.3	50.7	52.0	73.2	71.8	75.3	73.9
Helping others and volunteering	7.6	7.2	8.6	7.7	12.1	13.2	13.2	8.5
Meditating, praying, religious services	14.5	12.5	15.4	19.6	24.3	21.3	28.9	25.2
Computer	20.3	28.4	13.0	6.5	19.7	31.6	11.5	3.2
Sleep	204.5	203.7	205.1	206.5	194.8	196.4	194.5	191.3
Pet care	7.1	7.1	8.5	4.7	9.4	10.7	8.2	7.9
Managing finances	4.2	3.4	4.0	6.9	4.0	3.9	4.2	3.8
Work for pay	73.3	115.7	29.4	8.3	42.3	74.6	15.0	3.8
Total	681.2	714.8	636.5	644.6	731.0	758.0	736.1	663.4

due to the large drop in time spent working for pay among both sexes, which is not made up for by the slight increase in housework among men.

A few other patterns are worth pointing out. The time men dedicate to personal care increases sharply with age, and it is about the same as for women at advanced age (75 +); for women there is no age gradient. For them the number of hours of personal care remains close to 40 hours all along. Women engage in more socializing at all ages, and also in religious activities (meditating, praying, and attending religious services), while men spend more time exercising at all ages.

Of course, these averages mask variation by a number of other covariates. In the next two subsections we will illustrate this by the examples of education and self-rated health.

CATEGORIES OF TIME USE BY EDUCATION AS FRACTION OF TOTAL, EXCLUDING SLEEP AND WORK

The set of graphs included in Figure 12.2 presents the fraction of time spent in various activities other than working and sleeping by age, sex, and education. The rationale for excluding the time spent sleeping and working from the denominator is that in this section we are interested in patterns of time use as a function of total time at individuals' discretion. For example, a respondent who works many hours has necessarily less time to spend in socializing or any other activity. Our method adjusts for that.

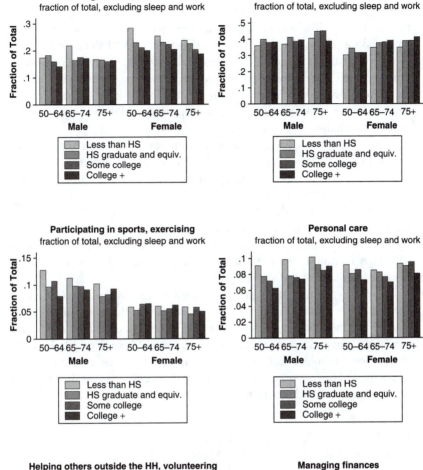

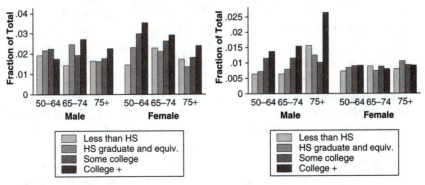

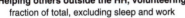

Figure 12.2   Activities as a Fraction of Total, Excluding Sleep and Work, by Education

Several interesting gradients emerge. For example, women with high education spend substantially less time running errands and doing housework than women with low education. Education being a proxy for wealth, the highly educated (and mostly more wealthy) women tend to substitute their own time with market-purchased goods and services. Conversely, women's time spent in leisure activities shows the gradient of the opposite sign; that is, the more educated women enjoy a greater fraction of their waking hours in leisure activities. The same is true for helping others and volunteering, and for praying, meditating, and attending religious services.

The category exercise shows an interesting pattern for men implying that men with lower education exercise more than men with high education and that this pattern holds across all age groups.[13] For women there is no discernible pattern of this kind.

Personal care includes as one of its subcategories "managing a medical condition of your own." Because education is strongly correlated with health, it comes as no surprise that time spent in personal care is much less for those with high education. This strong gradient is, however, less pronounced at advanced age (age 70 and above).

Managing finances among men exhibits a strong positive correlation with age and also a positive education gradient. However, this is not the case for women. At advanced ages, older women are mostly widows who need to take care of their own finances, at least in the absence of help from relatives. The observation that older women spend on average the same amount of time managing finances as women in their 50s and 60s suggests that they may not be attending adequately to them.

TOTAL HOURS SPENT ON CATEGORIES
OF TIME USE BY SELF-RATED HEALTH

Table 12.3 presents descriptive statistics of total hours spent on the various activities by age and self-rated health. The first thing to note is that total hours (sum of all activities) varies substantially by health status and age. For example, individuals in fair or poor health report lower totals by about 90 hours per month than those in excellent and very good health. This could be due either to people in worse health engaging less in simultaneous activities, like ironing while watching TV; or both age and health status being associated with greater difficulties to recall the information. Investigating the various categories for their association with health we find many of the expected relationships: Hours worked for pay are much lower for those in fair or poor health; and so is the time spent exercising. Interestingly, respondents in fair or poor health also systematically sleep less than their healthy counterparts. However, personal care (including treating a medical condition of one's own)

Table 12.3   Total Hours Spent Last Month on Specific Activities by Self-Rated Health Status (Weighted)

		Age Band			
Activity	Self-Rated Health	50–64	65–74	75+	All
All activities	Excellent or very good	763.3	723.9	678.7	734.8
	Good	743.2	660.5	664.3	696.9
	Fair or poor	673.8	670.4	582.6	644.9
	All	737.5	692.3	643.7	701.1
Work	Excellent or very good	110.4	26.4	8.4	71.7
	Good	96.7	17.6	4.3	53.0
	Fair or poor	39.9	13.3	3.0	22.8
	All	92.7	20.9	5.4	55.2
Errands, housework	Excellent or very good	86.4	102.4	97.1	92.5
	Good	88.2	95.4	97.9	92.5
	Fair or poor	92.7	97.0	77.6	89.9
	All	88.1	99.1	91.6	91.9
Leisure	Excellent or very good	151.4	179.0	181.2	163.6
	Good	154.0	176.8	192.8	169.4
	Fair or poor	154.0	178.4	157.9	161.8
	All	152.7	178.2	178.4	164.9
Sleep	Excellent or very good	204.2	208.5	198.4	204.5
	Good	198.2	191.4	201.9	197.2
	Fair or poor	189.3	188.0	188.8	188.8
	All	199.6	198.8	196.8	198.8
Personal care	Excellent or very good	30.1	32.8	34.3	31.5
	Good	32.4	34.9	40.7	35.1
	Fair or poor	46.9	49.3	40.6	45.9
	All	34.0	37.1	38.3	35.8
Exercise	Excellent or very good	36.7	39.2	35.7	37.2
	Good	35.5	29.0	31.9	32.8
	Fair or poor	27.3	32.6	22.8	27.6
	All	34.5	34.7	30.6	33.8
Managing finances	Excellent or very good	3.7	4.1	6.7	4.3
	Good	3.8	4.0	4.0	3.9
	Fair or poor	3.3	4.3	3.9	3.7
	All	3.7	4.1	4.9	4.0

(Continued)

Table 12.3 (Continued)

Activity	Self-Rated Health	Age Band 50–64	65–74	75+	All
Using the computer	Excellent or very good	38.2	16.0	6.0	27.1
	Good	23.6	8.4	4.2	14.8
	Fair or poor	18.1	8.8	2.6	11.4
	All	30.2	12.1	4.4	20.0
Socializing	Excellent or very good	63.2	69.6	71.1	66.2
	Good	61.3	61.5	67.9	62.9
	Fair or poor	70.5	61.2	57.3	64.4
	All	64.1	65.3	66.0	64.8
Helping others, volunteering	Excellent or very good	11.7	12.2	10.1	11.6
	Good	9.3	10.4	9.3	9.6
	Fair or poor	9.2	10.7	4.5	8.4
	All	10.5	11.3	8.2	10.3
Praying, meditating, religious services	Excellent or very good	15.9	20.5	23.0	18.2
	Good	17.5	21.2	21.1	19.4
	Fair or poor	21.7	32.8	25.8	25.8
	All	17.5	23.4	23.2	20.3
Pet care	Excellent or very good	9.3	8.3	6.8	8.7
	Good	8.9	8.2	7.0	8.3
	Fair or poor	8.8	8.5	6.4	8.1
	All	9.1	8.3	6.7	8.4

and spiritual activities, like praying and meditating, are significantly higher among those in fair or poor health. No such gradients are found in errands/housework, leisure, or in socializing.

Conclusion

The CAMS time use section is somewhat experimental, as it is aimed at gathering time use data in a self-administered questionnaire at low cost. As judged by the very high rate of item response and by the very reasonable patterns of completion times, the preliminary assessment of data quality is positive. This conclusion is reinforced by patterns of time use as a function of age, education, and health status in that they accord with prior expectations. For example, those in worse health spend more time attending to personal care.

Our comparison of CAMS with ATUS showed similar levels of time use by category, and similar variation by age. This suggests that for some purposes collection of time use by recall using a self-administered instrument is a good substitute for a diary method, and it is considerably cheaper. Of course, the CAMS method is no substitute for a diary when the research objective requires high frequency data collection or when it aims to relate time use to transient states such as affect.

Already the data show a number of interesting results. For example, time spent in managing finances increases with age among men, but not among women. Because the majority of older women are widows, this suggests that as they become responsible for their finances they may not be attending adequately to them.

Future work will integrate the time use data in retirement with economic data, including spending data from CAMS, in studies of household production. Because CAMS is embedded in the rich HRS longitudinal data, the time use data will permit many new types of analyses.

Notes

1. The first wave of HRS was collected in 1992, sampling 51- to 61-year-olds and their spouses. Other cohorts were added in subsequent waves of the survey so that beginning with HRS 1998 its sample covers the entire U.S. population age 51 and above.

2. The sample for CAMS wave 3, which was collected in the fall of 2005, included a refresher sample of 51- to 56-year-old respondents.

3. Funding has been committed to collect further waves of CAMS in 2007, 2009, and 2011.

4. CAMS wave 3, which was administered in 2005, included a separate time use questionnaire for the spouse of the addressee, so that we will have observations on time use from both spouses in a couple, once those data become available.

5. A copy of the questionnaires is available at http://hrsonline.isr.umich.edu/meta/2001/cams/qnaire/cams01abc.pdf for the first wave of CAMS, and at http://hrsonline.isr.umich.edu/meta/2003/cams/qnaire/cams2003.pdf for the second wave.

6. In 2003, questionnaires were mailed to 4,156 of the respondents who were sampled in the 2001 CAMS. The remaining 843 respondents were lost due to death ($n = 372$), loss to follow-up ($n = 173$), and exclusion from the 2003 CAMS because they were participating in other HRS supplemental studies ($n = 298$).

7. More specifically, in cross-tabulations the age pattern is U-shaped; that is, younger as well as older addressees are less likely to respond; response rates show a distinct gradient in self-rated health ranging from 83.1% for those in excellent health to 62.8% for those in poor health; across education groups, response rates are about 80% for all with the exception of those with less than a high school education, whose response rate is about 10 percentage points lower; the response rate among whites/Caucasians

is 80.2% compared to 64.4% among blacks/African Americans; across income quartiles 71.5% respond in the first quartile, 78.7% in the second and third, and 80.5% in the highest income quartile; wealth quartiles show a similar gradient in response rates ranging from 70.1% in the lowest quartile to 82.4% in the highest wealth quartile; couples are more likely to return the questionnaire. Their response rate is 81.1% compared to 73.3% for singles. This may be because in a couple, there is a chance that the spouse returns the questionnaire when the addressee is not inclined to. For singles there is no such backup option.

8. The fraction of full reporters ranges between 80.8% among the 50- to 64-year-olds to 67.5% among respondents age 75 and above. The education gradient is similar in magnitude: There are 65.4% full reporters among those with less than high school, while the fraction is much higher (84.8%) among those with college or more education. The group with four or more missing categories is not very large overall, but it varies with age and education by a factor of about 3. This group amounts to only 3.2% among the 50- to 64-year-olds, while it amounts to 9.9% among those 75 and above. Respondents with college or higher education have 3.0% with four or more missing categories whereas among those with less than high school this group makes up 9.5%.

9. For example, there are 73.2% full reporters among the group of respondents who took the least time (0–4 minutes) to complete the time use section of the questionnaire; 80.3% are full reporters among those who spent 15–19 minutes; and among those who took particularly long there are only 63.6% full reporters.

10. ATUS is sampled from households that completed their eighth interview with the Current Population Survey (CPS). The unit response rate in 2003 was about 58%, which does not take into account nonresponse to and attrition from the CPS. The combined response rate would be expected to be lower. Applying weights restores population representation along some dimensions, but may not be sufficient to correct for potential selection biases in statistics on time use. About 21,000 individuals aged 15 or over were interviewed in the ATUS 2003; that is, one individual per household chosen at random among those household members age 15 and over.

11. ATUS uses diaries covering the period from 4 a.m. of the previous day to 4 a.m. of the current day. The diary days are preassigned at random prior to the interview to obtain unbiased responses across the different days of the week. Only primary activities are recorded systematically, with the exception of child care. Respondents' reports on various activities are recoded and assigned a single 6-digit code using the ATUS Coding Lexicon (3-tier coding system of 17 broad activity categories, each with multiple second- and third-tier subcategories; the coding scheme encompasses a total of 438 distinct categories in 2003 the ATUS Coding Lexicon). It follows that in ATUS the assignment of activities to specific categories is subject to setup of the coding scheme and the decisions of the coding personnel. In CAMS, respondents decide for themselves how to allocate the activities across the provided categories. CAMS respondents are also encouraged to record secondary activities, even though these cannot be distinguished from primary activities.

12. For example, reading catalogues or reviewing ads or real estate information would be counted under "purchasing goods and services," while reading in relation to volunteering activities would be assigned to "volunteering." CAMS respondents might well choose to allocate many of these activities to "reading."

13. This pattern is not an artifact of looking at the fraction excluding sleep and work: The total number of hours spent exercising also shows this gradient.

Acknowledgment

We are grateful to NIA for financial support through Grant No. 1P01AG08291.

References

University of Michigan, Survey Research Center. (2001). *2001 CAMS questionnaire, Health and Retirement Study.* Retrieved June 10, 2008, from http://hrsonline.isr .umich.edu/meta/2001/cams/qnaire/cams01abc.pdf

University of Michigan, Survey Research Center. (2003). *2003 CAMS questionnaire, Health and Retirement Study.* http://hrsonline.isr.umich.edu/meta/2003/cams/ qnaire/cams2003.pdf

U.S. Department of Labor. (2005). *Time-use survey—First results announced by BLS.* Washington, DC: Bureau of Labor Statistics.

13

The Implementation of a Computerized Event History Calendar Questionnaire for Research in Life Course Epidemiology

Robert F. Belli, Sherman A. James,
John Van Hoewyk, and Kirsten H. Alcser

Introduction

Social epidemiologists have become increasingly interested in how childhood and adulthood socioeconomic conditions, separately and in combination, influence differential vulnerability of individuals or whole populations to premature disease and death in adulthood (Ben-Shlomo & Kuh, 2002; Berkman & Kawachi, 2000; Davey-Smith, 2003). While prospective study designs are clearly the preferred methodology, in which household or neighborhood social and economic conditions of individuals are collected when they are children, and then associations are tested between these early life conditions and the timing of declines in health as individuals grow older, such designs are logistically complex, time consuming, and expensive (Gordis, 2004). Hence, retrospective study designs, which request adults to recall the social and economic conditions of their childhood for the purpose of linking this information to existing or future health problems associated with aging will continue to be an important methodology for life course research on health disparities. However, if such retrospective studies are to make valid contributions to knowledge, major improvements in the way questions are structured to solicit information on early childhood circumstances will be needed (Burton & Blair, 1991; Cannell, Fisher, & Bakker, 1965; Jobe, Tourangeau, & Smith, 1993). This chapter describes using a computerized event history calendar (EHC) interviewing methodology as one promising approach to meeting this challenge. The work described in this chapter evolved as a collaborative effort among a cognitive psychologist with expertise in the structure of autobiographical memory and social epidemiologists interested in linking information on childhood socioeconomic conditions, obtained retrospectively, to health outcomes in African American adults in the Pitt County (North Carolina) Study. The latter is an ongoing investigation of social, economic, and behavioral precursors of cardiovascular disease in a cohort of Southern African Americans (Gerber et al., 1991; James et al., 1998; James, Fowler-Brown, Raghunathan, & Van Hoewyk, 2006; James, Keenan, Strogatz, Browning, & Garrett, 1992; James, Van Hoewyk et al., 2006; Strogatz et al., 1991; Strogatz et al., 1997).

Building upon basic cognitive psychological research demonstrating the importance of cues in eliciting otherwise forgotten material in autobiographical recall (Brewer, 1988; Wagenaar, 1986), and theoretical and empirical work on cuing mechanisms available in the structure of autobiographical knowledge (Belli, 1998; Conway, 1996; Means & Loftus, 1991), the EHC interviewing methodology has been shown to produce high-quality retrospective reports (Caspi et al., 1996; Freedman, Thornton, Camburn, Alwin, & Young-DeMarco, 1988). In EHC interviewing, respondents are encouraged to reconstruct intervals of social (e.g., places of residence, intimate relations), economic (e.g., employer names, periods of unemployment), or health-related (e.g., tobacco use, health status) episodes of activity or states of being, by using as cues chronological time and their own experiences that occurred earlier, later, or contemporaneously (Belli, Lee, Stafford, & Chou, 2004). To date, there have been several studies directly showing that the quality of retrospective reports using EHC interviewing methodologies is substantively better than reports obtained with traditional standardized conventional questionnaire (CQ) approaches. These studies include face-to-face and telephone modes, paper-and-pencil and computer-assisted interviewing methods, and life course and shorter reference periods (Belli, Shay, & Stafford, 2001; Belli, Smith, Andreski, & Agrawal, 2007; Engel, Keifer, & Zahm, 2001; van der Vaart, 2004; Yoshihama, Gillespie, Hammock, Belli, & Tolman, 2005; see also Yoshihama, Chapter 8, this volume). The Pitt County Study is one of the earliest panel studies to employ the computer-assisted EHC. Two previous epidemiological surveys of the Pitt County Study population, using standardized CQ approaches, were conducted in 1988 and 1993. In 2001, the EHC was employed in conjunction with a standard CQ approach in order to investigate socioeconomic influences over the life course on risk for hypertension and obesity, as initially recorded in 1988. While EHCs have been implemented in other epidemiologically related work (Kessler & Wethington 1991; Lyketsos, Nestadt, Cwi, Heithoff, & Eaton, 1994; Martyn & Belli, 2002), the Pitt County Study is the first in which a life course computerized EHC was integrated with standard CQ questions in a total computer-assisted interviewing package. Moreover, it is the first EHC in which questions were specifically designed to measure economic and psychosocial factors relevant to life course social epidemiology research. Details on the design, development, and application of the EHC are provided below, along with selective findings concerning its ability to accurately reproduce data collected from study participants in 1988.

Design and Development of the EHC

The computerized EHC (copyright 2000, Regents of the University of Michigan), was designed to assist respondents to use temporal and thematic cues available in the structure of autobiographical memory. The main thematic structures in the EHC are termed "domains," and each consists of events of the same type, such as membership in organizations, relationships with family members, or experiences with economic hardship. Temporally, the EHC presents timelines within each domain, with each calendar year of a respondent's life serving as a unit (from birth year to the interview year). In addition to years, corresponding ages are depicted, as the timing of events may be better remembered by the year of occurrence or by the age of the respondent, depending on the type of event and respondent preferences. Hence, within each domain, both thematic and temporal structures assist respondents in remembering which events happened and when, including cues to facilitate correct temporal ordering within domains, and cues that facilitate the association of event timing across domains, as may occur when changes in economic hardship occur more or less contemporaneously with changes in organizational membership. Moreover, the computerization of the EHC included the designing of several automatized prompts that provided warnings to interviewers of potential violations to response completeness and consistency.

The development of the computerized EHC followed the pretesting of two earlier versions. These pretests led to revisions in question wording to increase clarity and changes to certain domain structures to reduce interviewing time to a manageable level. An introductory domain was added for the purpose of orienting respondents to their entire life course by encouraging an individualized segmentation of different periods of life (childhood, adolescence, and adulthood).

INTERVIEWING

Interviews were conducted face to face from May 2001 to February 2002 with 1,209 participants, who consisted of a primarily working-class cohort of African American adults with an oversampling of middle-class persons. Participants are residents of Pitt County, North Carolina. Interviewer training was conducted on-site across 6 days in Pitt County with 23 interviewers. Interviewers were representative of the Pitt County community, included both African American and white individuals, and included individuals who varied in computer literacy. Training specific to the computerized EHC lasted 4 hours on one of these days. During interviewing, a regional field supervisor and three team leaders monitored the quality of interviewers' work. With regard to performance on the EHC, interviewers were continuously monitored, as needed, to determine whether the recorded response patterns followed rules of completeness and consistency. To minimize threats to data quality, monitoring of interviewer performance was most comprehensive during the first interviews that were conducted in order to correct interviewing problems as early as possible.

THE EHC INSTRUMENT

The final EHC instrument included eight conceptual domains that were designed to collect periods of stability and transitions between these periods for the entire life course. The domains focused on one important health behavior (cigarette smoking) and key dimensions of social and economic well-being, broadly defined as follows: household utilities; the family's exposure to economic hardship; social and material life conditions; organizational memberships; relationships with parents/guardians during the respondent's childhood; relationships with other family members; and the individual's exposure to unfair treatment. On average, the EHC required only 29.2 minutes to complete. Each domain consisted of at least one, and sometimes up to six, timelines. Interviewers were trained to introduce each domain with a script that could be read exactly as written or paraphrased as needed. Table 13.1 summarizes the content, and the average amount of interviewing time, for each domain. Figure 13.1 displays a computer screen for the life stages domain. Each domain was similarly represented with year and age timelines and specific domain timelines. To move across domains, interviewers located the appropriate domain tab near the bottom of the screen (see Belli et al., 2000, and Belli et al., 2007, for additional description of computerized EHC designs). The EHC was supplemented with CQ elements programmed in Blaise™ software that then were integrated into an overall interviewing package. Average total interviewing time for the entire research instrument was 75 minutes; the CQ portion consumed 45 minutes, on average. During the interview, only the interviewers could directly view the computer screen.

Table 13.1   Timeline Descriptions for Each Domain and Mean Minutes of
Interviewing Time per Domain

Domain	Timeline Descriptions	Mean Minutes
Stages	One timeline designed to assist respondents to orient themselves to a life review. Consisted of respondents' identifying years in which they went through life stages from young childhood to adulthood.	6.69
Utilities	Three timelines asking about times living in housing with and without indoor plumbing, electricity, and a refrigerator.	1.76
Economic hardship	Four timelines; three timelines collecting information on work history and periods in which respondent was unable to meet basic needs. One timeline asked about years in receipt of public assistance.	4.49
Sociomaterial conditions	Five timelines; two timelines asking about years of sufficient and insufficient heat and food, one timeline asking about ability to afford housing, one timeline on levels of neighborhood crime, and one timeline concerned with subjective social status.	4.80
Smoking	One timeline on cigarette smoking history.	0.88
Organizational membership	Three timelines; two asking about years of having membership in a church or other organizations, one asking about years of having a confidant.	2.37
Parents/guardian	Timelines designed to determine who were the primary breadwinners while respondent was growing up, and their educational and occupational backgrounds.	2.04
Family relations	Three timelines asking about levels of love and support, and experiences with verbal and physical abuse during the life course.	2.33
Unfair treatment	Six timelines asking about specific instances of having experienced unfair treatment at school, during employment, in regard to housing, in seeking to acquire resources and money, with the criminal justice system, or any other types of instances of unfair treatment.	3.89
Total minutes		29.24

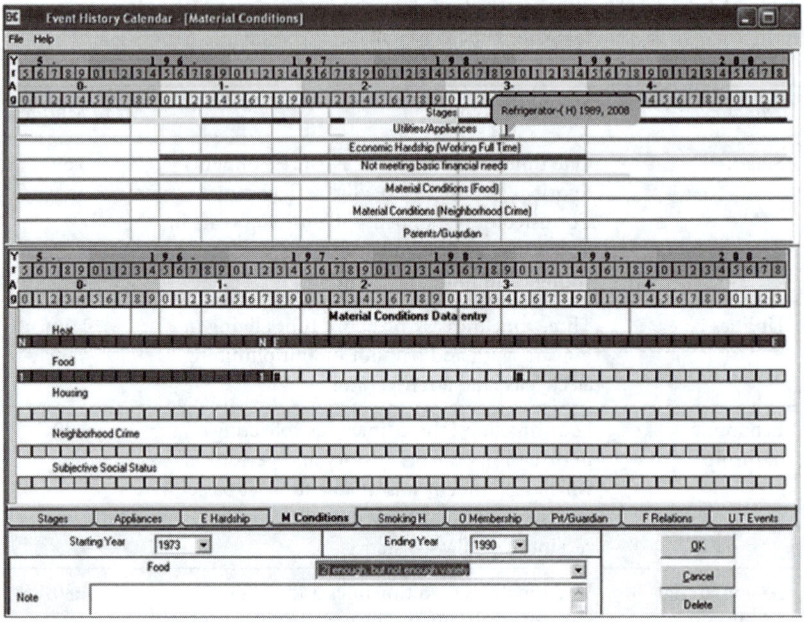

Figure 13.1   Black-and-White Screen Capture of Life Stages Domain in the Computerized EHC Questionnaire

SOURCE: The computerized instrument is copyrighted to the Regents of the University of Michigan; screen capture reproduced with permission.

Analyses

We assessed the accuracy of EHC data by comparing answers given in response to the EHC, in 2001, to answers respondents gave to comparable questions asked about contemporaneous behavioral, social, or economic conditions using the CQ format in 1988 and 1993. With a focus on each year of the respondent's life, six EHC variables were used for this methodological analysis. The first variable was number of cigarettes smoked: 0, 1–10, 11–20, and 21+. The second variable was part-time versus full-time employment: 0 = < 30 hours/week; 1 = > 30 hours/week. The third variable was working some versus not working at all: 0 = working some; 1 = not working at all. The fourth variable was church membership: 0 = not active; 1 = active. The fifth variable was other organizational membership: 0 = not active; 1 = active. And the sixth variable was indoor plumbing: 0 = no; 1 = yes.

The EHC also provided data to test substantive research questions concerning associations between social and economic deprivation during childhood (defined as birth to 13 years of age) and important indicators of health status (e.g., hypertension or obesity) or health behaviors (e.g., cigarette smoking) at varying points in adulthood. EHC data collected to examine these potential associations were organized into four major categories. The first category was Childhood Socioeconomic Position (SEP), indexed by the highest occupation held by the primary breadwinner of the household in which the respondent grew up: unskilled worker/farm laborer = 0; skilled/white-collar worker = 1.

The second category was an index of Negative Social Relationships, with scores based on answers to questions about exposure during childhood to unfair treatment (due to race, gender, social class, physical appearance, etc.), verbal abuse, physical abuse, withholding of familial love/support, lack of a confidant. Each of these five types of negative experiences was binary coded and the observed distribution of responses resulted in the following tertiles of Negative Social Relationships: score = 0 (good relationships, 36%); score = 1 (fair relationships, 33%); and score = 2–5 (poor relationships, 31%). The third category was a Socioeconomic Deprivation index, based on yes (score = 1) or no (score = 0) responses to the following four questions about childhood circumstances: raised by a single parent; experienced food insecurity at some point; felt unsafe in the neighborhood; and family received public assistance at some point. The observed scores produced the following tertiles of Socioeconomic Deprivation: score = 0 (low, 32%); score = 1 (medium, 44%); and score = 2–4 (high, 25%). The fourth category combined the index scores on Negative Social Relationships and Socioeconomic Deprivation to create a Cumulative Childhood Disadvantage Score, with values ranging from 2–6, organized into the following tertiles: score = 2–3 (low, 41%); score = 4 (medium, 30%); and score = 5–6 (high, 30%).

Results

EHC DATA QUALITY: CONCORDANCE

Table 13.2 provides *kappa* indices as indications of the extent of concordance between the retrospective EHC and contemporaneous CQ reports, providing an indication of the levels of data quality obtained in the EHC interviews. When comparing the concordance levels of the 2001 retrospective EHC reports to the 1988 and 1993 data collection waves, 13-year and 8-year retention intervals, respectively, are being examined. According to Fleiss (1981), *kappas* > .75 represent excellent agreement, *kappas* of .4 to .75 represent fair to good agreement, and *kappas* below .4 represent poor agreement. As

Table 13.2   Concordance Levels Measured as *kappa* Indices Between Reports Collected Contemporaneously in 1988 and 1993 via a CQ Methodology, and Retrospective Reports collected in 2001 via an EHC Methodology

Measure	kappa 1988	kappa 1993
Smoking (2 categories); 0 = not at all, 1 = at least one cigarette per day	.73	.81
Smoking (3 categories); 0 = not at all, 1 = up to one pack per day (1–20 cigarettes per day), 2 = more than one pack per day (21 cigarettes or more per day)	.65	.73
Smoking (4 categories); 0 = not at all, 1 = between 1–10 cigarettes, 2 = 11–20 cigarettes, 3 = 21 cigarettes or more per day	.51	.60
Working part-time vs. full-time; 0 = part-time, working < 30 hours/ week, 1 = full-time, working > 30 hours/week	.44	.54
Working some vs. not working; 0 = working some; 1 = not working at all	.41	.47
Church membership; 0 = not active; 1 = active		.42
Other membership; 0 = not active; 1 = active		.36
Plumbing; 0 = no plumbing; 1 = had plumbing	.35	

can be seen, the *kappa* indices demonstrate levels of agreement ranging from poor to excellent.

Clearly, the very best agreement (up to excellent) was obtained with smoking, a self-performed health behavior. In contrast, behaviors tied to social encounters, including labor histories and church membership, obtained fair to good levels of agreement. In the current study, the observed concordances for smoking and labor history with contemporaneously collected data are similar to those obtained with EHCs that have been examined in other methodological work (Belli et al., 2007). In addition, the patterns observed here with regard to lower observed kappas for the more remote years, and the decrease in *kappas* with greater refinements in the categorization of the smoking variable, were also observed in this other study (Belli et al., 2007).

The degree of concordance between the retrospective and contemporaneous reports as measured by *kappa* indices are constrained by an upper limit that is lower than perfection. Whereas the retrospective EHC questions use the calendar year as the smallest temporal reporting unit, their corresponding contemporaneous CQ questions, by asking what is currently occurring, are reflections of finer transitory states that can vary within a given calendar year.

In addition, the levels of agreement are compromised as the question wordings in some of the variables across waves express slightly different content. Consider especially the content for the employment question in 1988, which allowed the respondent to define full-time employment, whereas in 1993 and 2001 full-time employment was defined as working 30 or more hours per week. In addition, in 1993, respondents were asked to report the number of hours per week that they usually work, whereas in 2001 the EHC was designed to ask respondents whether or not they worked full-time, with full-time being defined as working an average of 30 or more hours per week. As another example, consider that whereas in 1988 respondents were asked to report on whether they had "complete plumbing facilities," in 2001 respondents were asked about "indoor plumbing." Such subtle differences in question wording can lead to different question meaning. Hence, in light of the constraints on the upper limits of possible concordance, the EHC appears to have performed well in eliciting retrospective reports that can be considered to consist of fair to excellent data quality.

EHC DATA QUALITY: SUBSTANTIVE FINDINGS

The quality of EHC data is also assessed by determining whether the retrospective reports that are collected lead to the discovery of relationships between early and later conditions of life. Demonstrating the utility of the EHC, retrospective reports of childhood SEP, which had been collected with the EHC instrument, significantly predict later life conditions associated with obesity, hypertension, and smoking. In addition, retrospective EHC reports of Childhood Cumulative Disadvantage also predict smoking behavior during later life.

EHC DATA ON CHILDHOOD SEP

Obesity

In analyses restricted to the 679 women in the Pitt County Study who were reinterviewed in 2001 (80% response rate), childhood SEP was a significant predictor of obesity status (BMI > 30.0) in 1988, the year of initial enrollment. The mean age (*SD*) of women in 1988 was 35.4 years (0.32). Of the 566 women from low childhood SEP backgrounds, 45.8% were obese, compared to 27.6% of the 113 women from less disadvantaged backgrounds. In multivariable analyses that controlled for age, marital status, alcohol consumption, cigarette smoking, regular physical activity, fruit/vegetable consumption, and adulthood SEP (measured by respondent's education, occupation, employment status, and home ownership), low childhood SEP women were 2.2 times more likely (odds ratio [OR] = 2.21, 95% confidence interval [CI]: 1.32, 3.68) to be obese than higher SEP women (James, Fowler-Brown, et al., 2006).

Hypertension

In analyses restricted to the 379 men reinterviewed in 2001 (75% response rate), the association between childhood SEP and hypertension status (mean blood pressure > 140/90 mmHg, or currently treated) in 1988 was investigated. The mean age (*SD*) of the men in 1988 was 35.1 (0.31). Among the 307 men from low childhood SEP backgrounds, the unadjusted prevalence of hypertension was 40.9%; it was 26.8% among men from higher SEP backgrounds ($p = 0.14$). In multivariable analyses controlling for age, marital status, alcohol consumption, cigarette smoking, regular physical activity, stress, social support, and adulthood SEP, men from low childhood SEP backgrounds were 60% more likely to be hypertensive (OR = 1.60, 95% CI: 0.75, 3.38) than their less disadvantaged counterparts (James, Van Hoewyk, et al., 2006).

Cigarette Smoking

In gender-specific analyses controlling for age, social desirability scores, and church membership during childhood, the relationship between childhood SEP and lifetime cigarette smoking status (i.e., ever vs. never smoked), in 2001, was investigated. Men from low childhood SEP backgrounds were 47% more likely to have ever smoked (OR = 1.47, 95% CI: 0.74, 2.91) than men from higher SEP backgrounds. Interestingly, the opposite pattern was observed for women; that is, those who grew up in low SEP households were significantly less likely than their more advantaged peers to have ever smoked (OR = 0.58, 95% CI: 0.30, 0.95) (S. A. James, 2005, personal communication).

EHC DATA ON CUMULATIVE CHILDHOOD DISADVANTAGE

Cigarette Smoking

In gender-specific analyses, again controlling for age, social desirability, and church membership during childhood, the relationship between Cumulative Childhood Disadvantage and lifetime cigarette smoking status (ever vs. never smoked), in 2001, was investigated. Scores on Cumulative Childhood Disadvantage were divided into tertiles—high, medium, and low. The low tertile was used as the referent category. Men in the highest tertile of Cumulative Childhood Disadvantage were 35% more likely to have ever smoked than men in the lowest tertile (OR = 1.38, 95% CI: 0.73, 2.58). Men in the medium tertile were 33% more likely to have ever smoked (OR = 1.33, 95% CI: 0.70, 2. 51) than men in the lowest tertile. Among women, the findings were again opposite those observed for men. Women in the lowest tertile of Cumulative Childhood Disadvantage were the most likely to have ever smoked: 69% more likely than women in the highest tertile (OR = 1.69, 95% CI: 1.07,

2.65) and 38% more likely than women in the medium tertile (OR = 1.38, 95% CI: 0.88, 2.16) (S. A. James, 2005, personal communication).

Strengths and Limitations of the EHC Methodology in Retrospective Study Designs

To the best of our knowledge, the 2001 Pitt County Follow-up Study is the first epidemiological study to collect retrospective reports of life course experiences via a computer-assisted interviewing EHC. It was demonstrated in this study that the EHC can produce retrospective data of reasonably high quality, as would be expected from an instrument that was designed to optimize the accuracy of autobiographical recall, especially when compared to conventional questionnaires (Belli, 1998; Belli et al., 2001; Belli et al., 2007; Engel et al., 2001; Yoshihama et al., 2005). The EHC in the current study also contributed valuable data to tests of original research questions in a population with many preventable risk factors for chronic diseases (Curtis, James, Strogatz, Raghunathan, & Harlow, 1997; James et al., 1998; James, Fowler-Brown, et al., 2006; James, Van Hoewyk et al., 2006; Strogatz et al., 1991). Moreover, the average administration time of 30 minutes, in the current study, attests to the practicality of this instrument in large-scale, community-based health research.

As EHC instruments, especially as displayed on computerized platforms, are emerging data collection methodologies, their implementation presents challenges not characteristic of CQ instruments. For example, currently, there are no software packages designed specifically to accommodate EHC instruments. Thus, they require customized programming, which adds to the overall research costs. It should be noted, however, that customization to deal with unique question characteristics and skip patterns is necessary even with CQ instruments that are programmed in existing packages. Customized interviewer training, for the specific EHC design, is also an added ingredient. Interviewers experienced in administering CQ instruments will be unfamiliar with the different requirements imposed by EHC designs. Interestingly enough, interviewers have expressed a preference for EHC-based interviewing over CQ interviewing, perhaps because the former is more conducive to natural conversational exchanges with respondents (Belli et al., 2001; Belli et al., 2007). Although computerization leads to advantages over paper-and-pencil EHC designs, especially with regard to automatizing data quality consistency and completeness checks, and with facilitating computerized data entry and management (Belli, 2000), computerized EHCs are disadvantageous in that paper-and-pencil designs facilitate respondents' viewing the calendar elements along with the interviewer, including the use of icons and other memory aids (Engel et al., 2001). Hence, design improvements are necessary to provide respondents with computer displays that they can see along with the interviewer (see Dijkstra, Smit, & Ongena, Chapter 15, this volume). This improvement, along with a number of others, may further optimize autobiographical recall.

Despite some remaining challenges associated with EHC interviewing, in the current study we have demonstrated the feasibility of including computerized EHC elements in an overall interviewing package for life course epidemiological research. With retrospective data produced by the EHC, we have observed potentially important associations between early life socioeconomic conditions and later life risks for obesity, hypertension, and cigarette smoking. Since the collection of retrospective data for life course epidemiological research will likely be necessary for many years to come, EHC methodologies represent a promising tool to pursue important questions across a wide variety of population groups.

Acknowledgment

This research was supported by National Institutes of Health Grants NIH/HL 065645 and 1R01AG/HD17977-01A1.

References

Belli, R. F. (1998). The structure of autobiographical memory and the event history calendar: Potential improvements in the quality of retrospective reports in surveys. *Memory, 6,* 383–406.

Belli, R. F. (2000). Computerized event history calendar methods: Facilitating autobiographical recall. *American Statistical Association Proceedings of the Section on Survey Research Methods* (pp. 471–475). Alexandria, VA: American Statistical Association.

Belli, R. F., Lee, E. H., Stafford, F. P., & Chou, C.-H. (2004). Calendar and question-list survey methods: Association between interviewer behaviors and data quality. *Journal of Official Statistics, 20,* 185–218.

Belli, R. F., Shay, W. L., & Stafford, F. P. (2001). Event history calendars and question list surveys: A direct comparison of interviewing methods. *Public Opinion Quarterly, 65,* 45–74.

Belli, R. F., Smith, L., Andreski, P. M., & Agrawal, S. (2007). Methodological comparison between CATI event history calendar and standardized conventional questionnaire instruments. *Public Opinion Quarterly, 71,* 603–622.

Ben-Shlomo, Y., & Kuh, D. (2002). A lifecourse approach to chronic disease epidemiology: Conceptual models, empirical challenges and interdisciplinary perspectives. *International Journal of Epidemiology, 31,* 285–293.

Berkman, L. F., & Kawachi, I. (2000). *Social epidemiology.* New York: Oxford University Press.

Brewer, W. F. (1988). Memory for randomly sampled autobiographical events. In U. Neisser & E. Winograd (Eds.), *Remembering reconsidered* (pp. 21–90). Cambridge, UK: Cambridge University Press.

Burton, S., & Blair, E. (1991). Task conditions, response formulation processes, and response accuracy for behavioral frequency questions in surveys. *Public Opinion Quarterly, 55,* 50–79.

Cannell, C. F., Fisher, G., & Bakker, T. (1965). Reporting of hospitalization in the Health Interview Survey. *Vital and Health Statistics* (PHS Publication No. 1000, Series 2, No. 6). Washington, DC: Government Printing Office.

Caspi, A., Moffitt, T. E., Thornton, A., Freedman, D., Amell, J. W., Harrington, H., et al. (1996). The life history calendar: A research and clinical assessment method for collecting retrospective event-history data. *International Journal of Methods in Psychiatric Research, 6,* 101–114.

Conway, M. A. (1996). Autobiographical knowledge and autobiographical memories. In D. C. Rubin (Ed.), *Remembering our past: Studies in autobiographical memory* (pp. 67–93). New York: Cambridge University Press.

Curtis, A. B., James, S. A., Strogatz, D. S., Raghunathan, T. E., Harlow, S. (1997). Alcohol consumption and changes in blood pressure among African Americans: The Pitt County Study. *American Journal of Epidemiology, 146,* 727–733.

Davey-Smith, G. (2003) *Health inequalities: Lifecourse approaches.* Bristol, UK: Policy Press.

Engel, L. S., Keifer, M. C., & Zahm, S. H. (2001). Comparison of a traditional questionnaire with an icon/calendar-based questionnaire to assess occupational history. *American Journal of Industrial Medicine, 40,* 502–511.

Fleiss, J. L. (1981). *Statistical methods for rates and proportions* (2nd ed.). New York: John Wiley.

Freedman, D., Thornton, A., Camburn, D., Alwin, D., & Young-DeMarco, L. (1988). The life history calendar: A technique for collecting retrospective data. In C. C. Clogg (Ed.), *Sociological methodology* (Vol. 18, pp. 37–68). San Francisco: Jossey-Bass.

Gerber, A. M., James, S. A., Ammerman, A. S., et al. (1991). Socioeconomic status and electrolyte intake in black adults: The Pitt County Study. *American Journal of Public Health, 81,* 1608–1612.

Gordis, L. E. (2004). *Epidemiology* (3rd ed.). Philadelphia: W. B. Saunders.

James, S. A., Fowler-Brown, A. G., Raghunathan, T. E., & Van Hoewyk, J. (2006). Lifecourse socioeconomic position and obesity in African American women: The Pitt County Study. *American Journal of Public Health, 96,* 554–560.

James, S. A., Jamjoum, L., Raghunathan, T. E., Strogatz, D. S., Furth, E. D., & Khazanie, P. G. (1998). Physical activity and non-insulin-dependent diabetes in African Americans: The Pitt County Study. *Diabetes Care, 21,* 555–562.

James, S. A., Keenan, N. L., Strogatz, D. S., Browning, S. R., & Garrett, J. M. (1992). Socioeconomic status, John Henryism and blood pressure in black adults: The Pitt County Study. *American Journal of Epidemiology, 135,* 59–67.

James, S. A., Van Hoewyk, J., Belli, R. F., Strogatz, D. S., Williams, D. R., & Raghunathan, T. E. (2006). Life-course socioeconomic position and hypertension in African American men: The Pitt County Study. *American Journal of Public Health, 96,* 812–817.

Jobe, J. B., Tourangeau, R., & Smith, A. F. (1993). Contributions of survey research to the understanding of memory. *Applied Cognitive Psychology, 7,* 567–584.

Kessler, R. C., & Wethington, E. (1991). The reliability of life event reports in a community survey. *Psychological Medicine 21,* 723–738.

Lyketsos, C. G., Nestadt, G., Cwi, J., Heithoff, K., & Eaton, W. E. (1994). The Life Chart Interview: A standardized method to describe the course of psychopathology. *International Journal of Methods in Psychiatric Research, 4,* 143–155.

Martyn, K. K., & Belli, R. F. (2002). Retrospective data collection using event history calendars. *Nursing Research, 51,* 270–274.

Means, B., & Loftus, E. F. (1991). When personal history repeats itself: Decomposing memories for recurring events. *Applied Cognitive Psychology, 5,* 297–318.

Smith, G. D. (2003). *Health inequalities: Life course approaches.* Bristol, UK: Policy Press.

Strogatz, D. S., Croft, J. B., James, S. A., Keenan N. L., Browning S. R., & Garrett J. M. (1997). Social support, stress and blood pressure in blacks: The Pitt County Study. *Epidemiology, 8*(5), 482–487.

Strogatz, D. S., James, S. A., Haines, P. S., Elmer, P. J., Gerber, A. M., Browning, S. R., et al. (1991). Alcohol consumption and blood pressure in black adults: The Pitt County Study. *American Journal of Epidemiology, 133,* 442–450.

van der Vaart, W. (2004). The time-line as a device to enhance recall in standardized research interviews: A split ballot study. *Journal of Official Statistics, 20,* 301–318.

Wagenaar, W. A. (1986). My memory: A study of autobiographical memory over six years. *Cognitive Psychology, 18,* 225–252.

Yoshihama, M., Gillespie, B., Hammock, A. C., Belli, R. F., & Tolman, R. M. (2005). Does the life history calendar method facilitate the recall of intimate partner violence? Comparison of two methods of data collection. *Social Work Research, 29,* 151–163.

Further Thoughts on Part III

Computerized data collection instruments, as illustrated by Phipps and Vernon (Chapter 7), Belli, James, Van Hoewyk, and Alcser (Chapter 13), and Dijkstra, Smit, and Ongena (Chapter 15), have several advantages in comparison to paper-and-pencil instruments. Some of these advantages avoid the possibility of interviewer error. For example, any contradictions that are reported by respondents, such as reporting two entirely different types of activities as having occurred at the same time (e.g., going shopping and watching television at home in a time diary; being employed and unemployed during the same period in a calendar) can be detected automatically and corrected by additional interviewer queries. Interviewers can also be notified automatically whenever a cueing opportunity arises, such as verifying the timing of events that were reported as occurring contemporaneously, or nearly so. Another advantage is that computerized applications are able to create data files automatically to researcher specifications as the data are being collected, avoiding a costly separate data entry phase that becomes increasingly burdensome with increases in sample size. Of course, the costs of programming are not trivial. Ultimately, however, computerization has opened the possibility of the self-administration of calendars and time diaries, perhaps via the Web, as more fully discussed by Stafford and Belli (Chapter 17).

Usually, but not always, calendar and time diary methods yield good to excellent data quality. As observed by Stafford (Chapter 2) and Belli and Callegaro (Chapter 3), in comparisons with conventional standardized "stylized" questions the data quality that emerges from calendars and time diaries is usually, but not always, better. Exceptions to these general findings beg for explanations and additional methodological research. In Chapter 11, Roberts and Mulvey found low concordance rates in calendar interviews. One possibility is that the population studied—respondents with known histories of substance use, violence, and involvement in the mental health system—will always provide unreliable reports, although design issues cannot be ruled out as being able to improve reporting among members of this population. As another example, Belli, Smith, Andreski, and Agrawal (2007) found that although calendar interviewing led to better retrospective reports for labor and cohabitation histories in comparison to a conventional standardized questionnaire, the opposite was true for reports of marriage history. One possibility, consistent with data, is that whereas the calendar interviews did not ask respondents how many times they were married—instead, they were asked to provide first names of all cohabitants, married or not—the conventional interviewing method did, and calendar respondents apparently failed to name some of their married partners. Deserving of additional methodological work, then, is ascertaining whether asking "how many times married" in a calendar interview will improve the retrospective reporting of past marriages.

Because any retrospective reporting is going to include inaccuracies and errors, one question that always arises with regard to data quality is how good is good enough? This is not an easy question to answer. Certainly, any improvements in data quality over existing methods is a welcome development, and hence researchers should have greater confidence whenever calendar retrospective reports are collected in lieu of reports collected via conventional standardized interviewing methods, such as serving as bridges between waves in a panel survey (see Belli & Callegaro, Chapter 3). Some researchers are becoming bolder; from retrospective life span data collected with calendar methods, Yoshihama (Chapter 8) and Belli, James, Van Hoewyk, and Alcser (Chapter 13) have tendered causal inferences. An optimistic view is that calendar methods are able to collect reliable low-cost life course data; contrast the almost instantaneous longitudinal data collected by a life course calendar versus the high cost and the number of years that are required to collect data in panel surveys. A pessimistic view is that the data may not be reliable enough to lend valid causal inferences. As with most research, these issues will be resolved only if data collected from a number of calendar interviews are able to converge with each other and other existing panel data on portraying a consistent pattern of life course relationships.

References

Belli, R. F., Smith, L., Andreski, P. M., & Agrawal, S. (2007). Methodological comparison between CATI event history calendar and standardized conventional questionnaire instruments. *Public Opinion Quarterly, 71,* 603–622.

PART IV

Methodological Issues in the Reliability, Validity, and Collection of Time-Based Data

Whereas the chapters in Part III seek to directly assess the data quality obtained by either calendar or time diary methods with another source of data that serves as a comparison, the chapters in Part IV concentrate on caveats about these assessments, either with regard to providing a more focused attention on the relationship between data collection methods and quality, or with regard to evaluating which analytic techniques are best suited to measure reliability and validity of timeline and event history data. On the data collection side of this equation, Stone and Broderick (Chapter 14) surprisingly find that compliance with self-administered diary instruments is poor despite participant reports that their compliance has been good, and that real-time electronic diaries are needed to ensure good compliance. In Chapter 15, Dijkstra, Smit, and Ongena highlight the challenges to interviewer training and instrument development that are unique to calendar instruments, and based on their experience, offer several useful suggestions for the design and implementation of both paper-and-pencil and computerized calendar instruments. In the final chapter in Part IV, Alwin (Chapter 16) discusses both the theoretical issues and the analytic methods for the assessment of reliability and validity with timeline and event history data, including the application of a latent Markov model to estimate reliability parameters of data collected in one of the first demographic studies that had administered calendar interviews, the Intergenerational Panel Study of Parents and Children.

14

Protocol Compliance in Real-Time Data Collection Studies

Findings and Implications

Arthur A. Stone and Joan E. Broderick

Introduction

Calendar and diary methodologies have been developed to provide researchers and clinicians with reliable and accurate information about people's life experiences in naturalistic settings (Belli, Alwin, & Stafford, Chapter 1, this volume). Experience captured by these methods can include a wide variety of events, behaviors, and subjective feelings or symptoms. A feature common to these methodologies is that they rely on respondents' self-reports, which are, in some cases, the only ways to collect experiential data. Calendar and diary methods can involve reports that are immediate or momentary and do not involve memory and recall. Often, though, they require respondents to summarize experience that has occurred over a designated period of time (e.g., day, week, or month). When data are retrospectively reported, there are a host of potentially serious threats to the validity of the reports (see Dijkstra, Smit, & Ongena, Chapter 15, this volume). It is these threats that have prompted the recommendation to minimize the reliance on memory and to have participants

AUTHORS' NOTE: Arthur A. Stone is the Associate Chair of the Scientific Advisory Board of invivodata, inc., a company that provides electronic data capture services to the pharmaceutical industry.

report on current experiences (Gorin & Stone, 2001). While this solution to recall bias has been widely adopted, it has recently become apparent that compliance with momentary reports of experience can be a significant challenge (Stone, Shiffman, Atienza, & Nebeling, 2007).

The focus of this chapter is on compliance with the collection of real-time, naturalistic data. There are many ways that real-time data may be collected; the most common method is the diary and there are two versions that are especially pertinent to the discussion of compliance: paper-and-pencil and electronic. Paper-and-pencil diaries are essentially pocket-size versions of standard paper questionnaires, albeit often shorter in length so they can be administered repeatedly without undue subject burden. Electronic diaries cover the same content as paper diaries, but are enabled with palm-top computers or personal digital assistants (PDAs) and present questions on touch-sensitive screens to record responses. Alternative, nondiary techniques for the collection of real-time data are interactive voice recording (IVR) (where questionnaires are administered over the telephone and responses are entered on the touch-tone keys), the Internet (where questions are completed online), and cellular telephones (either with live interviewers or in conjunction with IVR).

Regardless of the physical modality employed for data collection, a sampling protocol specifying the times and/or conditions for participants to complete diary entries is determined by the researcher based on a study's purpose. Three major classes of sampling protocols have been developed: random sampling, event-based, and time-based (Delespaul, 1995; Shiffman, 2007). Some protocols combine two or more sampling formats. Random sampling is the most common within-day protocol, and it is used when representative moments of a day's experience are desired, for example, when one wishes to characterize the experience of the entire day. Event-based protocols are useful when the research is addressing the antecedents or consequences of particular events (the occurrence of a symptom, behavior, or environmental condition). A combination of random sampling and event sampling is particularly useful for determining the unique conditions that precede targeted events by comparing data from target events with other randomly selected moments of the day. Time-based sampling protocols entail sampling according to time of day or a temporal window within a day; a common example is sampling morning, afternoon, and evening.

High levels of compliance with diaries are usually necessary to draw sound conclusions from real-time data. Regardless of the type of sampling scheme used in real-time data collection, deviations from the protocol (noncompliance) can threaten the validity of the data. The reason for this is that the value of real-time data capture is based on achieving a *representative sampling* of experiences the researcher is studying. If an outcome measure is meant to represent, for example, respondents' average or typical pain intensity over the course of a week, then a good approach for ensuring representative coverage of the period is to randomly sample over the week. If deviations from a protocol are entirely *random,* there would be little concern about systematic bias, yet there might be a concern that the number of samples taken was lower than planned, increasing variability and reducing statistical power. If deviations from the protocol are *nonrandom,* then bias is likely. Continuing with the example of assessment of weekly pain, some individuals might tend to ignore scheduled assessments when they are in extreme pain (e.g., during a flare of rheumatoid arthritis). These omissions will systematically bias the average weekly pain scores (the mean of all observations) to lower levels. Conversely, other respondents may believe that the researcher is interested only in times when they are experiencing pain and they may make a special effort to be compliant during painful periods. These individuals may choose to skip assessments when they are not in pain. This response pattern biases weekly averages upward.

These two examples of noncompliance are based on respondents' beliefs about the targeted variable (pain), but other social or physical environment characteristics may lead to poor compliance and biasing as well. Respondents with occupations requiring frequent meetings may often be unable to complete assessment prompts, and individuals who spend much of the day in their car may face the same problem. To the extent that these situations are systematically associated with different levels of the target variable compared with average circumstances, nonreporting during these situations will produce nonrepresentative data. At the opposite extreme, if an outcome variable has no association with situational or temporal factors and is actually constant across the week, then response patterns that result in missing data will be of little consequence. This will rarely be the case, since investigators employ momentary data capture when they know or suspect there is much variability in the targeted variable.

In addition to creating a summary for a period of time (a day, a week, etc.), real-time data are often employed to answer other kinds of questions, and compliance levels can affect the validity of the data for addressing those questions in various ways. Momentary data can be used to contrast experiences (e.g., pain) during various types of situations or circumstances, for example, at work versus at home or with a friend versus alone. Differential compliance in the compared situations could yield invalid conclusions. Similarly, real-time data have been used to study diurnal cycles of experience (e.g., Stone, Smyth, Pickering, & Schwartz, 1996), and noncompliance can have particularly pernicious effects on these analyses, especially if it occurs at the beginning and/or end of the day. This is likely because many studies have found higher rates of missing (noncompliant) data in the morning and evening hours, presumably because people are engaged in activities that preclude timely responses.

When respondents accurately indicate missing data in logbooks or diaries, noncompliance will be known to the researcher, who can then evaluate the impact of noncompliance on the data. Appropriate steps to handle the problem may be employed, such as by imputing data if noncompliance is infrequent or by entirely eliminating participants with unacceptable levels of noncompliance. A second type of noncompliance is when respondents submit diaries that appear to have been completed according to protocol, yet actually include entries that have been completed outside of the protocol assessment times (e.g., completing a scheduled 4 p.m. recording at 10 p.m. or on the following day). The problem with these data is that unless the researcher is able to detect instances of this kind of noncompliance, the validity of the data may be degraded.

To set the stage for studies of compliance with real-time, self-report protocols, we first present a summary of compliance issues pertaining to self-monitoring of various medical procedures. We then present recent work on compliance with paper-and-pencil self-report diaries, followed by a brief review of compliance with electronic diaries.

Compliance With Self-Monitoring in Medical Settings

While measures taken in the clinic are valuable, repeated measurements of physiological functions in patients' real-world environments can be even more informative. Two common examples of ambulatory monitoring are blood pressure and glucose. Both of these physiological variables are responsive to environmental and psychological events, and measurement exclusively in the clinic may not be adequate to make informed treatment decisions or to titrate medication dose. For this reason, ambulatory methods to assess blood pressure and glucose are now central to the management of hypertension and diabetes. With the acceptance and widespread use of ambulatory techniques has come an extensive literature of observations regarding compliance with these monitoring protocols and its implications for the data obtained. As the technological sophistication of physiological monitoring devices has advanced, many devices have incorporated microchips to time- and date-stamp when measures were taken. Comparisons of these data with patient written reports of when these measures were taken have often found substantial discrepancies; we discuss these findings below.

An especially rich compliance literature is in glucose monitoring by patients with diabetes. Several studies have compared the accuracy of glucose monitoring in diabetic patients' paper-and-pencil logbooks of their monitoring versus the electronic reading on their glucose meters. Among 19 diabetics who were unaware of the electronic data-capture feature of their glucose monitor across 12–14 days, Mazze et al. (1984) found that 26% of logbook recordings were inconsistent with the electronic meter, and, in two thirds of those cases, self-reported glucose levels were lower, indicating better than actual glucose control. A similar study of 14 diabetics for 21 days found that on average 19% of patients' records in the logbook contained "phantom values," that is, glucose recordings and values that were not found on the electronic monitor, and 12% of recordings on the monitor did not appear in the logbook (omissions; Ziegler et al., 1989). When means and variability statistics were compared for the logbooks versus the electronic monitor, significant differences were found. Gonder-Frederick and colleagues observed 30 diabetic patients for 2 weeks and found that only 23% of patients submitted diaries with no errors and only 47% of patients' logbooks were considered "clinically accurate," defined as ≤ 10% error (Gonder-Frederick, Julian, Cox, Clarke, & Carter, 1988).

The clinical impact of observations reported in patient logbooks compared with electronic data capture was further illustrated in a 2-year study of 22 diabetics. First, a glucose meter that did not have memory capacity was used for the 12 months and data were recorded by patients in a logbook. These data and clinical outcomes were compared in the second 12 months when a meter was used that stored glucose readings (Strowig & Raskin, 1998). Clinician access to more accurate readings during the second year was associated with significantly greater glycemic control (reversing a trend of poorer control during the first year) compared with use of patient logbooks in the prior year. Of significance, the degree of improved control was interpreted as yielding a 43% lower risk for retinopathy progression. As a result of these and other studies, electronic data capture of glucose monitoring has been widely adopted for diabetes care, and patient awareness of electronic monitoring has improved adherence to monitoring guidelines (Mazze, Pasmantier, Murphy, & Shamoon, 1985).

Discrepancies between patient logbooks and electronic monitoring have also received a good deal of attention in ambulatory blood pressure studies. Like the glucose monitors, ambulatory blood pressure monitoring devices are able to store the blood pressure readings. Studies comparing patient logbooks with the electronic data have found that discrepancies range from a low of 4% of reported values (Landert, Holm, Steurer, Bachmann, & Vetter, 2003) to as high as 32% (Johnson, Partsch, Rippole, & McVey, 1999), with the most commonly reported rate of 15%–25% (Cheng, Studdiford, Chambers, Diamond, & Paynter, 2002; Mengden et al., 1998; Nordmann, Frach, Walker, Martina, & Battegay, 2000). Not surprisingly, fictional or phantom data were more commonly generated by patients unaware that the monitor electronically captured the blood pressure recordings (Bachmann, Steurer, Holm, & Vetter, 2002; Landert et al., 2003). When data are aggregated over all recordings, some studies find important differences in the data reported by patients versus the electronic data (Johnson et al., 1999; Nordmann et al., 2000), whereas other studies find that the means are equivalent (Bachmann et al., 2002; Cheng et al., 2002).

This line of research prompted a recommendation from the 2000 International Consensus Conference on Self Blood Pressure Measurement to use electronic monitoring devices rather than patient self-report (Mengden, Chamontin, Phong Chau, Luis Palma Gamiz, & Chanudet, 2000).

A third example of compliance research with physiological assessment is monitoring collection of saliva samples in everyday life. The ability to assay a wide assortment of hormones in saliva (compared with the more invasive method of a blood draw) has resulted in burgeoning research in naturalistic settings. One stress hormone that is frequently measured is cortisol. Due to the biologically determined circadian cycle of cortisol production, precise recording of when the saliva samples are taken is essential for accurate interpretation of the data. Broderick and colleagues conducted two studies (one with healthy college students and the second with both healthy women and fibromyalgia patients) and found that self-report of saliva sampling deviated from electronically recorded sampling times at a level sufficient to alter the interpretation of the data significantly (Broderick, Arnold, Kudielka, & Kirschbaum, 2004; Kudielka, Broderick, & Kirschbaum, 2003). Jacob and colleagues in a 5-day study of 20 twin pairs and their sisters also found that verified compliance was lower than self-reported. Unlike the prior two studies, the noncompliant data did not alter the observed circadian cycle relative to analyzing only the compliant samples (Jacobs et al., 2005).

The most extensive line of compliance research in medical settings is that of adherence to medication administration instructions. In 1998, Urquhart and DeKlerk wrote, "Electronic and chemical marker methods provide the first reliable measurements of drug exposure in ambulatory trials. These data contradict the usual claim in published drug trials of > 90% of patients having been satisfactorily compliant with the protocol-specified dosing regimen" (Urquhart & De Klerk, 1998, p. 251). In fact, patients frequently inflate adherence in their logbooks or reports to their physicians (Boudes, 1998; Mallion, Baguet, Siche, Tremel, & de Gaudemaris, 1998; Urquhart, 1996). The terms "parking lot compliance" and "dumping" were coined to describe the common practice of off-loading medication just prior to a research or clinical visit so that the patient appears to have used the prescribed amount of medication since the last visit (Rand et al., 1992). The resounding conclusion of this research is that it is common for people to misrepresent their compliance with medication on self-report relative to objective indices, especially in chronic conditions when medication is prescribed for long periods of time (Osterberg & Blaschke, 2005).

Compliance With Paper Diaries

Compliance with physiological monitoring and medication has raised many concerns about reliance on patient self-report. Naturally, these concerns have been extended to the field of self-report diary research. Researchers and clinicians have been using paper-and-pencil diaries for decades in order to obtain detailed records of patients' medical symptoms and behaviors in order to avoid bias due to memory processes in retrospective reports. The advantage of diaries is to allow patients and research participants to generate a rich source of data over time as experience unfolds in naturalistic settings (Affleck et al., 1999; Eckenrode & Bolger, 1997; Stone, Kessler, & Haythornthwaite, 1991). However, since there is evidence from medical logbooks of a variety of omissions and falsifications of reports, could the same be true for diary reports about other types of experience? Until recently, the only empirical studies of compliance with paper-and-pencil diaries were based on patients' own reports of diary completion.

A few years ago our team undertook a study to determine compliance with paper diaries, and we developed an instrumented paper diary (IPD) to do this (see Figure 14.1). Physically, IPDs are composed of diary sheets in a small binder (DayRunner Organizer©, 17 cm × 11 cm × 3.5 cm) that can be zippered shut. The innovative feature of the IPD is that a series of discrete photo sensors were placed along the interior spine of the binder and these were connected to a wafer-thin computer located within the binder. This setup provided us with a detailed record of when the binder was open in a room with light and when it was either closed or open in a darkened room. Extensive testing prior to deployment in the field and testing both before and after field use ensured that the units were operating correctly. Diary pages were locked into the binder, so they could not be removed from the binder and completed elsewhere apart from the light sensor. Regarding completion of diary records, the data recorded by the IPD sensors provided definitive information about when diary records could not be completed, that is, when the binder was closed or was open in an area without light. The IPD could not verify when diaries were actually completed; rather, it confirmed only times when they might be completed, namely, when the diary was opened in a lighted area.

With the IPD in hand, we were equipped to design a study to test paper diary compliance. Many design decisions faced us, including the data collection sampling schedule, the length of the trial, and the participant sample. We chose a fixed-time schedule of three daily prompts, at 10 a.m., 4 p.m., and 8 p.m. By knowing the time of day that participants were instructed to make an entry, we could determine if the light sensor in the diary binder verified that the diary was open to make an entry at and around those times. If it was open, then there was the *possibility* of a compliant entry, although we could not know for certain that one was actually made. If the binder was closed, then no entry could have been made at the designated time. In this study, a diary entry was considered compliant if the binder was open during a targeted assessment time. More precisely, we defined two windows around the targeted times (1) ±15 minutes (30-minute window) and (2) ±45 minutes (90-minute window). Figure 14.2 shows a schematic of the design with the 30-minute window.

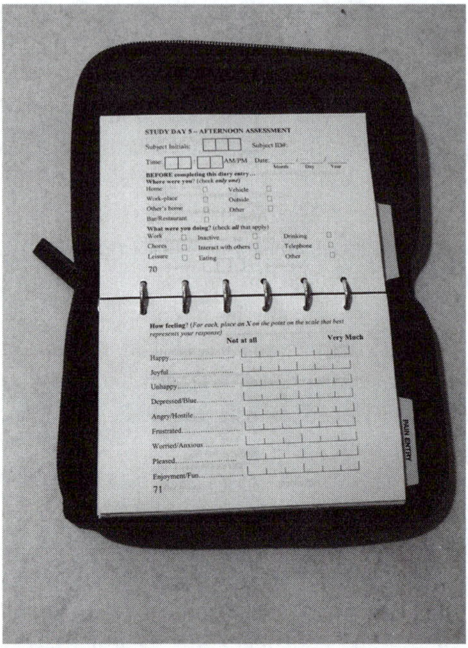

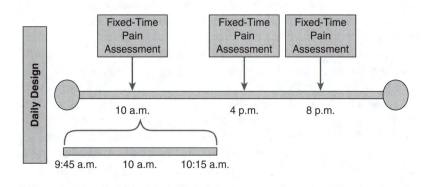

Figure 14.1   Instrumented Paper Diary

Figure 14.2   Design Schematic With 30-Minute Window

Forty rheumatology patients with chronic pain were recruited from a community rheumatology practice for the study. The primary focus of the diary was a multidimensional assessment of pain including pain intensity, sensory qualities of pain, and coping with pain. Additional questions about the psychosocial circumstances and respondent's affect were also assessed at the time of each diary entry. Patients were trained in the diary protocol in our laboratory, but they were not informed that their compliance was being monitored with the light sensor in order to make the trial similar to typical paper-and-pencil diary trials. They were instructed to make three diary entries per day at the designated times. After an initial 3-day familiarization period, participants used the diaries to record their pain for the next 21 days.

Compliance results were startlingly low: Within 30-minute windows around the designated times, respondents were compliant 11% of the time, and with the more liberal 45-minute windows, compliance was 20%. These statistics are in stark contrast to prior beliefs about compliance for paper-and-pencil diaries based upon the dates and times respondents typically indicate completing diary records. Indeed, when we analyzed the self-reported times and dates in our study, compliance was 91% for the 30-minute window, replicating prior studies.

One criticism of these analyses is that we were too stringent in the definition of acceptable compliance windows. However, further exploration of the data belies the overstringent criticism. Of the 710 days of data available for analysis in this study, we found that on 230 days (32%) the diary binder was not opened at all, precluding the completion of diary entries on those days. Nevertheless, paper diaries were submitted for all but 7 of these days, yielding an apparent compliance rate of 94%. These data provided convincing evidence that patients were completing the diary records either before or after the intended days for completion. On further investigation, we found considerable evidence of backfilling and, to our surprise, of *forward-filling*, the case where diaries were completed in advance of the targeted times (Stone, Shiffman, Schwartz, Broderick, & Hufford, 2002, 2003).

Results of this study provided the first direct evidence that paper-and-pencil diaries were not completed according to a study protocol and that inferences based on self-reported times and dates may not always be trustworthy. However, there are several considerations that must be taken into account when considering these results. First, a specific sampling design (fixed times, thrice daily) was examined. Perhaps other sampling schedules, for example, end-of-day or randomly scheduled throughout the day, would yield higher compliance rates. Second, a particular sample of patients was examined and perhaps other types of patients and/or nonpatient samples would yield better compliance. Third, participants were asked to make entries without any reminders. Perhaps an audio prompt, which is a common feature in electronic diaries, would produce higher and acceptable compliance levels.

We were particularly interested in the issue of reminders, because paper-and-pencil experience sample methods (ESM) (Csikszentmihalyi & Larsen, 1987) protocols typically employ an audible signal to let participants know when to complete a diary. The results reported above were likely to be underestimates of ESM compliance, because there was no reminder. To address this issue, we ran a one-group study that was essentially another arm of the study described above. The same patient population was recruited and the same thrice-daily sampling protocol was employed, but patients wore a programmable wrist watch that provided auditory reminders at the onset of and during the 15-minute windows surrounding each of the three targeted reporting times (Broderick, Schwartz, Shiffman, Hufford, & Stone, 2003). Compliance for the 27 participants in this study was indeed higher than was found in the prior study: It increased to 29% in the 30-minute window and to 39% in the 90-minute window. As in the prior study, the diary binder was not open at all on a large number of days, and self-reported compliance determined on the basis of the times and dates provided on the diary entries indicated high compliance rates (85%–91%) for those windows. Compliance rates were similar for 10 a.m. and 4 p.m. assessments, but were significantly lower for the 10 p.m. assessment. Furthermore, compliances rates dropped off about 10% over the course of the 3-week trial. A postparticipation questionnaire asked patients about how well they complied with the protocol. Unfortunately, their overall rating of compliance corresponded better with their self-reported compliance on the diary cards than with the verified compliance determined by the light sensor on the diary. Thus, asking participants about their compliance with a protocol is an inadequate substitute for actually measuring compliance.

In summary, these results should give considerable pause to investigators using or considering using paper-and-pencil diaries in their studies. None of the participants in the studies described above achieved compliances rates verified by the IPD that were above 80%, a figure that is informally discussed as a minimally acceptable group compliance standard for diary trials. One possible explanation for the low compliance rates observed in our studies is that the task of completing three prompts a day at specified times over a several-week period is simply too taxing for people. We will hold on this possibility until the next section of the chapter, because the results of studies using electronic diaries inform this discussion.

While we urge caution using paper diaries given these results, we again acknowledge that these results may not generalize to other samples of subjects, to other sampling protocols, or to other diary content. We do, however, advocate for proceeding with much caution when it comes to compliance with paper diaries. Perhaps prior pilot demonstrations that a paper diary in a particular protocol yields acceptable compliance using techniques that verify actual compliance would provide reassurance. In contrast, simply assuming that participants can be and will be compliant seems risky and could yield misleading findings.

As might be expected, our findings have generated considerable controversy in the diary field as they suggest the possibility that prior paper-and-pencil diary studies have not achieved anywhere near the compliance reported in those studies (based on respondents' self-reported completion of diaries). Some investigators do not believe that the compliance situation is as serious as our results suggest, and they have argued that high compliance with paper-and-pencil diaries is possible. They have further argued that even if compliance is not optimal, the resultant data may not be biased very much (the interested reader should see *Psychological Methods, 2006, 11,* for an empirical paper on these topics and three commentaries on the paper, including one by us, Broderick & Stone, 2006). We are fully in accord with the investigators who believe that additional parametric studies are needed to fully understand compliance with paper diaries and hope to see such work in the near future (Tennen, Affleck, Coyne, Larsen, & DeLongis, 2006). Despite the arguments, we nevertheless strongly suggest that researchers considering working with paper-and-pencil dairies carefully review the literature and determine the effect that low compliance could have upon the evaluation of their hypotheses.

Compliance With Electronic Diaries

Although compliance with paper diaries has been shown to be problematic in at least some paper diary protocols, well-designed electronic diaries have an outstanding record of verified compliance (Hufford & Shields, 2002). Researchers conducting real-time data collection with electronic diaries therefore will be likely to obtain reasonable compliance. But the most important point is that the researcher will know what the actual compliance rate is, because the diary will electronically verify the time and date of completion.

An important shortcoming in the diary compliance literature is our inadequate knowledge of the factors contributing to compliance. Questions naturally arising from the literature cited above are: What is it about electronic diaries that generates good compliance levels? And what is it about paper diaries that may result in poor compliance? Some of the possible reasons for these differences include participants' knowledge that their entries are being monitored and date- and time-stamped, the relative convenience of the small size of electronic diaries, and whether or not diary entries are signaled. Because evidence is relatively recent showing that compliance with paper diaries may not be acceptable, no systematic research is available to elaborate the factors that influence compliance. We hope this situation is remedied in the upcoming years.

Conclusion

We argue in this chapter that high levels of compliance with diary and other real-time data capture protocols are important for generating valid data about people's real-world experiences. If researchers are utilizing diaries in order to avoid the memory biases associated with reporting about occurrences distal to the event, then noncompliance with the assessment protocol is likely to be problematic. When researchers have knowledge of poor compliance, they may be able to take appropriate action to correct for potential bias. Diary protocols that do not incorporate verification of diary completion allow the possibility that study participants can misrepresent when diaries were completed, threatening the integrity of resulting data. As has been observed in physiological monitoring in medical settings, recent studies using the newly developed IPD have shown that completion times of paper diary entries are often misreported, and the entries are done at times that entirely defeat the purpose of real-time data collection. Electronic diaries and other forms of real-time data capture allow for the assessment of actual compliance and have yielded high protocol compliance rates in many studies.

References

Affleck, G., Tennen, H., Keefe, F. J., Lefebvre, J. C., Kashikar-Zuck, S., Wright, K., et al. (1999). Everyday life with osteoarthritis or rheumatoid arthritis: Independent effects of disease and gender on daily pain, mood, and coping. *Pain, 83*(3), 601–609.

Bachmann, L. M., Steurer, J., Holm, D., & Vetter, W. (2002). To what extent can we trust home blood pressure measurement? A randomized, controlled trial. *Journal of Clinical Hypertension (Greenwich), 4*(6), 405–407, 412.

Boudes, P. (1998). Drug compliance in therapeutic trials: A review. *Controlled Clinical Trials, 19*(3), 257–268.

Broderick, J., Arnold, D., Kudielka, B., & Kirschbaum, C. (2004). Salivary cortisol sampling compliance: Comparison of patients and healthy volunteers. *Psychoneuroendocrinology, 29*, 636–650.

Broderick, J., Schwartz, J., Shiffman, S., Hufford, M., & Stone, A. (2003). Signaling does not adequately improve diary compliance. *Annals of Behavioral Medicine, 26*(2), 139–148.

Broderick, J. E., & Stone, A. A. (2006). Paper and electronic diaries: Too early for conclusions on compliance rates and their effects—Comment on Green, Rafaeli, Bolger, Shrout, and Reis (2006). *Psychological Methods, 11*(1), 106–111; discussion 123–125.

Cheng, C., Studdiford, J. S., Chambers, C. V., Diamond, J. J., & Paynter, N. (2002). The reliability of patient self-reported blood pressures. *Journal of Clinical Hypertension (Greenwich), 4*(4), 259–264.

Csikszentmihalyi, M., & Larsen, R. (1987). Validity and reliability of the experience sampling method. *Journal of Nervous and Mental Disease, 175*, 526–536.

Delespaul, P. (1995). *Assessing schizophrenia in daily life: The experience sampling method.* Maastricht, the Netherlands: Universitaire Pers Maastricht.

Eckenrode, J., & Bolger, N. (1997). Daily and within-day event measurement. In S. Cohen, R. Kessler, & L. Gordon (Eds.), *Measuring stress: A guide for health and social scientists.* New York: Oxford University Press.

Gonder-Frederick, L. A., Julian, D. M., Cox, D. J., Clarke, W. L., & Carter, W. R. (1988). Self-measurement of blood glucose. Accuracy of self-reported data and adherence to recommended regimen. *Diabetes Care, 11*(7), 579–585.

Gorin, A., & Stone, A. (2001). Recall biases and cognitive errors in retrospective self-reports: A call for momentary assessments. In A. Baum, T. Revenson, & J. Singer (Eds.), *Handbook of health psychology* (pp. 405–413). Mahwah, NJ: Lawrence Erlbaum.

Hufford, M., & Shields, A. (2002, April). Electronic diaries: Applications and what works in the field. *Applied Clinical Trials,* pp. 46–59.

Jacobs, N., Nicolson, N. A., Derom, C., Delespaul, P., van Os, J., & Myin-Germeys, I. (2005). Electronic monitoring of salivary cortisol sampling compliance in daily life. *Life Sciences, 76*(21), 2431–2443.

Johnson, K. A., Partsch, D. J., Rippole, L. L., & McVey, D. M. (1999). Reliability of self-reported blood pressure measurements. *Archives of Internal Medicine, 159*(22), 2689–2693.

Kudielka, B., Broderick, J., & Kirschbaum, C. (2003). Compliance with saliva sampling protocols: Electronic monitoring reveals invalid cortisol daytime profiles in non-compliant subjects. *Psychosomatic Medicine, 65*, 313–319.

Landert, M., Holm, D., Steurer, J., Bachmann, L., & Vetter, W. (2003). Manipulation of blood pressure self-monitoring protocol values: A randomized controlled study. *Schweiz Rundsch Med Prax, 92*(23), 1075–1080.

Mallion, J. M., Baguet, J. P., Siche, J. P., Tremel, F., & de Gaudemaris, R. (1998). Compliance, electronic monitoring and antihypertensive drugs. *Journal of Hypertension, 16*(Suppl. 1), S75–S79.

Mazze, R. S., Pasmantier, R., Murphy, J. A., & Shamoon, H. (1985). Self-monitoring of capillary blood glucose: Changing the performance of individuals with diabetes. *Diabetes Care, 8*(3), 207–213.

Mazze, R. S., Shamoon, H., Pasmantier, R., Lucido, D., Murphy, J., Hartmann, K., et al. (1984). Reliability of blood glucose monitoring by patients with diabetes mellitus. *American Journal of Medicine, 77*(2), 211–217.

Mengden, T., Chamontin, B., Phong Chau, N., Luis Palma Gamiz, J., & Chanudet, X. (2000). User procedure for self-measurement of blood pressure. First International Consensus Conference on Self Blood Pressure Measurement. *Blood Pressure Monitor, 5*(2), 111–129.

Mengden, T., Hernandez Medina, R. M., Beltran, B., Alvarez, E., Kraft, K., & Vetter, H. (1998). Reliability of reporting self-measured blood pressure values by hypertensive patients. *American Journal of Hypertension, 11*(12), 1413–1417.

Nordmann, A., Frach, B., Walker, T., Martina, B., & Battegay, E. (2000). Comparison of self-reported home blood pressure measurements with automatically stored values and ambulatory blood pressure. *Blood Pressure, 9*(4), 200–205.

Osterberg, L., & Blaschke, T. (2005). Drug therapy: Adherence to medication. *New England Journal of Medicine, 353*(5), 487–497.

Rand, C. S., Wise, R. A., Nides, M., Simmons, M. S., Bleecker, E. R., Kusek, J. W., et al. (1992). Metered-dose inhaler adherence in a clinical trial. *American Review of Respiratory Disease, 146*(6), 1559–1564.

Shiffman, S. (2007). Designing protocols for ecological momentary assessment. In A. Stone, S. Shiffman, A. Atienza, & L. Nebeling (Eds.), *The science of real-time data capture: Self-reports in health research* (pp. 27–53). New York: Oxford University Press.

Stone, A., Shiffman, S., Atienza, A., & Nebeling, L. (Eds.). (2007). *The science of real-time data capture: Self-reports in health research*. New York: Oxford University Press.

Stone, A., Shiffman, S., Schwartz, J., Broderick, J., & Hufford, M. (2002). Patient non-compliance with paper diaries. *British Medical Journal, 324*(7347), 1193–1194.

Stone, A., Shiffman, S., Schwartz, J., Broderick, J., & Hufford, M. (2003). Patient compliance with paper and electronic diaries. *Controlled Clinical Trials, 24*(2), 182–199.

Stone, A., Smyth, J., Pickering, T., & Schwartz, J. (1996). Daily mood variability: Form of diurnal patterns and determinants of diurnal patterns. *Journal of Applied Social Psychology, 26*, 1286–1305.

Stone, A. A., Kessler, R. C., & Haythornthwaite, J. A. (1991). Measuring daily events and experiences: Decisions for the researcher. *Journal of Personality, 59*(3), 575–607.

Strowig, S. M., & Raskin, P. (1998). Improved glycemic control in intensively treated type 1 diabetic patients using blood glucose meters with storage capability and computer-assisted analyses. *Diabetes Care, 21*(10), 1694–1698.

Tennen, H., Affleck, G., Coyne, J. C., Larsen, R. J., & DeLongis, A. (2006). Paper and plastic in daily diary research: Comment on Green, Rafaeli, Bolger, Shrout, and Reis (2006). *Psychological Methods, 11*(1), 112–118; discussion 123–125.

Urquhart, J. (1996). Patient non-compliance with drug regimens: Measurement, clinical correlates, economic impact. *European Heart Journal, 17*(Suppl. A), 8–15.

Urquhart, J., & De Klerk, E. (1998). Contending paradigms for the interpretation of data on patient compliance with therapeutic drug regimens. *Statistics in Medicine, 17*(3), 251–267; discussion 387–389.

Ziegler, O., Kolopp, M., Got, I., Genton, P., Debry, G., & Drouin, P. (1989). Reliability of self-monitoring of blood glucose by CSII-treated patients with type I diabetes. *Diabetes Care, 12*(3), 184–188.

15

An Evaluation Study of the Event History Calendar

Wil Dijkstra, Johannes H. Smit,
and Yfke P. Ongena

Introduction

To obtain valid and reliable data in survey interviews, it is generally acknowledged that the interviewer's behavior should be standardized in order to provide each respondent with the same stimulus and prevent the interviewer affecting the answers of the respondent (Fowler & Mangione, 1990). Conducting an interview using an event history calendar (EHC), however, usually requires the interviewer to be much more flexible. Although completely structured interviews with an EHC have been done (Furstenberg, Brooks-Gunn, & Morgan, 1987), the more common approach is to use a semistructured format with an initial prescribed question for each (sub)domain (Freedman, Thornton, Camburn, Alwin, & Young-DeMarco, 1988). In such an approach, the interviewer is required to react to the respondent's answers, which in turn may produce unwanted interviewer variance and thus may endanger the quality of the data. Thus, interviewers on the one hand have to pose the questions as worded in the questionnaire, but on the other hand have to probe, for example asking whether a particular situation has changed, using their own words and based on their own judgment given the answers of the respondent. The flexible approach is especially expected to improve data quality with regard to resolving inconsistencies and checking the respondent's memory (Belli, Shay, & Stafford, 2001). However, such freedom may cause the interviewer also to perform nonstandardized behavior in cases where standardized behavior may have been more appropriate (e.g., using suggestive probes; see Smit, Dijkstra, & Van der Zouwen, 1997). Moreover, administering an EHC is quite a complex task. Interviewers have to grasp the essential ideas underlying the EHC method and apply techniques like parallel probing in an adequate way, whereas filling in the calendar itself is much less straightforward than filling in a usual questionnaire from a survey interview.

In this chapter we present two studies in the context of a large tobacco epidemiology study evaluating interviewer performance in administering an EHC. The first study concerns a paper-and-pencil version of the EHC; the second one a computer-assisted version. First we describe the underlying principles of the EHC and the task of the interviewer in more detail.

The Event History Calendar

EHC PRINCIPLES

The EHC is an extremely useful tool for collecting retrospective data on life events with respect to different life domains like residence change, marriage, occupation, medical history, and the like. The occurrence of simultaneous transitions in different domains is an important feature of the EHC. Transitions in one domain serve as cues that help the respondent (1) to remember transitions in other domains and (2) to locate those transitions exactly in time. The EHC also helps the interviewer to identify potential inconsistencies.

The basic idea of the EHC is that it uses the way events are apparently organized in memory. Remembering a particular event stimulates the respondent to remember related events or situations, that is, events serve as *cues* for other events. Three different types of cueing can be distinguished: top-down, parallel, and sequential cueing (Belli, 1998).

Top-down cueing refers to relationships between the top and the bottom of a hierarchy. In the EHC this cueing is reflected by first asking about the more general events in a domain, for example a timeline with names of employers, and next a timeline with more specific information, for example one's position. *Sequential* cueing refers to the chronological order of events within the same domain; events are organized in memory on the basis of what happened earlier versus later in time. *Parallel* cueing refers to associations that exist across domains; this memory process reflects the fact that many aspects of life impinge upon individuals simultaneously or nearly so. For example, a change in employment or getting married may affect the residential situation, finishing an education may affect employment status, and so on.

The Interviewer

In addition to the structure of the EHC itself, the interviewer plays an important role in the cueing process, and interviewer behavior should reflect all three principles. For example, the interviewer may ask: "When you worked for employer X, what was your first position?" (top-down cueing). An example of sequential cueing is, "Who was your employer after X?" Maybe the most important cueing mechanism is parallel cueing. For example, the interviewer may ask, "So when you started to work for employer X, that was in 1973, the same year that you moved to Amsterdam, when you were 28 years old?" Interviewers are expected to make frequent cross-checks across domains.

In administering the EHC, the interviewer has considerable freedom. Most interviewer behavior includes many kinds of probes, like probing for changes, and providing the respondent with cues. Such behavior is too complex to be strictly standardized as it depends to a large degree on the reports of the respondent. The interviewer is allowed to go back and forth between domains, as is sometimes necessary in order to cross-check whether particular changes in one domain coincide with changes in other domains. Thus, the EHC is much more flexible than a standardized survey interview that essentially consists only of scripted questions that should be read exactly as worded in a prescribed order, albeit with skip patterns. Moreover, the topics covered in an EHC usually mean that the interviewer is often provided with many details about the personal life of the respondent. In effect, administering an EHC is much more like a real conversation between an interviewer and a respondent. Although it has been shown that a conversational style of interviewing may improve data quality (Conrad & Schober, 2000), and an experimental comparison of EHC interviewing and strictly standardized conventional interviewing showed no evidence of a difference in interviewer variation in data quality (Belli, Lee, Stafford, & Chou, 2004), this flexibility nevertheless enhances the risk of inadequate interviewer performance. When using a flexible rather than a standardized approach, interviewers may be more likely to skip questions, probe insufficiently or suggestively, define key concepts in idiosyncratic ways, fail to read introductory texts or questions as worded, or enter data incorrectly.

Hence, the quality of the data obtained using the EHC procedure depends strongly on the performance of the interviewers. The present research is directed primarily toward checking the performance of the interviewer. Because this performance depends partly on the particular EHC instrument, our evaluation will also concern questionnaire design and EHC procedures. Our research questions are as follows:

- Do interviewers stick to rules of standardization, for example with respect to the wording of prescribed questions?
- Do interviewers grasp the concept of the EHC method and do they apply EHC techniques like parallel probing in an adequate way?
- Do interviewers enter data from the EHC correctly?
- To what extent is the EHC design responsible for interviewer errors?
- How do the paper-and-pencil and computer-assisted versions of the EHC compare?
- How should interviewers be trained to administer an EHC adequately?

Study 1: Paper-and-Pencil EHC

METHOD

The EHC

The paper-and-pencil (PAPI) EHC that was used in our first evaluation study was quite complex and covered a large number of domains and time-lines. For example, the residence domain consisted of addresses, setting (was the residence in a rural or urban setting), and the type of fuel used for heating and cooking. In total there were 35 timelines nested in eight domains: Residence (4 timelines), Life events (marriage, marriage events, and 4 other timelines), Education (2 timelines), Occupation (6 timelines), Tobacco history (5 timelines), Diet, alcohol, and weight (6 timelines in total), Medical history (5 timelines), and Life changes (1 timeline). The EHC covered the respondent's entire life (from birth until present), and the time unit was one year (Freedman et al., 1988). It will be clear that this EHC was a very complex one, requiring considerable interviewing skill.

Prior to administering the EHC itself, some introductory questions were posed (e.g., age, present residence). Next a cognitive test was administered, the SMMSE (Standardized Mini Mental State Examination) (Folstein, Folstein, & McHugh, 1975), and a criterion of performance on the SMMSE was set to determine whether respondents had the ability to complete an EHC. The EHC consisted of a large sheet of paper of about 80 by 30 centimeters (about 30.5 in × 11.8 in). In addition to the EHC, a paper-and-pencil questionnaire was available, including the introductory questions, the SMMSE, the introductory instructions and the prescribed initial questions for each domain and timeline of the EHC, and finally conventional (non-EHC) questions asking for information on socioeconomic status. This questionnaire also contained suggestions for probing behavior and cross-checking for each timeline. A booklet with response alternatives was available to the respondent throughout the questionnaire.

Interviewers and Training

Six experienced interviewers from a large research bureau in the Netherlands participated in the study. None of the interviewers had any prior experience with the EHC as an interviewing method. They all read an interviewer manual with background information about the EHC and how to administer the present EHC. The manual included detailed information about all domains and timelines. After reading the manual, the interviewers were instructed on the use of the EHC procedure during one day. The instruction was provided by an instructor from the research bureau. In order to check the adequacy of the instruction, we attended the instruction session as passive observers. Although the instructor was not acquainted with the EHC method and got most of his information from the interviewer manual, we were impressed with his performance. It was also clear that the interviewers did read the manual before the instruction session, and that they did grasp the essentials of administering the EHC. But we also felt that the interviewers lacked actual practice. Understanding the EHC concepts is a necessary but not sufficient condition for administering the EHC adequately.

Interviews

To evaluate the EHC procedure, 30 EHCs were administered to respondents aged 60 years or older. Respondents were interviewed at their home. All interviews were fully tape-recorded and transcribed. A 40-page checklist was constructed, covering all kinds of aspects of how the EHC was to be administered. Coders filled out this checklist for each interview, on the basis of the completed EHC and the transcribed interview.

Focus Group

After the interviews were conducted, a focus group meeting was held with the six interviewers, guided by the same staff member of the research bureau who gave the instruction. The session was fully recorded on videotape to enable us to study the session in more detail.

RESULTS

Focus Group

The focus group yielded a wealth of information, summarized below. Please note that these results are all based on self-observations by the interviewers.

Although the interviewers were very experienced, most of them felt quite uneasy with the EHC. It was felt necessary to have completed at least two interviews to become acquainted with the whole procedure and to feel comfortable with the EHC. They also sometimes felt uneasy when emotional life events came up (the death of partner, a divorce, etc.), especially if they observed resistance on the part of the respondent to report about these events. Nevertheless, they felt they could handle the situation, probably due to their prior interviewing experience.

Despite this uneasiness, the interviewers were very positive about the interview. They called the interview a "conversation," not an interview. They sometimes became so involved in the conversation that they forgot to turn the audiotape over to the next side. They were unanimously against the idea of splitting interviews into two parts if they took too long or the task became too burdensome for the respondent. During the interview, interviewers and respondents build up a personal relationship in the course of reviewing the respondent's life. Splitting the interview into two parts would adversely impact this relationship, and cross-checking across domains would be much less effective if the interview were split. Such remarks also showed that the interviewers were very well aware of the essential concepts underlying EHC interviewing.

Interviewers reported that respondents also liked the interview, looking back at their lives, remembering events that were nearly forgotten. Respondents did not complain about anonymity, privacy issues, or tape-recording the interview. Instead, they were very willing to provide all kinds of information, including irrelevant information, like describing their houses at previous addresses, troubles with a previous boss, and so on. Structuring the interview is necessary for purposes of efficiency; the interviewer should lead the discussion. All interviewers felt they were able to do so. Respondents often insisted that the interviewer enter *all* information: addresses where the respondent lived for only 2 months, jobs for one month, and the like. Respondents thought it important that all details they remembered with more or less effort should be recorded, and they were surprised, if not embarrassed, if the interviewer failed to record all that was reported (the EHC sheet simply did not allow for such detail). Interviews took about 1.5 hours, but were never experienced as too long or too burdensome by the respondents.

Interviewers found the EHC sheet too large; a lot of room on the table was needed in order to use the EHC together with all the other material (tape recorder, instructions, booklet with response alternatives). Most of the interviewers had trouble handling this large amount of materials. Some interviewers "solved" the lack of space by neglecting some of the materials, for example the questionnaire with prescribed introductions and questions. Instead, the domains and the timelines on the EHC sheet served as a guideline for the interview and they defined key concepts themselves. Other interviewers did not use the booklet with response alternatives at all, but used the questionnaire instead (the questionnaire also contained the response alternatives).

Despite its size, there was often not enough space on the EHC sheet to enter all information (e.g., if the respondent moved frequently in a short period of time, there was not enough room to enter all the addresses). Interviewers also reported that they sometimes found where and how to enter data difficult. For example, if a respondent married and divorced in the same year, how should this be entered into one and the same cell? They sometimes lost track of the correct column (the year) and suggested adding a row with year and age at the bottom of the EHC.

Interviewers reported that they used cross-checking heavily. They also reported that in many cases this led to corrections of earlier timelines. In general, the most problematic was not in remembering the events themselves, but remembering the years in which they occurred. Parallel probing was found very useful (e.g., reminding the respondent of the birth of a child in a particular year, etc.) to determine the year.

From information gained from the focus group we concluded that interviewers should practice EHC procedures during training. Just instruction is clearly not enough. A computerized EHC version may solve a number of data entry and "administrative" problems (i.e., the large amount of materials and the size of the EHC sheet).

The Interviews

Administering the EHC proper, excluding the introductory questions, the SMMSE, and the final questions, took between 45 minutes and 3 hours; on average about 1.5 hours. Although interviews with older respondents took somewhat longer than interviews with (relatively) younger respondents, the correlation between length and respondent age was not significant ($r = 0.20$). We also expected that the first interviews that were conducted by the interviewers would take more time than later interviews because of their becoming acquainted with EHC procedures. However, there appeared to be no correlation at all ($r = 0.02$) between length of interview and the order number of the interview.

The major instrument used to evaluate the EHC was a checklist that was filled out by coders based on the transcribed interviews and the completed EHC. The checklist was intended to compare the transcripts (what the respondent said) with the data entered in the EHC sheet to obtain information about EHC-related interviewer behaviors like cross-checking and probing, and to find causes of errors and poor interviewer performance.

The results of these checklists can partly be summarized by one of our coders who filled out the checklist. She wrote: "All questions were posed, the respondent gave sufficient information, but the EHC was incorrectly filled out, and doesn't represent the actual life course of the respondent."

We indeed were astonished by the large number of errors made by interviewers. A first type of error concerns incorrect data entry. For example, in some timelines the interviewers had to enter an X in the cell (e.g., to signify a marriage in a particular year). In other cases, the interviewer had to enter a number (e.g., to indicate the level of education). Interviewers entered X's where they should have entered numbers, and, more surprisingly entered numbers where they should have entered X's. Interviewers also entered information in wrong timelines, for example "births" on the "partner" timeline. Or they entered the same events in two adjacent cells to account for the respondent saying "maybe in 1996 or 1997."

Other errors concern entering information different from what the respondent said: wrong amounts, wrong years, wrong characters (e.g., "S" for separation instead of "D" for divorce on the marriage events timeline). Or they did not enter information at all; this error was usually caused by lack of space on the EHC timeline. For example, interviewers deliberately skipped addresses if there were a number of residential moves in a few years.

A second type of error concerns behavior that is not specific to the present EHC procedure, but reflects more general poor interviewer behavior, most notably unwarranted inferences (e.g., filling in complete timelines without even asking the respondent), and suggestive behavior (e.g., suggesting a year in which something could have happened, instead of stimulating the respondent to think of the year). Sometimes the booklet with response alternatives was not used at all; the interviewer just selected a response alternative based on an inference about the respondent's answer.

This list is far from exhaustive. Fortunately there is also good news. From the transcripts it was clear that the interviewers did grasp the essential idea of the EHC. They did make quite a lot of cross-references. Quite interestingly, it appeared that respondents often referred to events that were not part of one of the domains, especially World War II and the deaths of relatives and friends. Interviewers soon learned that such cues helped the respondent and cross-checked deliberately with such landmarks, like, "That was when your father died," or probed with, "Did that change during the war?"

CONCLUSIONS FROM STUDY 1

Data quality is hampered by numerous kinds of interviewer errors. A main cause of errors is insufficient interviewer training. The interviewers clearly had insufficient knowledge of all instructions and rules on how to fill in the EHC. It is of utmost importance that interviewers have the opportunity to practice with the EHC. Just instruction and an interviewer manual is not enough. It may be noted here that the research bureau was absolutely convinced that a single day of instruction would be sufficient.

In addition, interviewers should be trained in general interviewer skills. The flexible, conversational nature of the EHC interview indeed enhances the risk of poor interviewer behavior, for example, suggestive probing. Interviewers should be carefully trained to probe in a neutral way.

A more positive conclusion is that interviewers understood the essential idea of the EHC and acted accordingly. Cueing seems to improve the memory of the respondent. Moreover, the EHC was not too burdensome for the respondents, despite its length and the respondents' age.

Recommendations: Interviewer Training

An adequate interviewer training should contain the following elements:

Exercises. Scripts or scenarios describing in detail the life of a fictitious respondent are used by interviewers to fill out (parts of) the EHC.

Role-plays. Interviewers will interview each other about particular domains in role-plays. Special attention will be paid to probing techniques, parallel probing, and preventing suggestive behavior like leading questions. Use can be made of videotaping and later playing back parts of the interviews.

Practice interview. Interviewers should practice with a real respondent during training. The interview may be videotaped and should be discussed extensively.

Monitoring interviews. During the fieldwork, interviewer performance should be monitored. Parts of the interviews may be audiorecorded and subjected to a simple checklist. Intermediate data files can be checked for inconsistencies, interviewer variance, and the like.

Recommendations: EHC Design

For cueing purposes, we recommend adding a general timeline with landmarks to the EHC. Respondents often related the timing of events to such general events, most notably World War II, but other events were also mentioned, like the attacks on New York City and Washington, D.C., on September 11, 2001.

Private events were also mentioned, especially the death of a parent, but also retirement and severe illness. Adding a timeline for such private high-impact events is strongly recommended.

Data entry errors can be partly prevented if it is clearer to the interviewer what should be entered where. We recommend that *within* each timeline, in a light gray font, some essential reminders are entered, like "Life events: enter 'S' for separation and 'D' for divorce"; or "Birth: enter 'X' in the year of a birth."

Recommendations: A Computer-Assisted EHC

A better way to prevent data entry errors is a computer-assisted version of the EHC. For example, such a computer program might prevent the interviewer from entering an X if a number should be entered. It can also check for any unallowed gaps in a timeline; for example, the timeline designed to collect residential history should have no gaps. Introductory scripts can be adjusted depending on whether the respondent is male or female, or has a spouse or not, and so on, thus preventing complex sentences that include multiple possibilities like "he or she" or "If the respondent has a spouse then ask . . . ; if not, then ask . . ." Questions or timelines can be skipped if not applicable; for example, if the respondent does not have any children, the birth timeline can be skipped to prevent information from being incorrectly entered in it.

A computer-assisted version can also contain the introductory scripts, the response alternatives, suggested probes and cross-checks, and a help function where the interviewer can easily find information about how to handle difficult situations.

We decided to apply the recommendations above and to conduct another evaluation study, this time with a computer-assisted interviewing EHC.

Study 2: Computer-Assisted EHC

METHOD

The Computer-Assisted EHC

An advantage of the PAPI version of the EHC is that the life course of the respondent is constantly depicted on the EHC sheet, and thus visible to the respondent. This may stimulate the memory of the respondent and makes links between life events from different timelines and domains, as well as between subsequent events on the same timeline, directly visible, thus indirectly providing parallel and sequential cues to the respondent. A drawback of a computer-assisted (CAI) version, where the EHC is depicted on a laptop, might be the absence of such a visual aid for the respondent. Hence it was decided to use two laptops: one for the interviewer to enter data, and one laptop to serve as a visual aid for the respondent. As soon as the interviewer enters data, these data appear in the CAI-EHC, on both the interviewer's and the respondent's screens. When response options were available, these would be shown on the respondent's screen, while the interviewer poses the question. On request, the interviewer could also show the text of the questions (in case of hearing disabilities) and could adjust the font size (in case of visual problems).

The CAI device was developed by a software firm in close interaction with the researchers. The researchers continuously evaluated the device, for example, with respect to programming flaws (bugs), user friendliness, and appropriateness in view of the goal of the instrument. A small feasibility study was conducted with four respondents and research assistants as interviewers to test the ease of entering data in practice and the reactions of respondents to the respondent's screen. Figure 15.1 shows an example of the CAI-EHC.

It was also decided to record the interviews digitally (on the laptop itself to obtain high-quality recordings and to avoid an extra tape recorder) for purposes of monitoring interviewer performance during fieldwork. The programming work started about September 2004 and by about March 2005 the CAI version reached a final stage and was ready for the second evaluation study.

Interviewers and Training

Unlike the first study, which was conducted by a large research bureau, we conducted the present study. The main reasons were that we wanted to have

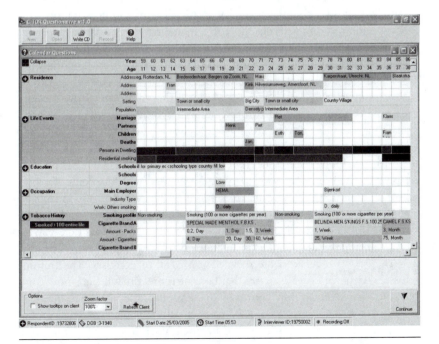

Figure 15.1   Example of EHC Screen

SOURCE: Copyright © Developed for the use of The Weinberg Group LLC by Kendle International. Used by permission.

first-hand experience with flaws in the training procedures and that the kind of training is very specialized (we probably would have had to train trainers from a research bureau before allowing them to train interviewers).

The interviews were administered by six interviewers. Three of them were very experienced interviewers who belonged to a regular pool of interviewers from a Free University project for large-scale surveys, and in particular had experience with interviewing older respondents. The three other interviewers were relatively inexperienced. They were graduate social science students and were hired because they got an introduction to the EHC method in one of their university courses. We wanted to have a mix of experienced and inexperienced interviewers to assess whether there would be any differences in performance associated with interviewer experience. All interviewers were female. The three experienced interviewers were aged between 58 and 59 years, the three relatively inexperienced interviewers between 22 and 27. All interviewers had computer experience.

A training manual was developed, describing general interviewing issues, a discussion of response effects (especially over- and underreporting and retrieval problems), and the respective roles of interviewer and respondent (i.e., interviewer tasks like question reading, showing interest, listening to the respondent, and judging the adequacy of answers). In addition, interviewing skills specific to administering the EHC, including theoretical backgrounds and the principles of cueing and probing techniques, were discussed. A separate computer manual describing the features of the computer program was developed by the programming team.

A training program was developed, consisting of 3 days of two sessions each. The training consisted of presentations by a trainer, highlighting and explaining particular issues, exercises, role-playing, and a practice interview with a "real" respondent. Exercises concerned written scenarios with detailed life stories, enabling the trainees to record responses in the EHC. The primary purpose of the exercises was to become acquainted with the computer program. Role-playing is done with descriptions of life events of respondents. In a simulated interview, two trainees play the roles of interviewer and respondent. Role-playing interviews are videotaped for later discussion. Role-playing scripts consisted of descriptions of fictitious situations for the "respondent."

The first two sessions are devoted primarily to exercises. The training schedule starts with easy exercises that become more difficult (i.e., more complex life events) during the course of the sessions. Role-playing is the main activity during sessions 3 to 5. Role-plays should take place in small groups (maximally four trainees), supervised by one trainer, in order for trainees to get sufficient opportunity for role-playing. The last session is devoted to interviewing a "real" respondent. Each trainee interviews the respondent with a part of the questionnaire; in this way the whole interview is administered. The interview is observed by the other trainees ("observers"). This interview is also videotaped and discussed afterward.

Interviews

Interviewing started immediately after the training. The interviews were conducted at the Free University. All respondents were 65 years or older. Each interviewer was expected to interview five respondents. We ended up with 25 interviews, however, because one respondent did not show up, and one interviewer withdrew herself after one interview. All interviews were videotaped.

Before they entered the interviewing room, respondents were informed that there were two laptops, one for the interviewer and one for the respondent, but that they were not expected to use their laptop. They were told the laptop was just for a visual display of the information they would be providing during the interview. Respondents were also told that the interview would be videotaped, unless they objected. Not a single respondent objected.

No special technical or logistical problems were encountered. In four cases the video recordings showed that an interviewer had some computer problems, which she was able to solve on her own. In one case, the assistance of a researcher was necessary. In general, however, the program and computers worked as expected and the audio recordings were of good quality.

Immediately after all interviews were finished, a focus group of the interviewees was organized; it was supervised by one of the trainers. The focus group took about 2 hours and was videotaped in order to be able to study the comments of the interviewers in more detail.

RESULTS

The Training

During the training we made a number of observations, assisting us to improve the training further. These observations are summarized in this section.

All interviewers were expected to read the manual before the training started. As in the first validation study, it was clear that they did. Actually, because the training started with a presentation introducing the study and the EHC method, most interviewers found this introduction partly superfluous. It was clear that it is not necessary to spend much time on such introductions during the training, thus saving valuable training time. Interviewers were very positive about the manual.

The exercises (filling in the EHC using written scenarios) served their purpose less well than expected, due to the complexity of the life events described in these scenarios. Actually, the scenarios were written to serve the purpose not only of learning the computer program, but a number of EHC principles as well. This was simply too much for the trainees: Exercises should be as simple as possible and serve only the purpose of learning the computer program.

Role-playing took much more time than planned because trainees, in their role of respondents, and especially the older experienced interviewers, tended to exaggerate their roles, extending the life events from the scripted role-plays with long (fictitious) stories. Due to lack of time, the video recordings of the role-plays were used less often than planned.

It very soon became apparent that there were large differences with respect to the computer skills of the interviewers. All student interviewers had sufficient computer skills, but this was less true for the older interviewers. Differences in computer skills also hampered the efficiency of the training: Trainees who finished their exercise just sat and waited until the other interviewers had finished their exercises.

The practice interview with the "real" respondent appeared to be an important addition to the training. After having interviewed a stranger, the interviewers felt much more comfortable and self-assured.

The Focus Group

Many of our own observations during the training were also made by the interviewers in the focus group, and we will not repeat them here. The most important goal of the focus group was to obtain information about how to improve the training.

The interviewers themselves liked the EHC interview and reported that the respondents' attitude toward the interview was positive. According to the interviewers, respondents liked the interview and it was not too burdensome for them; they were quite motivated to provide the required information. Most respondents also liked the respondent's screen unfolding their own life history. A few respondents did not seem to pay much attention to their screen.

The interviewers judged the manual with information about the study, general interviewing skills, and specific interviewing skills with respect to the EHC as quite adequate. Introductions at the start of the training should not be too long, since much is already covered by the manual; interviewers were eager to start with the "real" work. Sufficient attention was paid to emotional situations, although they realized that in an actual interview the impact of emotion-arousing events would be much greater than in a role-play situation. A 3-day training period was felt sufficient to train interviewers to administer the CAI-EHC. A longer training period would be less efficient because trainees (and trainers) are pretty exhausted after 3 days.

The interviewers did feel, however, that the training itself could be improved or made more efficient with respect to several aspects. In the next section we will give a number of recommendations based upon our own experiences during the training and the evaluation of the interviewers during the focus group meeting.

Recommendations With Respect to the Training

Exercises should be simple, describing a respondent with relatively few and nonproblematic life events. Exercises should be directed primarily toward using the instrument, not toward learning EHC principles. The first exercise should treat the whole questionnaire instead of covering only a small part, as was the case in the present study. In this way the interviewer becomes acquainted with the whole questionnaire in a relatively short time and a firmer base is laid with respect to the basics of handling the CAI device. Later exercises can add more complex life events.

Like the exercises, role-playing scripts should concern not-too-difficult situations (after all, it is not possible to confront trainees with all kinds of possible complications). Equally important, trainees should be better instructed about their roles as respondents. In addition, the role-play scripts we used contained information about only one particular domain (e.g., job history). Role-play scripts, however, should also have basic information about the timelines that precede the part of the EHC that the role-play addresses (e.g., education, marriage, and births) to give the trainee the opportunity to practice cross-checking.

Interviewers differed with respect to computer skills and in one case these skills were completely insufficient. Interviewers should have sufficient computer skills before entering the training. It is recommended that a short computer test be administered to candidate interviewers to check their computer skills.

The Interviews

The EHC part of the interviews (excluding introductory questions, SMMSE, and final questions concerning SES) took on average somewhat less than 1.5 hours (87 minutes). The shortest interview was nearly one hour, whereas the longest took a bit more than 2 hours. Like the first evaluation study, there was no significant correlation between length and order of interview ($r = -0.19$) or respondent age ($r = 0.01$).

A number of indications about the adequacy of the performance of the interviewers were derived from a systematic analysis of the audio- and videorecordings of the interviews. We discuss here a number of issues like question reading, parallel cueing, and probing in more detail.

The majority of the prescribed initial questions were read adequately (44%) or with only minor changes (39%). Generally, the interviewers performed better than the interviewers in the first evaluation study; nevertheless it is also clear that there is room for improvement. Table 15.1 shows some of the more astonishing examples of misread questions. From these examples it will be clear that the training should stress that questions be read as worded. This is also an issue for interviewer monitoring during fieldwork; especially when interviewers are made aware of monitoring and are given effective feedback, this is likely to influence their behavior positively (Cannell & Oksenberg, 1988).

From the conversation between interviewer and respondent we could infer that interviewers did not always show the response alternatives on the respondent's screen. We suggest that the CAI device be adjusted in such a way that the alternatives are displayed; for example, if alternatives are not shown, it will not be possible to enter data.

In contrast to findings in another study (Belli et al., 2004), interviewers used parallel cues reasonably often. In particular, the timelines "Addresses," "Employer," and, to a lesser degree, "Marriage events" were used for cueing. However, about 50% of the parallel cues were suggestive rather than neutral. Interviewers apparently found it difficult to distinguish between suggestive and nonsuggestive parallel cueing. For example, "Did you start smoking when your mother died?" is a suggestive cue. Cues should be *balanced*, like: "Did you start smoking before or after your mother died?"

In particular, the diagnosis of certain diseases was sometimes based upon changing food and smoking habits: Interviewers assume that when respondents quit smoking, drinking alcohol, or using fat products this is directly related to the diagnosis of a disease, and therefore suggest this in their probe.

Interviewers seldom used the landmarks, except World War II (especially with the diet timelines); most of the other landmarks were hardly helpful at all. Instead, personal life events that have a lot of impact, like the death of important persons, were much more helpful; this timeline should be extended with additional life events, like a car accident or a very special holiday.

During the interview, interviewers should probe often for changes. For example, while administering the "Diet" timeline, the interviewer should ask something like, "Did your diet change after that?" In many cases, however, the interviewer probed in a suggestive way, like: "And that was the same your whole life?" Because respondents tend to agree with such probes, data quality may be affected (note that incorrectly agreeing with "Did your diet change" is unlikely to affect data quality, because the respondent next has to indicate *what* changed). About 20% of the probes for changes were suggestive and occurred especially in the health domain (questions about diet and alcohol use; about 32% of the probes).

Conclusion

Comparing the PAPI version with the CAI version of the EHC showed that quite a lot of errors that occurred in the first evaluation study (the PAPI version) seldom appeared in the second one (the CAI version). Most notably,

Table 15.1   Examples of Questions Read With Major Change or Posed
Suggestively

Prescribed Wording	Interviewer Wording
• Have you ever lived with a partner as if married?	• Did you live together with your wife?
• I am also interested in how many people, including yourself, were living in the same household as you?	• How many persons were living in your house when you were born?
• Have you ever worked in any of the following professions or industries even for a short period of time?	• The work you did for Company X, was this an industrial work environment?
• Did you work indoors or outdoors? [If indoors:] To what extent were you exposed to other people's smoking while at your workplace?	• Can you tell me how was the smoking at work?
• Have you ever smoked 100 or more cigarettes in your entire lifetime?	• Are you a smoker?
• Please indicate, since at least age 13, whether you had diets high in fatty foods, moderate in fatty foods, or low in fatty foods.	• Do you eat a lot of fat?
• Did you ever consume more than 100 units of alcoholic beverages in your entire lifetime?	• Do you use alcohol?
• Has a doctor ever told you that you have any of the following types of cancer?	• Now some kinds of cancer happen to appear on my screen. Did you ever suffer from that cancer?

far fewer data entry errors were made. In this respect the CAI instrument performed much better than the PAPI version. The CAI program also reminded the interviewer in a number of cases that the EHC was not complete when the interviewer wanted to finish the EHC part. Moreover, notwithstanding the fact that in a number of cases questions were read quite inadequately, the majority of questions were read correctly, and to a larger extent than in the PAPI version.

With respect to the degree of parallel cueing and other specific EHC techniques, the differences between the PAPI and CAI versions were not very large. We suspect that this is partly because not all interviewers mastered the computer program sufficiently, thus distracting them from other tasks. Neither was there much difference in the average duration of the interview between administering the PAPI version and the CAI version. Here, too, we expect improvement if interviewers become better acquainted with the computer program.

Moreover, the CAI version eliminates time involved in data entry that is required for PAPI-EHCs: The data from a PAPI-EHC still need to be entered into a computer.

Of utmost importance is adequate interviewer training. On the basis of our experiences with the training in the second evaluation study we completely revised the interviewer training. By now we have given this training a number of times to different trainees and are quite satisfied with its quality. In addition, we set up a scheme of refresher trainings. These one-day courses appear to be extremely helpful. It seems that during a refresher course the interviewers suddenly really grasp the ideas behind the EHC, the difference between suggestive and neutral probing, and the options provided by the computer program.

Finally, we set up a scheme for interviewer monitoring by systematically coding interviewer behavior using the audiorecorded interviews. Interviewers who perform inadequately may be completely retrained, take an extra refresher course, or just be provided with feedback.

The procedures we have discussed—conducting evaluation studies, developing a computer-assisted instrument, setting up trainings, monitoring the performance of interviewers—are no doubt costly and time-consuming. Nevertheless, we think this is the only way to obtain data of high quality. If such requirements are fulfilled, the EHC method appears to be an extremely valuable instrument for obtaining life course data. If training is not adequate, using an EHC is a waste of money as it will not represent the actual life course of the respondent, as one of our coders observed in the first evaluation study.

Acknowledgment

This research was carried out with the financial support of Philip Morris International.

References

Belli, R. F. (1998). The structure of autobiographical memory and the event history calendar: Potential improvements in the quality of retrospective reports in surveys. *Memory, 6,* 383–406.

Belli, R. F., Lee, E. H., Stafford, F. P., & Chou, C.-H. (2004). Calendar and question-list survey methods: Association between interviewer behaviors and data quality. *Journal of Official Statistics, 20,* 185–218.

Belli, R. F., Shay, W. L., & Stafford, F. P. (2001). Event history calendars and question list surveys: A direct comparison of interviewing methods. *Public Opinion Quarterly, 65,* 45–74.

Cannell, C. F., & Oksenberg, L. (1988). Observation of behavior in telephone interviews. In R. Groves, P. Biemer, L. Lyberg, J. Massey, W. Nicholls II, & J. Waksberg (Eds.), *Telephone survey methodology* (pp. 475–495). New York: John Wiley.

Conrad, F. G., & Schober, M. F. (2000). Clarifying question meaning in a household telephone survey. *Public Opinion Quarterly, 64,* 1–28.

Folstein, M. F., Folstein, S. E., & McHugh, P. R. (1975). Mini-mental state: A practical method for grading the cognitive state of patients for a clinician. *Journal of Psychiatric Research 12,* 189–198.

Fowler, F. J., & Mangione, T. W. (1990). *Standardized survey interviewing: Minimizing interviewer-related error.* Newbury Park, CA: Sage.

Freedman, D., Thornton, A., Camburn, D., Alwin, D., & Young-DeMarco, L. (1988). The life history calendar: A technique for collecting retrospective data. *Sociological Methodology, 18,* 37–68.

Furstenberg, F. F. J., Brooks-Gunn, J., & Morgan, P. S. (1987). *Adolescent mothers in later life.* New York: Cambridge University Press.

Smit, J. H., Dijkstra, W., & Van der Zouwen, J. (1997). Suggestive interviewer behaviour in surveys: An experimental study. *Journal of Official Statistics, 13,* 19–28.

16

Assessing the Validity and Reliability of Timeline and Event History Data

Duane F. Alwin

Introduction

In recent years, a great deal of theory and research has paid attention to the life span development of individuals and how events and experiences earlier in life contribute to developments later on (Elder, Johnson, & Crosnoe, 2003; Elder & Shanahan, 2006; Kuh & New Dynamics of Ageing (NDA) Preparatory Network [Kuh & NDA], 2007). Empirically linking earlier and later events and experiences over time within individual lives, or showing the unfolding of the nature and structure of the life course and its consequences, requires that we have valid and reliable reports about the events and experiences in people's life histories (Elder, 1985, 2000; Scott & Alwin, 1997). From a measurement perspective, it is clear that event history calendars and daily diaries of events and experiences represent two of the most promising avenues for gathering information on event occurrences over time (Belli, 1998, 2000; Freedman, Thornton, Camburn, Alwin, & Young-DeMarco, 1988; Juster, 1985).

In keeping with the general goals of this volume, this chapter focuses on methods for assessing measurement quality in timeline and event history data. It is evident from even a cursory review of the methodological literature on this topic that there are a number of different methods that have been used to assess data quality in calendar and diary research. Some strategies focus on the success of data collection by examining such things as the extent of incomplete data and respondent adherence to investigator protocols (see, e.g., Stone & Broderick, Chapter 14, this volume). Such approaches are essential to the evaluation of the quality of event and timeline measurement.

Data quality in survey research can also be evaluated using techniques rooted in the psychometric concepts of *reliability* and *validity* (see Alwin, 2007; Saris & Gallhofer, 2007). Although there are a number of different approaches to assessing data quality in these terms, the typical approach involves an examination of the extent of correspondence of multiple assessments of the same events and experiences (see, e.g., Belli, Shay, & Stafford, 2001; Belli, Smith, Andreski, & Agrawal, 2007; Freedman et al., 1988). Measures of agreement are used to assess correspondence or consistency across multiple assessments, and these are used to interpret relative performance of measurement approaches across domains of content. In this latter type of research, the concept of validity refers to the extent to which measures capture the intended construct of interest, whereas reliability refers to the consistency of measurement (American Educational Research Association, American Psychological Association, & National Council on Measurement in Education [AERA, APA, & NCME], 1999). In other words, validity refers to *what* we are measuring—reliability refers to *how well* we are measuring it, regardless of what it is. As I note below, reliability provides an upper bound on the level of validity that can be empirically assessed (Alwin, 2007).

Using these ideas as its foundation, this chapter discusses methods for the evaluation of the quality of event history and timeline data collected in survey interviews. The chapter is motivated in part by the observation of a general level of confusion among survey researchers about the concepts of reliability and validity and what they have to do with survey measurement. One of the goals of this chapter, therefore, is to clarify their nature and their applicability to the measurement of life course events and experiences in sample surveys. In this chapter I, thus, first briefly review the concepts of reliability and validity as they can be applied in the context of survey research. Second, I discuss the research design requirements for assessing the quality of survey measurement as guided by psychometric concepts, and therein I stress the importance of using longitudinal designs for measuring data quality. Third, I discuss approaches used to quantify the quality of measurement of diary and timeline data—typically involving reports of discrete events and experiences—including levels of agreement, correlation, and reliability, and ultimately I consider estimates of the conditional probabilities of particular observations, given membership in latent event classes. In this context I illustrate some of the advantages and disadvantages of these approaches for assessing the quality of event data, using data from the Intergenerational Panel Study of Parents and Children, a longitudinal study begun in 1962 in Detroit, Michigan, that has since 1985 collected event history data across multiple domains of experience (see Freedman et al., 1988).[1]

The Concepts of Reliability and Validity

In some ways, data collected in diary and timeline assessments are no different from other types of information collected using survey questionnaires, and the methods for assessing their validity and/or reliability are in principle not different from evaluating survey data in general (see Alwin, 2007). However, the models often proposed for assessing reliability and validity are primarily applicable to survey measures in which the underlying, or latent, variable of interest is continuous in nature, for example, household income, or level of satisfaction with the economy. In other words, in the majority of research on survey measurement quality, available methods of validity and reliability assessment primarily involve cases wherein the measures assess an underlying variable defined as consisting of an interval scale, that is, a continuous variable. However, when the latent variable is a set of latent classes, the classical continuous variable models for reliability and validity assessment are inappropriate, and other strategies are needed. Hence, in discussions of assessing the reliability or validity of calendar and event history data, it is therefore important to distinguish between measures of latent continuous variables and those assessing latent categories (see Alwin, 2007). I return subsequently to the distinction between continuous and categorical latent variables—first I discuss the concepts of reliability and validity in relation to issues of measurement in survey research.

OBSERVED AND LATENT VARIABLES

Whatever the nature of the metrics of the variables involved—categorical or continuous—it is necessary for our purposes to distinguish between *observed* (or manifest) variables and *unobserved* (or latent) variables and to conceptualize the linkage between the two levels of discourse. This distinction between latent and manifest variables allows us to define the concepts of reliability and validity in terms that are familiar to most researchers. First, it is important to think of a response to a survey question to be an "observed" variable that reflects some "latent" variable or construct of interest, and our interest is in conceptualizing the relationship between the two. If we define the response variable as a random variable (Y), observed in some population of interest, that has a latent counterpart (T), which is also a random variable in the given population, and which in part is responsible for the production of the response, that is, $T \rightarrow Y$, we can readily define the concepts of reliability and validity, as in the following: By definition, the observed variable in this case is literally what we can think of as a "survey response" (see Groves, 1989), and the "latent" or "unobserved" variable is what the survey question is intended to measure. We may think of T as a part of (or a component of) Y. There is no necessary identity between the two, however, as we know, there are a number of types of "survey measurement errors," which we can define globally using the notation E, that are also a part of Y. In this sense, we can conceptualize Y as having two major parts that contribute to the survey response, a "true" and "error" component: $T \rightarrow Y \leftarrow E$.

Note that while Y is observed, both T and E are unobserved, or latent, variables. This type of formulation allows us to think in terms of two general considerations when examining the variation observed in survey responses; one is the variation in the underlying phenomenon one is trying to measure, for example, income or employment status, and the other is the variation contributed by "errors of measurement." The consideration of each of these parts—the part concerning the construct one is trying to measure as well as the part concerning survey measurement errors—is a worthy effort.

It is important to note that this formulation is intended to be very general, allowing for a range of different types of Y and T random variables, Y and T variables that represent discrete categories, as well as Y and T variables that are continuous. There are a number of different cases or types of situations involving different types of variables at each level. If Y and T are continuous random variables in a specified population of interest, for example, and if it is assumed that E is random with respect to the latent variable, that is, T and E are uncorrelated determinants of Y, we have the case that is represented by *classical true-score theory* (CTST), where the T latent variable is referred to as a true score and measurement error is simply defined as the difference between the true score and the observed score: $E = Y - T$ (see Alwin, 2007; Groves, 1989).

In general, there is no constraint on the covariance properties of E and T, although in the CTST case, E is considered to be random, that is, uncorrelated with T. This assumption underlies the development of psychometric approaches to estimating reliability, as I discuss below. Although we generally find the CTST to be quite valuable in many situations, it has certain limitations, especially when it comes to assessing the reliability and validity of event and calendar data. For this reason, we insist on a more general conceptualization that permits T to be either a set of latent nominal classes, a set of latent ordered classes, or a latent continuous variable, *and* a conceptualization that permits Y also to be a nominal, ordinal, or interval response variable (see Alwin, 2007, pp. 128–130).

Before developing the idea of reliability further, however, it is important to add more complexity, in order to eventually incorporate the concept of reliability into the discussion of validity. Indeed, in addition to reliability, and perhaps of greater interest, is the concept of validity—the extent to which the investigator is measuring the theoretical construct of interest. In a more general sense, measurement validity refers to the extent to which measurement accomplishes the purpose for which it is intended, that is, are you measuring what you think you are measuring? Validity is a somewhat more elusive concept than reliability, given the absence of adequate criteria for its evaluation (see AERA, APA, & NCME, 1999). Although matters of validity are often thought to be capable of solutions on an abstract level, as with the notion of "content" or "face" validity, on an empirical level the issue of validity can be defined only with respect to some criterion that is related to the purpose of measurement. Often, the validity of measurement is assessed with respect to its correlation with criterion variables that lie outside the particular survey, and that are considered to be associated with the survey measurement. In addition, validity is often defined at the level of the construct, that is, the relationship between T (or the latent variable being measured) and the construct of interest, C, or, $C \rightarrow T$. Of course, without a direct measure of this "construct of interest" one often must fall back on notions of *criterion-related validity*.

I should note at this point that, although some will mistake it for validity, when traditional psychometric approaches refer to the *reliability* of measurement *on a conceptual level*, they refer to the closeness of the correlation between Y and T. Thus, when one is dealing with measurements that are reliable, it is assumed that the measurement error part of Y is minimal, and in a "variance accounting" framework, mostly due to latent "true" variation. By contrast, when measures are unreliable, it is because there is a great deal more "error of measurement" than "true variation," that is, much more "noise" than "signal," to use a metaphor from radio telegraphy. Validity, on the other hand, refers to the extent of correlation between T and C. High reliability is important in part because validity depends on reliability—without highly reliable measures, high validity is impossible. Reliability of measurement is a sine qua non of all social science research, and it is readily shown that reliability is a necessary although not sufficient condition for validity (see Alwin, 2007, pp. 291–292).

It turns out that the best estimate of this correlation between Y and T is the correlation between two identical measures of T, say Y_1 and Y_2, and hence we tend to think of reliability in terms of the way we assess it, namely as the consistency in two identical efforts to measure the same thing. I return below to the problem of estimating reliability and validity via the implementation of research designs that permit these types of interpretations. It is important for present purposes that we distinguish between the "conceptualization" of reliability and validity on one hand and the "estimation" of them on the other. It deserves emphasis that the concepts of reliability and validity are often confused with the methods we use to measure them.

Finally, it is important to understand the relationship between reliability and validity. It can be shown that the *criterion validity* of a measure—its correlation with another variable—cannot exceed the reliability of either variable (Alwin, 2007; Lord & Novick, 1968). There is a mathematical proof for this assertion (Alwin, 2007, pp. 291–292), but the logic that underlies the idea is normally accepted without formal proof: If our measures are unreliable, it is difficult to establish their validity, and they cannot be trusted to detect patterns and relationships among variables of interest. Thus, it needs to be emphasized that when such a relationship between T and C is assessed via examination of the relationship between two forms of measurement of the same events (e.g., Belli et al., 2001; Belli et al., 2007), this comparison is constrained by the reliability of both sets of reports, and their observed relationship will be attenuated due to unreliability of measurement.

To summarize, for our present purposes we take reliability to refer to the relationship between Y and T (as stated above), whereas validity has to do with the relationship between T and C, that is, between the latent variable being measured and the theoretical construct of interest. When one has another measure, such as a "record of the variable" or a "gold standard" for this theoretical construct, then one can examine the relationship between T and C, where C is represented by another variable (say X), referred to as a criterion (and, hence, this is called criterion-related validity). Such designs are relatively rare, but when available, they can be very useful (I return to a brief discussion of these below). As already noted, both measures of "gold standards" and of "alternative methods" contain measurement error, so such correlations or measures of agreement must always be interpreted in light of reliability of measurement in both variables.

Research Designs for Assessments of Data Quality

With respect to assessment, according to Campbell and Fiske (1959) both concepts of reliability and validity require that agreement between measurements— *validity* is supported when there is correspondence between two efforts to measure the same trait through *maximally different* methods; *reliability* is demonstrated when there is agreement between two efforts to assess the same thing using *maximally similar*, or replicate, measures (Campbell & Fiske, 1959, p. 83). Thus, both types of studies involve assessing the correspondence between measures—studies of reliability focus on the consistency of repeating the measurement using replicate measures, whereas researches on validity are concerned with the correspondence of a given measure to some criterion of interest, taking into account the reliability of either measure.

VALIDATION STUDIES

Establishing the validity of survey measurement is difficult because within a given survey instrument there is typically little available information that would establish a criterion for validation. In the psychometric tradition, the concept of validity has mainly to do with the utility of measures with respect to getting at particular theoretical concepts. This concept of validity is difficult to adapt to the case of survey measures, given the absence of well-defined criteria representing the theoretical construct, but several efforts have been made. There is a well-known genre of research situated under the heading "record check studies" (Marquis, 1978), where the investigator compares survey reports with a set of record data that may exist for the variables in question in a given population (see Bound, Brown, Duncan, & Rodgers, 1990). This is an important design that has been used for studying validity, and although rare, such studies can shed light on survey measurement errors; as stressed earlier, however, correlations among multiple sources of information are limited by the level of reliability involved in reports from either source (Alwin, 2007, pp. 48–49).

Another design that has been used in the study of nonfactual content, for example, attitudes, beliefs, and self-perceptions, involves the application of multitrait-multimethod (MTMM) measurement designs, where the investigator measures multiple concepts using multiple methods of measurement. In recent years, a great deal of attention has been paid to a model originally proposed by Campbell and Fiske (1959) involving the measurement of multiple concepts or "traits," each measured using multiple "methods"—hence, the multitrait-multimethod measurement design (MTMM) (see Alwin, 1997, 2007; Saris & Gallhofer, 2007; Scherpenzeel & Saris, 1997). Using this design, methods have been developed for separating validity and invalidity in survey reports. Its use has been limited to the study of components of variance in measures of attitudes, beliefs, and self-descriptions primarily because there are often not multiple measurement formats for gathering factual data. The inherent value of the logic of these MTMM designs for the present case of event and timeline measurement should be obvious.

A third type of validation study is what has been referred to as "gold standard" studies, where an alternative approach to measurement, for instance, an event history calendar, is compared to data gathered on the same people using the method that represents the *gold standard* or the accepted or standard approach to measuring particular content (see, e.g., Belli et al., 2001). All of these qualify under the definition of validity studies, in that they all three are aimed at examining the correspondence between responses to a particular survey question and the "true" or "best" indicator of the construct it is intended to measure. All of these validation designs embody the principle articulated by Campbell and Fiske (1959), that the best evidence for validity is the convergence of measurements employing maximally different methods.

RELIABILITY STUDIES

With respect to studies of reliability, there are several standard methods of reliability estimation in common use in survey research; however, many of these approaches are in general inadequate for purposes of dealing with the reliability of survey data, and are limited with respect to assessing the reliability of event and calendar data in particular. Strategies of reliability estimation for continuous variables are well developed, and because they are discussed at length elsewhere, we only briefly consider these models here—see Alwin (2007) for a detailed discussion of these models.

The basic model for reliability assessment is derived from a set of definitions about the true score of a fixed person as an expected value of that person's propensity distribution (see Lord & Novick, 1968). The classical literature on reliability estimation states that "the correlation between truly parallel measurements taken in such a way that the person's true score does not change between them is often called the *coefficient of precision*" (p. 134). In this case the only source contributing to measurement error is the unreliability or imprecision of measurement. The assumption here, as is expected in all such designs, is that "if a measurement were taken twice and if no practice, fatigue, memory, or other factor affected repeated measurements," the correlation between the measures reflects the precision, or reliability, of measurement (p. 134).

What is problematic in survey questionnaires is the inability or difficulty of obtaining replicate or multiple measures of the same interview. Cronbach (1951) developed a measure of what is often referred to as "internal consistency reliability" (ICR), which assumed that the measures are univocal (i.e., measures one and only one thing) and that the property of tau-equivalence (i.e., measures having equal true scores) holds for the measures; this is frequently used by survey researchers to estimate the reliability of survey data. There have been alternative ICR approaches that generalize Cronbach's models to the general case of weighted linear composites (see, e.g., Alwin, 2007, pp. 51–53; Greene & Carmines, 1979; Jöreskog, 1971). These ICR models are not technically estimates of reliability in models where tau-equivalence does not hold, and there are several limitations as an approach to assessing reliability. First, given this relatively stringent set of requirements on the design of survey measures, they are often unrealistic for purposes of assessing the reliability in survey measurement. Second, and increasingly, research on survey methodology has been moving in the direction of assessing the reliability of single survey questions rather than composite variables (e.g., Alwin, 1989, 1992, 1997, 2004, 2007; Groves, 1989; Saris & Andrews, 1991; Saris & Gallhofer, 2007; Saris & van Meurs, 1990; Scherpenzeel & Saris, 1997). Third, the idea of using coefficients that assume a composite measure of the underlying variable is unrealistic, and certainly so for assessing the reliability (or validity) of event or timeline data in the vast majority of cases. Standard internal consistency approaches, for example, coefficient α, make no sense in such cases.

In past years, another method considered superior to the ICR approach, the test-retest method, was considered a superior design for assessing reliability (see Siegel & Hodge, 1968) in terms of Lord and Novick's (1968, p. 134) standards of "repeated measurement" and the coefficient of precision. Early in the survey methods literature, serious issues were raised about the utility of the test-retest approach (Moser & Kalton, 1972). In some cases, it can be a quite valuable design; however, when the reinterview time period is so short that respondents can remember their earlier response, or when the reinterview period is so long that the respondents change, there are problems (see Alwin, 2007, pp. 96–101). It is probably worth noting in this regard that the test-retest design is not mentioned in the current set of standards for educational and psychological testing (AERA, APA, & NCME, 1999). Investigators interested in the study of measurement error in survey data using longitudinal methods have turned to alternative designs and other models for reliability estimation. One such design is the use of multiple (three or more) reinterviews within the framework of a longitudinal design, and a class of autoregressive models— the quasi-Markov simplex models—have been developed for application to multiwave panel models using structural equation methods (Alwin, 2007). These models are linked to Coleman's (1964, 1968) now classic work on the measurement of change, which dealt with the separation of change from unreliability of measurement. These models were further developed for the continuous latent variable case by Heise (1969), Jöreskog (1970), and Wiley and Wiley (1970). They go well beyond the classic test-retest method (Moser & Kalton, 1972; Siegel & Hodge, 1968) in that they specify errors of measurement in the observed scores and permit change in the latent true variable underlying these measures (see Heise, 1969; Jöreskog, 1970; Wiley & Wiley, 1970). The quasi-Markov simplex models have seen increasing application, given that the statistical identification issues were readily dealt with using structural equation modeling strategies; however, in the case of event history data, the logic is applied to latent classes rather than continuous variables. As I discuss in the following section, one must turn to latent class models (see Alwin, 2007).

Reliability Assessment for Event Data

Some measures obtained from the application of event history calendars and time diary methods are considered to measure latent continuous variables, and some of the above methods may be appropriate for estimating the reliability and validity of such data. However, I assume that in general "event data," by which I mean discrete state measurement, are more often than not categorical in nature. In cases where the investigator cannot, because of the essential nature of the data, or for other reasons, assume the underlying latent variable of interest is continuous, the classical psychometric methods are less valuable. Event history data are frequently categorical in nature, for example, whether or not a person occupied a particular state, such as marriage or coresidence with parents; or a report of whether the household head is employed or not. Consequently, such kinds of event data are perhaps best thought of as measures of latent classes or categories, corresponding to the nature of the phenomenon of interest, rather than as states along some continuum of interest.

In this part of the chapter, I review several common methods for the reliability assessment of event history data, including measures of "percent agreement," coefficients of agreement, such as Cohen's κ (*kappa*), and applications of classical true score theory, where ordinality can be assumed. There is nothing in principle wrong with any of these bivariate methods; it will be seen that each has certain advantages and disadvantages. Ultimately, however, I argue that we need to go beyond these bivariate assessments and consider a set of latent class models that are uniquely suited to assessments of reliability of event history data.

PERCENT AGREEMENT

There are several intuitively based approaches to defining reliability in the case of categorical variables. One might think, for example, that the percentage of cases that agree in response disposition for a set of individuals across two occasions of measurement might be a sensible approach to reliability. Such approaches have been used in response to the obvious inappropriateness of applying methods of reliability estimation for continuous variables and/or the perceived lack of available reliability models for categorical data. The approach that computes the "percent agreement" among two or more measures of the same latent variable is problematic because the extent of agreement clearly depends on the number of categories involved (see Alwin, 1992, p. 105, fn. 19). In general, this is not a desirable feature of a way to assess differences in reliability across domains of measure, as it confounds the domain of measurement with the number of categories used to describe the variable.

COEFFICIENTS OF AGREEMENT

Another measure that has been applied to assessing consistency among event measures is known as Cohen's κ (*kappa*). *Kappa* was developed as a measurement of interrater agreement; it is considered to be a better measure than the simple percent agreement. With an interest in measuring interrater agreement, Cohen (1960) developed a measurement of agreement for categorical variables that he argues takes into account the agreement occurring by chance. If there is complete agreement, κ will equal 1.0, and as there is less agreement, then κ approaches zero.

The κ coefficient was developed for the agreement among two sets of ratings. Where more than two variables are involved, other techniques are available

(Fleiss, 1981). It has been criticized for its claim that it is a "chance-corrected" measure of agreement, in that this is based on the assumption of statistical independence of raters. It has also been suggested that κ is not comparable across studies, procedures, or populations (Uebersax, 1982). Regardless of its limitations, it has seen some use in assessing the validity and/or reliability of event data (see Belli et al., 2001; Belli et al., 2007). Although these approaches have a certain degree of appeal, in this chapter I argue that ultimately it is more productive to approach the problem within the framework of a model that specifies observed variables as reflections of latent variables and a measurement design that provides a means of estimating the relationship between observed and latent variables.

AN EXAMPLE FOR EVENT DATA

As I noted earlier, a typical approach to examining the reliability and/or validity of event data involves an examination of the extent of correspondence of multiple assessments of the same events and experiences (see, e.g., Belli et al. 2001; Belli et al., 2007; Freedman et al., 1988). All of the measures of agreement discussed in the foregoing have been used in this research to assess the relative performance of measurement approaches across domains of content. In what follows I present an example of how these techniques can be applied to event history data with the goal of assessing the reliability of measurement. I employ data from the Detroit Longitudinal Study (DLS), a longitudinal study begun in 1962 in Detroit, Michigan, with a probability sample of 1,304 married white women who had borne a child the previous year. The study became intergenerational in 1980 as these children reached age 18 and were included in data collection. Table 16.1 presents the data for 1980 and 1985 from the DLS, for measures of two variables—educational status and employment status—wherein the 1980 data were obtained from a standard question list concerning enrollment and employment, and in 1985 the information was obtained from an event history calendar (Freedman et al., 1988).

In Table 16.2, I present three measures for each of the event classes that assess the correspondence of measures—percentage agreement estimation (see Freedman et al., 1988, pp. 62–65), the calculation of Cohen's κ, and an estimate of reliability using CTST models (see Scott & Alwin, 1997, pp. 120–121). The results are, of course, not comparable across the rows of the table inasmuch as these various measures of consistency are not measuring the same thing, but for our purposes it is possible to compare across domains of measurement, in this case school status and work status. In this case, all of these methods show the same pattern of results—a much higher level of consistency in the measurement of school status, compared to work status.

Table 16.1   Cross-Tabulation of 1980 and 1985 Responses About School Attendance and Employment Observed in the Intergenerational Panel Study of Parents and Children

(1) School Attendance[a]

| | 1980 Response | | | | | | | |
| | Full-Time Attendance | | Part-Time Attendance | | No Attendance | | Total | |
1985 Response	N	%	N	%	N	%	N	%
Full-time attendance	**358**	93	22	33	14	4	394	49
Part-time attendance	13	3	**20**	30	14	4	48	6
No attendance	14	4	25	37	**316**	92	355	45
Total	385	100	67	100	345	100	797	100

(2) Employment[b]

| | 1980 Response | | | | | | | |
| | Full-Time Employment | | Part-Time Employment | | No Employment | | Total | |
1985 Response	N	%	N	%	N	%	N	%
Full-time Employment[c]	**249**	83	63	27	55	17	367	42
Part-time Employment[d]	31	10	**153**	65	56	17	240	28
No Employment	20	7	20	8	**221**	66	261	30
Total	300	100	236	100	332	100	868	100

NOTE: The numbers of respondents who gave identical answers in both interviews are in bold text.

a. This analysis excludes the 85 respondents who said in 1980 that they were in high school, since these respondents were not asked whether they attended full or part time. In 1985, 75 of these respondents (88%) said that they were attending school in the month of the 1980 interview.

b. This analysis excludes the 10 respondents who said in 1980 that they were in the military.

c. Full-time employment is 30 or more hours per week.

d. Part-time employment is less than 30 hours per week.

These results reinforce a number of notions that occur in the literature on consistency estimates for event data. First, levels of agreement between multiple reports of event data can be quite high, despite the problems inherent in retrospective reporting (see Scott & Alwin, 1997). Second, these methods are useful in pointing to differences among domains in the ability of events to be reported precisely, and they help raise issues about the

Table 16.2   Results From Three Bivariate Approaches to Measuring Consistency in Survey Reports of Event Statuses in the Intergenerational Panel Study of Parents and Children

Estimated Consistency	School Status	Work Status
% Agreement	87%	72%
Cohen's *kappa*	.771	.575
CTST reliability	.900	.620

adequacy of certain question forms. In this sense, these approaches are compatible with current approaches to assessing the reliability of survey data as a means for improving the design of questions (see Alwin, 2007). Finally, it should be pointed out that while these approaches give an overall or global account of the amount of consistency among various sources of reports, they cannot say anything about category-specific reliability. I now turn to a class of models that can handle this. The following discussion stresses the importance of this distinction and focuses mainly on the measurement of latent event categories.

The Latent Class Model for Event Data

Although the above approaches are perfectly reasonable for assessing the relative quality of data across domains of measurement, there are several limitations. Central among these is the fact that, except for the approaches based in CTST, these models do not explicitly formulate the problem in terms of measurement of latent variables. While there have been efforts to develop estimates of composite reliability (analogous to coefficient α) for use with latent class models (see Bartholomew & Schuessler, 1991), the problem of estimating reliability for individual survey measures that measure latent classes has been relatively neglected. We turn now to a brief discussion of a variety of latent class models that in fact formulate the problem in terms of the relationship of the observed responses, and a set of latent classes that can be used to assess the extent of measurement error in measures of categorical variables (Clogg, 1995; Clogg & Goodman, 1984; Goodman, 2002; Lazarsfeld & Henry, 1968). These models have not found wide application to date, in part because they are relatively unknown or poorly understood, but they are increasingly discussed in the literature on assessing survey measurement reliability (see Alwin, 2007; Alwin & McCammon, 2006; Langeheine & van de Pol, 2002; van de Pol & de Leeuw, 1986).

LATENT CLASS MODELS

Figure 16.1 presents three models involving latent classes. We do not dwell extensively on these here, as they are discussed elsewhere (Alwin, 2007, pp. 263–287). In theory, these provide an analogue to the conceptions of reliability and validity involved in models based on classical psychometric theory (e.g., Clogg & Manning, 1996). Essential to the formulation of a notion of reliability consistent with that used in the case of continuous latent variables is the definition of a set of conditional probabilities relating the observed measures to the latent variables. These probabilities are defined based on the nontrivial assumption of local independence, an assumption common to all model-based assessments of reliability (see Clogg & Manning, 1996, p. 172).

It is important for purposes of reliability estimation that there is an isophormism between the number of latent classes and the number of categories of the observed measures (see Wiggins, 1973, p. 26). Consider the case, for example, where there are three dichotomous measures of the same underlying latent variable, X, that has two classes—classes that are identical to the categories of the observed measures (see Figure 16.1a). Following the Clogg-Manning notation, we denote these three measures of X as A, B, and C, and refer to their levels using subscripts i, j, and k, respectively.[2] Similarly, we denote the number of latent classes by T (in this case $T = 2$), the levels of which are indexed by t. One need not restrict the model to dichotomous measures, but doing so in the present case facilitates discussion of the model.

Recall that in the continuous case, reliability is defined as a function of the correlation between the latent variable and the measures, and there is a parallel in latent class models. A schematic diagram of the relationships between the observed and latent variable distributions in the latent class model is given in Figure 16.1. There are three versions of the latent class model given in this figure. The latent class model given in model (a) is analogous to the single factor model in the case of continuous variables, where multiple indicators of a single latent variable are used to draw inferences about the quality of measurement. This is the model developed by Clogg and Manning (1996). The development of a latent class model in model (b) that is analogous to the classical true score model employs "multiple measures" rather than "multiple indicators," that is, the same survey measure at multiple occasions, rather than several different survey items thought to measure the same underlying construct measured at a single point in time (see Alwin, 2007, pp. 272–277).

The essential problem with interpreting relationships between multiple indicators of the same underlying concept in cross-sectional surveys has to do with the acceptability of the assumptions of univocity (that the indicators measure one and only one thing) and independence of measurement error. Except for the classic writings by Coleman (1964, 1968) and a pioneering book

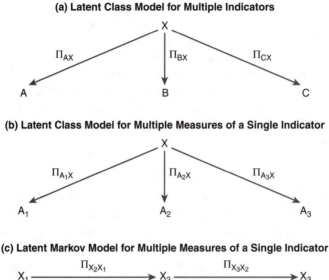

(a) Latent Class Model for Multiple Indicators

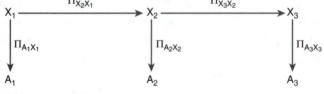

(b) Latent Class Model for Multiple Measures of a Single Indicator

(c) Latent Markov Model for Multiple Measures of a Single Indicator

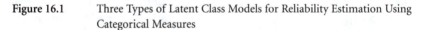

Figure 16.1   Three Types of Latent Class Models for Reliability Estimation Using
Categorical Measures

by Wiggins (1973), which formulated the basic ideas behind the longitudinal
approach to reliability estimation, little attention has been devoted to reliability and its estimation for measures of categorical latent variables using longitudinal survey designs. The work of Wiggins (1973) combines features of the
latent class model and the simple Markov chain, and although this model
shares some features with the latent class model, it is quite different. Indeed,
the latent Markov model—see model (c) in Figure 16.1—addresses an important deficiency in the static latent class model, namely the possibility that
membership in the latent classes can change over time. As pointed out below,
however, one may think of the latent class model as a special case of the latent
Markov model.

The latent Markov model (LMM) depicted in model (c) in Figure 16.1 is
a dynamic version of the latent class model. It is an analogue to the quasi-
Markov simplex model discussed above (see Wiggins, 1973, pp. 97–106). In
this case the model retains the property of a one-to-one correspondence

between categories of observed and latent classes, which is an essential ingredient of models that provide information on reliability. At the same time, an important component of this model is its allowance for individuals to move in and out of the latent categories over time. Thus, where the categories of the observed variable can be assumed to be identical to the categories of the latent variable and where the unit of analysis can change membership in the latent classes over time (e.g., marital status, school enrollment, or employment status), the LMM is an appropriate candidate for analyzing change while at the same time assessing the level of measurement error.

There are two sets of parameters of interest in this model: (1) The matrices of conditional probabilities linking the observed and latent classes can be designated as $\Pi_{A_1 X_1}$, $\Pi_{A_2 X_2}$, and $\Pi_{A_3 X_3}$, and (2) the matrices of transition probabilities linking the latent categories over time, designated as $\Pi_{X_2 X_1}$ and $\Pi_{X_3 X_2}$. The relationships between the latent classes and manifest response categories in the model in Figure 16.1c are comparable to the interpretation of the matrices $\Pi_{A_1 X}$, $\Pi_{A_2 X}$, and $\Pi_{A_3 X}$ in Figure 16.1b, which represents the situation in which there are three identical measures (A_1, A_2, and A_3) of X. In contrast to the coefficients in Π_{AX}, Π_{BX}, and Π_{CX} in Figure 16.1a, note that here we have three identical measures, and the response probability matrices can therefore more readily be interpreted in terms of the reliability of measurement.

The latent transition probabilities in this model embody the same intent of the quasi-Markov simplex model, as developed for the continuous case, in that the model allows for change at the unit of observation level while examining the reliability of survey measures. Indeed, Wiggins (1973) developed this as an approach to reliability estimation for the case in which the latent variables were categories—latent classes—and the unobserved processes that entailed movement between latent classes were conceptualized in terms of a Markov process (Langeheine & van de Pol, 2002; van de Pol & de Leeuw, 1986). Just as the quasi-Markov simplex model allows for change in the latent variable, here the model allows change in the latent distribution and expresses change in the form of a latent transition matrix. At the time Wiggins (1973) published his work, approaches to estimation were still relatively underdeveloped.[3] Recent developments in estimation have made the application of these models possible (see Langeheine & van de Pol, 2002; van de Pol & de Leeuw, 1986). As we noted in the discussion of the latent class model above, the utility of these models for reliability estimation stems from the fact that the latent classes are put into a one-to-one correspondence with the manifest classes (Wiggins, 1973, p. 26), and the probabilities linking the observed and latent categories are estimated in the presence of changes in the membership in the latent classes.

I present an example of the estimates obtained from the LMM using the DLS, specifically the data from the 1980, 1985, and 1993 child interviews. In 1980, information on current school and work statuses were collected using a question list approach. Regarding school status, respondents were first asked, "Are you going to school at all now?" Those answering in the affirmative were then asked, "What kind of school do you attend?" Finally, respondents attending a school other than high school were asked, "Are you attending school full-time or part-time?" Work status was measured with the following items: "Next, some questions about jobs. Are you doing any work for pay at the present time?" and if so, "About how many hours do you work on your main job in an average week?"

In 1985 and 1993, this information was collected using a life history calendar. In 1985, information was collected for the period from the fall of 1976 through the month of the interview, while in 1993, the period from the month of the 1985 interview up through the month of the 1993 interview was covered.[4] In 1985, the life history calendar was completed with regard to schooling using these prompts: "Were you enrolled in any school the September after your fifteenth birthday, either full or part time?" "Was that full or part time?" "When did you stop attending school for a month or more, either because you dropped out or had a vacation which lasted a month or more?" Following from these questions, the calendar was completed for each monthly period.

In the 1985 interview, the questions used to enter the life history calendar regarding work status read, "Aside from home chores, have you had a regular job for pay, either full or part-time after you turned fifteen which lasted for a month or more?" and if so, "When did that employment begin?" "Was that employment for 1–9 hours per week, 10–29 hours per week, or 30 or more hours per week?" and finally, "When did your employment situation change—either because you changed the number of hours you worked or quit working for a month or more?"

In 1993, the prompt for the schooling portion of the life history calendar was dependent on the respondent's schooling status at the time of the 1985 interview. Those previously enrolled were asked, "In (month of previous interview), 1985, you told us you were going to school (full/part) time. In what month and year did you stop attending school for one month or more, either because you dropped out or had a school vacation?" Respondents not previously enrolled were asked, "Since (month of previous interview), 1985, were there ever any times that you were enrolled in school, either full- or part-time?"

Like the schooling section of the life history calendar, the work status questions for the 1993 interview were dependent on the respondent's work status in 1985. Those previously working were asked, "In (month of previous interview), 1985, you told us you were working (1–9/10–29/30 or more) hours per week. In what month and year did your employment situation change, either because you changed the number of hours you worked or quit working for a month or more?" Respondents not previously working were asked, "Since (month of previous interview), 1985, have you had a regular job for pay, either full-time or part-time, which lasted one month or more?"

The focus of the present analysis is on the reliability of the assessment of the respondents' current work and school statuses at three points in time. Thus, while the 1985 interview collects information on these statuses for the month of the 1980 interview, and the 1993 interview collects information on these statuses for the month of the 1985 interview, only the data collected on current school and work statuses at the time of the 1980, 1985, and 1993 data collections are used.

RESULTS

Table 16.3 presents the results of our estimation of a three-wave LMM for two separate event history processes, school and work status, from the DLS. The table presents the observed distributions, the estimated latent distributions, and estimated response probabilities linking the two for each wave of observation. The top panel of the table presents results for school status and the lower panel the results for work status. These results were obtained under the constraint that the within-time matrix of response probabilities, which contains probabilities of levels of response condition on latent class membership, equal over time. In other words, the model assumes the equality of reliabilities over time: $\Pi_{A_1 X_1} = \Pi_{A_2 X_2} = \Pi_{A_3 X_3}$.

There are several tests of hypotheses that interest us here with respect to the reliability of measurement as conceptualized in terms of the response probability results. First, with respect to the Π_{AX} parameter matrix, standard errors are available from modern software applications, and it is possible to test specific hypotheses about population parameters. We do not explore these here, but in general these can be quite valuable with respect to evaluating the nature of the results. In one case, for school status observed as "not enrolled in school," the model produced a "boundary solution" and some parameters were fixed at 1.0 and 0.0. If these values are close to reflecting the true state of affairs, this is somewhat reassuring, because it suggests that those who are not enrolled in school can accurately report it. The problem of measurement error tends to occur among people who are enrolled in school, where there is a .75 probability of reporting enrollment among those whom the model considers "enrolled" at the latent level.

This ability to make declarations about the quality of measurement as "class-specific" phenomena (e.g., enrolled vs. not enrolled), and not necessary for the measure as a whole, is one advantage of the latent class model. In other words, it is possible to arrive at different declarations about measurement quality that pertain to a specific category of the phenomenon being measured. However, this hypothesis is testable, and thus, a second set of hypotheses that we test using this model construction examines whether the category-specific reliabilities are equal. We use the term *reliability* in the sense of Clogg and

Table 16.3   Observed Distributions, Estimated Latent Distributions, and Estimated Measurement Response Probabilities From a Latent Markov Model of School Enrollment and Work Status Observed in the Intergenerational Panel Study of Parents and Children in 1980, 1985, 1993

School Enrollment (N = 798)

Wave	School Status	Observed Distribution	Response Probabilities		Latent Distribution
			Not Enrolled	Enrolled	
1	Not enrolled	0.431	1.000	0.259	0.243
1	Enrolled	0.569	0.000	0.751	0.757
2	Not enrolled	0.768	1.000	0.259	0.690
2	Enrolled	0.232	0.000	0.751	0.310
3	Not enrolled	0.898	1.000	0.259	0.865
3	Enrolled	0.102	0.000	0.751	0.135

Work Status (N = 872)

Wave	Work Status	Observed Distribution	Response Probabilities		Latent Distribution
			Less Than Full-Time	Full-Time	
1	Less than full-time	0.649	0.836	0.212	0.699
1	Full-time	0.351	0.164	0.788	0.301
2	Less than full-time	0.276	0.836	0.212	0.104
2	Full-time	0.724	0.164	0.788	0.898
3	Less than full-time	0.284	0.836	0.212	0.115
3	Full-time	0.716	0.164	0.788	0.885

Manning's (1996) "reliability as predictability," and ask whether from a statistical viewpoint there is an equivalence in the probability of the item response given the latent class. This amounts to the test of the equality of diagonal elements of the Π_{AX} parameter matrix. Tests of equality of diagonal elements of these parameter matrices were carried out by placing a linear constraint on the threshold logits for the latent response function. The constraint is analogous to the typical equality constraints used for model testing in structural equation models; in this case the constraint takes the form $t_{01} = -t_{11}$. The test statistic in this case is distributed as χ^2 with 1 degree of freedom. The application of this test in the case of work status yields nonsignificant differences ($\chi^2 = 0.135$, $p = .713$), and we therefore cannot conclude that the quality of measurement varies by category of the variable.

Another interesting feature of the LMM is that it provides estimates of latent distributions for the latent classes at each point in time, as shown in Table 16.3. There are at least three potentially meaningful comparisons of these latent class distributions. First, it may be meaningful to compare the latent distributions for a given measure across time. In the present example, the analyses for schooling yield the finding that school enrollment changes dramatically over the period studied, from a proportion of .24 not enrolled in school in 1980 to .69 in 1985 to .86 in 1993. There also appears to be a change in the latent distribution for work status, beginning with .30 working full-time in 1980 to .90 in 1985 to .88 in 1993.

It may be useful in some circumstances to compare the latent distributions with the observed distributions, and these differences may interact with time. What we find in the present case that the observed distributions overestimate the proportion not enrolled at every time point, but decreasingly so over the period studied. In the case of work status, those not working full-time are underestimated in 1980, but in 1985 and 1993 there is considerable overestimation of the "not working full-time" category in the observed variables. In some cases the observed and latent distributions can be quite different, and this difference may change across occasions of measurement.

Conclusion

In the study of reliability methods for time diary and event history data, a fundamental distinction must be made between measures of latent continuous variables and those assessing latent categories. Regardless of whether measures are continuous or categorical, if the latent variable is continuous, approaches based on classical true-score models are appropriate, but when the latent variable is a set of latent classes, the classical methods will not work. To this point the systematic study of measurement error in survey research has focused primarily on the continuous latent variables, and I have not covered these in any depth here. Rather, in this chapter I discussed models for categorical latent variables, which are appropriate for event history data, where movement in and out of latent categories is an essential ingredient in the processes involved. Clogg and Manning (1996) argue that the latent class model provides an analogue to the conception of reliability involved in models based on classical theory, but there are several limitations to this approach. By contrast, Wiggins (1973) developed a latent class model for just this purpose. His model incorporated measurement parameters and permitted changes in latent class membership. Despite the existence of these models, little work on the estimation of the parameters of latent change models has occurred until recently. I argue that the special properties of these models make them particularly well suited to the investigation of issues of validity and reliability for event history data.

I provided an example of the analysis of reliability of event history data using the Wiggins (1973) model, which is now called the "latent class Markov chain model," or the Latent Markov Model (LMM), or the "hidden Markov model." Although this model has existed in the sociological literature for several decades (see Coleman, 1968; Wiggins, 1973; van de Pol & de Leeuw, 1986; van de Pol & Langeheine, 1990; van de Pol, Langeheine, & de Jong, 1991; Vermunt, Langeheine, & Böckenholt, 1999; Langeheine & van de Pol, 2002), to my knowledge it has been used sparingly in the assessment of reliability. The main limitations appear to be the flexibility of statistical software that can place the necessary restrictions on the model. Our preliminary analyses indicate that for the kind of single-variable models one normally wants to estimate for dynamic latent class models, these models are workable and can be estimated in cases where there are three or more occasions of measurement. There are several available software packages for estimating these models, including the PANMARK computer program for latent class analysis (van de Pol, Langeheine, & de Jong, 1991), M*plus* (Muthén & Muthén, 2004), and *WinLTA* (Collins, Flaherty, Hyatt, & Schafer, 1999).

My example illustrated that for those event classes that are allowed to change, reliability estimation for categorical variables is a useful application of latent class modeling techniques. Models permitting change in the composition of latent classes are essential for the purpose of separating assessments of reliability from assessments of latent true change. I discussed the prospects offered by the LMM for these types of data. In the present example, we have shown that the measurement of school status and work status, as gathered in the context of event history measurement, can be usefully modeled using the LMM approach. Our analysis examined several aspects of the process of movement across these statuses over time, while at the same time examining the quality of measurement (see Alwin & McCammon, 2006). I found that the nature and extent of measurement errors can vary across levels of the latent categorical variable, a feature that is unique to the latent class approach. I illustrated how these models can be used to detect and test for these differences. Although these models have not been widely applied to date, I expect these circumstances to change in future studies of the reliability of measurement involving categorical latent variables.

Consideration was also given to assessing the consequences of measurement error and the extent of differences between the observed distributions of categorical variables. My results pertain to life course statuses and processes that were undergoing considerable change during the period of study, particularly involving the transition to adulthood (in this sample between 1980 and 1985; see Alwin & McCammon, 2006). I found differences in the latent and observed levels in regard to the degree of change, but in both educational and employment realms there was substantial change between the ages of 18 and 23. These results reinforce the fact that models used to assess the reliability of data serve well to the extent they can rely on replicate measures embedded in longitudinal designs that permit change over time.

Notes

1. For present purposes I refer to this as the Detroit Longitudinal Study (DLS).

2. I use the notation introduced by Clogg and Manning (1996), as extended by Alwin, (2007; see also Alwin & McCammon, 2006) in order to maintain consistency with that literature; it is not intended to be compatible with notation used previously in this chapter.

3. Wiggins's (1973) work was based on a 1955 Ph.D. dissertation completed at Columbia University under the direction of Paul Lazarsfeld. Langeheine and van de Pol (2002, p. 325) note that "it took nearly 30 years until problems of parameter estimation were solved for the latent Markov model."

4. The analysis presented here uses data on current work and school status at the time of each data collection (1980, 1985, and 1993). As a result, the model assumes equal reliability for question list and calendar approaches. While the 1985 data did include retrospective calendar reports on work and school status for 1980, only data on current status from each occasion of measurement are used here.

Acknowledgment

Research presented here was supported by these grants: "The Reliability of Survey Data," from the National Science Foundation (SES-9710403), and "Aging and the Reliability of Measurement," from the National Institute on Aging (R01-AG020673). The author acknowledges the collaboration of Ryan McCammon in the development of this project, the help of Pauline Mitchell and Alyson Otto in the preparation of the tables and figures, and the detailed comments of Bob Belli on a previous version of this chapter.

References

Alwin, D. F. (1989). Problems in the estimation and interpretation of the reliability of survey data. *Quality and Quantity, 23,* 277–331.

Alwin, D. F. (1992). Information transmission in the survey interview: Number of response categories and the reliability of attitude measurement. In P. V. Marsden (Ed.), *Sociological methodology 1992* (pp. 83–118). Washington, DC: American Sociological Association.

Alwin, D. F. (1997). Feeling thermometers vs. seven-point scales: Which are better? *Sociological Methods and Research, 25,* 318–340.

Alwin, D. F. (2004). Reliability. In K. Kempf-Leonard (Ed.), *Encyclopedia of social measurement.* New York: Academic Press.

Alwin, D. F. (2007). *Margins of error: A study of reliability in survey measurement.* New York: John Wiley.

Alwin, D. F., & McCammon, R. J. (2006, June). *Reliability estimation for event measurement in surveys.* Paper presented at the PSID conference on event and calendar measurement, Ann Arbor, MI.

American Educational Research Association, American Psychological Association, & National Council on Measurement in Education. (1999). *Standards for educational and psychological testing.* Washington, DC: American Educational Research Association.

Bartholomew, D. J., & Schuessler, K. F. (1991). Reliability of attitude scores based on a latent-trait model. In P. V. Marsden (Ed.), *Sociological methodology 1991* (pp. 97–123). Oxford, UK: Blackwell.

Belli, R. F. (1998). The structure of autobiographical memory and the event history calendar: Potential improvements in the quality of retrospective reports in surveys. *Memory, 6,* 383–406.

Belli, R. F. (2000). Computerized event history calendar methods: Facilitating autobiographical recall. In *American Statistical Association Proceedings of the Section on Survey Research Methods* (pp. 471–475). Alexandria, VA: American Statistical Association.

Belli, R. F., Shay, W. L., & Stafford, F. P. (2001). Event history calendars and question list surveys: A direct comparison of interviewing methods. *Public Opinion Quarterly, 65,* 45–74.

Belli, R. F., Smith, L. M., Andreski, P. M., & Agrawal, S. (2007). Methodological comparisons between CATI event history calendar and standardized conventional questionnaire instruments. *Public Opinion Quarterly, 71,* 603–622.

Bound, J., Brown, C., Duncan, G. J., & Rodgers, W. L. (1990). Measurement error in cross-sectional and longitudinal labor market surveys: Validation study evidence. In J. Hartog, G. Ridder, & J. Theeuwes (Eds.), *Panel data and labor market studies.* Amsterdam: North-Holland.

Campbell, D. T., & Fiske, D. W. (1959). Convergent and discriminant validation by the multitrait-multimethod matrix. *Psychological Bulletin, 6,* 81–105.

Clogg, C. C. (1995). Latent class models. In G. Arminger, C. C. Clogg, & M. E. Sobel (Eds.), *Handbook of statistical modeling for the social and behavioral sciences* (pp. 311–359). New York: Plenum.

Clogg, C. C., & Goodman, L. A. (1984). Latent structure analysis of a set of multidimensional contingency tables. *Journal of the American Statistical Association, 79,* 762–771.

Clogg, C. C., & Manning, W. D. (1996). Assessing reliability of categorical measurements using latent class models. In A. von Eye & C. C. Clogg (Eds.), *Categorical variables in developmental research: Methods of analysis* (pp. 169–182). New York: Academic Press.

Cohen, J. (1960). A coefficient of agreement for nominal scales. *Educational and Psychological Measurement, 20,* 37–46.

Coleman, J. S. (1964). *Models of change and response uncertainty.* Englewood Cliffs, NJ: Prentice Hall.

Coleman, J. S. (1968). The mathematical study of change. In H. M. Blalock, Jr., & A. B. Blalock (Eds.), *Methodology in social research* (pp. 428–478). New York: McGraw-Hill.

Collins, L. M., Flaherty, B. P., Hyatt, B. P., & Schafer, J. L. (1999). *WinLTA user's guide* (Version 2.0). University Park: Pennsylvania State University, The Methodology Center.

Cronbach, L. J. (1951). Coefficient alpha and the internal structure of tests. *Psychometrika, 16,* 297–334.

Elder, G. H., Jr. (1985). Perspectives on the life course. In G. H. Elder, Jr. (Ed.), *Life course dynamics: Trajectories and transitions, 1968–1980* (pp. 23–49). Ithaca, NY: Cornell University Press.

Elder, G. H., Jr. (2000). The life course. In E. F. Borgatta & R. J. V. Montgomery (Eds.), *Encyclopedia of sociology* (2nd ed., Vol. 3, pp. 1614–1622). New York: Macmillan Reference USA.

Elder, G. H., Jr., & Shanahan, M. J. (2006). The life course and human development. In W. Damon & R. M. Lerner (Eds.), *Handbook of child psychology: Vol. 1. Theoretical models of human development* (6th ed., pp. 665–715). New York: John Wiley.

Elder, G. H., Jr., Johnson, M. K., & Crosnoe, R. (2003). The emergence and development of life course theory. In J. T. Mortimer & M. J. Shanahan (Eds.), *Handbook of the life course* (pp. 3–19). New York: Kluwer Academic/Plenum.

Fleiss, J. L. (1981). The measurement of interrater agreement. In *Statistical methods for rates and proportions* (2nd ed., chap. 13). New York: John Wiley.

Freedman, D., Thornton, A., Camburn, D., Alwin, D. F., & Young-DeMarco, L. (1988). The life history calendar: A technique for collecting retrospective data. In C. C. Clogg (Ed.), *Sociological methodology 1988* (pp. 37–68). Washington, DC: American Sociological Association.

Goodman, L. (2002). Latent class analysis: The empirical study of latent types, latent variables and latent structures. In J. A. Hagenaars & A. L. McCutcheon (Eds.), *Applied latent class analysis* (pp. 3–55). New York: Cambridge University Press.

Greene, V. L., & Carmines, E. G. (1979). Assessing the reliability of linear composites. In K. F. Schuessler (Ed.), *Sociological methodology 1980* (pp. 160–175). San Francisco: Jossey-Bass.

Groves, R. M. (1989). *Survey errors and survey costs.* New York: John Wiley.

Heise, D. R. (1969). Separating reliability and stability in test-retest correlation. *American Sociological Review, 34,* 93–101.

Jöreskog, K. G. (1970). Estimating and testing of simplex models. *British Journal of Mathematical and Statistical Psychology, 23,* 121–145.

Jöreskog, K. G. (1971). Statistical analysis of sets of congeneric tests. *Psychometrika, 36,* 109–133.

Juster, F. T. (1985). The validity and quality of time use estimates obtained from recall diaries. In F. T. Juster & F. P. Stafford (Eds.), *Time, goods, and well-being* (pp. 63–91). Ann Arbor: University of Michigan, Institute for Social Research.

Kuh, D., & the New Dynamics of Ageing (NDA) Preparatory Network. (2007). A life course approach to healthy aging, frailty, and capability. *Journal of Gerontology: Medical Sciences, 62A,* 717–721.

Langeheine, R., & van de Pol, F. R. J. (1990). A unifying framework for Markov modeling in discrete space and discrete time. *Sociological Methods & Research, 18,* 416–441.

Langeheine, R., & van de Pol, F. R. J. (2002). Latent Markov chains. In J. A. Hagenaars & A. L. McCutcheon (Eds.), *Applied latent class analysis* (pp. 304–341). New York: Cambridge University Press.

Lazarsfeld, P. F., & Henry, N. W. (1968). *Latent structure analysis.* Boston: Houghton Mifflin.

Lord, F. M., & Novick, M. L. (1968). *Statistical theories of mental test scores.* Reading, MA: Addison-Wesley.

Marquis, K. H. (1978). *Record check validity of survey responses: A reassessment of bias in reports of hospitalizations.* Santa Monica, CA: RAND.

Moser, C. A., & Kalton, G. (1972). *Survey methods in social investigation* (2nd ed.). New York: Basic Books.

Muthén, L. K., & Muthén, B. O. (2004). *M-Plus: The comprehensive modeling program for applied researchers: User's guide.* Version 2.0. Los Angeles: Muthén & Muthén.

Saris, W. E., & Andrews, F. M. (1991). Evaluation of measurement instruments using a structural modeling approach. In P. B. Biemer, R. M. Groves, L. E. Lyberg, N. A. Mathiowetz, & S. Sudman (Eds.), *Measurement errors in surveys* (pp. 575–597). New York: John Wiley.

Saris, W. E., & Gallhofer, I. N. (2007). *Design, evaluation, and analysis of questionnaires for survey research.* Hoboken, NJ: John Wiley.

Saris, W. E., & van Meurs, A. (Eds.). (1990). *Evaluation of measurement instruments by meta-analysis of multitrait multimethod matrices.* Amsterdam: North-Holland.

Scherpenzeel, A. C., & Saris, W. E. (1997). The validity and reliability of survey questions: A meta-analysis of MTMM studies. *Sociological Methods and Research, 25,* 341–383.

Scott, J., & Alwin, D. F. (1997). Retrospective vs. prospective measurement of life histories in longitudinal research. In J. Z. Giele & G. H. Elder, Jr. (Eds.), *Methods of life course research: Qualitative and quantitative approaches* (pp. 98–127). Thousand Oaks, CA: Sage.

Siegel, P. M., & Hodge, R. W. (1968). A causal approach to the study of measurement error. In H. M. Blalock, Jr., & A. B. Blalock (Eds.), *Methodology in social research* (pp. 28–59). New York: McGraw-Hill.

Uebersax, J. S. (1982). A generalized kappa coefficient. *Educational and Psychological Measurement, 42,* 181–183.

van de Pol, F., & Langeheine, R. (1990). Mixed Markov latent class models. In C. C. Clogg (Ed.), *Sociological methodology 1990* (pp. 213–247). Oxford, UK: Blackwell.

van de Pol, F., & de Leeuw, J. (1986). A latent Markov model to correct for measurement error. *Sociological Methods and Research, 15,* 118–141.

van de Pol, F., Langeheine, R., & de Jong, W. (1991). *PANMARK user manual: PANel analysis using MARKov chains.* Voorburg: Netherlands Central Bureau of Statistics.

Vermunt, J. K., Langeheine, R., & Böckenholt, U. (1999). Discrete-time discrete-state latent Markov models with time-constant and time-varying covariates. *Journal of Educational and Behavioral Statistics, 24,* 179–207.

Wiggins, L. M. (1973). *Panel analysis: Latent probability models for attitude and behavior processes.* New York: Elsevier Scientific.

Wiley, D. E., & Wiley, J. A. (1970). The estimation of measurement error in panel data. *American Sociological Review, 35,* 112–117.

Further Thoughts on Part IV

As detailed by Dijkstra, Smit, and Ongena (Chapter 15), a key concern of survey researchers in interviewer-administered data collections is the extent to which interviewing errors are biasing the reports of respondents. Certainly, interviewer training can reduce interviewing errors, as noted by these authors. There are several issues at play, however, when considering the flexible nature of calendar interviewing. Belli and Callegaro (Chapter 3) present theoretical arguments and empirical data that illustrate the advantages of flexible interviewing in comparison to standardized approaches by promoting more effective retrieval cues and permitting the beneficial aspects of ordinary conversation to disambiguate meaning. To what extent might interviewer training, if not done carefully, inhibit the benefits of calendar interviewing that are derived from its flexibility? To what extent do interviewer errors actually impact on data quality in calendar interviews, if at all (the coding of verbal behaviors, and associating behaviors with data quality, may help to answer this question; see Stafford & Belli, Chapter 17)? Answers to these questions will ultimately lead to best interviewer training practice.

Another related issue derives from a comparison of flexible calendar interviews with conventional standardized interviews on interviewer variance, that is, the extent to which interviewers impact the quality of respondent reports. Because calendar interviewing is more flexible and, by definition, interviewers will show greater within-interview variance whenever interviewing is allowed to be less standardized, some survey methodologists have assumed that such flexibility will show costs in terms of increasing interviewer variance in terms of greater variability in the quality of interviewing in calendar methods in comparison to standardized approaches. In other words, whereas enforcing standardized procedures is believed to ensure that all interviewers behave in basically the same way, with flexible approaches it is assumed that some interviewers will perform markedly better, and others remarkably worse. There are a number of points to be made here. First, although calendar interviewing is more flexible, there are constraints as to what interviewers can do because there is only a limited—if undefined—set of queries that will be able to satisfy questionnaire objectives, which are structured. Second, as noted by Dijkstra et al. (Chapter 15), interviewer training will be able to make interviewing practice more consistent among calendar interviewers. Third, the empirical work that has been done comparing the level of interviewer variance between standardized and calendar interviews has found no significant differences between these types of interviews, although descriptively it does appear that calendar interviews may lead to modestly higher interviewer variance (Belli, Lee, Stafford, & Chou, 2004; Sayles, Belli, & Serrano, 2008). Finally, any increases of interviewer variance in calendar interviewing in comparison to standardized approaches is more than offset if, overall, there is an increase in data quality, as the empirical evidence shows to date (see Belli & Callegaro, Chapter 3).

References

Belli, R. F., Lee, E. H., Stafford, F. P., & Chou, C.-H. (2004). Calendar and question-list survey methods: Association between interviewer behaviors and data quality. *Journal of Official Statistics, 20,* 185–218.

Sayles, H., Belli, R. F., & Serrano, E. (2008). *Interviewer variance between event history calendar and conventional questionnaire interviews.* Manuscript submitted for publication.

PART V

Looking Ahead

Chapter 17   Future Directions in Calendar
and Time Diary Methods

Although time diaries and calendars have been administered since the early- and mid-20th century, respectively (see Stafford, Chapter 2, and Belli & Callegaro, Chapter 3, this volume), to our knowledge this is the first book that has been devoted solely to these flexible interviewing approaches that seek to use cues available in the structure of autobiographical knowledge to improve the quality of retrospective reports. The authors who have contributed chapters to this volume represent many different disciplines, and each provides examples of how to use these methods to study processes that govern the life course. Most of this work would be best described as quantitative research, although some of these researchers use techniques in qualitative paradigms as well. Various methods and modes are represented, including paper-and-pencil and computerized instruments, and data collection in face-to-face, telephone, and self-administered modes. Among those who have used an interviewer-administered mode, there exist varying degrees of including strictly standardized questions to be presented to respondents exactly as written, although research that has directly compared flexible time diary and calendar interviewing approaches with conventional standardized questionnaires (also referred to as "stylized" questions in the time diary literature, and "question-list instruments" in the calendar data collection literature) have generally found better quality retrospective reporting with the more flexible approaches. The flexible, more conversational techniques are better able to use autobiographical memory cues in comparison to standardized ones.

In this final chapter, Stafford and Belli (Chapter 17) point to some of the directions that characterize current cutting-edge research in calendar and time diary approaches, and those directions that will continue to characterize these methods in the future. Adaptations to more diverse samples and new settings, advancements in data collection methods in light of ongoing technological developments, new methods for processing rich diary and calendar data, and broadening the types of questions regarding the life course with diary and calendar methods are explored.

17

Future Directions in Calendar and Time Diary Methods

Frank P. Stafford and Robert F. Belli

T he chapters in this volume demonstrate that calendars and time diaries are becoming applied to large, national infrastructural databases as well as more focused, investigator-initiated research projects within a variety of social and health science disciplines. We foresee continued adaptation to more diverse samples and new settings in which calendars and time diaries are applied. Included in the future for calendar and time diary methods is continuing methodological work on instrument design issues to determine more specifically what interviewing properties improve the quality of the retrospective reports that are collected, and with the growing availability of Web-based data collection, how best to implement calendar and diary methods within a self-administered Web-based platform. Companion methods for processing the rich diary and calendar data will grow within both research communities and applications outside of traditional research realms.

Varied Samples

In conjunction with application to more diverse samples, different variants of time diary instruments have emerged and are likely to continue emerging. To illustrate, the American Time Use Survey (ATUS) (see Phipps & Vernon, Chapter 7, this volume) provides a national sample and a particular model for data collection. Investigators working with diaries for special populations can compare their descriptive results with ATUS. This will provide a benchmark for situations where their sample or methods give rise to how generalizable their study findings may be.

As an example of a more focused study, the Child Development Supplement (CDS) of the Panel Study of Income Dynamics (PSID) has collected time diary data on children 0–12 as of 1997, 6–18 as of 2002/2003, and age 11–18 in 2007/2008. Since ATUS has diaries on individuals in the age range of 15 and older, some comparisons of those in the common age, 15–18, can be made between CDS and ATUS. In a similar fashion, market work hours as measured in the work hours collected via calendar interviewing in the PSID can be compared to market hours as reported in the Current Population Survey (CPS). For innovative designs such as the Consumption and Activities Mail Survey (CAMS) (Hurd & Rohwedder, Chapter 12, this volume), measures of the time estimates can be compared with ATUS.

Instrument Design Innovations

There can be no doubt that Web-based platforms will become increasingly used as a source of data collection in the near and more distant future. Because of the potential to program a Web-based application with design features that promote accurate autobiographical remembering, a more precise understanding of those interviewing properties that are most beneficial to autobiographical recall can assist in the design of self-administered Web-based platforms to the extent that these properties are programmable. With the advent of intelligent agents (Graesser, van Lehn, Rosé, Jordan, & Harter, 2001; Sen & Weiss 1999), at this juncture it appears that almost any property that is uncovered can be implemented in a Web-based design.

With regard to interviewing properties, although calendar methods have been hypothesized to promote those retrieval cues and conversational narrative structures that permit a more thorough and accurate remembering from one's autobiographical past (Belli, 1998), and although calendar methods have been shown to produce better retrospective reports in comparison to conventional standardized questionnaires (Belli & Callegaro, Chapter 3, this volume), there has been little work examining whether the hypothesized structures are actually in play. Belli, Lee, Stafford, and Chou (2004) have found through the coding of verbal behaviors from transcribed audiotaped calendar and conventional standardized questionnaire interviews that calendar interviews promote significantly more retrieval cues and strategies in comparison to standardized ones, and that, in turn, the use of retrieval cues and strategies is associated with better quality retrospective reports, but only in calendar interviews. This work has also suggested that conversational components, such as interviewers requesting and providing clarification, also improves data quality in calendar interviews. Yet these data, although they are provocative and provide support for specific roles of retrieval and conversational properties in calendar interviews, are at best preliminary.

Ongoing behavioral coding work (Marincic & Belli, 2006) is examining in greater depth the types of verbal behaviors that are engendered in calendar and standardized interviews, and which of these behaviors are associated with improvements in the quality of retrospective reports. Greater depth is approached in two ways. First, behaviors are identified within small units; in this case these units are conversational turns, which are defined as a stream of continuous talking by either the interviewer or the respondent. Second, a wider variety of behaviors that adhere to several categories is being examined. Of course, one key category defines the various types of retrieval probes that are implemented by interviewers and the spontaneous retrieval strategies that are observed in respondents.

It is possible to identify behaviors associated with parallel, sequential, and top-down probing and retrieval as shown in Marincic and Belli (2006). Within sequential retrieval, they have observed the use of (1) timing, in which *when* an event took place is probed and remembered; (2) duration, in which *how long* events occurred are discussed; and (3) undifferentiated sequential, in which *what happens next* is asked or remembered. These researchers have also observed an assortment of conversational behaviors, including, among interviewers, verifications, clarifications and seeking clarification, directive probes, feedback following responses or attempts at responding, digressions, and laughter. Among respondents, agreements or disagreements to verifications and directive probes, expressions of cognitive difficulty, explanations, and also digressions and laughter have been observed.

Figure 17.1 shows an excerpt of a calendar interview that provides examples of many of these behaviors. There exists a considerable interplay of behaviors that are retrieval and conversational in their orientation. As this excerpt illustrates, calendar interviewing is characterized by the use of retrieval mechanisms within a natural conversational exchange between interviewers and respondents that (1) associate events that have happened contemporaneously in parallel, (2) associate events that happened sequentially, and (3) recover detailed elements of an event (data element retrieval), which is in line with those retrieval mechanisms hypothesized to reside within the structure of autobiographical knowledge (Belli, 1998).

It is important to note that behavior coding analyses have yet to be conducted with time diaries. The kinds of retrieval and conversational properties that are revealed by behavior coding may mirror what has been observed with calendar interviews, except on a smaller time scale (see Belli & Callegaro, Chapter 3, for speculations concerning this notion), or perhaps surprises will be in store. In any event, an important outcome of such analyses will be to

I: And how long did you stay there please? *Duration probe*

R: Until, um, October of '92. *Timing response*

I: Okay. And then, um, in October of '92, did you take another job? *Sequential probe*

       Duration response ——————————————— *Sequential response*

R: I took another job of—but it lasted for, like, a month and then I went to work some place else – you're interested in—

I: Not that month one then, we'll take the next. *Clarification*

       Sequential response   *Explanation*

R: Okay, um. The next job was at, um, let's see. Trying to think of the name of the place, they changed their name. Um. They used to be called employer 10?

                          Data element

I: Employer 10? *Verification probe*

R: Yes. *Verification agreement*

       Timing probe   *Directive*

I: And when did you start working for them? In '92?

Directive agreement   *Timing dual*

R: Um. Yes, December of '92 until May of '93.

                    Sequential probe

I: Alright. December of '92 until May of '93. And then in May of '93 did you...?

        Parallel response *Data element response*   *Explanation*

R: Um, I went to work in state 3 for employer 11, but I'm trying to think how long I worked there. It wasn't—it

                                  Sequential response

was—it was until—let's see. I came to state 3 in August—I must have gone for a job—oh, I guess I started in January of '94, and I only worked for 6 weeks, and then I went on disability.

       Parallel response   *Timing response*   *Duration response*

Figure 17.1   Excerpt of Calendar Interview With Identified Behaviors to Collect Data on Life Course Labor History

learn what specific behaviors are being assumed by interviewers and respondents. As with our work with calendar interviewing, it would be especially helpful to have some form of validation data so that insights can be gained regarding which behaviors, and which combinations of behaviors, promote the best recall.

Although an interviewer is not present in Web-based self-administered designs, there is recognition that self-administered questionnaires may be programmed to include conversational properties that are not unlike those that occur in implementation of interviewer-administered instruments (Conrad, Schober, & Coiner, 2007). In principle, then, one can incorporate the types of retrieval and conversational properties that are found to promote better recall in calendar and time diary interviewer-administered designs in Web-based self-administered ones. The degree of conversational and retrieval flexibility that characterizes calendar interviews, and that likely characterizes time diary interviews, poses challenges to implementation, however.

Because of its ability to incorporate flexible elements, calendar data collection methodologies can, and have, been implemented on the Web. One recent example is the Web-based calendar that is collecting reports of childhood events associated with the domains of schooling, parental relationships, and residential changes, in the American Life Panel study. This calendar displays several timelines with bars to represent periods of stability, and icons that are placed on specific timelines to represent the timing of transitions (such as a split between silhouettes of a man and women to represent a divorce). Respondents are also provided with textual questions that ask for these transitional timings, such as "At what age did you move?" This design apparently does not permit an active implementation of specific probes that are provided for respondents to consider as in actual interviews, although respondents can examine the calendar for contemporaneous events across domains if they so choose.

In a mixture of standardized and calendar elements in an interviewer-administered computerized instrument, Reimer and Matthes (2007; see Figure 3 in their article) have used a graphic-user interface similar to the Web-based display being used in the American Life Panel, although the design of Reimer and Matthes (coined as "TrueTales") is to be viewed by interviewers, and not by respondents. The similarities arise in there being a timeline display and textual questions. The differences arise in that the questions in TrueTales are tailored with fills that specifically seek respondents to engage in sequential and/or parallel retrieval. The fills are specified by inconsistencies in respondents' reports that have arisen earlier during the interview, such as gaps or overlaps.

One can envision from the Reimer and Matthes design, which combines tailored textual questions with timelines, an even more flexible Web-based application that is optimized to use effective probes that are governed by programmed intelligent agents. As noticeable from Figure 17.1, in interviewer-administered calendars, interviewers may alternate between duration, timing, and sequential probes (and parallel ones as well), and respondents may prefer to answer in terms of timing or durations, or seek to think sequentially or about contemporaneously occurring past events. From an examination of verbal behaviors, it may become better understood which alternations of these different retrieval cues and strategies are most effective in promoting accurate recall. Further, it may be possible for Web-based applications to be programmed not only with this intelligence, but also with an intelligent agent that, with practice, acquires knowledge concerning which specific probe will work best based on the question-and-response history that has already occurred.

Time diaries, as well as calendar approaches, are open to these sophisticated possibilities, although their feasibility remains somewhat uncertain at this point in time. In a sense, the 24-hour time diary is a type of calendar, which becomes more evident with timeline portrayals of the sort reported by Stafford (Chapter 2, this volume). In comparison to time diaries, calendars have the property of more fully capturing coincident activities of interest. Unlike time diaries, where there have been ongoing issues of how to treat secondary and even tertiary activities, with calendars it is normally the case that several domains of activity or states prevail at a given time and that within each domain there can be multiple activity forms. So a person can be a student and work at the same time, and one could hold two jobs simultaneously to support the ongoing school enrollment. Note that such a calendar provides far richer information than simple questions like, "Did you work last year (month)? Did you go to school last year (month)? Are you in school now? Are you working now?" Depending on the purpose such short questions may be better, but calendars (or time diaries) provide a great deal more information in a clearer layout, even if one is interested in overall schooling or work activity of different population groups.

As is evident from this volume, calendars have been applied to a very wide and growing range of time windows, ranging from large segments of a person's entire life to shorter periods. Educational histories seem particularly well suited to data collection via calendar applications. People have spells of education, or within a spell there are changes in the subject matter studied, and there are distinct events such as graduation or dropping out temporarily or otherwise. In each instance, such periods of stability and transitions between these trajectories would facilitate their collection via calendar data collection. Again, one may be content with much less information, such as what is the highest grade the respondent has attained as of the date of the interview.

As another example, health histories illustrate another area of application. For example, the 2007 Panel Study of Income Dynamics survey (see ftp:// ftp.isr.umich.edu/pub/src/psid/questionnaires/q2007.pdf, pp. 114–115) has implemented a calendar application to obtain health conditions and events of an individual's youth. For illnesses with a distinct onset and treatment period the calendar seems well suited. However, some conditions, such as arthritis, may come on gradually so there is not a distinct event that marks the onset. Health history calendars may be refined to capture the distinction between onset and diagnosis for pertinent health conditions such as arthritis, which may provide important information regarding the actual onset of chronic disease.

Expanding Data Collection Capabilities

In panel surveys, calendars can be administered during the successive interviews of each wave and collect information that ultimately leads to a continuous timeline. In dependent interviewing, each successive calendar would begin at its most remote time points by reminding respondents of answers that were provided at the most recent time points of the previously administered calendar during the prior wave. With a succession of such calendars one could create a long timeline, that is, a life course depiction, of activities and experiences. While dependent interviewing is in use outside of calendar methods, there are questions to be answered about methods for reconciling any differences between the respondent's current remembrance if it is not consistent with the endpoint information from the prior calendar collection. If the respondent is informed of the endpoint responses that were provided from the last interview, this may conflict with the contents of what the respondent remembers, creating a potential seam bias. Not mentioning the prior endpoint may produce goodwill with the respondent, but perhaps an even larger seam bias.

A similar issue of respondent interaction arises over within-period inconsistencies. In a computerized version, as information comes in to complete a time segment, calculations can be made to check logical inconsistencies: one that is common in both calendars and traditional methods is the allocation of the 52-week year into different labor market states. In common definitions the states are mutually exclusive and can be added up to compare with 52 weeks. If there are minor or more notable discrepancies, should the respondent be engaged in a reconstruction with the interviewer?

How far can one go across domains? In practice, one could think of residence and employment as complementary domains for a calendar. New employment often leads to a change of residence and a new employment position may provide a different income level that induces a residential change— even at the same employer. At the same time it can be argued that family structure and residence and employment are complementary domains in a calendar. As additional domains are added, what are the limits—the points at which the losses from comprehensiveness offset the gains from a type of content complementarity? This may not be a problem for a study with a well-defined set of measures, but may be a question for larger scale infrastructural studies. The research purposes matter, and shape the domain choices. For a study seeking to understand the connection between welfare, school, and work, the inclusion of the domains in a single calendar seems best suited to study of the temporal dependencies.

An area where calendars may come to have a great payoff is in medical compliance and clinical trials. A possibility is that clinical trials could employ calendar and time diary variants to collect data. If a clinical trial extends over many months, the reports from the patients provide information on compliance or connection to other medical and life events—such as work, other hospitalizations, or episodes during which side effects were experienced. In the application of such trials one can imagine a software, say, "CLIN-CALENDAR," that would capture the timelines of interest in terms of compliance and related domains of interest.

The resulting calendar data could provide far better information to assess an array of clinical outcomes and could be combined with lab and clinic measurements through time. Many drugs have initial side effects that dissipate with time, or, conversely, some side effects may show up only after a substantial duration, as with cumulative effects of exposure to the medication. A further aspect of such a calendar would be one mentioned earlier—namely, dependent interviewing. In this setting, as the patient revisited the care provider, the calendar entries up to the point of the last visit could be reviewed, and in this way subsequent data collection would extend an unbroken timeline of information in the various domains as well as possibly reframing some specific episode timing. The specifics of effective ways in which to obtain a cooperative response to the alignment of the preload and the new measures would need substantial exploration as to best or better practice. Time diary methods could be applied to such clinical trials, especially the Day Reconstruction Method (see Schwarz, Kahneman, & Xu, Chapter 9, this volume) to include measures of affect to assess the satisfaction or discomfort from treatments. Some equally effective medical therapies may differ dramatically in terms of patient burden or well-being.

Other applications of calendars could be in the construction and maintenance of employment records. Here there could be a synthesis of information from personnel records that could be supplemented with periodic calendar reports from the employee. The joint information could provide a far richer database on the employee's connection to the employer. Here, too, as in the clinical trials illustration, a set of companion software types and procedures for analysis of the data at both the level of the individual record and to provide data for statistical analysis would need development.

Once extended timelines via calendar methods have been collected, perhaps supplemented by time diary information, the statistical methods for analyzing the duration of events and timing of transitions would involve methods such as event history analysis and would also require effective designs for processing, organizing, and documenting the collected data. One task would be to recover some simple basic descriptive statistics before working with more structured analysis. The resulting studies based on continuous timeline information could provide a far better type of data model than that available with temporally discrete measures. And there may be strong cross-application benefits as innovations in the design, collection, and analysis of temporally continuous data would benefit researchers in quite separate substantive domains.

Acknowledgment

We are grateful to National Science Foundation Grant SES 0094942 and National Institutes of Health Grants AG019802, HD033474, and 5R01AG/HD17977-05 for financial support.

References

Belli, R. F. (1998). The structure of autobiographical memory and the event history calendar: Potential improvements in the quality of retrospective reports in surveys. *Memory, 6,* 383–406.

Belli, R. F., Lee, E. H., Stafford, F. P., & Chou, C.-H. (2004). Calendar and question-list survey methods: Association between interviewer behaviors and data quality. *Journal of Official Statistics, 20,* 185–218.

Belli, R. F., Shay, W. L., & Stafford, F. P. (2001). Event history calendars and question list surveys: A direct comparison of interviewing methods. *Public Opinion Quarterly, 65,* 45–74.

Conrad, F. G., Schober, M. F., & Coiner, T. (2007). Bringing features of human dialogue to Web surveys. *Applied Cognitive Psychology, 21,* 165–187.

Graesser, A. C., van Lehn, K., Rosé, C. P., Jordan, P. W., & Harter, D. (2001). Intelligent tutoring systems with conversational dialogue. *AI Magazine, 22*(4), 39–51.

Marincic, J., & Belli, R. F. (2006, November). *Do you hear what I hear? Verbal behavior coding of event history calendar and conventional interviews.* Poster presented at the annual meeting of the Midwest Association for Public Opinion Research, Chicago.

Reimer, M., & Matthes, B. (2007). Collecting event histories with TrueTales: Techniques to improve autobiographical recall problems in standardized interviews. *Quality & Quantity, 41,* 711–735.

Sen, S., & Weiss, G. (1999). Learning in multiagent systems. In G. Weiss (Ed.), *Multiagent systems: A modern approach to distributed artificial intelligence* (pp. 259–298). Cambridge: MIT Press.

Further Thoughts on Part V

A mong the biggest challenges in any scientific discipline, including life course research, is to document and account for the variability that exists in the entities that are studied. Humans show variability in their circumstances, in their behaviors, and in their thoughts and memories. As entities that are the subject of scientific inquiry, accounting for such human variability is a mighty challenge, indeed.

The researchers who contributed chapters to this edited volume have sought common strategies to document and account for human variability in their adoption of calendar and time diary data collection methods. These methods are based on the notion that using human interaction and language to collect information on human variability necessitates permitting a certain level of variability—of flexibility—in the manner in which information is queried and reported by respondents. Others will disagree with this notion, arguing that a strict form of standardized data collection is the only means to ensure that the variability in what is measured can be attributed solely to the experiences of the respondents, and not to the methods with which the data had been collected. Some may seek a compromise approach by being intent on increasing the level of standardized interviewing methods in calendar and time diary approaches.

This volume is not positioned to address these issues fully. But we have provided insight into these issues by presenting in the various chapters that compose this volume a number of examples of how calendar and time diary data collection strategies can be valuable tools in life course research. We have also exposed the methodological challenges that are posed by these data collection approaches, and have shown that there is considerable room for additional methodological research for purposes of improving the quality that is collected by these methods beyond what is already observed. We also hope, largely because of the promise of calendar and time diary methods, that substantive researchers in the behavioral, social, and health sciences will learn "by example" and be more likely to entertain adopting calendar and time diary methods in their own work.

Author Index

Subject Index

About the Editors

Robert F. Belli is Professor of Psychology and Graduate Chair of the Survey Research and Methodology Program at the University of Nebraska–Lincoln and Adjunct Research Professor of the Survey Research Center at the University of Michigan. He is also North American Editor of *Applied Cognitive Psychology*. His most recent interests include the application of principles from cognitive psychology—especially autobiographical memory and conversational processes—to reduce response errors in retrospective survey reports.

Frank P. Stafford is Professor of Economics, Director of the Panel Study of Income Dynamics at the Institute for Social Research (ISR) of the University of Michigan. His active research areas include issues of time allocation, the economics of child care, and cross-national comparative studies on the role of information technology. Other research interests include family decisions about wealth, pensions, and savings as they relate to individual mental and physical health through time.

Duane F. Alwin is the inaugural holder of the Tracy Winfree and Ted H. McCourtney professorship in Sociology and Demography at Pennsylvania State University, where he is affiliated with the Population Research Institute and the Survey Research Center. Prior to moving to Penn State in 2002, he held an appointment for 23 years in the Survey Research Center of the Institute for Social Research at the University of Michigan. His research interests include a wide range of phenomena connected with aging and the life course, and he is best known for his innovative work on the connections among human development, social structure, demography and social change.

About the Contributors

Sangeeta Agrawal received her master's degree in applied statistics from the University of Western Ontario, London, Canada. She is currently working at the College of Nursing, University of Nebraska Medical Center, as a statistical coordinator/instructor. She has also worked as statistical consultant for the Fostering Self Change Program at the Centre for Addiction and Mental Health, Toronto, Ontario. Prior to this, for 7 years she was at the Addiction Research Foundation in Canada, where she was a research associate.

Kirsten H. Alcser is survey director in the Survey Research Center of the University of Michigan's Institute for Social Research (ISR). She has more than 20 years of experience designing and directing surveys across multiple modes and has served as coinvestigator and survey director on several epidemiological projects at ISR and at the UM School of Public Health.

David M. Almeida is Professor of Human Development and Family Studies at Pennsylvania State University. He is a life span developmental psychologist, with a primary focus on stress and coping during middle adulthood. His research interests center on the general question of how daily experiences within the family and other social contexts, such as work and leisure, influence individual health and well-being.

Joan E. Broderick is Research Associate Professor in the Department of Psychiatry and Behavioral Science at Stony Brook University. She recently completed a National Cancer Institute–funded project involving several methodological studies investigating paper and electronic diaries for self-report of pain and fatigue in patients with chronic illness.

Mario Callegaro is Survey Research Scientist at Knowledge Networks in Menlo Park, California. He obtained a Ph.D. in Survey Research and Methodology at the University of Nebraska–Lincoln. His work, publications, and conference presentations include topics such as event history calendar methodology, non-sampling errors in surveys, impact of mobile phones on survey practice, and mode effects in collecting data.

Eric M. Camburn is Assistant Professor and Senior Researcher at the Consortium for Policy Research in Education at the University of Wisconsin. His current research centers around understanding efforts to improve instruction in urban schools, including programmatic efforts to improve instruction; the organizational factors that support such improvement efforts; the impact such change efforts have on leadership practice, instruction, and student achievement; and on assessing the validity of self-reports of teaching and leadership practice. Much of his research involves the use of multilevel statistical models and measurement models, but he has also conducted a number of mixed-method investigations.

Richard Correnti is Assistant Professor at the Learning Policy Center in the School of Education at the University of Pittsburgh. His research interests include the measurement and determinants of instruction (e.g., professional development), how educational innovations impact instruction, and how instruction affects student learning.

Wil Dijkstra is Professor in Methods of Data Collection in the Social Sciences at the Department of Social Research Methods at the Free University of Amsterdam. His main research interest is the interaction between interviewer and respondent in survey interviews. More recently, he became involved in the event history calendar method and obtained a grant from the Dutch National Science Foundation (with W. van der Vaart, Ph.D.) to improve this method.

Michael D. Hurd is Senior Economist at the RAND Corporation, the Director of the RAND Center for the Study of Aging, a Research Associate at the National Bureau of Economic Research, and Research Professor at the Mannheim Research Institute for the Economics of Aging. His broad research area is the economics of aging, including the structure of private pensions and Social Security and their effects on retirement decisions, the economic status of the elderly, the determinants of consumption and saving, the use of health care services, methods of assessing uncertainty in a population; bracketing and anchoring effects in the elicitation of economic information; and the relationship between socioeconomic status and mortality. He is a Co-Principal Investigator of the Health and Retirement Study and a consultant to the English Longitudinal Study of Ageing and to the Survey of Health, Ageing, and Retirement in Europe.

Sherman A. James is the Susan B. King Professor of Public Policy Studies in the Terry Sanford Institute for Public Policy at Duke University. He also holds professorships at Duke University in Sociology, Community and Family Medicine, and African and African American Studies. A social epidemiologist, his research focuses on the social determinants of racial and ethnic health inequalities, with special emphasis on the role of chronic stressors due to poverty and racial/ethnic discrimination.

Daniel Kahneman is Eugene Higgins Professor of Psychology at Princeton University and Professor of Public Affairs at Princeton's Woodrow Wilson School. He is a fellow of the National Academy of Science, the American Academy of Arts and Sciences, and a Nobel laureate in economics. His research focuses on judgment and decision making and their implications for policy, with a current focus on time use and well-being.

Kristy K. Martyn is Associate Professor, Chair of Health Promotion & Risk Reduction Programs, and a family and pediatric nurse practitioner at the University of Michigan School of Nursing. She has more than 20 years of extensive experience in primary health care clinical practice and research with low-middle-income adolescents. During the past 9 years, she has conducted extensive preliminary work to develop the event history calendar (EHC) and examine its use with adolescents and in primary care settings.

Edward P. Mulvey is a Professor of Psychiatry and Director of the Law and Psychiatry Program at Western Psychiatric Institute and Clinic at the University of Pittsburgh School of Medicine. He has done work on how clinicians make judgments regarding the type of risk posed by adult mental patients and juvenile offenders. Currently, he is the principal investigator for a large, multisite longitudinal study, "Pathways to Desistance," examining how serious adolescent offenders make the transition from adolescence to adulthood.

Yfke P. Ongena is Assistant Professor of Research Methods in the Department of Political Science and Research Methods at the University of Twente. Her research interests and expertise focus on methods of behavior coding, interviewer–respondent interaction, and cognitive aspects of survey interviews.

Polly A. Phipps is a behavioral scientist at the U.S. Bureau of Labor Statistics (BLS). Her interests include survey methodology and public policy issues, and she has pursued a combination of those interests while working at the RAND Corporation, the Washington State Institute for Public Policy, and the BLS. She is currently conducting research on survey nonresponse and measurement error at the BLS.

Jennifer Roberts is Associate Professor of Criminology at Indiana University of Pennsylvania. She was a predoctoral fellow with the National Consortium on Violence Research, where she worked on a life events calendar project that interviewed male inmates about their experiences with violence. Her current research is focused on examining the efficacy of the life events calendar using a sample of mental patients who are at high risk for violence.

Susann Rohwedder (Ph.D., Economics, University College London) is an Economist at RAND and Associate Director of the RAND Center for the Study of Aging. Her research focuses on the economics of aging in the areas of household consumption and saving behavior, retirement, pensions, Social Security, and expectation formation. She is involved in several data collection efforts: She is jointly responsible for the design of the Consumptions and Activities Mails Survey (CAMS), an experimental module of the Health and Retirement Study, and for several modules of the American Life Panel (ALP).

Brian Rowan is the Burke A. Hinsdale Collegiate Professor in Education and Research Professor at the Institute for Social Research at the University of Michigan. His scholarly interests lie at the intersection of organization theory and school effectiveness research. His current research includes studies of a variety of school improvement initiatives as well as continuing work on the measurement of teaching and teachers' knowledge.

Norbert Schwarz is Charles Horton Cooley Collegiate Professor of Psychology at the University of Michigan, Professor of Marketing at Michigan's Ross School of Business, and Research Professor at the Institute for Social Research. He is a fellow of the American Academy of Arts and Sciences, the Association for Psychological Science, and the American Psychological Association and recipient of the Wilhelm Wundt Medal of the German Psychological Association. His research focuses on human judgment, including its implications for social science methodology.

Johannes H. Smit is Associate Professor of Survey Methodology and currently affiliated with the Vrije Universiteit Medical Centre, the Netherlands. His interests focus on the quality of data collection in large longitudinal studies in "difficult populations," including the elderly and patient cohorts (osteoporosis and mental health). He has consulted on fieldwork for large epidemiological studies, has investigated nonresponse, and has been active exploring the interactions between interviewers and respondents in relation to data quality and statistical modeling for longitudinal data.

Linda Carter Sobell is Professor and Associate Director of Clinical Training at the Center for Psychological Studies at Nova Southeastern University (NSU) in Ft. Lauderdale, Florida. She is known nationally and internationally for her work on the assessment and treatment of addictions, particularly brief motivational interventions, the process of self-change, and assessment instruments including the Timeline Followback method.

Mark B. Sobell is Professor at the Center for Psychological Studies at Nova Southeastern University (NSU) in Ft. Lauderdale, Florida. He is known nationally and internationally for his research on alternatives to abstinence, assessment and treatment of addictions, particularly brief motivational interventions and preventing alcohol-exposed pregnancies in high-risk women, and assessment instruments, including the Timeline Followback method.

Arthur A. Stone is Distinguished Professor and Vice-Chair of the Psychiatry Department and Director of the Applied Behavioral Medicine Research Institute at the medical school at Stony Brook University. His recent interests focus on a fine-grained understanding of the interplay between environmental influences and physiological processes, especially the hypothalamic-pituitary-adrenal axis. He has been involved with the development of Ecological Momentary Assessment, a technique for intensively monitoring individuals in their natural environments.

John Van Hoewyk is a Senior Research Associate in the Survey Research Center at the University of Michigan. His current interests include the imputation of item missing data in large-scale data sets, the role of incentives in survey participation, disclosure risk in public release data sets, and public attitudes toward data sharing.

Margaret K. Vernon is Senior Project Manager for United BioSource Corporation (UBC)'s Center for Health Outcomes Research in Bethesda, Maryland. Her research interests include adolescent well-being and health, with a particular focus on positive social and emotional outcomes during the adolescent years. She also has expertise and formal training in both qualitative and quantitative methods.

Elaine Wethington (Ph.D.) is Associate Professor in the Departments of Human Development and Sociology at Cornell University, and Co-Director of the Cornell Institute for Translational Research on Aging. As a medical sociologist, she specializes in the sociology of mental health and illness. Her research interests are in the areas of (1) situational determinants of exposure to stress, access to social support, and successful coping in midlife through old age; (2) the epidemiology of mental and physical illness, particularly in relationship to exposure to severe life stressors; and (3) developing methods to encourage more rapid translation of basic social science research into programs and policies that will benefit aging people.

Jing Xu is Assistant Professor of Marketing at the Guangha School of Management at Peking University in Beijing, China. Her research focuses on consumer judgment and choice and their implications for well-being.

Mieko Yoshihama is Associate Professor of Social Work at the University of Michigan. Her research focuses on women's experiences of violence, coping, and well-being over their life course, and she has conducted numerous research projects, including a multicountry study of domestic violence and health coordinated by the World Health Organization, a nationwide survey in Japan, and a study of Japanese American women in Los Angeles. Recently, she applied the life history calendar method to better understand the cumulative effects of domestic violence on women's well-being over time in community-based studies in Michigan as well as Japan.